The thought of John Austin
Jurisprudence, Colonial Reform,
and the British Constitution

The thought of
JOHN AUSTIN
Jurisprudence, Colonial Reform, and the British Constitution

WILFRID E. RUMBLE

THE ATHLONE PRESS

London and Dover, New Hampshire

First published in Great Britain 1985
by The Athlone Press, 44 Bedford Row, London WC1R 4LY
and 51 Washington Street, Dover, NH 03820

British Library Cataloguing in Publication Data
Rumble, Wilfrid E.
The thought of John Austin: Jurisprudence,
Colonial Reform, and the British Constitution
1. Austin, John, 1790–1859
I. Title
340'.109 K230.A92

ISBN 0-485-11292-2

Library of Congress Cataloging in Publication Data
Rumble, Wilfrid E.
The thought of John Austin: Jurisprudence,
Colonial Reform, and the British Constitution

Bibliography: p.
Includes index.
1. Austin, John, 1790–1859. 2. Jurisprudence.
3. Law—Great Britain. I. Title.
K230.A862R86 1985 340'.109 84-28302
ISBN 0-485-11292-2

Typeset by Inforum Ltd, Portsmouth
Printed in England at the University Press, Cambridge

to Kirkie

The Author and the Publisher are grateful to the Salmon Fund of Vassar College for help in the publication of this book.

Contents

Acknowledgments

1 Introduction 1

2 Austin's life and its relationship to his thought 9

3 Divine law, utilitarian ethics, and positivist jurisprudence 60

4 Judicial legislation and legal positivism 109

5 The reform of Malta 144

6 A defence of the British Constitution 193

7 Conclusion 218

Notes 221

Selected bibliography 262

Index 272

Acknowledgments

It is a genuine pleasure to acknowledge the large number of persons who contributed to this book. A special vote of thanks is due to the Committee on Research of Vassar College, which granted me a subvention from the Salmon Fund. H. Partick Sullivan, Dean of the College, and his assistant Judith B. Hanna, were especially helpful in this regard. Gordon Waterfield was very gracious, encouraging, and informative. Mildred Tubby did her usual splendid job as the typist of several drafts of the manuscript. Shirley A. Maul, Readers' Service Librarian at Vassar, was instrumental in securing material on interlibrary loan. Helen Mary Hill, my former research assistant, performed numerous tasks with her characteristic efficiency, good cheer, and high degree of competence. Deborah A. Chew rendered yeoman service in the correction of the proofs, to which Catherine, Bill, and Cynthia Rumble also contributed. Wendy L. Tedmon, my current research assistant, Helen Lefroy of The Athlone Press, and Carolyn Priest-Dorman helped in a variety of different ways. Finally, my wife Kirk prepared a substantial portion of the index. Her other, more subtle contributions are too numerous to mention.

I would also like to thank Yale University Library for permission to reproduce John Austin's letter of 25 December 1844 to John Stuart Mill, in the John Stuart Mill Collection there; the Controller of HM Stationery Office for quotations from Crown Copyright papers in the Public Record Office; and The Library, University College, London, for permission to quote the following letters: John Austin, 5 November 1830, and 12 November 1830 (College Correspondence); Sarah Austin to Lord Brougham, 26, 541; 26, 524; and 38, 601 (Brougham mss).

1 *Introduction*

This book is an analysis of certain ideas of John Austin, the English jurist who lived from 1790 to 1859. The standard image of him is as a philosopher of law, but he was much more than that. He was also the author of significant contributions to ethics, political theory, and colonial reform. At least this conception of his importance as a thinker underlies this study. Its purpose is to develop a better understanding than now exists of Austin's thought on legal, and a limited number of other, subjects. This book presumes, thus, that his ideas are sufficiently important to warrant detailed analysis. The aim of this introductory chapter is to explain the basis of this presumption and the organization of this study.

1

Although Austin is not a dominant figure in contemporary jurisprudence, his philosophy of law is important for several reasons.[1] To begin with, it is a basic component of the background to current developments in legal philosophy. The reason for Austin's significance in this respect is *not* universal support for his ideas. Indeed the response to many of them in the last thirty or thirty-five years has tended to be highly critical. Even so, contemporary jurists take him seriously and feel obliged to address his ideas. This is evident from the writings of the two most influential contemporary figures in Anglo-American jurisprudence. H. L. A. Hart allocated three of the ten chapters of *The Concept of Law* to discussion of ideas virtually identical with Austin's.[2] While Ronald Dworkin nowhere discusses Austin's ideas with the same thoroughness as Hart, he began his influential critique of positivism with an explanation of them.[3]

Moreover, the value of what Austin attempted to do is substantial. His objective was nothing less than to elucidate the basic concepts of jurisprudence and the structure of a legal system. He was convinced that erroneous or unclear ideas about law were widespread. He also believed that these conceptual mistakes or lack of clarity had perniciously affected both legal theory and practice. The result of his efforts to cure these ills is a coherent and lucid set of ideas for understanding and studying law. To say this is not to imply that his analysis is wholly satisfactory, which is not the case. Even so, his painstaking attempt to unveil the secrets of the 'mysterious science' is an impressive intellectual achievement. The objective of conceptual clarification that he set for himself also remains a most valuable goal, whatever the limitations of his own attempts to achieve it.

Aside from this, Austin's legal philosophy has educational value for students of his thought. He once said of himself that 'if he had any special intellectual vocation, it was that of "untying knots" '.[4] His efforts to unravel them required him to explain in minute detail the complexity and 'numerous ambiguities' of legal concepts.[5] Although his powerful, unusually thorough, and precise analysis may be unacceptable in a number of respects, close examination of it is extremely useful. In particular, careful study of his work encourages students of it to clarify if not to develop their own ideas on a number of the most basic questions of jurisprudence. This experience is beneficial no matter how different these ideas may be from Austin's own conceptions.

Commentator after commentator on Austin has emphasized the utility in this sense of study of his work. It is invaluable, John Stuart Mill stressed, for developing 'the difficult art of precise thought'.[6] Despite his criticisms of Austin's style, Walter Bagehot argued that the student of his ideas 'will find that he has gained something which he wanted, but something which he did not *know* that he wanted; he has clarified a part of his mind which he did not know needed clarifying.'[7] No one put the matter better than Sir Henry Maine: 'There is not the smallest necessity for accepting all the conclusions of these great writers [Bentham and Austin] . . . but there is the strongest necessity for knowing what those conclusions are.' They are indispensable, Maine continued, at least for the purpose of 'clearing the head'.[8]

Austin's philosophy of law is also important because of its pivotal role in the development of legal positivism. Although this tradition of jurisprudence is subject to very different interpretations, legal positivists share a distinctive cluster of ideas. To say this is not to suggest that they constitute a monolithic school of thought. Rather, it is to argue that the label 'legal positivism' signifies the existence of an identifiable pattern of thought.[9] It includes at least two distinctive strands, one of which is a belief in the positivity of law. Law is something that is laid down, posited, set, or 'created and annulled by acts of human beings'.[10] In short, law is made rather than discovered. The other basic characteristic of legal positivism is a sharp distinction between the law as it is and the law as it ought to be. While positivists disagree on the basis of this distinction, they share the view that the validity or existence of the law that is does not depend upon its conformity to the law that ought to be. For the legal positivist, in brief, 'all laws owe their origin and existence to human practice and decisions concerned with the government of a society, and . . . have no necessary correlation with the precepts of an ideal morality.'[11]

This conception of legal positivism implies that it has no necessary connection with analytical jurisprudence. The latter entails the 'clarification of the meaning of law, the identification of the characteristic structure of a legal system, and the analysis of pervasive and fundamental legal notions'.[12] Analytical jurisprudence is thus an *approach* to the study of law. As such, it is consistent with various non-positivist conceptions of law or its relationship to morality. 'Logically, a scholar can engage in analytical work without espousing any of the [different] . . . "positivist" doctrines.'[13] Similarly, a legal positivist can take a sociological, ethical, or other non-analytical approach to the study of law. At the same time, many legal positivists have espoused analytical jurisprudence. This is true not only of Austin, but such preeminent twentieth-century philosophers of law as Hans Kelsen and H. L. A. Hart.[14] Legal positivism and analytical jurisprudence often appeal, thus, to the same jurist.

Austin's *Lectures on Jurisprudence* may be, at any rate, the best single expression of these strands of thought in the Anglo-American jurisprudence of the nineteenth century. To be sure, he borrowed liberally from his predecessors such as Thomas Hobbes and Jeremy Bentham. Also, few contemporary positivists accept Austin's particular conceptions of law, sovereignty, or legal obligation. Still, they tend to agree with him that law is made rather than discovered. They also share his opinion of the great value of an analytical jurisprudence and the need to distinguish clearly between the law as it is and as it ought to be.[15] To this extent, contemporary forms of legal positivism may be interpreted as a continuation of the Austinian tradition.

Finally, Austin's philosophy of law is important because of its powerful, if delayed, impact upon English jurisprudence. The only book that he published during his lifetime was *The Province of Jurisprudence Determined* (1832). It did not receive much recognition during his life, a situation that dramatically changed after his death in 1859. In fact, his reputation may never have been higher than it was a decade or two after his demise. Lord Brougham wrote in 1860 that Austin was 'the most able and learned cultivator of the science [of jurisprudence] in our day'.[16] One year later James Fitzjames Stephen asserted that as long as jurisprudence is studied, Austin's work 'will remain . . . an imperishable monument of the conscientious labour, profound thought, and extraordinary powers of mind which its author bestowed on it.'[17] An anonymous writer claimed in 1863 that Austin's 'remarkable acuteness and analytical power . . . make every relic of his studies most welcome to all who can appreciate his rare qualities.'[18] An American reviewer of Austin's *Lectures on Jurisprudence* maintained in 1865 that he is 'conspicuous among the most distinguished jurists of . . . [this] century'.[19] Fifteen years later Albert V. Dicey argued that Austin's name should never be mentioned without 'profound respect' and that it is impossible to speak 'too highly' of his merits.[20] In the same year Thomas Erskine Holland wrote that Austin is the person to whom 'most Englishmen are indebted for such ideas as they possess of legal method.'[21]

Almost three-quarters of a century later, H. L. A. Hart ascribed an even stronger impact than this to Austin's ideas. 'Within a few years of his death,' Hart writes, 'it was clear that his [Austin's] work had established the study of jurisprudence in England.' Indeed, his influence on this field of thought was 'greater than that of any other writer. For English jurisprudence has been and still is predominantly analytical in character.'[22] Carleton Kemp Allen went so far as to claim that Austin was the author of 'the characteristic jurisprudence of England'.[23] Of course, the publication in 1961 of Hart's influential *The Concept of Law* probably requires qualification of this last statement. If an American may be permitted a judgment, his philosophy of law seems to me to be more characteristically English than Austin's. Nevertheless, Allen's assertion indicates the strong influence of Austin on the jurisprudence of his native country.

To say this is not to deny that Austin might have been much less influential if Jeremy Bentham had published his *Of Laws in General* during his life.[24] At least it is the opinion of H. L. A. Hart that if this master-work of analytical jurisprudence had been published in Bentham's 'lifetime, it, rather than John Austin's later and obviously derivative work, would have dominated English jurisprudence.'[25] It may also be the case that Bentham was 'a far more profound and original thinker, and a much greater philosopher of law' than Austin.[26] Nevertheless, Austin rather than Bentham exerted the strong influence on the actual development of English jurisprudence. Moreover, Austin was regarded for many years as the great philosopher of law of the utilitarians. No one expressed more clearly than

Sir Henry Maine the dominant impression, until very recently, of the roles of the two men:

> Bentham in the main is a writer on legislation. Austin in the main is a writer on jurisprudence. Bentham is chiefly concerned with law as it might be and ought to be. Austin is chiefly concerned with law as it is. Each trespasses occasionally on the domain of the other.[27]

If Austin was the dominant figure in English jurisprudence well into the twentieth century, he evidently had little effect on European jurisprudence. Still, his work is similar in several respects to the influential theory of law developed in this century by Hans Kelsen. In fact, Kelsen believes that his structural analysis of positive law does not differ essentially from analytical jurisprudence. 'Where they differ', Kelsen writes, 'they do so because the pure theory of law tries to carry on the method of analytical jurisprudence more consistently than Austin and his followers.'[28] The impact of his ideas is also evident in the writings of such major American jurists as Justice Holmes and John Chipman Gray, both of whom had read Austin carefully.[29] If the legal realists were much less familiar with Austin than either Holmes or Gray, he foreshadowed a number of distinctive themes of the realist movement.[30] Indeed, Ronald Dworkin has claimed that Austin's theories are 'now accepted in one form or another by most working and academic lawyers who hold views on jurisprudence.'[31]

These considerations explain the rather extensive scholarly literature about Austin's philosophy of law. The most impressive recent interpretation of it is W. L. Morison's *John Austin*, which is the first book about Austin published in the English language for over half a century.[32] It is also a work of high quality, a judgment that applies to many of the other studies of his jurisprudence.[33] Even so, these various writings suffer from a number of limitations.

To begin with, interpreters of Austin's philosophy of law almost invariably dismiss his utilitarian ethics as irrelevant to his jurisprudence. If the thesis defended in the third chapter of this study is well-founded, this interpretation is mistaken. Awareness of why it is erroneous is essential for understanding the basis and distinctiveness of Austin's version of legal positivism. Moreover, his valuable analysis of judicial legislation has never received the kind of detailed examination that it merits. This belief underlies the fourth chapter of this book, the focus of which is Austin's account of judge-made law. Finally, the extant descriptions of his legal thought are incomplete.

His analysis of laws of libel and trial by jury, for example, receives little or no attention in the literature. The fifth chapter of this study attempts, among other things, to fill this gap.

2

If Austin's philosophy of law has its limitations, it has 'never been . . . ignored'.[34] The ideas that he developed on other subjects have suffered a very different fate. The almost total neglect of them is unfortunate because of the importance of these dimensions of his thought. Although his contribution to the philosophy of law constitutes his most impressive achievement, it is not his only one. He was an ardent utilitarian who wrote a valuable exposition and defence of this influential ethical theory. His interpretation of it elicited words of praise from no less a figure than John Stuart Mill. He wrote in 1832 that Austin had discussed certain branches of the question of the nature of the standard of right and wrong 'in a manner which we have never seen equalled'.[35] 'Of all views I have yet seen taken of the utilitarian scheme,' Mill wrote in 1834, 'I like Austin's best.'[36] Toward the end of his life Mill reiterated that Austin's defence of the principle of utility was 'most able and instructive'.[37] Almost a century later an American philosopher praised Austin's writings on ethics as 'one of the nicest formulations of the theory of restricted utilitarianism'.[38]

Austin not only contributed to the development of utilitarian ethical theory. In addition, his utilitarianism provides the underlying unity and coherence to his diverse writings. Despite the truly remarkable changes in his political opinions, for example, he retained a utilitarian perspective on politics until his death. He began his career as an arch-Benthamite. His political outlook veered pointedly to the right in the latter stages of his life. This development culminated in his publication in 1859 of *A Plea for the Constitution*, which was highly critical of proposals for the democratic reform of Parliament.[39] Some of Austin's objections to this possibility adumbrated the position subsequently taken by much better known Victorian critics of democracy. His pamphlet therefore merits more attention than it has received from students of this movement of political thought. Moreover, Austin's work illustrates the wide differences of opinion that are possible among utilitarians.

Austin also published four very long articles.[40] They addressed such topics as primogeniture and entails, unlimited liability for joint-stock companies, free trade, and centralization. His discussion of these matters is important for at least two reasons. To begin with, it reveals very clearly his position on several policy questions of the day. In his articles he did *not* focus on an exposition of the law that is to the exclusion of the law that ought to be. Instead he also criticized existing law and recommended certain changes in it. In other words, he played the roles of critic and reformer. Furthermore, the policies that he advocated in his articles tended to be enlightened or prophetic, or both. He criticized entails and primogeniture, defended the rule of limited liability for partners in joint-stock companies, extolled the principle of free trade, and praised widespread popular participation in local government.

Most of the Benthamites had a deep interest in problems of colonial reform.[41] Austin not only shared this concern, but had an opportunity to do something about it. He and George Cornewall Lewis were appointed Royal Commissioners to the British colony of Malta in 1836. Austin was the senior, and dominant, partner in their collaboration. He and his colleague developed a sweeping programme of reform for Malta that deserves a much more comprehensive analysis than it has ever received.[42] The work of the Commissioners has been described by a historian of the Island as 'one of the landmarks in Maltese history'.[43] Many of their proposals were accepted by the British government. Their very able reports and recommendations are also a fascinating example of utilitarianism-in-action. Finally, the reforms of the Commissioners disclose Austin's ideas on problems about which he wrote little or nothing elsewhere.

These considerations provide the rationale for the detailed examination of the Commissioners' reforms in Chapter 5 below. Their plans for the expansion of public education, the employment of natives, the abolition of censorship, and the enactment of a comprehensive law of libel receive special emphasis. Austin and Lewis not only proposed this last change, but drafted the law that the colonial government eventually enacted. They also wrote a very detailed and revealing commentary on this measure. Chapter 6 is an analysis of Austin's inflexible opposition to extension of the suffrage in Great Britain, criticism of which is the main thrust of *A Plea for the Constitution*.

Since Austin's ideas about law are his most notable achievement, they receive somewhat more attention in this study than other dimensions of his thought. Even so, this book is not a comprehensive exposition of his legal philosophy. While some of the major themes of his *Lectures on Jurisprudence* are explained in detail, others are discussed only briefly or not at all. The most important examples of the latter are his various classifications of the *corpus juris*, including his fundamental distinction between the law of things and the law of persons. Furthermore, this book does not attempt to explain *all* of the important ideas that he developed on non-legal subjects. Although studies of this kind are desirable, this work has a more limited objective. Still, fulfilment of its purpose should enhance appreciation of the varied contributions of a man whose ideas need additional study.

The primary obligation of the author of a book about the thought of someone is to explain it as accurately and clearly as is possible. Fulfilment of this duty requires careful analysis of the writings of Austin, which are the focus of this work. Unlike most previous treatments of his thought, this study examines both his published and unpublished works. The latter are essential for understanding his proposals for the reform of Malta. An appreciation of his life and the historical context of his ideas also facilitates understanding of his thought. This conviction is the rationale for Chapter 2, which is a more detailed account of Austin's life than has yet to be published.[44]

Some of the chapters of this book explain Austin's ideas, while others both elucidate and evaluate his thought. The second and third chapters fall into the first of these categories. The other chapters contain appraisals of his views that probably will not be acceptable to all right-thinking men and women. A scrupulous attempt has been made, however, to separate the explanation of Austin's ideas from the evaluation of them. The reader will thus be in a good position to reach his or her own conclusions about their merits. At any rate, a balanced appraisal of Austin's thought requires an accurate understanding of it. The primary objective of this study is to contribute to the satisfaction of this requirement. It should therefore be useful for both proponents and critics of Austin's ideas, as well as persons who are unfamiliar with his writings.

2 *Austin's life and its relationship to his thought*

Sarah Austin has accurately written that the life of her husband was 'passed in the shade'.[1] She meant that he had spent his sixty-nine years out of the public limelight. Since relatively little is known about many phases of his life, much of it is now in the shade in another respect. This lack of knowledge is due partly, though not entirely, to the small number of primary sources about his life which are extant. The bulk of his letters were destroyed during the Second World War.[2] Their destruction means that many of the details of his life are likely to remain in the shade.

These considerations raise the question of whether a biography of Austin is possible, if it were desirable. The answer seems to me to depend on the kind of account of his life which is attempted. On the one hand, a comprehensive biography based upon a rich supply of original sources is out of the question. The kind of study of Austin that Richard Cosgrove has recently written of Albert Venn Dicey, for example, is impossible.[3] On the other hand, an accurate reconstruction of the general outline and some of the details of Austin's life is possible. If the relevant sources do not contain a wealth of data, they are not barren. In fact, the available material provides the basis for a more detailed biography of Austin than has hitherto been published.[4]

The development of such an account is desirable for several reasons, one of which is that Austin's life is not without a certain amount of interest or significance. More important than this, knowledge of his life facilitates understanding of the origins, context, and evolution of his thought. At least this perspective underlies the subsequent pages of this chapter.

1

Austin was born on 3 March 1790, and died on 17 December 1859. His life therefore almost completely overlapped what one historian has dubbed the Age of Improvement, the period from 1783 to 1867. It was an era marked by 'formative changes in the structure of the English economy, the shape of English society and the framework of government'.[5] If the end result of these changes was the alleviation of the human estate, the process was often difficult and painful. It was characterized by stubborn resistance to change, protracted social conflict, and a substantial amount of human misery. As a result, the prospects for human betterment sometimes seemed quite dim. J. H. Plumb described the situation in 1815, when Austin was twenty-five, in these terms: 'Great Britain seemed on the edge of bankruptcy and social revolution. Starvation was driving the poor to wreck . . . machinery . . . and the government . . . repressed brutally what . . . it could not comprehend. To thinking men the horizon was dark and foreboding.'[6] Despite how ominous the future at times appeared, the need for change became more apparent to a larger number of persons. 'In the first quarter of the nineteenth century,' G. Kitson Clark writes, 'it was becoming increasingly clear that what was politically, socially, intellectually and spiritually a new society was growing up in England for which neither the institutions, nor the ideas, that had been inherited from the eighteenth century would suffice.'[7]

John Austin was one of the persons who became convinced of the insufficiency of many of these institutions and ideas. Since very little is known about his childhood, whether or how it influenced this conviction is uncertain. He was the eldest of the seven children of Jonathan and Anne Austin, who may be placed within the broad middle-class of English society. Of course, such a classification may obscure more than it reveals. G. Kitson Clark has emphasized, and properly, the significant economic and cultural differences between identifiable groups within the 'middle class'.[8] Nonetheless, the term itself retains a certain utility. At the least it denotes a very broad category of persons who fall somewhere between the nobility and landed gentry, on the one hand, and manual labourers, on the other hand. Moreover, the phrase 'middle class' was highly significant for any number of men and women in the nineteenth century. They included John Austin, who praised highly this 'rational class' of English society. This does not mean, however, that his jurisprudence was a rationalization of middle-class interests.[9]

In any case, Austin's parents belonged to this admittedly 'large section of society'.[10] Jonathan Austin was a prosperous Suffolk miller and corn merchant. He was a self-educated, but intelligent and informed man. He apparently enjoyed reading and became knowledgeable in history and political economy. He may have been inspired in this respect by his wife, who has been described as 'well-educated, gently nurtured, and possessed of exceptional abilities'.[11] According to Janet Ross, the granddaughter of John Austin, his mother was also a deeply religious person with a strong 'tinge of melancholy'.[12] It is possible that she transmitted this last quality to her son. His disposition resembled, at any rate, that of his mother.

Jonathan Austin attempted to provide the best education that he could afford for his children. His two daughters were evidently 'clever and well-read women'.[13] His sons were, according to John Stuart Mill, 'of more than common ability and all eminently gentlemen'.[14] Joseph Austin died as a young man as a result of yellow fever contracted during a tour of duty with the British navy. Alfred Austin was Assistant Poor Law Commissioner and Secretary to the Board of Works. George Austin had a flair for languages and lived in Freiburg for most of his life. Charles Austin, who was born in 1799, was better known during his lifetime than any of his brothers.

Charles Austin was a highly energetic and intelligent person, a brilliant orator and conversationalist, and the possessor of a remarkable force of will and character. These varied assets explain the profound impression that he made upon his contemporaries. John Stuart Mill was so impressed that he believed that Charles Austin was capable of 'dominating the world'.[15] The poet John Moultrie was sufficiently inspired to write a poem that described Charles Austin in these terms: 'No keener wit, no intellect more subtle, none more bold, was found in all our host.'[16] Like his older brother, Charles Austin was an ardent Benthamite in the 1820s. He was also a very persuasive exponent of this form of utilitarianism. He evidently influenced a number of his fellow undergraduates at Cambridge University, as well as other young men, to embrace the faith.[17]

Charles Austin followed in the footsteps of his older brother to the extent that he became a barrister. Unlike John Austin, Charles Austin's practice of law was highly successful. A contemporary described him as 'the first lawyer in England'.[18] His income was extraordinary. Estimates of it for 1857 ranged from 40,000 to 100,000 pounds. His success required an enormous expenditure of energy that eventually took its toll of his health. He evidently shared with his oldest brother a nervous and delicate constitution. It was so taxed by overwork that, in 1848, he felt that he was dying. He therefore retired from the practice of law and lived for the remainder of his life off the fortune that he had accumulated. His death in 1874 apparently surprised many of his old friends, who believed that he had 'long ago passed away'.[19]

Although John Austin spent the final eleven years of his life in seclusion, his career was in other respects quite different from that of his younger brother. Most of John Austin's early years were closely intertwined with the Napoleonic wars. From 1793 to 1815 Great Britain was in a virtually continuous state of war with France. This conflict not only provided Jonathan Austin with an opportunity to make large profits from his milling business, but directly conditioned the life of his eldest son. He was brought up in Ipswich, which was then a garrison town. He was apparently 'filled with military zeal by the bands and marching troops. At the age of seven he was found kneeling in the garden praying earnestly to God that he might be given a bow and arrow.'[20] Whether his prayers were answered is not known, but in 1807 he enlisted in the British army. He served as an officer under Sir William Bentinck in both Sicily and Malta.

Austin kept a diary during the last years of his military service. This document illuminates his disposition, character, and ambitions. An entry dated 31 December 1811 expressed his dissatisfaction with the manner in which he spent the year. 'During that period', he wrote, 'the waste of money, of time and of health has been enormous; and indolence – always the prominent vice of my character – has within the last nine months assumed over me an empire I almost despair of shaking.'[21] Even so, Austin decided to rouse himself from this lethargy. He became convinced that his happiness was 'commensurate with and inseparable from . . . progress . . . in the acquisition of knowledge'.[22] Despite relapses, he read extensively during this period.

Austin resigned his commission in 1812. Some of his critics have argued that his military service influenced the ideas about law that he subsequently developed. F. J. C. Hearnshaw maintained, for example, that it 'probably impressed upon his mind a permanent tendency to over-emphasize the element of command in law, and to stress unduly the indivisible and illimitable character of supreme authority. His jurisprudence always smacked of the drill-sergeant.'[23] Speculation of this sort has been fuelled by Sarah Austin's description of the effect on her husband of the five years he spent in the army.

> At a very early age Mr. Austin entered the army, in which he served for five years; a fact which would have no place here, but for the permanent traces it left in his character *and sentiments* . . . he retained to the end of his life a strong sympathy with, and respect for, the military character, as he conceived it. The high and punctilious sense of honour, the chivalrous tenderness for the weak, the

> generous ardour mixed with *reverence for authority and discipline*, the frankness and loyalty, which were, he thought, the distinguishing characteristics of a true soldier, *were also his own; perhaps even more preeminently, than the intellectual gifts for which he was so remarkable*[24] (emphasis added).

Sarah Austin was a gifted person who knew her husband better than anyone else. Her explanation of the effects of his military service must therefore be taken seriously. Even so, her account is inaccurate to the extent that it attributes to her husband a life-long *reverence* for authority and discipline. Such is the case, at least, if this word means 'deep respect and veneration for some thing, place, or person regarded as having a sacred or exalted character'.[25] John Austin did not revere authority, in this sense of the word, in the 1820s and early 1830s. Although he believed that authority was both necessary and desirable, he did not impute to it a sacred or exalted character.

This is apparent from certain themes of *The Province of Jurisprudence Determined*, which was published in 1832. To some extent, it was a clarification and defence of the principle of utility. Since Austin was an ardent utilitarian, he evaluated laws and governmental policies on the basis of their effects on the general happiness.[26] These *effects* determine whether legal or political authority has a justifiable *claim* to respect, which is not intrinsic. Aside from this, various other ideas that Austin expressed in this book are incompatible with reverence for authority. He was a strong proponent of the utility of free discussion and criticism of laws and policies.[27] He was convinced that the 'most pernicious laws . . . have been and are continually enforced as laws by judicial tribunals.'[28] He even believed that resistance to government could be justified on utilitarian grounds.[29]

These are not the characteristic ideas of a person who *reveres* legal or political authority. A letter which Austin and George C. Lewis wrote in 1837 also expressed a less than reverential attitude toward *military* authority:

> The habits of absolute command, to be followed by implicit obedience, which military men contract, render them in most cases unfit for performing those functions of civil government, which consist in consulting the opinions and feelings of the governed, and in satisfying their reason before requiring their obedience.[30]

This evidence points strongly to the conclusion that Austin did not revere authority when he wrote his famous book. If this inference is warranted, then a reverential attitude toward authority could not explain his ideas about law. Of course, he eventually developed a very different attitude toward the powers-that-be than he expressed in the 1820s and 1830s. The conservative views which he subsequently held may have distorted Mrs Austin's perception of the effects of his military service. In any case, *reverence* for authority and discipline is incompatible with some of the most characteristic ideas which he expounded in the only book that he published in his lifetime.

Whatever the effects of John Austin's military service were, he resigned his commission and decided to study law. Legal education, in its modern form, was non-existent at this time. Instruction in law, such as it was, was intensely practical. The law student was 'obliged to get his knowledge of law by means of undirected reading and discussion, and by attendance in chambers, in a law office, or in the courts.'[31] The men whose offices Austin attended are not known with any certainty, though they apparently included Godfrey Sykes. Austin evidently envisaged even as a student the role which he was subsequently to play. At least Sir John Patterson recalled this incident in the pupil room at Mr Sykes' office:

> One day a singular man entered . . . for the first time, and presently announced to his companions that he had come there, not only to qualify himself as a special pleader, but to study and elucidate the principles of Law. This was John Austen.[32]

Austin's apprenticeship included a stint in the chambers of an equity draughtsman. This experience may have influenced certain characteristics of his style of writing. An equity draughtsman was a barrister who 'drafted equity pleadings. In those days . . . the bill in equity, or first pleading, was frequently a tiresome and repetitious document in nine parts, each of which had to be very exact in its language.'[33] Although Austin's writing was almost always clear and could be eloquent, at times it was tiresome and very repetitious. His publications also reflected his penchant for the maximum possible degree of accuracy and precision. A famous letter that he wrote to his fiancée in 1817 provides some evidence that his experience as an equity draughtsman contributed to these tendencies:

> I almost apprehend that the habit of drawing will in no short time give me so exclusive and intolerant a taste (as far, I mean, as relates

to my own productions) for perspicuity and precision, that I shall hardly venture on sending a letter of much purpose, even to you, unless it be laboured with the accuracy and circumspection which are requisite in a deed of conveyance.[34]

Some of Austin's letters to Sarah Taylor, to whom he became engaged in 1814, indicate that he was an apt prophet. They include his proposal of marriage, the formality and pretentiousness of which mark it as one of the most remarkable documents in the history of this ancient institution.[35] If the tone of this letter upset Sarah Taylor, her annoyance was not strong enough to induce her to turn down Austin's proposal. They were married in 1819, one year after John Austin was called to the bar. His bride was a remarkable person in her own right. She also deserves some of the credit for whatever success her husband achieved. G. M. Young has cited her as an example of the 'notable Victorian woman', a 'blend of the great lady and the intellectual woman, not yet professional'.[36] Sarah Austin shared with her husband middle-class origins, good looks, intelligence, and ability. The differences between the Austins were probably more striking than these similarities. John Austin was a nervous, insecure, and apparently humourless man who was subject to long periods of lethargy and despondency. His wife was ambitious, energetic, lively, and gregarious. She was also an able translator who possessed a very graceful style of writing.[37] She was in some respects a stronger person than her husband, who quite accurately foresaw that she would be his 'prop and comforter'.[38] Sarah Austin turned out to be much more than that. She not only comforted and encouraged her husband, but functioned as a kind of secretary and literary agent for him. Her greatest service to him may have been to edit his lectures on jurisprudence, which were published posthumously.[39] It was a task that John Austin was either unwilling, or unable, to undertake.

The Austins moved to London, at any rate, shortly after their marriage. Their home was the focus of an active social life throughout most of their married life. Sarah Austin's proclivity, and gift, for entertainment were nowhere more apparent than in London. Despite very limited resources, the residence of the Austins in Queen Square Place 'soon collected within its walls as remarkable an assemblage of persons as ever met in a London drawing-room'.[40] They included Jeremy Bentham and James Mill, who lived in the same neighbourhood as the Austins. This proximity no doubt facilitated the intimate friendship that developed between the Austins and their famous neighbours. According to Alexander Bain, the young lawyer and his wife were 'the closest of [James] Mill's . . . friends'.[41] Their friendship continued 'to the last'.[42] Although the personal relationship between Bentham and the Austins cooled somewhat in the late 1820s, it was quite intimate in the preceding years.

The significance of the relationship that John Austin developed with Mill and Bentham is difficult to exaggerate. To begin with, their ideas strongly influenced the spectacles through which Austin saw much of the world. Moreover, his association with the leading utilitarians placed him at the cutting edge of a vital reform movement. To be sure, Bentham and his circle did not monopolize the impulse for reform of English society. The author of a recent study points out, for example, that the reformers belonged to various schools of thought.[43] Still, John Roach maintains that the utilitarians were the most important group of secular reformers. He also gives them the highest ranking among 'political and social thinkers in nineteenth-century England'.[44]

If James Mill is best known as Bentham's lieutenant, he was a formidable person in his own right. He had a forceful personality, a powerful intellect, a gift for lucid expression, and an almost puritanical zeal for reform. His opinions 'gave the distinguishing character to the Benthamic or utilitarian propagandism of that time'[45] and he was 'more than anyone else . . . the theorist of the new brand of radicalism'.[46] Its supporters included a 'little knot of young men' who were subsequently known as the 'philosophic radicals'.[47] According to John Stuart Mill's classic explanation of their mode of thinking, they combined 'Bentham's point of view with that of the modern political economy, and with the Hartleian metaphysics'. The philosophic radicals were also enthusiastic advocates of Malthus's principle of population, which provided the basis of the only path to the 'indefinite improvability of human affairs'. Finally, they shared James Mill's 'almost unbounded confidence in the efficacy of . . . representative government, and complete freedom of discussion'. The philosophic radicals also agreed with his support for a democratic suffrage and his 'sternest disapprobation' of aristocratic rule.[48]

John Stuart Mill's account of the creed of the philosophic radicals may under-emphasize their diversity. William Thomas's recent study of them stresses, for example, 'the variety both of theoretical outlook and of political response within the group'.[49] Even so, Austin held most, if not all, of the tenets of the philosophic radicals as portrayed by Mill. Austin was a great admirer of Bentham, a strong proponent of modern political economy, a believer in Hartleian metaphysics, and a most enthusiastic Malthusian. The only areas in which he may *possibly* have disagreed with the philosophic radicals were their *unbounded* confidence in representative government, their faith in *complete* freedom of discussion, and their support of a democratic suffrage. The available evidence simply does not establish, with complete certainty, Austin's views of these matters in the early 1820s. The available evidence does indicate, however, the *probability* that at this time he even agreed politically with the philosophic radicals. At least in 1859 he expressed the view that he once was 'a Radical' who accepted Bentham's political opinions 'without sufficient examination'.[50]

This interpretation does not imply that Austin was strongly influenced, if he was influenced at all, by James Mill.[51] The point is, rather, that Austin had 'attained, by reading and thought, a considerable number of the same opinions [as James Mill], modified by his own very decided individuality of character.'[52] His friendship with James Mill and persons under his influence may also have reinforced the points of agreement between the two men.

The influential figure in Austin's intellectual development was not James Mill but Jeremy Bentham. Austin was indeed both a student of Bentham and an 'enthusiastic admirer, almost a worshipper, of him'.[53] In fact, the word 'disciple' is not too strong a term to use to describe the early relationship of Austin to Bentham. This is apparent from a letter that the former wrote to the latter in 1819. Austin not only explicitly described their relationship in these terms, but also wrote:

> for though I have long revered you, and though my deep conviction of the importance of your doctrines has long inflamed me with an earnest desire to see them widely diffused and generally embraced; still, these feelings . . . have been not a little enhanced by the regard which you have shown for *myself*. If these feelings remain unimpaired . . . I shall not be the least zealous amongst those preachers of the gospel who . . . are daily increasing in numbers and in faith.[54]

The religious language of this letter – the use of such words as 'zealous', 'preachers', 'gospel', 'disciple', and 'faith' – is highly significant. It indicates that Austin perceived Bentham's doctrines as the key to the salvation of mankind. The remainder of Austin's letter provides further support for this interpretation. This is evident from the 'secret' which, he wrote, he would not disclose to anyone else but

Bentham and Bingham. The essence of it was his intention to practise law only in order to accumulate enough money to support himself and his wife in 'independence and comfort', after which he would feel 'no violent desire for any other object than that of disseminating your [Bentham's] doctrines'. Austin expressed the need to keep this 'scheme' a secret for two reasons, one of which was to prevent his father from disinheriting him. The other was his expectation that he would have little chance to make money as a lawyer if he held up 'the absurdity of the system to public view'.[55]

The very great extent to which Austin was, in the mid-1820s, an ardent Benthamite is also apparent from his first and second publications. These articles not only appeared in journals controlled by the Benthamites, but clearly illustrate the spirit of their reforms of English law. At least this inference may be drawn if A. V. Dicey was warranted in claiming that Bentham and his disciples 'sounded the attack upon every restriction, not justifiable by some definite and assignable reason of utility, upon the freedom of human existence and the development of individual character.'[56]

Austin published his first article in 1824[57] and it reflected a more egalitarian outlook than any of his other writings. The article itself was a long, detailed, and important critique of primogeniture from a Benthamite perspective. Although the precise origins of this rule are unclear, Sir Frederick Pollock claimed that it 'obtained . . . a more complete and lasting success [in England] than anywhere else. . . . Primogeniture . . . drove its rivals into corners, and became the common law of English landed property.' Even so, he pointed out that 'the power of testamentary disposition [also] became unlimited; so that the rule of intestate descent is now [1883] comparatively unimportant in its effects.'[58] If the effects of primogeniture were relatively insignificant by 1883, it proved to be very difficult to abolish. In fact, the periodic attempts to eliminate it did not succeed until 1925. Resistance to the change was fuelled by the highly emotional support for the rule demonstrated by its supporters. They defended primogeniture for intestate descent on grounds that 'any tampering with [it] . . . must, by leading to the division of estates, destroy "that fair and reasonable influence which the property and aristocracy of the country was [sic] allowed to possess." '[59]

If primogeniture had defenders in the nineteenth century, it seldom lacked critics. The system of entails by means of which land was tied down to the same family for generations, if not centuries, was also subject to attack. The ranks of critics and reformers of these laws and practices included John Austin. His article on the subject was a response to an essay by Ramsay McCulloch on the French law of succession published in the *Edinburgh Review*,[60] the voice of the Whigs. He had not only defended the custom of primogeniture and the English law of entail on the basis of their utility,[61] which was bad enough in the eyes of Bentham and the philosophic radicals. In addition, McCulloch had committed the cardinal sin of extolling the British aristocracy. He expressed his view in these terms:

> Far from joining in the outcry that has so frequently been raised against the magnitude of the property in the hands of the aristocracy, we consider the existence of a numerous and powerful body of landed proprietors, without artificial privileges, but possessed of great natural influence, as essentially contributing to the improvement and stability of the public institutions of such densely peopled countries as France and England; and as forming the best attainable check to arbitrary power on the one hand, and to popular frenzy and licentiousness on the other.[62]

This *apologia* was anathema to Bentham, James Mill, and the philosophic radicals. Bentham himself excoriated the 'corrupted and corrupting aristocracy', under whose rule the condition of 'the poor people is day by day approaching nearer and nearer to the condition of the negro and the horse'.[63] Although James Mill expressed his opposition to the aristocracy in more guarded language, there is no doubt about his disapproval of its political power. Aside from a deficiency in intellectual ability, he argued, the few who rule use their power to benefit themselves at the expense of the people.[64] Any comparatively small number of persons who monopolized political power would exercise it for the same purpose. The existence of an aristocratic ruling class thus defeats the very *raison d'être* of government, which is to secure the greatest happiness of the greatest number. Mill therefore concluded that the unfitness of the established aristocracy to rule may be deduced from the known laws of human nature and, as such, 'rests on demonstration'.[65]

This analysis underlies the opposition of Bentham and Mill to the political power of the British aristocracy. The *Westminster Review* had been founded in 1823 in order to provide an organ for expressing and promoting their doctrines.[66] It was thus a natural place for Austin to publish his article on primogeniture. He began from the same premise as McCulloch, a premise to which Austin adhered throughout his life.

The long and short of it was that 'an institution or custom must be praised or blamed as it tends to increase or diminish the sum of happiness. In a word, the test to which it must be submitted is *utility*.'[67] Austin was so strongly committed to this standard that he even criticized David Ricardo for his occasional deviations from it. To be sure, political economy is indebted to his 'piercing and comprehensive genius . . . for its pretensions to the name of a science.' Even so, in his treatment of the causes which 'accelerate or retard accumulation, he sometimes forgets, for a moment, that accumulation, like every thing else, is subordinate to the great end, happiness.'[68]

If Austin and McCulloch began from the same utilitarian premise, they strongly disagreed about its application to the case of primogeniture. Austin claimed that this institution is anything but expedient. He also assailed the power of entailing or substituting, which prevented 'the owner from selling, giving away, or encumbering the land as well as from disposing of it by will.'[69] Austin was particularly critical of entails because of his conviction that they were the basis of, and perpetuated, the custom of primogeniture. Although English law limited the duration of restrictions on alienation, he claimed that these limitations were largely ineffective. As a matter of fact, 'property in large masses is transmitted from generation to generation almost as certainly as ever.'[70]

Austin criticized primogeniture on various grounds. His most fundamental objection was its substantial contribution to 'aristocratical ascendancy and . . . misgovernment'.[71] Primogeniture not only perpetuates aristocratic power, but fosters a 'most terrible abuse' of it.[72] The underlying reason for this pernicious state of affairs is the need of the aristocracy to provide for their younger children. This necessity explains the existence of bloated establishments,[73] unnecessary and wasteful wars,[74] enormously expensive and useless colonies,[75] the award of military positions on the basis of familial connections rather than merit,[76] and the imposition of excessive taxes to maintain an established church.[77] In short, the custom of primogeniture explains the tendency of the aristocracy to tax and pillage the people 'with little moderation, though, certainly, with much of decorum'.[78]

This critique strongly conditioned the system of testamentary disposition that Austin himself favoured. His general view was that insofar as 'happiness is the effect of wealth, those institutions and customs are most to be praised, which most conciliate augmentation in the quantity of wealth with equality in the distribution of it.' He maintained that these ends are 'conciliated amongst the middling class in England as far as they can be.'[79] He also argued that prohibition of all restrictions on alienation of real property was the best means to achieve these ends. In other words, elimination of these restraints is the most effective way to augment wealth and ensure equality in its distribution. Finally, he maintained that the abolition of entails would cause the custom of primogeniture to wither away. He summarized his position in these terms: 'We think that every person of mature age and sound mind should be left to dispose of his property at his own discretion, subject only to the simple and not severe condition of imparting the same absolute dominion to the object or objects of his bounty.'[80]

This argument raises the question of *why* the prohibition of entails would have the benefits that Austin attributed to it. To begin with, he claimed that it would augment wealth by promoting a much more efficient use of land. The system of entails encourages short leases unacceptable to 'multitudes of wealthy capitalists, who would willingly invest their capital under more enduring interests.'[81] If entails were abolished, capitalists would either lease land for long terms or buy it. The result in either case would be to increase the proportion of the capital of the community efficiently invested in agriculture.

Austin explained how the abolition of entails would foster a more equal distribution of wealth by analyzing two sorts of countries. One was a nation that was 'ill-governed', a not too oblique reference to England. Even in such a country, the prohibition of restrictions on alienation would have egalitarian effects. While one proprietor might dissipate or impair his property, another 'would be inclined to divide it for the rational and humane purpose of dealing equally with his children. And as these and other inducements to alienation would always be backed by the instant power of alienating, a large fortune would rarely or never be transmitted to any very distant descendant of the person who had originally acquired it.'[82] The testator's perception that the bulk of his real property would be unlikely to remain in the family would lead to the same result. On the one hand, the temptation to bequeath his property to a single child would be negligible. On the other hand, he would be subject to 'those sentiments of even-handed justice, which dictate the testamentary dispositions of men of the middling class.'[83]

The beneficial effects of the prohibition of entails would be even greater in a country that was well-governed. The most significant consequence would be to extinguish 'at once, and for ever . . . the pernicious custom of primogeniture'.[84] Austin cited the experience of the United States in support of this judgment, in which respect he was following the practise of Bentham. He came to extol the virtues of the American republic as 'the only form of government which ever had, or ever could have had, for its end in view, the greatest happiness of the greatest number.'[85] Accordingly, Bentham cited American experience whenever it was useful to support his reforms and Austin followed the example of his mentor. While it may appear 'romantic' to a 'rapacious and sordid oligarchy', public offices in America are filled on the basis of merit rather than family influence. Every testator must therefore decide whether to provide for his younger children from his own estate, or to leave them unprotected. Austin was confident of the choice that would be made: 'Every parent would bequeath his property with a view to equality amongst his children; and . . . properties would be reduced, in the course of a single generation, to those moderate dimensions which comport with the general happiness.'[86]

Austin published his second article in 1826[87] and it provides additional evidence of his strong commitment to the cause of legal reform. His essay was in essence a far-sighted critique of the unlimited liability of partners in joint-stock companies. Prior to the statutory changes enacted in 1844 and 1855, English law 'virtually prohibited joint-stock enterprise for ordinary trading and manufacturing purposes'.[88] Peter Mathias points out that each partner in an enterprise was personally liable for the debts of the partnership 'to the last guinea, to the last acre'. Individual firms could only limit the liability of their partners by Royal Charter, Letters Patent or a Special Act of Parliament. Such dispensations were rarely given to manufacturing concerns.[89]

Austin criticized this system as both 'needless and pernicious'.[90] The unlimited liability of partners was harmful because it deterred investments useful to investors and the public. A cautious man would not invest in a joint-stock company regardless of how successful he thought it would *probably* be. Since he could lose everything if the company failed, the 'merest chance of incurring this fearful evil, outweighs the probability of gain'. Although Parliament or the Crown could exempt partners from unlimited liability, Austin felt that this remedy was almost worse than the disease. The Crown may withhold its permission and thus prevent useful undertakings. If immunity were granted, the applicants were subject to 'needless vexation, and loaded with unnecessary expense'. Austin claimed that exemption by

Parliament was even worse than by the Crown. 'The negligence, the impudent injustice, with which pretended inquiries have been managed by honourable committees, have extorted expressions of indignation and scorn from the most temperate and discreet.'[91]

Austin argued that the rule of unlimited liability is not only pernicious, but unnecessary. For one thing, it is not required in order to protect creditors. If joint stock companies were properly registered, their potential creditors would have sufficient information to make intelligent decisions about lending money. For another thing, unlimited liability is not necessary in order to protect investors from their own folly. Austin claimed that the disadvantages of trading in companies are 'so great and obvious, that the rule is unnecessary as a check upon improvident enterprise'.[92] In short, unlimited liability presumes a paternalism of which Austin was highly critical. He expressed his objections to it in terms which illustrate very clearly the individualistic spirit of the broader movement in which he participated:

> Every ignorant ruler is mightily given to rule. Not satisfied with protecting the governed from the harm which they might do to one another, the impertinent meddler must needs protect them from the harm which they might do to themselves. But in spite of all that may be thought by drivelling and presumptuous legislators, the great majority of mankind are prudent, as well as laborious. The cheering truth is established by the progress of all large communities from poverty to comparative opulence . . . capital could never accumulate in quantities worthy of the name, if most of those who are able to save were not habitually saving, and their savings were not applied to the business of production with habitual skill and discretion.[93]

These considerations were the basis of the reforms that Austin advocated in the established law. They included a requirement for the registration of joint-stock companies and their partners, permission for these companies to sue and to be sued 'effectually and with ease',[94] and establishment of the right of partners to limit their liability without approval of Parliament or the Crown. Austin thus recommended many of the changes subsequently enacted by Parliament in 1844, 1855, 1856 and 1862.[95] To this extent, his article was prophetic and quite persuasive. At the same time, he insisted that limited liability would not be as beneficial as it could be unless the laws of usury were also abolished. Both these laws and the law of partnerships imposed 'needless and mischievous restraints upon the discretion of lenders and borrowers. The removal of either restriction would mitigate the evil of the other; but in order to obtain the full complement of good, both of them must be abolished.'[96]

If Austin's first and second articles do not constitute exciting reading, they tend to express liberal and progressive ideas. These writings also indicate the great extent to which he was an orthodox Benthamite in the mid-1820s.[97] His intellectual debt to Bentham extends far beyond, however, the themes of these articles. Austin appears to have inherited, or at least been subject to the strong influence of, Bentham's dissatisfaction with theories of the moral sense and natural rights,[98] his uncompromising commitment to utilitarianism,[99] his command conception of law, his theory of sovereignty, and his sharp distinction between the law as it is and as it ought to be.[100] Austin also derived from Bentham an intense dissatisfaction with English law and its apologists such as Blackstone,[101] a very high evaluation of legal certainty,[102] and an enthusiasm for codification.[103]

This interpretation does not signify that only Bentham influenced Austin, or that their views were identical. Austin's legal philosophy reflected the impact of Hobbes, his prescriptions for social reform embodied the teachings of Malthus, and his ideas about economics corresponded almost completely to the doctrines of the classical political economists. It is therefore not surprising that Austin praised highly Hobbes,[104] Malthus,[105] Adam Smith,[106] and Ricardo.[107] John Stuart Mill may have had these men in mind when he accurately observed that Austin 'had made Bentham's best ideas his own, *and added much to them from other sources and from his own mind*' (emphasis added). Mill was also impressed by the extent to which Austin was free of the 'youthful fanaticism' of the philosophic radicals and differed from the other Benthamites. They included Charles Austin, who presented the Benthamic doctrines in 'the most startling form of which they were susceptible'. Unlike his brother, John Austin attacked 'narrower interpretations and applications of the principles they both professed'.[108]

The extent to which Austin was his own man became apparent in the late 1820s. His unwillingness to restrain expression of his disagreement with Bentham evidently led to a break in their personal relationship which was similar to the split that developed between James Mill and Bentham.[109] This was a period of Bentham's life, after all, in which he became less tolerant of disagreement with his ideas. 'If

Bentham had been remarkably flexible and undogmatic for the better part of his life,' James Steintrager has written, 'the last fifteen years were marked by a growing inflexibility and dogmatism, characteristics matched by the increasing tendency to treat his personal associates with vituperation and scorn.'[110]

Although the specific issues about which Austin and Bentham disagreed are unknown, some of their views were quite different. Their most substantial differences of opinion were political. Austin eventually became far more conservative than he was in the early and mid-1820s. The change in his political outlook may have begun in the late 1820s and could have been the source of his friction with Bentham. At least it is the view of Gordon Waterfield that Austin 'argued in Bentham's study that it was a fundamental error to think that the people themselves had no "sinister interest", and that these were quite as dangerous as the "sinister interests" of the governing classes.'[111] Unlike Austin, Bentham became more radical in the latter stages of his life. He did not become a democrat, for example, until he was over forty. Moreover, his 'original conversion' to democracy in 1789–90 appears to have been 'very ephemeral'. 'Three or four years later . . . [he] was writing *against* parliamentary reform,' A. J. Dinwiddy points out, 'and he subsequently forgot that he had ever written the fragment of 1790 in support of it. . . . The really fruitful turning-point in the development of his political thought came in 1809.'[112] In short, it did not come until he was sixty-one years old.

If the most basic differences between Bentham and Austin were political, their positions on various other issues also differed. Austin's interpretation of utilitarianism diverged in certain respects from Bentham's, he had a narrower conception of the functions of government than his mentor, and he criticized certain of Bentham's ideas about law.[113] Of course, Austin expressed his 'great admiration'[114] for Bentham, whom he was 'prone to follow'. Even so, Austin refused to adopt his predecessor's 'dogmas' with 'blind and servile submission'.[115] Indeed Austin claimed that only impostors 'exact from their disciples "prostration of the understanding". . . . A man of Mr Bentham's genius may provoke inquiry; and may rest satisfied with the ample and genuine admiration which his writings will infallibly extort from scrutinizing and impartial judges.'[116]

The extent to which Austin practised what he preached is evident from his *Lectures on Jurisprudence*, which contain numerous criticisms of Bentham. They include the judgments that he mistakenly applied the term sanctions to rewards as well as punishments,[117] unjustifiably blamed judges for legislating,[118] inadequately defined independent political society,[119] overstated the degree of simplicity that law may achieve,[120] expressed 'ignorant disdain' for the law of things of the classical Roman jurists,[121] subjected status to an 'inconsistent and obscure' analysis,[122] severed substantive from procedural law,[123] and erroneously conceived of title.[124]

Moreover, these criticisms do *not* reflect the only significant differences between the two men. Both the range and approach of Austin's published writings about law are, for example, narrower than Bentham's. Austin not only concerned himself with a relatively small number of problems, he was also more the expositor than the censor or reformer of law. In contrast, Bentham 'wrote on almost every conceivable subject to which the application of utilitarian principles can make a difference. . . . On nearly all of these subjects he offered both searching, detailed analysis and constructive criticism, and so played the dual role of what he himself termed Expositor and Censor.'[125] Aside from this, Austin's and Bentham's attitudes toward inventing new terminology to replace the ambiguities of established expressions differed. Bentham occasionally utilized neologisms, while Austin was critical of this practice.[126] Although they shared the same *goal* of clarifying legal concepts, their *means* to achieve this end were not always identical. Finally, their conceptions of sovereignty differed in several respects.[127]

This analysis may underestimate the extent to which Austin eventually disagreed with Bentham's ideas about law. Such an interpretation draws a certain amount of support, at least, from a pamphlet that Austin published in 1859. While he acknowledged his youthful admiration for Bentham, he also pointed out that he had become more critical of his great predecessor with the passage of time:

> I have since dissented from many of his [Bentham's] views of law and of the various subjects immediately connected with it; although my admiration of his genius has increased in intensity as my increasing knowledge has rendered it less undiscerning.[128]

This evidence clearly establishes that Austin was no mere parrot of Bentham. To say this is not to suggest, however, that they disagreed about fundamentals. Although Austin chipped away at the edges of Bentham's doctrines, he accepted the essentials of most of them. In short, he owed a substantially larger intellectual debt to Bentham than to anyone else.

2

The years from 1825 to 1835 constitute one of the most significant periods of Austin's life. At the outset of this span of time he decided to quit the practise of law. Subsequently, he began what appeared to be a most promising career as a teacher of jurisprudence. He also completed and published *The Province of Jurisprudence Determined*. One disappointment after another marked the final years of this ten-year period. The most significant one was the termination of Austin's career as a teacher. The corollary of this development, and others, was a disenchantment with England that strongly conditioned the decision of the Austins to live abroad.

Austin's failure as a practising lawyer was very different from the bright prospects that had been predicted for him – if the account of Janet Ross is accurate. Lord Brougham, Sir John Romilly, and Sir William Earle told her that they entertained the highest expectations for Austin's success. These men were particularly impressed, she has recounted, by his clear mind, exact memory, and the 'extraordinary vigour and precision of his language.' As a result, they expected Austin to reach 'the highest place in the profession'.[129] These expectations proved to be unfounded and in 1825 he gave up the practise of law.

Austin evidently practised law as an equity draughtsman in Lincoln's Inn.[130] Unfortunately, almost nothing is known about his experiences at the bar. Any explanation of his lack of success is therefore highly speculative. Sarah Austin explained her husband's failure on the basis of his delicate health and the 'constitution of his mind'.[131] His health certainly could have been an important factor. Sydney Smith once described Austin as 'the Opprobrium Medicorum. Nothing and Nobody seems to do him any good.'[132] He was subject throughout most of his life to severe 'feverish attacks',[133] the symptoms of which were very similar to migraine headaches. According to Janet Ross, the 'travail of the brain reacted on the digestive organs, produced sickness and fever, and culminated in excruciating headaches which laid the powerful thinker . . . prostrate.'[134] Aside from poor health, Austin's disposition and temperament probably contributed to his failure as a practising barrister. He was not only a nervous, sensitive, proud, and conscientious man who tended to lack self-confidence. In addition, he was hyper-sensitive, unduly proud, and a perfectionist. As long as he 'could descry the smallest error or ambiguity in a phrase,' Sarah Austin wrote, 'he recast it again and again till his accurate mind could no longer suggest an objection or a difficulty.'[135] Of course, this last trait was responsible for some of the virtues of Austin's writings on the subject of jurisprudence. It is also a trait which could have redounded to his credit as a practising lawyer, if he had not possessed it in such an extreme form. Nevertheless, the cluster of traits which formed the man in all likelihood impeded his success in the practise of law.

The impact upon Austin of this experience is difficult to gauge. Sarah Austin attempted, in one place, to minimize its significance. She claimed that John Austin's lack of success in the practise of law was 'nothing, and would never have been regretted by himself or those who cared for him'.[136] Although this statement may be entirely accurate, I doubt that it states the whole truth. Austin devoted seven years of his life to the attempt to practise law. It is inconceivable to me that his inability to succeed did not discourage and disappoint him. Still, his failure at the bar does pale in comparison with his lack of success as a teacher of jurisprudence.

If Austin was disappointed by his failure at the practise of law, his spirits must have been lifted enormously in 1826. In that year he was appointed to the Chair in Jurisprudence and the Law of Nations at the University of London. The University had just been established and its major purposes were

> to provide higher education for those persons unable to go to Oxford or Cambridge, and . . . to afford an opportunity for the study of those subjects neglected at Oxford and Cambridge. Oxford and Cambridge were exclusive, expensive, and narrow. London was to be open and cheap, and to remove the reproach 'that learning only means, in its common acceptation, a knowledge of the dead languages and mathematics.'[137]

The subjects neglected at Oxford and Cambridge included professional courses for the study of law and medicine. The founders of the University of London believed that one of its greatest contributions would be to fill this gap. The Governing Council of the University particularly emphasized the great potential of the study of law in London. The Council issued a statement in 1827, for example, explaining why the University would pay special attention to the department of law. No other projected course of study afforded 'a greater field for usefulness, especially as regards those young men who are destined to practise as attorneys, many hundreds of whom come annually to London from offices in the country.' The Council stressed the necessity of 'giving the young men brought up to this branch of the profession, that high tone of moral sentiment which a liberal and enlightened education is best calculated to impart.'[138] The location of the University was also expected to facilitate an interchange between practitioners and academicians which would be beneficial to both. Finally, the Council expressed the hope that the professor of law would, in effect, utilize the case method urged half a century later in the United States by Christopher Columbus Langdell. The teacher of law might learn ' "to illustrate his prelections . . . by practical discussions of cases actually tried in the Courts of London and Westminster – as the Medical teachers explain the practical application of their science by Clinical Lessons." '[139]

Although Austin's lectures at the University did not entirely neglect actual cases, he said relatively little about them.[140] At any rate, he was evidently chosen by 'common consent'[141] to fill the Chair. The reasons for his selection are not known with certainty, but two factors probably influenced the decision to appoint him. One was his association and identification with Bentham and his circle. If Leslie Stephen is correct, Austin was regarded by 'all' the utilitarians as 'the profoundest of jurists'.[142] Some of the most prominent Benthamites played very important roles in establishing and governing the University of London. James Mill and George Grote were, for example, among the six or seven most active members of the Council.[143]

This analysis does not mean that Bentham, his followers, or his ideas dominated the University of London. Bentham himself may have been active behind the scenes, but he 'took no public part in the discussions and manoeuvres which prepared the way for the opening of the new institution. . . . the evidence leaves us with the unexpected and disappointing picture of a peripheral, or at best a background figure.'[144] Moreover, his teachings were not the only influence upon the educational policies of the University. Its founders also 'drew their inspiration . . . from the University of Edinburgh and the traditions of Scotland [and] . . . from that liberal movement of which Priestly is a representative.'[145] Even so, Bentham cast a very large shadow over the University. J. H. Burns has pointed out that

> many of the College's antecedents bring us . . . near Bentham himself. It is not simply the presence on our first Council of such avowed Benthamites as Mill, Grote, Tooke, and Warburton; nor merely the early prominence of men like Brougham who gave

practical effect to so many of Bentham's ideas, and Hume – described by Bentham in 1821 as 'the only Member of Parliament who thoroughly deserves that name'. Behind these personal associations lies the affinity between the London University project and so much of what Bentham fought for. [It includes] [e]ducational reform, the progress of science, and a chance to wipe the eye of the Established Church.[146]

This evidence indicates why Austin's association and identification with the Benthamites may have influenced his appointment to the Chair in Jurisprudence and the Law of Nations. He certainly could be relied upon to spread the gospel about a field to which the utilitarians attached the highest importance. Another factor was probably at least as influential, however, in securing Austin's appointment. This was the widespread perception of him as unusually well-qualified for the position.[147] If Lord Brougham is correct, Austin's qualifications included 'profound learning, great reach and force of mind, and a wonderful faculty of exposition'. Of no less importance was Austin's keen sense of duty and his unrelenting pursuit of the truth, which was 'ever his first object; the diffusing a knowledge of it his next'.[148]

In addition to these virtues of a truly great teacher, Austin was, or could be, a very effective public speaker.[149] He was also a prince of conversationalists, a skill that could have contributed to his pedagogical effectiveness. In fact, his mastery of the art of conversation was legendary. Janet Ross found evidence of it in his childhood. She recounted that he was so eloquent in dinner-table conversation with his father that 'the worthy miller never noticed that John drank up his glass of beer.'[150] This story may be apocryphal, but the testimony of Austin's contemporaries to his prowess as a conversationalist is real. Leslie Stephen was probably understating the case when he wrote that Austin was 'famous for his conversational powers'.[151] James Stephen believed that he had not encountered 'in conversation . . . a more interesting or eloquent man'.[152] No less a figure than Macaulay said of Austin: 'He is a speaker of very eminent ability, and in conversation I hardly know his superior.'[153] John Stuart Mill expressed the view of many others when he wrote that Austin's friends 'would be quite satisfied if he would write the very words which he talks.'[154] To be sure, not all of the persons to whom he talked necessarily enjoyed listening to him. Mrs Grote wrote in some irritation that 'the presence of a listener (or listeners) will revive him like magic. . . . It is the indispensable condition of his existence; *talk*, and *monological* talk.'[155]

Nevertheless, most of the persons with whom, or *to whom*, Austin talked derived considerable pleasure from his remarks. Indeed, John Stuart Mill believed that few men contributed more than Austin 'by their individual influence *and their conversation* to the formation and the growth of a number of the most active minds of this generation'[156] (emphasis added). To Mill, this contribution may have been an adequate 'set-off' for Austin's inability to realize fully his very great potential.[157]

Despite his qualifications as a teacher of jurisprudence, Austin faced no small difficulties in preparing his lectures. They included the need to familiarize himself with all of the relevant literature on the subject. This problem was accentuated by the lack of a useful model that he could follow, or at least use, for his particular purposes. These problems underlie the decision of the Austins to visit Germany, where they spent the autumn of 1827 and the winter of 1828. Their sojourn there had two purposes, one of which was to enable Austin to learn the German language and to master the achievements of the great German jurists. The second was to facilitate preparation of his lectures, which were scheduled to be delivered in the autumn of 1828.

The Austins resided in Bonn for most of the six months that they spent in Germany. Their residence in this city was one of the happiest periods of John Austin's life. Bonn was the seat of a newly-established university whose faculty included a number of distinguished scholars, such as Niebuhr and Wilhelm von Schlegel. The Austins found the atmosphere of this university town very congenial to their tastes. In particular, they reacted favorably to its inhabitants' 'respect for knowledge, love of art, freedom of thought, and simplicity of habits'.[158] The cordial reception that the Austins received in Bonn no doubt contributed to their pleasant experiences. They rather quickly became 'familiar figures . . . in legal and philological circles'.[159]

Although John Austin did not complete the preparation of his lectures, he did master the German language. He also was exposed to new currents of thought and scholarship. If the precise impact of this exposure is difficult to calculate, it probably had an important effect upon both his legal and non-legal thought. This is also the conclusion of Andreas Schwarz, the author of the best study of this phase of Austin's life and its relationship to his thought. Schwarz believes that Austin's familiarity with German scholars and books 'contributed in many ways to stimulate his mind, to enrich his learning, and to develop his reflection.'[160] Admittedly, his stay in Germany had little effect on the foundations of his philosophy of law. He derived all of the inspiration that he needed in this respect from English sources such as Hobbes, Locke, and Bentham. Austin also felt that German philosophy of law was in a 'backward state'.[161] Still further, he lamented the 'thick coat of obscuring jargon with which [the German jurists] . . . have wantonly incrusted their necessarily difficult science.'[162] Nonetheless, his residence in Germany probably influenced his thought in a number of respects.

German jurisprudence in 1827 was in a period of transition from natural law to the historical school, the leader of which was Karl von Savigny. The result was a somewhat confusing, but stimulating, atmosphere. It included 'older and more recent books on natural law, different kinds of legal philosophy, legal encyclopedias and methodologies, treatises on the common or pandect law . . . and . . . recent historical and systematic descriptions of . . . Roman law'.[163] Austin's favourable reaction to at least some of this work is evident from his praise of the 'instructive and admirable books which many of the German jurists have certainly produced'.[164] He particularly admired their enthusiasm for Roman law and the fruits of their labours in this area. He viewed the newly-discovered Institutes of Gaius as a 'clear, concise and elegant exposition of the Roman law'. He also expressed his admiration for the high quality of the exposition of Roman law in German textbooks. He wrote to George Grote that the expository books of the German jurists, particularly on Roman law, were 'models of arrangements, and . . . abound with learning'.[165]

These comments indicate that Austin's exposure to German scholarship probably reinforced his interest in Roman law, to which he had introduced John Stuart Mill in 1822. This exposure may also have contributed to Austin's very great admiration for the achievements of the Roman jurists. To be sure, he had nothing but disdain for their philosophy of law. He wondered how 'men of such admirable discernment should have displayed such contemptible imbecility'. Nevertheless, he indicated that their legal philosophy was 'the only part of their writings which deserves contempt'.[166] He particularly admired their systematic exposition of Roman law. He believed that they 'have seized its general principles with great clearness and penetration, have applied these principles with admirable logic to the explanation of details, and have thus reduced this positive system of law to a compact and coherent whole.'[167] In other words, the Roman lawyers did for Roman law what Austin was attempting to do for the science of jurisprudence.

Roman law thus provided Austin with a model of what could be achieved for law as a whole. From this perspective English law seemed useless. At least he took the position that Roman law is 'greatly and palpably superior, considered as a system or whole, to the Law of England'. This attitude may explain why his lectures referred to Roman law almost as much as English law. At any rate, he claimed that to turn from the one to the other is to 'escape from the empire of chaos and darkness, to a world which seems by comparison, the region of order and light'.[168] Aside from this, Austin found some of the ideas developed by the Roman lawyers for *their* purposes to be extremely useful for *his* purposes. The most important example is the distinction which he drew between rights *in rem* and *in personam*. He attached the highest importance to this notion, the origins of which he traced to the 'penetrating acuteness of the classical Roman jurists'.[169]

Austin's residence in Bonn may also have reinforced the prime importance that he ascribed to legal theory. The basis of this very speculative judgment is the strong emphasis on theory in German legal education at the universities. 'The object purposed to be attained', a Select Committee on Legal Education reported in 1846, 'is thorough and extensive knowledge of theory.'[170] This goal explains the nature of the courses which introduced the student to the law. He

> usually begins with an outline of the science, or what is termed the 'Encyclopedia' (Methodologie), common to all other branches of study, and though not obligatory, of considerable advantage. . . . The 'Naturrecht' (Natural Law, or the Philosophy of Jurisprudence) then follows. . . . These lectures illustrate the abstract principles of Jurisprudence, by frequent reference to the practice of different countries, and are well calculated to give the student a general idea at least of its philosophy.[171]

Austin's residence in Germany not only had a significant impact upon his legal thought, but his overall 'views of life'. This is at least how John Stuart Mill described the changes that he observed in Austin upon his return to England. He demonstrated a less militant and polemic disposition, developed a new interest in 'the poetic and contemplative', attributed less significance than he had demonstrated earlier to external changes without a 'better cultivation of the inward nature', and manifested a strong dislike for the 'general meanness of English life'.[172]

Another change in Austin that Mill noted concerned his attitude toward the progress of popular institutions. This development is particularly important because it marks the first major stage in the evolution of his political conservatism. Although the six months that he spent in Germany did not affect his outlook as much as his residence in Europe from 1840 to 1848, it had an impact. This is apparent from his very favourable comparison of the Prussian monarchy with English representative democracy. The former not only displayed more 'practical good government' than the latter, but the Prussian monarchy demonstrated much more care than the English democracy for 'the education and mental improvement of all ranks of the people'. Austin attached tremendous significance to this achievement. He was convinced that the true security 'for good government is "un peuple éclairé" '. In fact, he attributed so much significance to popular education that he even rejoiced in the progress of socialism. Despite his highly critical attitude toward it, he believed that the growth of this movement would have the beneficial effect of compelling the 'powerful classes to educate the people, and to impress on them the only real means of permanently improving their material condition, a limitation of their numbers'.[173] Socialism would thus be the unintended spur for the development of attitudes to which Austin, as a convinced Malthusian, attached the highest importance.

Austin was scheduled to begin his lectures in November 1828. This date is also frequently described as the time when he began teaching at the University of London. He did not actually begin to deliver his lectures, however, until 1829. He requested a delay on two grounds, one of which was ill-health. The other was the difficulty of preparing lectures on jurisprudence 'without a model'.[174] He apparently began to doubt that he would ever deliver his lectures, but these problems were eventually overcome. The course that he began to teach in the autumn of 1829 could not have begun under more auspicious circumstances. He expressed considerable satisfaction with the quality of his students, which was indeed high. Alexander Bain even surmised that Austin's course 'had perhaps the most distinguished attendance that ever honoured any lecturer'.[175] If the accuracy of this judgment is impossible to confirm, many of Austin's students were distinguished. They included John Stuart Mill, Edwin Chadwick, John Romilly, J. A. Roebuck, C. P. Villiers, George Cornewall Lewis and Charles Buller.[176]

Thirty-two students enrolled in the course that Austin taught in 1829. Their reaction to it was apparently favourable. The Governing Council of the University reported in February 1830 that it continued 'to derive the greatest satisfaction from the success which has attended the Law Department'.[177] Austin concluded that 'even if the University were to fail, he should by that time have established a reputation as a teacher of Law which would always enable him to get a class somewhere.'[178] Some evidence of the inaccuracy of this prediction appeared in November 1830. No students showed up for the first lecture in Austin's course. A letter which he subsequently wrote to the University no doubt understated his disappointment:

> If I shall have no Class during the present session, I shall be somewhat surprised as well as discouraged. For my Class last session consisted of thirty-two; most of them were strangers to me, though some were my friends, and acquaintances; and my Lectures (generally speaking) were regularly attended, and seemed to make an impression not unfavourable.
>
> If I shall have a Class, though never so small, I shall certainly Lecture to them regularly, and with all the vigour and ability which I can put forth. This I think is required from me by my engagements to the University.[179]

Although a few students eventually enrolled in the course, Austin postponed the delivery of his lectures until January 1831. He was very discouraged by the 'pitiable' enrolment[180] in his class, which attracted only six or seven students. This small number frustrated his elaborate preparation, wounded his vanity, and imperilled his future at the University. Most of the professors had a guaranteed income during the first three years of their appointment. Their remuneration would thereafter depend upon, and vary with, the number of students who took their courses. 'Scottish experience was held to have proved', Hale Bellot writes, 'that men lectured best when they were hungry. Imminent destitution was a necessary spur to intellectual activity.'[181] If Austin had to live only from the money that he derived from teaching, he would have starved to death. The last year that he offered his course his fees amounted only to £32.[182] He delivered his final lecture in June 1833.[183] He decided in October to stop teaching, at least for a year or two. He resigned his Chair at the beginning of 1835.

The reasons for the failure of Austin's course are varied. Of course, the use of the word 'failure' to describe it is not entirely accurate. His lectures were anything but a failure in a number of respects. They had a definite impact on some of the brightest young men of the time, such as John Stuart Mill and George Cornewall Lewis. The lectures were also posthumously published in volumes which were to exert a profound influence on English jurisprudence. Nevertheless, Austin's course was a failure in the sense that it did not attract enough students to enable him to earn a living by teaching. To be sure, private parties in 1831 raised sufficient funds to endow a salary of £200 per annum for him for the academic years 1831, 1832 and 1833.[184] Nevertheless, this possibility apparently was not attractive enough to overcome his disenchantment with the low enrolment in his course. The endowment was only for three years, after which Austin might well have had no more students than he did in 1832–3.

The reason for the low enrolment in Austin's course could have been his ineffectiveness as a teacher. The available evidence, such as it is, indicates that this explanation is inaccurate. To begin with, his attitude toward the course was very positive. He was most enthusiastic about the prospect of delivering lectures on jurisprudence to young men, many of whom might become active in public affairs. Furthermore, he prepared for his course with his usual conscientiousness and thoroughness.[185] In addition, he used a number of promising techniques for establishing rapport with his students and eliciting their attention. He attempted to learn the names of each member of the class so that he could address them individually,[186] he encouraged discussion and even invited criticism of his lectures, and he tried to develop the habit of lecturing extemporaneously.[187]

Aside from this, the extant comments about Austin's course are very favourable. Lord Brougham asserted that it was 'admired by all'.[188] 'I hear delightful accounts of your lectures,' Nassau W. Senior wrote to Austin in 1829, '& wish they were at an hour that wd admit of my hearing them.'[189] John Stuart Mill claimed that the lectures, which he faithfully attended, 'left an indelible impression on the minds of those who heard them delivered'.[190] Of course, even Mill was not wholly uncritical. He believed that Austin's lectures were unnecessarily repetitive. He also expressed regret that their author was unable to complete his course. Still, Mill maintained that the members of the class were 'extremely delighted with the course as far as it went'.[191]

Although none of this evidence is conclusive proof that Austin was an effective teacher, it strongly supports this judgment. If this conclusion is justified, then other factors besides his performance in the class-room were responsible for the low enrolment in his course. An understanding of them requires a brief explanation of the subject matter of his lectures. They were an exposition of his philosophy of positive law, or law 'as it necessarily is'. His conception of general jurisprudence will be explained in the next chapter of this book, but its focus was the 'principles and distinctions which are common to various systems of particular and positive law.'[192] He distinguished this science from particular jurisprudence, the subject matter of which is 'any . . . system of positive law as now actually obtains, or once actually obtained, in a specifically determined nation, or . . . nations'.[193] While Austin illustrated some of the ideas that he discussed by reference to the actual law of particular nations, the heart of his lectures consisted of elucidation of the basic concepts of general jurisprudence.

A course of this highly theoretical nature laboured under severe handicaps in terms of attracting students. These obstacles included the practical spirit of most actual or prospective English lawyers. Their attitude had a number of sources, one of which was a perception of law as a means for the economic advancement of the practitioner. From this point of view Austin's lectures were of little direct use. In 1861 a reviewer of *The Province of Jurisprudence Determined* accurately wrote that it does not 'impart that species of information which could immediately be coined into guineas. The generality of lawyers care little for general or abstract jurisprudence.'[194] English lawyers were also born and bred in a common-law tradition that tended to de-emphasize the significance of abstract theories or broad generalizations. A major characteristic of the tradition was the development of case law through the judicial resolution of concrete human problems. The actual or future decision of a court was from this perspective far more important than any theory.

This particularistic, case-by-case approach had little appeal for Austin. He was highly critical of its effects on English law, his dissatisfaction with which was pronounced. He candidly stated that 'no other body of Law, obtaining in a civilized community, has so little of consistency and symmetry as our own.'[195] Austin made no secret of his opinion that the body of English law was a 'chaos' of incoherent details of 'matchless confusion and obscurity'.[196] He also derided the knowledge of the typical English lawyer. It is 'nothing but a beggarly account of scraps and fragments. His memory may be stored with numerous particulars, but of the Law as a whole, and of the mutual relations of its parts, he has not a conception.'[197]

It was this knowledge of law as a whole that Austin attempted to develop and explain to his students. If the attitude of the prospective lawyers in his course was similar to that of actual practitioners, his attempt probably had little appeal. A second reason for the low enrolment in Austin's course was the undeveloped state of legal education. The tenor of instruction in the law was not only 'severely practical',[198] but very little legal education in its modern form took place. Sir William Holdsworth described its status in the eighteenth century as a 'very melancholy topic', which it remained for the first part of the next century. Although this last period was an age of law reform, legal education was 'almost the last thing to be reformed'.[199]

The very limited role of the universities and Inns of Court in legal education fully supports Holdsworth's analysis. Their minimal contributions are evident from the Report in 1846 of a Select Committee on Legal Education. It took extensive testimony from legal educators in the universities, which it summarized in these terms:

> Dr Phillimore [of Oxford] states, that the course of lectures on Civil Law is mere form, the lectures are nominal, the examination nominal both in Civil and Common Law. There is no Chair of Common Law, no instruction for pupils in Arts; in fine, in plain terms, no system of Legal Education. . . . The opinion entertained as to the legal education at Cambridge by its own professors, is not more favourable. Mr Starkie, Professor of Civil Law in Downing College, states that he has no attendance on his lectures, and that with the exception of some few lectures of Dr Geldart on Civil Law . . . (whose lectures too . . . are unaccompanied by questions or examination), 'there are no lectures given, and no attendance whatever'.[200]

If the universities failed to provide a system of legal education, the Inns of Court did nothing to fill the gap. Lord Brougham described the situation in these terms:

> The Inns of Court have for ages past never affected to educate their members; and a person is called . . . to the bar, merely because his name has been five years upon the books, or three if he has a degree of Master of Arts, and because he has what is called kept twelve terms, which means being present at the time that grace is said, for a minute or two, a certain number of days in each term during those three years.[201]

While vestiges of requirements of legal qualifications remained, they had become mere formalities. Brougham cited the 'Exercises' as an example. 'Those are now reduced to the merest form: a paper is put into the hands of the student, containing a proposition in law. . . . he then comes before one of the Benchers, and begins, and as soon as he has uttered the first words . . . the Bencher bows, and the student retires, and he has kept "his exercise." ' Brougham emphasized that 'anything, therefore, more entirely nugatory, and more of a mockery, as a test of legal acquirements, cannot possibly be imagined.'[202]

These conditions underlie the conclusions of the Select Committee. They include the judgment that 'no Legal Education, worthy of the name, of a public nature, is at this moment to be found in either country [England and Ireland].'[203] Also, the bulk of the members of the legal profession evidently did not view this situation as a reproach. At least C. H. S. Fifoot attributes to them satisfaction with the *status quo*,[204] an attitude that may have persisted long after Austin's death. In 1883, for example, Albert V. Dicey expressed the opinion that,

> If the question whether English law can be taught at the Universities could be submitted in the form of a case to a body of eminent counsel, there is no doubt whatever as to what would be their answer. They would reply with unanimity and without hesitation that English law must be learned and cannot be taught and that the only places where it can be learned are the law courts or chambers.[205]

Under these circumstances, the odds were heavily stacked against the success of Austin's novel course. If his lectures had been delivered in a situation in which legal education were academically developed, a larger number of students might have attended them. William Holdsworth attributed the failure of Austin's course, for example, 'principally . . . to the fact that legal education had sunk to so low a level, that it was hardly to be expected that any great number of lawyers would feel any interest in an attempt to expound the theory of law.'[206] While philosophically or theoretically inclined students such as J. S. Mill and George C. Lewis were attracted by this attempt, they were the exceptions who proved the rule.

To say this is not to deny that other factors may also have contributed to the limited enrolment in Austin's course. They include the small number of students who matriculated at the University of London. Although the fledgling institution had been expected to enroll 2,000 students, eighty years were required before this expectation was fulfilled. A mere 630 students enrolled for the session of 1829–30. By the next year the position had become 'alarming. Financial embarrassment was immediately felt.'[207] Another factor may have been Austin's periodic illnesses, which forced him frequently to cancel or postpone his lectures. This development must have discouraged at least some students from taking his course. Even so, the prevailing temper of the legal profession and the state of legal education were the basic reasons for the low enrolment in Austin's class.

Whatever the reasons for it, the failure of Austin's course was the 'real and irremediable calamity of his life – the blow from which he never recovered.'[208] The blow was so devastating for a number of reasons, one of which was the frustration of his laborious efforts to prepare his lectures. He expended a vast amount of time and energy on them, at the price of considerable psychological stress. Both the labour and the anxiety seemed to be fruitless. Another reason for the severity of the blow that he received was the unflattering implications of the low enrolments in his course for his future as a teacher of jurisprudence. He dearly wanted to teach this subject and seemed admirably qualified for the position. If the reaction to his course did not completely shatter his prospects as a teacher, it cast grave doubts upon them.

A third factor also contributed to the psychological damage which Austin suffered as a result of the failure of his course. This experience magnified the disappointment that he suffered from the reaction to *The Province of Jurisprudence Determined*. The basis of this work, which was published in 1832, was the first ten lectures in Austin's course (the book also included a revised edition of *An Outline of a Course of Lectures on General Jurisprudence or the Philosophy of Positive Law*, which Austin had published in 1831). The idea for publishing his introductory lectures as a book apparently originated with Sarah Austin. At least she wrote to a friend:

> At first he [John Austin] quite rejected the idea; but on my placing before him many arguments which appeared to me weighty, he consented, only saying that he could incur no risk, neither could he send for a publisher, but that if I would find one and negotiate everything, he would print them. You may imagine I was not slow to undertake nor to accomplish this.[209]

The purpose of Austin's book was to clarify the province of jurisprudence, a subject that he believed to be mired in confusion. The proper focus of this science was positive law, or law 'strictly so-called', which he conceived of as the commands of the sovereign. The introductory chapter of his book is an exposition of his famous command conception of law, or law 'properly so-called'. The second, third, and fourth chapters are an explanation and defence of the principle of utility. These portions of the book are also a very revealing indication of Austin's attitude towards a variety of social, economic, and other problems. The fifth chapter is a detailed analysis of the relationships between law and morality. The final and longest chapter is an elucidation of Austin's controversial theory of sovereignty. This chapter also includes a significant analysis of the origins and forms of government, including a lengthy critique of the theory of the original contract.

Austin's book was not reviewed by either the *Edinburgh Review* or the *Quarterly Review*, which were the most influential journals of the time. This fact was the basis of Sarah Austin's judgment that the initial reception of her husband's book was 'not encouraging'.[210] At the same time, it was not entirely ignored. Indeed, it received several laudatory reviews that would have encouraged almost anyone but John Austin. A reviewer in the *Westminster Review* maintained, for example, that the province of jurisprudence determined 'claims the same place in a course of ethical studies, as Euclid's Elements in Mathematical.'[211]

A favourable review of Austin's book by the *Westminster Review*, which was *the* journal of the Benthamites, is not surprising. Even more laudatory reviews appeared, however, in publications that this group did not control. A good example is *The Times*, which extolled Austin's achievements:

> To great patience in investigating this abstruse and uninviting science, and eminent skill in developing the results of his labours, he adds an ardent love of truth, which breathes throughout his work. . . . Apart from its utility . . . the treatise . . . fairly entitles the author to rank high among original and profound thinkers, and those worshippers of science who have preferred the rare honours which are to be gained in the more difficult paths, to the easy fame which can be won in the more beaten tracks.[212]

The review in the *Law Magazine Review* also acclaimed Austin's book. The reviewer praised his style and his 'very high order of intellect', which was both 'expansive and penetrating'.[213] His book was 'deep', 'clear', 'high toned', 'eloquent', and comprehensive.[214]

Indeed, it 'must certainly rank as the best book on jurisprudence, and one of the best books (speaking generally) of the day.'[215] The reviewer strongly recommended the work to anyone who wished to think clearly about ethics and politics. He especially praised its value for all students of law who wish to master 'the scientific knowledge of it'.[216]

Despite these laudatory notices of his book, Austin was disappointed by the reaction to it. Several of his other experiences during this period of life also disillusioned him. In 1833 he accepted an appointment to the Criminal Law Commission established in that year. The creation of this body was 'an innovation in the history of criminal law and the movement for its reform. It was a Benthamite conception, a group of experts called in by the government, with the approval of Parliament, to discharge a task demanding both specialized knowledge and prolonged consideration.'[217] The terms of reference of the Commission were:

> to digest into one statute all the enactments concerning crimes, their trial and punishment; and to digest into another statute all the provisions of the Common Law touching the same; and to enquire and report how far it might be expedient to combine both these statutes into one body of the Criminal Law, repealing all other statutory provisions; or how far it might be expedient to pass into a law the first-mentioned only of those two statutes.[218]

Austin's appointment to the Commission appeared to be a Godsend for him. The remuneration of the Commissioners was so handsome that it evoked frequent complaints in Parliament.[219] The work of the Commission seemed to John Stuart Mill to be of a type which Austin 'most likes, and for which he is best fitted'.[220] If he was well-suited to serve on the Commission, he soon became discouraged by its meetings. The other Commissioners were practical lawyers who took the position that Austin's views were 'too abstract and scientific'.[221] He also believed that the Commission lacked authority to propose the 'fundamental reforms from which alone any good could come'.[222] He was convinced that he could achieve alone what the Commission would fail to accomplish. 'If they would give me two hundred a year for two years,' he told his wife, 'I would shut myself up in a garret, and at the end of that time I would produce a complete map of the whole field of crime, and a draft of a Criminal Code.'[223]

This not immodest statement may or may not have been justified. At least Lord Brougham expressed deep regret that Austin did not have the opportunity to draft 'a complete map of the whole field of criminal law', a task which he was 'most capable of doing'.[224] Austin reached the conclusion, however, that he could not continue to be paid for public funds for service on a Commission whose work he believed to be of little benefit to the public. He therefore resigned his post.

In 1834 Austin had another opportunity to demonstrate his genuine promise as a teacher of law. In that year he was engaged to deliver a series of lectures on jurisprudence at the Inner Temple. Although John Stuart Mill believed that this engagement placed Austin 'in the best circumstances . . . for *him*',[225] they turned out not to be good enough. The number of lectures which he actually delivered is uncertain, as is the reaction of the students who attended them. At any rate, Austin decided that completion of the lectures would serve no useful purpose. The position apparently did not afford him the kind of security and confidence that he needed, or desired. His health also broke down under the strain of preparing the lectures and the anxiety of delivering them. He therefore became convinced of 'the inutility of struggling against such obstacles'.[226]

The disappointment that Austin experienced as an author, teacher, and Commissioner had a profound impact upon him. The most serious effect of them was to convince him that he had little or no future as a teacher of jurisprudence or a legal theorist. 'I was born out of time and place,' he told his wife, 'I ought to have been a schoolman of the twelfth century – or a German Professor.'[227] Despite the self-serving character of this judgment, it had a certain foundation in the facts. At least this inference may be drawn from a very significant opinion expressed in 1846 by the Select Committee on Legal Education. It maintained that the emphasis on the practical and mechanical in legal education

> has had the effect of discouraging, as profitless, the higher and doctrinal departments of the Profession, and produced two striking evils: it has deprived the study of Law of its scientific character, and gradually thrown out of the race, by the experience of how little such attainments are appreciated, those very intelligences who were most capable of bringing back the Profession to its original purposes and character. The consequence has been, that in this country we have, generally speaking, but few examples of that important class of thinkers and writers who, in other countries, standing on the summits of the profession, and disengaged from the

turmoil and labour of its daily technical duties, have . . . [the] opportunity to keep the profession up to the intellectual height to which it should be its proudest boast to aspire.[228]

Although the Report of the Select Committee did not mention Austin, its members may well have had him in mind. A better example of the kind of person to whom the Report refers is difficult to cite. Austin attempted to study law scientifically, he had the capacity to raise the intellectual level of the profession, and his attainments were little appreciated. Most important of all, the reaction to his work convinced him that the further development of it was useless. No audience existed for his particular approach to law and its study.

This conviction was one of several reasons why Austin published nothing about the philosophy of law after 1832. His inability to write on this subject was not due to either lack of time, encouragement, or desire. He was not gainfully employed from 1838 until his death in 1859. He was asked more than once to prepare a second edition of his book, or simply to reprint it. He refused the requests on the ground that the work contained numerous defects which had 'escaped the criticism of others'. Although this perception of these imperfections is unknown, he concluded that his book must be 'entirely recast and rewritten'.[229] He also expressed the intention to complete a *magnum opus*, the purposes of which were

> to show the relations of positive morality and law . . . and of both, to their common standard or test; to show that there are principles and distinctions common to all systems of law (or that law is the subject of an abstract science); to show the possibilities and conditions of codification; to exhibit a short scheme of a body of law arranged in a natural order; and to show that . . . English Law, in spite of its great peculiarities, might be made to conform to that order much more closely than is imagined.[230]

Unfortunately, Austin was either unable or unwilling to do the work required in order to write this treatise. Of course, factors other than his unhappy experience in the 1830s contributed to this problem. They include his recurring illnesses, his unusually high standards, and the difficulty that he *always* experienced in writing *anything*. What can only be called a flaw in his character probably also played a role. The most accurate way to describe it is as loss of nerve, or a certain lack of courage. A stronger person than Austin would have reacted very differently to the adversity that he suffered. Such an individual might have been inspired to ever greater efforts to demonstrate that his ideas merited the attention they had not received. Although Austin's very different reaction is understandable, it does not reflect well on a certain dimension of his character.

At least Sarah Austin in effect drew this inference in 1857. She pointed out to M. Guizot that her husband had been for many years disgusted with his fellow-men, their judgments, and their affairs. She indicated that he had used this as an excuse, at least to himself, 'for obeying his own reluctance to set about work'. She agreed with him that 'time was when nobody worked harder, and that had he then met with encouragement or even justice, he should have accomplished great things.' She also shared his view that he had been 'shamefully treated'. Nevertheless, she concluded this part of her letter with this remark: 'you and I know that there is another way of avenging oneself on the injustice of men.'[231] John Austin was unable or unwilling to choose this other mode of avenging injustice, an inability or unwillingness that even his wife found criticizable.

3

All but one or two of the final twenty-four years of Austin's life were indeed passed 'in the shade'. The particulars of his daily routine for most of these years are unknown, but the general pattern of his unenviable life is clear enough. It consisted of periodic illnesses and depressions, social isolation, fits and starts of work, and waste of large amounts of time. M. Barthelemy St Hilaire, who became a devoted friend of Sarah Austin after their meeting in 1840, described John Austin in these terms: 'Intensely nervous and often ill, he loved solitude, and even in his own house no one saw him until dinner, at which he did not always assist. Sad by nature, and a deep thinker, he spoke little, but when he did it was with extraordinary vehemence and eloquence.'[232] An even less flattering picture of Austin emerges from some of the letters of his wife. She wrote in 1842, for example, that the 'first three months of the year passed by (like so many others) in attacks of illness and fruitless attempts at work. . . . Is life so long that one can afford to throw away years? To vegetate, without any sphere of usefulness, any interchange of ideas, any society?'[233] Almost eight years later she described her husband's lack of productivity in these terms:

> [He] . . . gets books and exhausts their whole contents, turning every part of his subject over a thousand times in his mind; but though the head works, the hand is absolutely inert. And then he takes refuge in a sort of *découragement* – as if there were nothing to be done for mankind.[234]

If John Austin's hand was absolutely inert for most of the period from 1835 to 1859, it was not entirely motionless. In fact, he was sufficiently productive to make these years important for the student of his thought. Although he wrote nothing that focused on the philosophy of law, he produced a number of works on other subjects. They include reports about Malta that he and George C. Lewis co-authored in 1837 and 1838, the quality of which was very high. The preparation of these documents required an outburst of energy, the only equivalent of which in Austin's life were his efforts to prepare his lectures on jurisprudence. Within the next ten years he published two articles on significant economic and political problems. In 1859 he completed his conservative defence of the British constitution. It reflected a belief in the value of an established aristocracy which was probably influenced by his residence in Germany and France from 1840 to 1848.

The Austins' decision to live abroad was apparently prompted by both psychological and financial considerations. John Austin left England disillusioned by a country 'where worldly success is not only the reward, but the test of merit'.[235] This bitterness no doubt contributed to the Austins' decision to move to Boulogne in 1835. The fact that they could live more cheaply there than in England probably also played a role. Boulogne has at least been described as a 'favourite resort for the English with small incomes, and for those who wished to escape their creditors in England.'[236]

John Austin had lived in Boulogne for about a year and a half when he accepted an offer to be a Royal Commissioner to Malta. The other Commissioner was George Cornewall Lewis, a former student and great admirer of Austin. The quality of their reports on Malta was high and many of their recommendations for change were accepted by the Colonial Office. Despite this, Austin's experience as a Commissioner ended on an unhappy note. The termination of the Commission was abrupt and without explanation. Moreover, he failed to receive 'a single word of recognition of his services'.[237] Finally, the British government resisted compensating him for his services. He eventually was paid, largely because of the importunities of Sarah

Austin. She described the situation in these words:

> My poor husband was made so ill he could not leave his bed, and I had to do strange things for a woman, *contro il nostro decora* (against our decorum), certainly; but a woman fighting for her husband is always in the right.[238]

At any rate, the Austins had decided to live on Malta in order to observe first-hand conditions on the island. They remained there for slightly less than two years and returned to England in 1838. In 1840 they visited Carlsbad for the purpose of reviving John Austin's deteriorating health. The legendary waters of this famous town had the desired effect. The Austins were so pleased that they spent the summers of 1841, 1842 and 1843 in Carlsbad, while the intervening winters were passed in Dresden and Berlin.

John Austin's residence in Berlin apparently stimulated his interest in the political questions of the day. His concern with these problems was a major reason for his attempt to write an article about free trade. The effort was not easy. He encountered the same difficulties that plagued his attempts to write on any subject. He also found it difficult to reduce the length of his article to publishable dimensions. The initial draft of it was apparently three times as long as the final version published in the *Edinburgh Review*.[239]

Austin's article was published in 1842, four years prior to the repeal of the Corn Laws. He was highly critical of these measures and his article represented, in a sense, his contribution to the movement for their repeal. His essay was a detailed critique of Friedrich List's *The National System of Political Economy*. List was an influential writer whose book became 'the textbook of late nineteenth-century protectionists'.[240] He was a staunch advocate of the German Customs Union and the exclusion of foreign manufactured goods from German markets. He was also very critical of England and its restrictions on trade 'for the protection of the landed interest'. He even urged other nations to exclude English manufactured goods from their markets. Worst of all, he 'contemptuously rejects the principle of free international trade; and he looks upon Turgot and Adam Smith, with the other political economists by whom the principle is maintained, as drivelling and ridiculous dreamers.'[241]

List was thus an advocate of policies that cut deeply against the grain of principles to which Austin accorded the highest significance. This is evident from his profound admiration of the 'inestimable science of political economy', the truths of which he believed to be of 'ineffable moment'.[242] Popular knowledge of the leading principles of the science would be, he felt, of immense public utility. He thus described in the most enthusiastic terms the beneficial results of the development of widespread understanding of the reasons for the institution of property and the effect of population on wages.

These benefits included solution of a problem of great import to Austin's generation. It is at least the opinion of John Roach that 'the overmastering concern in men's minds between 1780 and 1830 was the problem of poverty, which men saw as the nerve centre of the whole social question.'[243] Austin's conception of the efficacy of popular understanding of the science of political economy as a means to eliminate this evil is difficult to exaggerate. Indeed his optimistic projections rival Karl Marx's vision of the splendour of the second and higher stage of communism. If the great mass of the people understood the basic truths of this science, Austin claimed, they

> would be raised from penury to comfort; from the necessity of toiling like cattle, to the enjoyment of sufficient leisure; from ignorance and brutishness, to knowledge and refinement; from abject subjection, to the independence which *commands* respect.[244]

This faith was a fundamental part of the intellectual equipment that Austin used to analyze social problems. It also included his life-long adherence to the principle of free trade, to which he ascribed as much value as Richard Cobden, John Bright, and the Manchester School. While their defence of the principle reflected a religious fervour that is absent from Austin's writings,[245] he shared their vision of free trade as an indispensable condition for national and international progress. Austin therefore denounced List's views in the strongest possible terms. Even Albert V. Dicey, who greatly admired Austin and was a strong proponent of free trade, was struck by the 'dogmatic tone' of his article.[246] Various factors contributed to the intensity with which Austin criticized List, one of which was the latter's challenge to basic articles of the former's credo. Another factor was Austin's perception that List's book was symptomatic of 'the mischievous and malignant prejudices which are now raging in every part of the Continent'.[247] A third consideration was the desire to change English policies which contributed to this unfortunate situation. Austin put the matter this way in a letter to John Stuart Mill:

> The landlords, and other partizans of our own prohibitive system, have no conception of the feeling of hostility which their rascally and stupid policy has excited in other countries. My dissection of his [List's] book . . . may possibly alarm them; and as the article is written in a mightily patriotic tone, and with great care to give them no offense, they may possibly pay some attention to the warnings which it conveys. If they persist in their restrictive system, . . . they will provoke all other countries to exclude our manufactured goods.[248]

Austin's strong reaction against this 'suicidal policy' explains his enthusiasm for its 'absolute abandonment'.[249] He stressed that Great Britain must abolish all of her laws that are designed to prohibit or restrain imports. Accordingly, he expressed his approval for repeal of the Corn Laws. He criticized them for causing a fluctuation in the English demand for foreign corn, the effect of which was the reduction of any 'considerable demand for English manufacturers in foreign corn-growing countries'. Austin claimed that other disadvantages of the Corn Laws pale in comparison with this 'obvious objection'.[250]

Various factors conditioned Austin's steadfast support for the principle of free trade. One of the most influential forces was his deep conviction of the inexpediency of governmental interference with the interests and concerns of individuals. To be sure, he fully acknowledged the necessity or utility of particular governmental actions. They include the enactment of laws, the administration of justice, defence against foreign enemies, the construction of public roads, and support of education. Still, these cases are exceptions to the general rule of non-interference.[251]

Austin was convinced that trade between nations falls under the rule rather than the exceptions to it. Although he believed that it was unnecessary for him to prove the utility of free trade, an unshakable faith in its advantages pervades his article. Indeed, he explained the benefits of this policy in terms that rival those of Richard Cobden. He extolled the principle of free trade as an almost talismanic force which

> shall act on the moral world as the principle of gravitation in the universe – drawing men together, thrusting aside the antagonism of race, and creed, and language, and uniting us in the bonds of eternal peace. . . . In the dim future . . . the effect will be to change the face of the world, so as to introduce a system of government

entirely distinct from that which now prevails. . . . the desire and the motive for large and mighty empires, for gigantic armies and navies, for those materials which are used for the destruction of life and the desolation of the rewards of labour, will die away.[252]

Austin fully agreed with this assessment of the wondrous effects of free trade. The benefits that he attributed to it included the development of an international division of labour, the extinction of slavery, a demonstration of the inexpediency of colonies, and the prevention of wars. If free trade were universal, the interests of nations would be 'thoroughly interlaced'. Any disturbance of their mutual commerce would therefore be disastrous. Since war is the most pernicious of all conceivable disturbances, it would be 'feared and detested by the productive population of the world.'[253]

Austin's other article was a lengthy study of political centralization.[254] He conceived of this phenomenon as the practical dependence of the subordinate authorities in a state on the sovereign power. The conditions of centralization include the specification and limitation of the powers of local governments, the territory and population of which must not be a 'large fraction' of the entire country. The administrators of the sovereign national government must also be subject to a good table of organization. The ideal is an 'unbroken chain of subordination [that] connects the lowest functionary with the central authority.'[255]

Austin was unable to perceive any evils in centralization. He viewed it as a product of advanced civilizations and a harbinger of social progress. He claimed that the disadvantages often attributed to it are in reality the effect of other causes, such as over-government. The basic reason for over-government is not centralization, but false opinions of the '*legitimate province of government*'. Over-government itself is an anachronistic legacy of the dark ages in which centralization was inconceivable:

The obvious truth is, that the over-governing imputed to centralization descends from states of society in which centralization was impossible. It comes from the crude conceptions of the legitimate province of government, which were naturally entertained by the middle ages and the ages immediately following them – ages which were just as incapable of centralized and regular government, as of conceiving the advanced science and the advanced industry which (like centralization) are products of a high civilization.[256]

These ideas would probably not surprise anyone familiar with Austin's theory of sovereignty. The same cannot be said of certain other themes of his article, one of which was his claim that centralization will be *encouraged* if the sovereign follows the 'reasonable policy' of *delegating* a substantial number of its legislative and administrative powers. The sovereign government should limit itself to the enactment of laws on 'matters of general and permanent concern'. Austin also took the position that uniform institutions are undesirable if they are reluctantly accepted by 'considerable portions of the governed.'[257] In that case the attempt to force the people to accept disliked institutions would be counter-productive. Austin believed that the policies of Great Britain toward her 'dependent populations' confirmed this hypothesis:

> From her vast experience in colonial government, she has learned to respect their opinions and manners, and to touch their institutions with a cautious and tender hand. To this policy, not less prudent than magnanimous and humane, we must mainly attribute her wonderful success in attaching her Hindoo subjects to her naturally invidious rule; and in tincturing an Asiatic people whose prejudices were all but indelible, with the morality and the knowledge of Christian and civilized Europe.[258]

Aside from this, Austin strenuously denied that centralization was incompatible with subordinate governments of 'local and popular origin'. In fact, he ardently defended strong local governments in which 'a *considerable* fraction of the population in each locality should take a *considerable* part in the administration of the local affairs, or in the appointment and control of the local administrators'[259] (emphasis added). Although he failed to explain what constituted a *considerable* fraction of the population, he defended such participatory democracy on grounds that would have excited the admiration of Thomas Jefferson. Despite the administrative inefficiencies of local governments of a popular nature, Austin argued that they would compensate for this 'partial inconvenience, by their tendency to invigorate the mind, and elevate the morality of the country'.[260] He was therefore critical of the excessive control exercised by some sovereign governments, or general administrations, over local governments.[261]

This analysis indicates a paradoxical quality of Austin's legal and political thought, the full dimensions of which will become evident subsequently in this study. On the one hand, he had an unshakable conviction of the universality and necessity of a sovereign of legally unlimited powers. This person or body is not, and cannot be, 'restrained by positive law from dealing with all things within its territory at its own pleasure or discretion'.[262] On the other hand, he was a firm believer in the utility of a substantial amount of delegation of power and local control. He was also an avid proponent of a limited role for the state, which most definitely should *not* deal with some things. The possibility that his theory of sovereignty might facilitate or rationalize policies of which he disapproved never seems to have occurred to him.

If Austin had lived several decades longer, he might have become more conscious of this possibility. At least it was very evident to Dicey. In spite of his acceptance of Austin's theory of sovereignty, his strong opposition to collectivism, and his self-description as 'an old, an unconverted, and an impenitent Benthamite',[263] he emphasized that the Benthamites 'had forged the arms most needed by socialists'.[264] These weapons included the theory of an all-powerful Parliament of which Dicey himself gave the classic account. He explained the argument in these terms:

> The omnipotence of Parliament, which Bentham learned from Blackstone, might well, considered as an abstract doctrine, command the acquiescent admiration of the commentator. But the omnipotence of Parliament – turned into a reality, and directed by bold reformers towards the removal of all actual or apparent abuses – might well alarm, not only adventurers . . . but also statesmen . . . uninfluenced by any sinister interest.[265]

Although this passage refers to 'commentators' and 'statesmen', it obviously reflects a certain tension between Dicey's own legal and political ideas. This conflict was not acute enough, however, to lead him to abandon his famous and very Austinian theory of parliamentary sovereignty. How Austin would have resolved the same tension, if he perceived it, is uncertain. The chances are that he would not have abandoned his theory of sovereignty, but would have developed a number of other arguments. They include the claim that the pernicious *exercise* of Parliament's illimitable powers is no argument against their *existence*. The powers exist regardless of their use for good or ill. He also might have argued that the remedy for the misuse of power is not to limit sovereignty, which is impossible. Instead, it is to educate legislators and the public in the truths of political science and political economy. At least he fully endorsed this position, to which he adhered throughout his life. He explicitly exonerated Hobbes, for example, from the charge of being an apologist for tyranny on the ground that scarcely

> a single advocate of free or popular institutions, even in these latter and comparatively enlightened ages, perceives and inculcates so clearly and earnestly as he, the principle [sic] cause and preventive of tyrannous or bad government. The principle [sic] cause . . . is ignorance, on the part of the multitude of sound *political science* . . . that is to say, *political economy*, with the two great branches of *ethics*, as well as *politics*. . . . And if such be the principal cause of tyrannous or bad government, the principal preventitive of the evil must lie in the diffusion of such knowledge throughout the mass of the community. Compared with this, the best political constitution that the wit of man could devise, were surely a poor security for good or beneficent rule.[266]

4

The Austins moved to Paris in 1844.[267] This great city particularly appealed to John Austin because of the opportunity that it provided to meet and socialize with French intellectual luminaries. Sarah Austin's penchant for, and talent at, entertainment helped to insure that the opportunity was not wasted. Wherever she went, Gordon Waterfield writes, 'she had her "salon"; just as the eminent collected in the Austins' house at Queen Square, so it was at Bonn and at Paris.'[268]

Auguste Comte was among the illustrious Frenchmen whom John Austin met. The interchange of ideas that may have taken place between them would have been fascinating to observe. Of course, Comte's *Cours de Philosophie Positive* had no influence upon Austin's philosophy of law, and little or no impact upon subsequent legal positivists.[269] The observation of Karl Bergbohm is amply justified: 'Mit dem "Positivismus" und der positiven Philosophie Aug. Comtes . . . hat dieser Terminus naturlich nichts zu thun.'[270] Nevertheless, Austin and Comte shared certain attitudes, such as a common dissatisfaction with theology and metaphysics. Austin also thought highly of Comte. He was a man of 'merit', 'great sincerity', 'uprightness', and 'generous and affectionate temper'.[271] This opinion no doubt strongly influenced Austin's willingness to intervene with M. Guizot on behalf of Comte.[272] At the same time, Austin was critical of Comte's dogmatism and imprudent expressions of contempt for religion. Austin wrote to John Stuart Mill that, in these respects, Comte continually reminded him of Jeremy Bentham: 'But of all the men I ever saw (excepting Mr Bentham) he is the most confident in his own capacity and views, and the least inclined to attend to the suggestions of others.' Austin felt that Comte was 'so wedded to his own devices and so full of presumptuous contempt for all which has been done by others', that attempts to persuade him to be more reserved about religion would be unsuccessful.[273]

M. Guizot was another prominent Frenchman whose friendship the Austins cultivated. He was a distinguished historian and the influential Minister of Foreign Affairs under Louis-Philippe from 1840 to 1848. Alfred Cobban has described him as 'perhaps the most intelligent and high-minded minister ever to preside over the ruin of a political system.'[274] The relationship that he and the Austins developed was much more intimate than the latter's acquaintance with Comte. Sarah Austin wrote in 1857 that during her residence in Paris, Guizot and his family were 'more like the most affectionate relations or the oldest friends than comparative strangers.' She profoundly admired his 'great, amiable & eminent qualities'.[275] John Austin held much the same opinion of Guizot. 'Though his talents and acquirements are great, various, & imposing,' Austin wrote, 'I am far more struck by the elevated moral character which seems to break out spontaneously in his conversation & manners.' In fact, Austin was so impressed that he beseeched the heavens that Guizot would not be 'depraved by ambition'. 'I have such a longing and need for believing in somebody,' Austin confessed to John Stuart Mill, that if Guizot 'committed a baseness for the purpose of keeping or recovering political power, I should almost die (or fall sick) of despair and misanthropy.'[276]

The Austins were living in Paris when the French Revolution of 1848 erupted. John Austin's observations of Paris, which was the centre of the storm, had a profound impact upon his political thought. The essence of it, which will be explained in detail in the sixth chapter of this book, was to accentuate his increasingly conservative outlook. The highly negative reaction of both of the Austins to the French Revolution of 1848 strongly influenced, at any rate, their decision to return to England.

The Austins eventually settled in Weybridge, Surrey, for the final eleven years of John Austin's life. The comments of Sarah Austin indicate that these years were not only the happiest period in the life of her husband, but of their marriage. She once wrote that her married life had been filled with 'numerous' and 'various' trials, some of which were 'hard to bear'.[277] They evidently included a certain lack of tenderness on the part of John Austin toward his wife. 'Ill-health, disappointment, and anxiety had naturally enough made all things distasteful to him.'[278] This behaviour and attitude no doubt contributed to the secret 'affair', if that is the right word, that Sarah Austin developed with Prince Puckler-Muskau in the 1830s. He was a German aristocrat whose *Tour in England, Ireland, and France* she had translated.[279] Their relationship was evidently conducted solely through the post and Sarah 'fell in love . . . without ever having seen him'.[280] In fact, they did not meet until her ardour had cooled to the point where an indiscretion on her part was unlikely. Even so, her letters to the Prince express a very passionate yearning for him.[281]

If John Austin demonstrated a lack of tenderness toward his wife for much of their marriage, this situation apparently changed dramatically in the 1850s. He evidently spent his time reading, walking, meditating, and quite literally cultivating his garden. His health and disposition improved remarkably, as did his relationship with his wife. Indeed, the peace of mind that he finally achieved may have converted him into the ideal husband. At least Sarah Austin described him in these terms after his death in 1859:

> But since he had given up the conflict with fortune, and especially since we settled down in our quiet retreat, he had gradually come to a state of mind and temper which I can only call *heavenly*, so gentle and noble, so without all alloy of unsatisfied cravings, or vain repinings, or harsh passions, or low desires was it! In this blessed frame of mind all his youthful and passionate love for me seemed to return, mingled with a confidence and intimacy which only a life passed together can produce. I was too happy! It pleased God, after many years of care and toil, and suffering, to permit me to taste of this tranquil happiness – only to lose it.[282]

Despite his withdrawal from the world, Austin retained a strong interest in political events. Various proposals for the reform of Parliament had surfaced, all of which he opposed. This dissatisfaction was the basis of *A Plea for the Constitution*, which was published in 1859.[283] It involved a defence of the British aristocracy and constitution which was most unusual for a nineteenth-century British utilitarian. As such, his final work marked the culmination of a train of thought that was influenced by, if it did not originate during, his residence in Paris.

Austin became seriously ill in November 1859 and died on December 17th. If his wife's account is accurate, he faced the end of his life with equanimity and serenity.[284] She subsequently decided to edit for publication his lectures on jurisprudence, as well as his notes, tables, and unpublished essays on this subject. Since John Austin had refused to permit even the reprinting of his only book, this decision was not easy for her to reach. The task of editing his work was also formidable. To be sure, the preparation of a new edition of *The Province of Jurisprudence Determined* and an *Outline of the Course of Lectures* was relatively easy. The production of a suitable edition of his other papers was a different story. This material was in an 'imperfect', 'half-legible', 'fragmentary', and 'confused' state.[285] Sarah Austin, who was sixty-six when her husband died, was not in the best of health. She also felt obligated to preface her edition of his work with a brief description of his life. The writing of this account was extremely painful for her. 'I have written a good deal,' she wrote to M. Guizot, 'but it is written between bursts of grief, and interrupted by tears and sobs. . . . What a life of unbroken disappointment and failure!'[286]

Sarah Austin, who died on 8 August 1867, devoted the final eight years of her life to the process of editing and re-editing her husband's papers on jurisprudence. She overcame her doubts about whether she should even attempt this task for various reasons. They included the belief that the imperfections of John Austin's unpublished papers were outweighed by their merits, which 'no defect of form or arrangement can destroy'. The publication of this material would, she believed, benefit her husband's 'country and . . . mankind'.[287] Aside from this, she concluded that she was in a better position than anyone else to produce an accurate and complete edition of his papers. Still further, she feared that if she did not undertake this job no one else would.

Sarah Austin may also have been motivated by a quite different consideration: the wish to demonstrate that her married life had not been wasted. 'I never wish to be mentioned', she wrote to Lord Brougham in 1862, 'but as Mr Austin's wife. The only distinction I desire is that of having been thought worthy to be his companion in weal & woe, his obedient & respectful & affectionate helpmate.'[288] A person with such views could not be expected to approve of the liberation of women from marital 'bondage', which Sarah Austin criticized. She articulated very clearly her position in another letter to Lord Brougham:

> I cannot too loudly and emphatically utter my protest against every project for disturbing the great relation between Man & Woman which began at the creation and underlies the whole fabric of society –
>
> I have always felt that my highest honour, my greatest privilege, was to be the servant (I am not afraid of the name) of a noble-hearted, great minded & not very fortunate man; & all schemes that could emancipate me from that servitude, are . . . odious and shameful.[289]

Sarah Austin practised what she preached. Despite this, John Austin's actual achievements did not meet her high expectations. The result was a disappointment which she once described as '*bitter*'. Its basis was *not* the fact that John Austin had been unable to coin 'his talents into gold or risen upon them to power or greatness.' Rather, Sarah Austin was bitterly disappointed because her husband 'will depart out of the world without having done for the great cause of Law and Order, of Reason and Justice, what he might have done.' 'To enable him to do this,' she went on to say, 'I should have been proud and happy to share a garret and a crust with him.'[290]

If Sarah Austin did not share a garret and a crust with her husband, she certainly did sacrifice a good deal for him. The motives which explain the final, great, and difficult service that she rendered him were no doubt varied. Still, the desire to prove that her sacrifices had not been in vain may have influenced her. At the least she wrote in 1865 of her edition of her husband's *Lectures on Jurisprudence*: 'The having been permitted to do that work is the greatest consolation of my dreary life.'[291] Unless she had done it, the bulk of John Austin's fifty-seven lectures on jurisprudence might never have been published. The same is true of his other notes, tables, and essays on this subject. Although he might have exerted a potent influence on the course of English jurisprudence without the publication of this material, its appearance in print certainly facilitated the strong impact that he eventually had. His *Lectures on Jurisprudence* are also invaluable for understanding certain dimensions of his philosophy of law that are discussed briefly, if at all, in *The Province of Jurisprudence Determined*. His analysis of judicial legislation and codification are examples. To this extent, Sarah Austin not only bears some of the responsibility for the belated influence of John Austin's writings on jurisprudence. In addition, her labours as an editor enhanced understanding of the very nature of his philosophy of law.

5

Despite the credit that Sarah Austin deserves for her editorial work, she should never have had to assume this responsibility. John Austin had ample opportunity to complete the *magnum opus* that he contemplated, or at least to edit himself his lectures on jurisprudence. His inability or unwillingness to do either symbolizes the frustrations and lost opportunities of this gifted but unhappy man. If his life was not a record of unbroken disappointments and failure, he had more than his share of both. He was unsuccessful in the practice of law, he was unable to attract many students as a teacher of jurisprudence, and he was not nearly as productive a writer as he could have been. Since he had the ability to be a successful barrister, a popular teacher, and a very productive writer, there is almost a tragic quality to his lack of success in these endeavours.

Various factors influenced Austin's failure to realize more fully his great potential. The most basic causes of it were the nature of the culture in which he lived and the kind of person that he was. The culture contributed to his lack of success for several reasons, one of which was the virtual absence of organized legal education. Another was professional indifference, or outright hostility, to theory. If Austin had lived in a culture more sympathetic to his efforts as a teacher and writer, his achievements might have been much greater than they were.

Although the cultural obstacles that Austin confronted were steep, they were not insurmountable. The 'personal equation' cannot therefore be ignored in any explanation of the gap between his potential and accomplishments. The single most important personal characteristic that limited his success was the lack of real strength of character or will. He differed graphically in this respect from James Mill, whom Alexander Bain has described in these terms:

> He was a man of strong Will, in the best sense of that somewhat indefinite phrase. The basis of will is necessarily the active temperament; and Mill was, by nature, a truly energetic character. Activity was natural to him; he would never be found lounging and musing in idleness. But Will, in the highest sense, is activity confined to proper channels, by a few great leading motives; these having their source in the feelings, regulated by the intellect. It is when a man has conceived some great ends of life with such intensity that they engross all the available active energy, that he is

> said to have Will in the higher meaning of purpose, persistence, steadiness of pursuit, as contrasted with intense fits of desultory application.[292]

Austin was the example *par excellence* of a person who lacked strength of will, at least as Bain conceived of it. If Austin had been more energetic, persistent, and steadier in the pursuit of his great ends, he might have achieved more than he in fact did. To say this is neither to condemn him nor to belittle the value of his actual accomplishments. Rather, it is to facilitate understanding of his inability to accomplish more than he did.

3 *Divine law, utilitarian ethics, and positivist jurisprudence*

Despite Austin's legendary precision and thoroughness, nagging questions remain about the basis of or rationale for some of his most distinctive ideas.[1] Uncertainty about the foundations of his conceptions of law and sovereignty is probably the most important example. These notions are basic premises of his jurisprudence, from which he deduces implications of the utmost importance. At the same time, he wrote very little about the reasons for his belief in these ideas. Nor do students of Austin agree on the basis of these crucial elements in his philosophy of law.[2] They are virtually unanimous, however, that his utilitarian ethics are wholly unrelated to his jurisprudence. This belief persists even though three of the six chapters of *The Province of Jurisprudence Determined* are a discussion of ethics.

The prevalence of this interpretation of Austin is not difficult to explain or to document. He almost never explicitly justified his conceptions of law and sovereignty by utilitarian arguments. His approach in this respect contrasts markedly with that of his great predecessor, Jeremy Bentham. He demonstrated no reluctance to discuss the implications of the principle of utility for almost anything. Austin also advocated a sharp division of labour between students of the sciences of ethics, one subdivision of which is legislation, and jurisprudence. The exclusive concern of the latter is positive law as it *is* rather than as it *ought to be*.[3] Aside from this, he insisted that the existence of human laws is independent of their goodness or badness. For these reasons Austin's discussion of ethics has appeared to many jurists to be irrelevant to his jurisprudence. It is, Sir Henry Maine once pointed out, 'consistent with *any* ethical theory'.[4] According to Lord Bryce, the theory of utility 'has nothing to do with the Analytic Method, nor with Positive Law'.[5] No less sympathetic a student of Austin than John Chipman Gray found it 'hard' to defend his 'consistency in . . . giving up so large a part of the volume to a discussion on the test of morality.'[6] If Wolfgang Friedmann is correct, the principle of utility 'has no influence whatsoever on the main principles of Austin's doctrines.'[7]

Although this belief is widespread and understandable, it is unwarranted. This is the only inference to be drawn, at least, if the interpretation to be defended in this chapter is accurate. Its purpose is to demonstrate *that*, and to explain *how*, Austin's utilitarian ethics and political theories are related to his jurisprudence. The impact of these ideas was, it will be argued, *one* reason for his conceptions of law and sovereignty. His chapters on ethics are therefore highly relevant to his particular kind of positivist jurisprudence. They are not an aberration, but a necessary introduction to his philosophy of law. This chapter implies, in short, that his book is a unified whole rather than unrelated parts.

This interpretation of Austin could be criticized on two very different grounds, one of which would be that it is inaccurate. Ample evidence will be adduced later in this chapter to show that this particular criticism is unfounded. The other criticism would be that whether the interpretation is accurate or inaccurate is unimportant. After all, very few contemporary jurists regard Austin's conceptions of law and sovereignty as satisfactory. H. L. A. Hart, who is probably the most distinguished Anglo-American philosopher of law in the post-World War II era, is the most significant example.[8]

This second criticism of the central thesis of this chapter seems to me to be unacceptable. Despite widespread dissatisfaction with Austin's conceptions of law and sovereignty, an understanding of their utilitarian basis is important. To begin with, *some* of his most fundamental ideas about law and its study still have highly intelligent and well-informed supporters, such as Hart.[9] Austin's insistence on the value of an analytical jurisprudence is one example. His sharp distinction between the law as it is and the law as it ought to be is a second example. This chapter will demonstrate that his utilitarianism strongly influenced this last aspect of his thought. His ethical theories even had an impact, it will be argued, upon his conception of general jurisprudence. Furthermore, the very errors that Austin is alleged to have committed reinforce the need to understand the basis of his thought. If his command conception of law and theory of sovereignty are mistaken, this fact raises the obvious question of why he believed so firmly in these notions. Although this study will not provide the only possible answer to this question, a plausible response to it will be developed.

These considerations are not the only reasons for the importance of understanding the utilitarian basis of Austin's conceptions of law and sovereignty. In addition, this interpretation means that his philosophy of law is not as ethically and politically neutral as it has usually been thought to be. If this thesis is sound, it also has an important implication for the evaluation of Austin's notions of law and sovereignty. His critics usually assume that the proper way to object to these doctrines is to show how they conflict with law as it in fact exists. H. L. A. Hart's penetrating critique is probably the most important recent illustration of this tendency.[10] Nothing argued for in this study implies that his criticisms are improper. One probable reason for Austin's conceptions of law and sovereignty was his belief that they reflect the way things are. Determination of whether this belief is justified is therefore relevant to an evaluation of these concepts. It is likely, however, that utilitarian considerations of what ought to be also influenced these key elements of his thought. In particular, the chances are that his conviction of the utility of commands and sovereigns had an impact. Determination of whether this belief is justified is therefore also proper in the evaluation of his concepts of law and sovereignty.

In any case, the aim of this chapter is not to *evaluate* these ideas. Rather, it is to *explain* how they are related to Austin's ethical and political theories. A final reason for the importance of this explanation is its utility for understanding the distinctiveness of his version of legal positivism. His interpretation of this influential philosophy of law is by no means identical with subsequent statements of it, most notably that developed by Hans Kelsen.[11] One reason for the differences between the two positivists is Austin's commitment to utilitarian ethical and political theories. Yet, the very important implications of this commitment for his jurisprudence are veiled. Accordingly, the fact that he straddles earlier and later forms of legal positivism has been obscured. On the one hand, his conceptions of law and sovereignty have a utilitarian foundation. Both their content *and* basis are quite similar to that of the great seventeenth-century philosopher, Thomas Hobbes.[12] To this extent, Austin has one foot in the rather distant past. On the other hand, the ethical and political foundations of his concepts of law and sovereignty are not readily apparent. He could thus adumbrate, if he did not inspire, forms of legal positivism which eschew any discussion of ethics or politics. To this extent, Austin has a much more visible foot in the future. In short, his place in the development of positivism is more ambiguous than has generally been recognized.

1

The purpose of this section is to explain the ethical and political theories of Austin which influenced his philosophy of law. Since his ideas about ethics have deep roots in the past, a brief review of the tradition of British thought upon which he drew is desirable. An elucidation of his utilitarianism is necessary, in any case, prior to a demonstration of its impact upon his jurisprudence. For the meaning of this influential moral philosophy is not self-evident. Nor do proponents of it entirely agree in their conceptions of utility or how to evaluate particular actions. If the varieties of utilitarianism are not as numerous as the versions of natural law, different interpretations certainly exist.[13] Furthermore, Austin's discussion of ethics includes a defence of the necessity of rules and authority for ethical decision-making. The case which he makes mirrors a view of human nature or behaviour which also conditioned his conceptions of law and sovereignty.

A number of Austin's predecessors at least adumbrated and very probably influenced some of his ethical theories. John Locke, whom Austin extolled as the 'greatest and best of philosophers',[14] is a most important example. Although his moral philosophy is not wholly consistent, some elements of it fit into a utilitarian mould.[15] There is, to begin with, a certain amount of both psychological and ethical hedonism. The search for pleasure and the avoidance of pain not only 'constantly . . . operate and influence all our actions without ceasing,'[16] but are the measure of good and evil. What is apt to produce 'any degree of pleasure' is 'in itself good; and what is apt to produce any degree of pain . . . evil.' In addition to this, Locke firmly denied the existence of 'innate practical principles'. Still further, he insisted that ethics is a science capable of demonstration. The rejection of innate ideas does not in any way invalidate the truth of moral principles or a science of morality. Finally, he classified law into three basic types. They are divine law, 'the only true touchstone of *moral rectitude*'; civil law, which 'no body overlooks'; and the law of opinion or reputation, the most influential of the three.[17]

William Paley was an influential eighteenth-century English clergyman, educator, and 'theological utilitarian'.[18] Despite his conservative political outlook, he played a very important role in the development of utilitarianism. In fact, it 'first became widely known in England through [his] work'.[19] His *Principles of Moral and Political Philosophy* (1785)

rapidly because the classical manual of morals at Cambridge University, where Paley lectured for seven consecutive years. Here for

> some time past Locke's philosophy had been taught, but it was henceforth to be replaced by 'Locke and Paley'. Paley remained for half a century the acknowledged representative of the Utilitarian morality. The 'Paleyans' came to be denounced long before the 'Benthamites'.[20]

Although Austin was critical of some of Paley's ideas, others induced a very different reaction. The most important example is his conception of the relationship between Divine law and the principle of utility. His famous definition of virtue was ' "*the doing good to mankind, in obedience to the will of God, and for the sake of everlasting happiness.*" ' He was critical of the moral sense as a means to know the laws of God, which must be determined in other ways. They include examination of His express declarations in Scripture. Since these precepts are very incomplete, Paley argued that the Divine will must also be gathered from God's work or the 'light of nature'. Such knowledge requires utilitarian calculations of the ' "tendency of the action to promote or diminish the general happiness." '[21] For the Divine character is such that 'what promotes the general happiness is required by the will of God'. In other words, 'whatever is expedient, is right. It is the utility of any moral rule alone, which constitutes the obligation of it.'[22]

In accordance with these ideas, Paley insisted on the necessity of general rules for moral conduct. He also sharply distinguished between the particular and general consequences of actions. An action that is useful in a particular case is bad if it conflicts with a rule necessary for the general happiness. Determination of what is expedient requires, in short, calculations of *all* of the effects of *courses* of action. To be justifiable on utilitarian grounds an action must be useful *as a rule* and 'on the whole, at the long run, in all its effects, collateral and remote, as well as . . . immediate and direct.'[23]

The teachings of Jeremy Bentham are the most obvious source of Austin's utilitarian ethics. The ethical theories of both men are similar in numerous respects. They shared at least the following attitudes or concepts: the notion that pleasure or avoidance of pain is the ultimate purpose of every act; the idea that only pleasure is intrinsically good and that only pain is intrinsically bad; the belief that the *effect* of laws or governmental actions on the *general* happiness is *the* political standard; a critical attitude toward the evaluation of actions on the basis of their motives, none of which is intrinsically bad; a dissatisfaction with the "phantom" of justice as a criterion for appraising laws or governments; and the conviction that substantive ethical questions are reducible to calculations of future facts. Ethics is an inductive science and ethical issues should be resolved 'in the same manner that all other questions of fact are to be decided, by testimony, observation, and experience'.[24]

At the same time, Austin's ethical theories are not simply a carbon copy of Bentham's. If the similarities in the views of the two men are marked, certain differences are also discernible. On the one hand, Austin does not employ some of Bentham's most distinctive ethical concepts. The most notable examples are his 'hedonistic calculus' and the formula of the greatest happiness 'of the greatest number'. On the other hand, Austin emphasizes certain themes which Bentham does not stress and might well criticize. A brief explanation of each of these ideas is therefore essential for understanding the distinctiveness of Austin's ethical theories.

One of the most notable elements of Austin's utilitarianism is the conspicuous role of Divine law. This fact unmistakably indicates his debt to Locke and the 'theological utilitarians'. Austin's use of Divine law also clearly differentiates his ethical theories from either Bentham's or J. S. Mill's. In their interpretations the principle of utility is logically, and explicitly, independent of the law of God.[25] The relationship between the two concepts is quite different if the words of John Austin are taken at their face value.[26]

Divine law is the stated foundation of his ethical system. Laws 'properly so-called' are general commands or orders, the precise nature of which will be explained in detail later. These commands are divisible into two basic types: divine and human. Imperatives of this second class are either positive laws or positive moral rules. Divine law is the ultimate 'test' or 'measure' of both kinds of human law. To that extent, it is the ultimate source of the rules which should govern human actions. The laws of God also impose religious duties, the violation of which are sins. The sanctions for these transgressions are 'the evils, or pains, which we may suffer here or hereafter, by the immediate appointment of God, and as *consequences* of breaking his commandments.' The threat of such punishments constitutes motives for obedience which are 'paramount to all others'.[27]

Austin followed Paley in classifying the laws of God into two groups, revealed and unrevealed. His express commands are 'signified . . . through the medium of human language; and uttered by God directly, or by servants whom he sends to announce them.' Unfortunately, Austin said nothing more about *who* the ministers of God in this world are and *how* they can be identified. In any case, the Supreme Commander's unrevealed laws are also very important. They are the only commands which God has 'set to that portion of mankind who are excluded from the light of Revelation.' Moreover, 'many' of the duties which God has imposed upon us are not expressly revealed.[28] This fact raises the problem of how to identify these commands and the duties which they impose.

Austin perceived only two possible resolutions of this difficulty. The tacit commands of the Deity may be known by either the principle of utility or the 'moral sense'. Virtually all the utilitarians rejected the latter, which Austin also criticized. He subsumed under this label virtually all ethical theories other than utilitarianism, regardless of their basis. It may be 'innate practical principles', 'common sense', 'conscience', or natural law and rights. No matter, all of these theories presuppose the existence of a moral sense. This faculty is the alleged basis of mankind's universal approval, or disapproval, of certain actions. The moral sense engenders certain sentiments that arise 'spontaneously, instantly, and inevitably'.[29] These feelings are proof, supposedly, that the actions which excite them are enjoined or prescribed by the Deity.

Austin cited various objections to this theory. To begin with, we are frequently uncertain about how we ought to act and what our duty is. If a moral sense exists, the sentiments that it engenders are neither spontaneous nor instantaneous.[30] Aside from this, the moral sense is a highly subjective standard for the appraisal of human actions. To evaluate an action is to imply that it agrees with or deviates from an assumed standard. The moral sense is a very unreliable standard for making such judgments. The only measure that it proposes is an individual's like or dislike for a particular act.[31] Finally, the actual moral sentiments of real persons vary tremendously *between* and *within* different ages or nations. While the moral sentiments of most men have been uniform with respect to actions of a 'few classes', their sentiments toward other kinds of actions pass through 'every shade or degree, from slight diversity to direct opposition'. If the dictates of the moral sense are therefore the standard of what should be done,

> God has not set to men a *common* rule. If they are different with different men, there is no *common* test of human conduct: there is no test by which one man may try the conduct of another. It were folly and presumption in *me* to sit in judgment upon *you*. . . .

> There is no broad sun destined to illumine the world, but every single man must walk by his own candle.[32]

This statement is indicative of a second distinctive feature of Austin's ethical theories, an emphasis upon conformity to rules. A major part of his discussion of ethics is an explanation of how to determine the utility of an action. The main alternatives which he examines are reducible to act- and rule-utilitarianism, though Austin does not use these labels. Act-utilitarianism entails the direct application of 'considerations of utility to *this* act in *this* situation'.[33] Rule-utilitarianism means that the decision to act in a particular way must be deducible from a rule. Considerations of utility are relevant only for the determination of which rules should be followed. The major difference between the two forms of utilitarianism is thus the place of rules in ethical decisions. The act utilitarian claims that the conformity of an action to a rule is not required for the justification of the action. The rule or restricted utilitarian believes that such conformity is a necessary condition of ethically justifiable behaviour.

Throughout most of his first chapter on ethics Austin explains, *and justifies*, rule-utilitarianism of a sort similar to Paley's. Austin not only argued that human conduct *is* guided by rules, but that it *ought to be.* No nineteenth-century utilitarian expressed more clearly than Austin the relationship between conduct, rules, and the principle of utility. The 'true' theory of utility means that

> our conduct would conform to *rules* inferred from the tendencies of actions, but would not be determined by a direct resort to the principle of general utility. Utility would be the test of our conduct, ultimately, but not immediately: the immediate test of the rules to which our conduct would conform, but not the immediate test of specific or individual actions. Our rules would be fashioned on utility; our conduct, on our rules.[34]

Austin criticized act-utilitarianism as both superfluous and mischievous. Ethically correct decisions are deducible from rules grounded in the principle of utility. These generalizations are discovered by calculating and comparing the probable effects of alternative courses of action on the general happiness. These computations are the basis for choosing the pattern of behaviour, the sum total of the effects of which is most beneficial. The existence of such rules means that direct application of the principle of utility to particular acts is unnecessary. Aside from this, the effects of attempting to reach decisions in this fashion are pernicious. For one thing, measurement of all the effects of alternative actions is 'too slow and uncertain to meet the exigencies of our lives'. For another thing, 'on-the-spot' calculations and comparisons of effects are likely to be mistaken.[35] Finally, direct application of the principle of utility would encourage exceptions to useful rules. Certain acts which are in general mischievous may appear useful or harmless if considered by themselves. One example is the theft by a poor man of the property of his rich neighbour. A second is evasion of payment of taxes to a good government. Similarly, certain acts which are in general useful appear harmful if considered only by themselves. The punishment of a criminal is an example.[36]

Austin feared that direct application of the principle of utility would open the floodgates to these kinds of exceptions to generally useful rules. One reason for his apprehensiveness was the 'weakness' of our judgments. A second, he significantly added, is the 'more dangerous infirmity of our wills'. Human beings tend to 'grasp at present enjoyment, and to turn from present uneasiness'. This tendency is the 'habitual inclination of us all'.[37]

These criticisms imply that no exceptions to rules are ever justifiable. Austin also explicitly asserts that God forbids classes of actions '*without exception*'.[38] To take this position is, however, to advance a kind of rule-fetishism which appears intrinsically unreasonable. Perhaps for this reason, even Austin had to admit that only 'most' of the commands of the Deity are 'general, and commonly inflexible'.[39] Some cases require exceptions to rules and direct application of the principle of utility. Unfortunately, this qualification seems to raise very serious difficulties for rule-utilitarianism. Determination of how to act in any particular situation would appear to require calculation of specific consequences. Otherwise, the individual could not *know* whether the good effects of deviation from the rule outweigh the bad consequences. If this is the case, then qualified rule-utilitarianism raises the same problems which Austin perceived in act-utilitarianism.

His ethical theories also raise the problem of *who* is to determine *which* rules should guide human actions. It is one thing to demonstrate *how* individuals should reach ethically justifiable decisions. It is another thing to explain *who* is to select the rules which are the basis for such decisions. After all, these generalizations rest on complex calculations and comparisons which could generate substantial disagreement.

At least two resolutions of this issue are possible, one of which is to say that each person can and should formulate his or her own rules without the guidance of others. Austin rejects this possibility for reasons which will become apparent. The other alternative is for some authority to make the rules to which others could, and should, defer. It is this kind of solution to the problem which Austin develops and which is a third distinctive element of his ethical theories. This dimension of his teachings also reflects a concept of human nature which to some extent conditioned his conceptions of law and sovereignty.

Austin's view of who should formulate ethically justifiable rules presupposes a distinction between *legal* and *ethical* authority. The former necessarily involves the power to *enforce* standards, while the latter is entitled only to *recommend* rules. To be subject to an ethical authority means voluntarily to defer to the standards which it suggests. Such a body merits deference if it is trustworthy, the mark of which is the '*unanimous or general consent of numerous and impartial inquirers*'. Austin admitted that, unfortunately, no such group of ethical experts now exists. Past writers on ethics have tended to lack that '*indifferency* in the pursuit of truth which is so earnestly inculcated by Mr Locke'.[40] Even so, the situation is far from hopeless. A trustworthy authority in ethics can be developed if certain requirements are met. They include the use of geometrical methods of logical rigour, a precise style, and the spirit of dispassionate inquiry. Public education, the beneficial effects of which Austin extolled, is no less important.[41]

Austin justified the need for an ethical authority on utilitarian grounds. The effects of this institution on the general happiness are preferable to the results of unguided individual judgments. If the decisions of the 'multitude' are not based upon authority, they are likely to be incorrect. Most people lack the leisure which is necessary for the development of ethical knowledge. Their ability to calculate and compare the consequences of possible courses of action is small. Indeed, 'much' of ethical science will always either be 'hidden from the multitude' or taken on authority or trust.[42] In fact, even the educated 'few' must in general rely on authority if they are to act for the common happiness. No single person can comprehend the tendencies of all of the numerous classes of human actions. Even the most knowledgeable of men cannot therefore completely dispense with authority. For 'many of the rules of conduct, which were actually observed or admitted, would be taken, *by the most instructed* [emphasis added], on *authority*, *testimony*, or *trust*.' After all, 'many' mathematical truths are 'probably taken upon trust by deep and searching mathematicians'.[43]

Austin's utilitarian ethics strongly conditioned, at any rate, his conception of the end for which sovereign governments ought to exist. It is the greatest possible advancement of human happiness. He interpreted this principle in highly individualistic and hedonistic terms. The good of an individual is the sum total of the pleasures which he or she enjoys. The good of England is the aggregate of the pleasures enjoyed by Englishmen 'considered individually or singly'.[44] The good of mankind is the balance of the pleasures experienced by the members of the human race. In short, the proper end or purpose of government is the maximization of human happiness defined in terms of pleasure.

Austin thus conceived of the end of government in universalistic terms which subordinate national to international goals. The end of government is not the good of a particular independent political society, but the good of mankind. Nevertheless, he argued that this universal end should not be the immediate objective of a sovereign government. Rather, it usually should attempt to advance as far as is possible the welfare of its own citizens.[45] Austin justified this policy on the ground that it is ordinarily the only way in which the good of mankind can be advanced.

Austin took a similar position with respect to the rule that individuals should follow in order to promote the general good of their society. The essence of it is that they should attempt to foster their own happiness rather than the general happiness. This course of action is desirable because it is the only effective way to maximize happiness within a society. The good of an individual is a much more determinate or precise purpose of action than the general good. Aside from this, individuals have much stronger and steadier motives for pursuing their interests rather than the interests of others. Most important of all, each person is as a rule 'the best possible judge of his own interests'. His knowledge of these interests and how to promote them is 'intimate', while his knowledge of the interests of others is 'vague conjecture'. A person whose motive for action was the desire to advance the happiness of others would thus be unlikely to achieve his or her goals. Such a person would also tend to manage his or her own interests 'unskilfully'. Since the general good is an aggregate of individual enjoyments, it would be diminished rather than advanced by this course of action. The best if not the only way to advance the general good is therefore for each individual to attempt to promote his or her interests.[46]

Austin recognized that this rule is not universally applicable. In fact, he took the position that the utilitarian end frequently requires unselfish actions. Occasions arise in which the love of self should yield to love of family, love of family to love of country, love of country to love of mankind. Under these circumstances, general utility should be the *motive* for conduct rather than simply the *test* of its value. Nevertheless, these cases are exceptions to the general rule that individuals should pursue their own self-interest instead of the interests of others.[47]

The same line of reasoning underlies Austin's belief that sovereign governments should as a rule attempt to promote the happiness of their subjects rather than the happiness of mankind. The ends of national self-interest and the good of mankind 'never or rarely conflict'.[48] Focus on the particular end is for nations, as for individuals, the only way as a rule in which the general end can be advanced. The danger from this point of view is not that either individuals or nations will act selfishly. Rather, it is that they will attempt to advance their respective interests stupidly rather than intelligently.

2

Austin devoted a significant portion of his book to an exposition of these and other ethical and political theories. The vast majority of the commentators on his work believe, it has been pointed out, that this exposition is an aberration. The purpose of this section is to explain some of the reasons for a very different interpretation of *The Province of Jurisprudence Determined*. It is one which emphasizes the close and substantial relationship between Austin's ethical, political, and legal theories. Subsequent sections of this chapter will provide additional support for this interpretation of his thought.

Although the standard interpretation of Austin's book is inaccurate, it is not entirely unreasonable. In fact, it draws a certain amount of support from a number of basic elements of his philosophy of law. One of them is his view of the province of jurisprudence, an understanding of which requires a brief explanation of his conception of law. He conceived of law 'properly so-called' as a class of commands, which are the '*key* to the sciences of jurisprudence and morals'.[49] These imperatives are significations of desire, the author of which must be a determinate and rational being or beings. Persons incapable of expressing or intimating their desires cannot issue orders. The form by which a command is signified is irrelevant to its status as a binding order. A commander may express his desires as pleas or requests, while a subject may communicate his wishes in the imperative form. Even so, the communication of his desires is not a command. For a subject lacks what the commander possesses, which is the 'power and the purpose . . . to inflict an evil or pain in case the desire be disregarded.'[50] Unlike the former, the latter is able to impose sanctions for the disregard of his wishes. In other words, he has the power to inflict an evil or pain independent of the consent of the persons to whom the command is signified. This liability to a sanction is the long and short of legal obligation. Anyone who is subject to a command is by definition *bound*, *obliged*, or *obligated* to obey it.

Commands thus necessarily imply the existence of superiors and inferiors. Austin emphasized, however, that as he used the term it did not denote high social status, wealth, or virtue. The superiority implied by the notion of command 'signifies *might*: the power of affecting others with evil or pain, and of forcing them, through fear of that evil, to fashion their conduct to one's wishes.'[51] Commands may also be either general or particular. They may oblige a *class* of persons to a *course* of conduct, or they may oblige a specific person to a *particular* action. The rule that all thieves shall be hung by the neck until dead is an example of a general command, or rule. The judicial order that a particular thief shall be hung is an example of an occasional or particular command.[52] Aside from this, the commander may signify his wishes either expressly or tacitly. If he permits a subordinate to issue general orders, he tacitly expresses his desire that these orders shall be obeyed. Such tacit expressions of desire are as much law as the explicit orders of the commander.[53]

Law 'properly so-called' takes various forms, one of which is divine law. A second consists of certain rules of positive morality which, unlike other positive moral rules, are genuine commands. A third type consists of positive law, or law 'strictly so-called'.[54] These imperatives are the express or tacit commands of the sovereign, Austin's conception of which will be explained later in this chapter. Positive law is, in any event, the subject of jurisprudence. The only other types of laws which fall within its province are legislative actions that explain or repeal positive laws, or create rules without sanctions. The 'space' which these 'improper laws' occupy in the science of jurisprudence is, however, 'comparatively narrow and insignificant'.[55]

Austin divided this science into national or particular and general jurisprudence. The specific subject-matter of national jurisprudence is the positive laws of a particular community. They are so interrelated as to constitute a system of law, the nature of which varies somewhat from one country to another. Other principles, notions, and distinctions are common to all legal orders. They characterize both 'the scanty and crude systems of rude societies, and the ampler and maturer systems of refined communities'.[56] The latter also share certain principles, notions, and distinctions which form the subject-matter of general jurisprudence. Its exclusive or appropriate object is the *exposition* of these principles.

Austin further subdivided the principles of general jurisprudence into those which are necessary and unnecessary. To say that some are necessary means that 'we cannot imagine coherently a system of law . . . without conceiving them as constituent parts of it.'[57] He cited many examples of these fundamental notions, which include duty, right, liberty, injury, punishment, and redress. The relationship of these concepts to each other and to law, independent political society, and sovereignty is also 'necessary'. Other principles which inhere in the very idea of a legal system are the distinction between written and unwritten law, various classifications of rights and obligations, and the differentiation between civil and criminal law.[58]

Certain principles, notions, and distinctions that fall within the province of general jurisprudence are not necessary in this sense. A system of law could coherently be visualized without reference to them. Nevertheless, these principles do very generally characterize mature and ample legal systems. The distinction between the law of persons and the law of things is an example. The ultimate basis of these widespread similarities between different legal systems is the 'common nature of mankind', which provides a 'common foundation' for '[a]ll systems of law'.[59] This common nature explains the similar grounds of utility which 'extend through all communities', which are 'palpable . . . in all refined communities',[60] and which are the immediate basis of the conceptual uniformities of different legal systems. Nothing indicates more unmistakably than this analysis the dependence of Austin's very conception of jurisprudence upon his utilitarianism. The one provides the foundation without which the other could not stand.

Austin insisted, at any rate, that the elucidation of legal language was an essential prerequisite of an exposition of the basic principles of jurisprudence. The necessity for such clarification stemmed from several considerations. One was the 'purely verbal puzzle[s]' generated by 'mysterious jargon',[61] while another was the 'numerous ambiguities' of terms such as 'law', 'right', 'obligation', 'injury', 'sanction', 'person', 'thing', 'act', and 'forbearance'. A final factor was the unsatisfactory definitions of these words by many writers about law. Most of their definitions 'instead of shedding light upon the thing defined . . . involve it in thicker obscurity'.[62]

Austin could have attempted to overcome these difficulties by coining new terms. If he had done so, he would have followed in at least some of the footsteps of Jeremy Bentham. Although Bentham tried to restrain his inclination to mint new terms, he did not wholly succeed.[63] Austin not only specifically criticized some of Bentham's neologisms, but preferred 'to adhere to the established terms, and in the pithy language of Hobbes *snuff* them with apt distinctions and definitions, and when, being snuffed, they give light, then to use them.'[64] This preference reflected his perception that the rejection of established words is seldom possible or expedient. While the meaning of these terms may be obscure, it is usually less obscure than that of new words. A neologist also runs the substantial risk of using his newly-invented terms ambiguously.[65] Finally, these words are

> open to a great inconvenience from which established though ambiguous expressions are completely exempt. They are open to that undiscerning, yet overwhelming ridicule, which is poured upon innovations in speech by the formidable confederacy of fools: who being incapable of clear and discriminating apprehension, cannot perceive the difficulties which the names were devised to obviate, though they know that their ears are tingling with novel and grating sounds.[66]

Austin conceived of general jurisprudence, in any case, as involving the exposition of two different kinds of principles or notions. Concepts which are absolutely essential for the study of any legal system are one type. To this extent, the business of general jurisprudence is to formulate what today would be called a 'conceptual framework'. Empirical generalizations are the other type of principle. Their inclusion within general jurisprudence means that it entails more than the elucidation of basic legal terms or concepts. In addition, it involves the exposition of substantive similarities between different legal systems. In short, general jurisprudence has a 'sociological' dimension. While Austin was an ardent believer in the necessity for conceptual and linguistic analysis, he did not limit the business of this science to the purely analytical exposition of legal principles.

This fact also constitutes one difference between Austin and Bentham. The latter distinguished between local and universal expository jurisprudence, the subject of which is the laws of all nations. Neither the substance nor the forms of the laws of any two nations are exactly identical. The only universal links between legal systems are terminological. For this reason the scope of books on universal jurisprudence is very narrow and their task is wholly analytical.[67] Austin did not explicitly disagree with this view, which he acknowledged to be literally correct.[68] He did, however, significantly qualify his agreement with Bentham. Although the only *universal* similarities between legal systems are terminological, very *widespread* substantive likenesses exist.

Two sources seldom, if ever, used for the study of Austin clarify further his conception of these similarities. One is his personal copy of Bentham's *An Introduction to the Principles of Morals and Legislation*. The book includes this pencilled comment next to Bentham's statement about terminological similarities between legal systems: 'The same remark applies to all these Institutions which owing to the common nature of man are everywhere nearly the same. Father and son.'[69] The second source is a catalogue description by Austin of his course of lectures at the University of London. This account is also the best extant indicator of the kinds of legal systems which he felt to be 'rude' and 'mature'. Although it is difficult not to detect an ethnocentric bias in his words, they are too important not to quote at length:

> The principles and distinctions which the mere being of Law suppose, are the matter of Universal Jurisprudence. Taken in its *literal* import, it lies within a narrow compass. So different is Law amongst barbarians from Law amongst civilized men . . . Law in Mahometan from Law in Christian communities, that Jurisprudence would be confined to the definitions of a few leading terms, supposing it confined to the matter which is *common* to *all* systems. But in the positive systems of Law which are worthy of accurate examination (in the positive systems, that is, of the civilized European Nations), *common* distinctions and principles, though they take very various forms, are sufficiently numerous to constitute the subject of a science. Accordingly, these are the subjects of the *Universal* Jurisprudence which is the purpose of the Lectures to expound.[70]

Austin insisted, in any case, that determinations of the worth of positive laws are beyond the scope of the science of *jurisprudence*. Its 'exclusive' and 'appropriate' object is the *exposition* of 'principles abstracted from positive systems. . . . With the goodness or badness of laws, as tried by the test of utility (or by any of the various tests which divide the opinions of mankind), it has no immediate concern.'[71] This insistence is, surely, a recurring theme of the legal positivism on the development of which Austin had such a strong impact.[72] To say this is not to suggest, however, that he regarded determinations of the worth of positive laws as unimportant or arbitrary. Unlike some subsequent legal positivists such as Hans Kelsen, Austin was not an ethical non-cognitivist.[73] Since he was an ardent utilitarian, he believed that evaluations of positive laws are capable of rational proof. His argument was only that such appraisals are the business of the science of legislation rather than jurisprudence. Ethics is a *science* the purpose of which is to determine 'the nature of the index to the tacit commands of the Deity'. One subdivision of ethics is the *science* of legislation, the business of which is to determine 'positive law as it ought to be.'[74]

This conception of the province of jurisprudence appears to support the prevailing interpretation of Austin. The same is true of his analysis of the relationship between legislation and jurisprudence. Since 'knowledge of what ought to be, supposes a knowledge of what is, legislation supposes jurisprudence, but jurisprudence does not suppose legislation. What laws have been and are, may be known without a knowledge of what they ought to be.'[75] A third and related theme of Austin's legal positivism also seems to show the irrelevance of his exposition of ethical and political theories. Nothing is more characteristic of his work than a sharp distinction between the law as it is and the law as it ought to be. He strongly emphasized that the validity of positive law, its existence as law, is independent of its goodness or badness. The 'simple' and 'glaring truth' is that

> the existence of law is one thing; its merit or demerit is another. Whether it be or be not is one enquiry; whether it be or be not conformable to an assumed standard, is a different inquiry. A law, which actually exists, is a law, though we happen to dislike it, or though it vary from the text by which we regulate our approbation and disapprobation.[76]

These ideas explain why countless students of Austin have criticized his chapters on ethics as unrelated to, or inconsistent with, the rest of his book. This criticism is impossible to reconcile, however, with a large number of facts. To begin with, Austin sometimes refers to the principle of utility in order to answer questions that he raises. His analysis of the layman's knowledge of law is an excellent illustration of this tendency. He began from the premise that 'not one in a thousand [laymen] knows the laws which bind him'.[77] Even lawyers have no real knowledge 'of any branch of law but that which they have peculiarly studied'.[78] These considerations raise the issue of how to explain the tendency of the behaviour of laymen to conform to legal precepts. Austin's response to this problem was to argue that

> some laws are so obviously suggested by utility, that any person not insane would naturally surmise or guess their existence; which they could not be expected to do, where the utility of the law is not so obvious. And most men's knowledge of the law is mostly of this kind. They see that a particular act would be mischievous, and they conclude that it must be prohibited. The conduct of nineteen men out of twenty, in nineteen cases out of twenty, is rather guided by a surmise as to the law, than by a knowledge of it.[79]

Moreover, Sarah Austin claimed that her husband felt jurisprudence and ethics to be closely related. She maintained that the 'whole structure' of his philosophy of law is based upon 'the only sure test [utility] to which the goodness or badness of laws can be brought'.[80] His firm belief in the intimate connection between legal theory and ethics was also the major reason for his intention to rewrite completely *The Province of Jurisprudence Determined*. This felt need originated largely from his deep conviction that 'until the ethical notions of men were more clear and consistent, no considerable improvement could be hoped for in legal or political science, nor, consequently, in legal or political institutions'.[81]

Austin thus believed that ethical clarity and consistency were essential for legal and political, as well as scientific, progress. He was also convinced that only utilitarianism provided the requisite clarity and consistency. This is evident from his explanation of why it 'really *is* important . . . that men should think distinctly, and speak with a meaning'.[82] One reason for the importance of such thought and speech is its value as a means to reduce or eliminate unnecessary social or political conflicts. Austin cited the American Revolution as an example. He argued that it could have been avoided if Englishmen had approached the problem of American independence from a utilitarian perspective. Then they would not have talked of the *sovereignty* of the mother country and her so-called *right* to tax her colony. Instead, they would have used the utilitarian cost-benefit analysis employed by Edmund Burke. He

> would have taught them better: would have purged their muddled brains, and 'laid the fever in their souls', with the healing principle of utility. He asked them what they would get, if the project of coercion should succeed; and implored them to compare the advantage with the hazard and the cost.[83]

There is even more compelling evidence than this of Austin's belief in the close connection between ethics and jurisprudence. It is his explicit claim that 'in a chain of systematical lectures concerned with the *rationale* of jurisprudence, such an exposition [of ethical theories] is a necessary link.' Although the sciences of legislation and jurisprudence are different, they are also '*connected by numerous and indissoluble ties*' (emphasis added). Determination of the nature of the index to the tacit commands of the Deity is therefore not only an 'all-important object of the science of legislation'. In addition to this, it is 'a fit and important object of the kindred science of jurisprudence'.[84]

Austin defended this position by several arguments, one of which reflects a particular theory of the causal impact of utilitarian considerations on legislation. Understanding of the meaning of positive laws requires, he claimed, a clear explanation of their purposes. They are, in turn, incapable of being understood without an appreciation of the nature of the principle of utility. For it 'not only ought to guide, but has commonly in fact guided the legislator. The principle . . . well or ill understood, has usually been the principle consulted in making laws.' An elucidation of the principle of utility is necessary, therefore, in order to explain accurately the coverage and purpose of a law. Otherwise, its meaning may be unintelligible. This fact explains, Austin maintained, why his discussion of utility was *not* a deviation from the subject of his book.[85]

This argument implies that causal explanations of positive law are a proper concern of the student of jurisprudence. To that extent, it indicates one way in which Austin's version of legal positivism differs from that of Hans Kelsen. The former's concept of jurisprudence is, in a word, more 'sociological' than the latter's. Kelsen's 'pure' theory of law excludes causal explanations, which belong to the province of the sociology of law. Such propositions are as foreign to the structural analysis of positive law, he claimed, as moral or political evaluations.[86] The major reason for Austin's quite different attitude is, clearly, his commitment to utilitarianism.

In any event, this argument for the consistency of Austin's discussion of utilitarianism has a certain cogency. The purpose of his discourse on ethics was not to enable the student of jurisprudence to determine the worth of positive laws. Rather, his goal was to facilitate understanding of the law that is. If the principle of utility has the causal impact which he attributed to it, then explanation of it is essential for achieving this aim. To be sure, the existence of positive law is not *logically* dependent upon its ethical correctness. Still, the existence of law commonly depends upon the legislator's *perceptions* of utility, well- or ill-understood.

To say that this response is somewhat persuasive is not to imply that it is wholly acceptable. The basis of Austin's argument is a causal explanation of legislation, the accuracy of which is open to very serious question. It is one thing to say that the desire for happiness is part of the constitution of human nature. All of the classical nineteenth-century British utilitarians accepted one version or another of this doctrine. It is another thing to contend that the *general* happiness has in fact been the motivation of *legislation*. This contention assumes that socially undesirable laws are simply the result of ignorance, which is dubious. Toward the end of his life, at least, Bentham firmly rejected any such explanation of law-making.[87] Some of Austin's comments are also difficult, if not impossible, to reconcile with this assumption.[88]

His argument for the inconsistency of his discussion of ethics is also not completely satisfactory for another reason. The principle of utility may or may not have the causal impact which Austin attributed to it. No matter, explanation of the scope and purport of positive laws does not require the *kind of discussion of the principle of utility in which he engages*. Full understanding of the impact of this principle requires only an *elucidation of its meaning*. Austin's discussion of the principle is much more, however, than an *explanation* of what it is. He not only elucidated the meaning of the principle, he also defended it as *the* index to the tacit commands of God. He *criticized* the theory of the moral sense. He *explained* how the rules which *ought* to guide human conduct can be discovered. He *justified* the *need* for rules and an ethical authority. He emphasized both the 'importance' *and* the 'truth' of the principle of utility, which he ardently wished to commend to others.[89] His discourse on ethics crosses the line, thus, which divides 'meta-ethical' *explications* from 'normative' *prescriptions.*[90] The latter were unnecessary in order to explain the causal impact of the principle of utility on legislation.

Austin's other defence of the consistency of his discussion of ethics, to be explained momentarily, is not subject to this criticism. This argument does more than explain why an *elucidation* of utilitarianism is necessary for understanding positive laws. In addition, this contention indicates why jurisprudence requires *justification* of the principle of utility. This response is therefore fully compatible with the actual nature of Austin's discussion of ethics.

The study of jurisprudence in his sense of the term involves numerous principles, notions, and distinctions. 'Many' of them, he points out, could not be expounded 'correctly and clearly' without analysis of the 'seemingly irrelative' ethical theories.[91] Unfortunately, Austin does not explain in any detail precisely what these statements mean. They could denote the need for utilitarian calculations in evaluating or choosing between some juristic *concepts.* The choice between them must be in part made, it could be argued, on the basis of their *effects* on the general happiness. The principle of utility, properly understood, is the only correct test of these effects. An explanation *and defence* of it is therefore necessary in a book on jurisprudence. Otherwise, students of this science would not know how to evaluate certain legal concepts. This consideration could explain why the determination of the true index to the tacit commands of God is 'a fit and important object of the . . . science of jurisprudence'.[92] If this is what Austin means, then his discussion of ethics is not inconsistent with *his* version of legal positivism. The purpose of this discourse is not to facilitate evaluations of *positive laws* as good or bad, which is the business of the science of legislation. Rather, the aim is to provide a basis for evaluating *concepts of jurisprudence.* Achievement of this objective requires an explanation *and* justification of the principle of utility.

The only example which Austin gives does not, admittedly, confirm this interpretation.[93] Yet, his celebrated or infamous separation of law from morality does support it. For one of his criticisms of the confusion of law as it is and as it ought to be is its pernicious *effects.* A sharp distinction between the two is for this reason *socially desirable.* Moreover, the desirability of this distinction is a recurring theme of legal positivism in any of its forms. To be a legal positivist *means* to emphasize the absolute necessity of distinguishing between law and morality.[94] Austin's utilitarian argument for the separation does not appear, however, in the literature of most subsequent legal positivists.[95] The existence of this argument thus indicates one more way in which his utilitarianism makes him a special kind of positivist.

Explanation of this point requires an elucidation of Austin's controversial distinction between law and morality. To say that he separated the two is not to imply that he totally divorced them. In fact, he acknowledged a large number of actual and possible connections between positive law and positive morality or divine law. The content of these different types of rules may overlap.[96] Moral or ethical concepts influence the creation and enforcement of positive laws.[97] The law of God is the model on which human laws *should* be based. Positive law *is* 'in a great measure founded' on positive morality,[98] and there are 'numerous' cases in which law and morality are 'intimately and indissolubly allied'.[99] This alliance is indeed so intimate that it is 'sometimes expedient to include in the *corpus juris* a part of what is really positive morality, because positive law is not intelligible without it.'[100] Austin claimed that international law does *not* fall into this category,[101] but he expressed a different attitude toward public law, or the portion of it that related to the sovereign or constitution of the state. He justified this exception on the ground that the positive law of England is unintelligible in the absence of knowledge of the constitution of Parliament and the rules by which it legislates. At the same time, it is 'manifest' that 'much' of this part of the public law of England consists of 'either mere law imposed by the opinion of the community, or merely ethical maxims which the body spontaneously observes'.[102]

These ideas indicate why the use of the word 'separation' to describe Austin's conception of the relationship between law and morals is misleading. The term that much more accurately describes his views is 'distinction' between law and morality. Despite the many links between them, they have different natures and should be carefully distinguished. This distinction is imperative, Austin insisted, because the *existence* of positive laws is not logically *dependent* upon their moral or ethical goodness. These laws *exist* though they 'vary from the text, by which we regulate our approbation and disapprobation'.[103] To make the goodness of positive laws a necessary condition for their existence creates only confusion.

The main example of this confusion that Austin cited was Sir William Blackstone's famous conception of law. While Austin did not specifically cite this famous passage from the *Commentaries on the*

Laws of England, he obviously was referring to it. According to Blackstone:

> This law of nature, being coeval with mankind, and dictated by God himself, is of course superior in obligation to any other. It is binding over all the globe, in all countries, and at all times: no human laws are of any validity, if contrary to this; and such of them as are valid derive all their force, and all their authority, mediately or immediately, from this original.[104]

The crime of murder illustrates the relationship which Blackstone imputed to natural and human law. The commission of this offence is not wrong because it is prohibited by human law. Rather, individuals are obligated not to commit murder because it is 'expressly forbidden by the divine, and demonstrably by the natural law'. Indeed, if 'any human law should allow or enjoin us to commit it, we are bound to transgress that human law, or else . . . offend both the natural and the divine.'[195]

Austin interpreted this conception of law to mean that 'no human law which conflicts with the Divine law *is a law*'. He criticized this assertion on two very different grounds. To suggest that no human law which conflicts with Divine law is a law is, to begin with, 'stark nonsense'. Any such proposition conflicts with a number of indisputable historical facts. The most pernicious laws 'have been and are continually enforced as laws by judicial tribunals'.[106] To be sure, this argument seems to contradict Austin's assessment of the causal impact of the principle of utility. Nonetheless, it is the argument which he advances and for which he adduces slavery as an example. Despite his 'utmost abhorrence' of this institution, he argued that denial of the actual or possible existence of a *legal* right to own slaves is absurd. For it has been established by positive law 'in every age, and . . . almost every nation'.[107] The right to own slaves illustrates the numerous legal rights which have been 'generally pernicious'.[108]

Austin also criticized Blackstone's assertion for a very different and much more political reason. To say that human laws that conflict with divine laws are not laws is not only 'puerile', but 'mischievous'.[109] The most pernicious of its bad effects is anarchy, a state of affairs of which Austin strongly disapproved. Although he did not formally define this term, he used the word to denote a society without government. This condition would exist if the bulk of a society did not habitually obey a common and determinate human superior.

Austin's criticism of Blackstone obviously assumes that anarchy in this sense is highly undesirable. Otherwise, it would not be a criticism of the learned commentator to claim that to take his position is to preach anarchy. Unfortunately, Austin did not explain in detail why a society without government is undesirable. He probably assumed that any such explanation was unnecessary in a book about law. Several of his predecessors had also criticized anarchy at some length. They include Hobbes and Bentham, both of whom Austin profoundly admired. At any rate, his scattered remarks on the subject indicate that he objected to anarchy for several reasons. To begin with, he expressed grave reservations about the possibility of a society without government. While such a state of affairs is conceivable, 'we cannot look forward to its being realized'. Moreover, the conception of society without a 'guiding or directing' body is impossible. The reason for its impossibility is the vagueness of positive morality. It is 'necessarily so uncertain that it cannot serve as a complete guide of conduct, nor can it be sufficiently minute and detailed'.[110] Finally, the social effects of the absence of government are bad. This is why, Austin claimed, 'obedience to established government is enjoined generally by the Deity. For, without obedience to "the powers which be", there were little security and little enjoyment.'[111]

Austin's statement that the Deity *generally* enjoins obedience means what it says. Exceptional circumstances may arise in which resistance to the established government is justifiable on utilitarian grounds. The difference between a bad and a good government is, he argued, 'so momentous . . . that *if it would lead to a good one*, resistance to a bad one would be useful'.[112]Determination of whether it is useful requires calculation and comparison of the effects of resistance. They include: the evils of the established government; the likelihood that resistance will produce a better government; the evils of this course of action, which always produces some bad effects; and the advantages of successful resistance.[113] Since its effects may be beneficial, resistance is ethically justifiable. The failure to appreciate this is one of the few limitations, Austin maintained, of Hobbes' political philosophy. His 'extreme timidity' obscured his awareness that in certain anomalous cases disobedience is 'counselled by that very principle of utility which indicates the duty of submission'.[114]

At the same time, Austin emphasized the difficulty of knowing whether resistance was justified in any particular case. The root of the problem is the uncertainty which would probably characterize estimations of its expediency. A cost-benefit analysis requires calculations and comparisons of the varied and numerous effects of resistance. Different persons would be likely to reach different conclusions about the results of this course of action. 'What appears pernicious to one person may appear beneficial to another.'[115] Wise, good, and brave men will therefore probably disagree about whether resistance, in a particular situation, is justified. 'A Milton or a Hampden might animate their countrymen to resistance, but a Hobbes or a Falkland would counsel obedience and peace.'[116]

This uncertainty means that even utilitarians are likely to disagree about whether resistance is justified in a particular case. Although the principle of utility is preferable to any other index to the Divine will, it is an 'obviously insufficient' index.[117] Nevertheless, Austin believed that general utility provides an 'intelligible test', the use of which will encourage a 'just solution'. A utilitarian approach to resistance also fosters peaceful compromise of differences rather than revolutionary violence. A cost-benefit analysis would force each side to 'compare the worth of its object with the cost of a violent pursuit'. Both upholders of the *status quo* and its critics might therefore decide that compromise of their objectives was preferable to violence. General utility is thus vastly superior as a standard of resistance to the 'unmeaning abstractions' or 'senseless fictions' that dominate political rhetoric. Examples of this kind of 'jargon' are the appeal to the rights of man, inalienable liberties, eternal and immutable justice, or the original contract. Parties to political disputes who use these 'fustian phrases . . . must . . . take to their weapons, and fight their difference out'.[118]

Another such 'phrase' for which Austin had little use was natural law. While this ancient notion played an important part in Blackstone's legal philosophy, Austin had only contempt for it. The modern conception of natural law has 'thoroughly perplexed and obscured the sciences of Jurisprudence and Ethics'.[119] This idea is so 'utterly indefinite' that it would 'justify resistance to government under any pretext whatever'. The same is true of the cognate idea of natural rights, which is mere jargon involving 'stupendous absurdities'. This principle is subject to 'any interpretation' and therefore offers a pretext for rebellion against 'any government whatever'.[120] The notion of natural law or natural rights is in this respect similar to the moral sense, innate practical principles, or conscience. These phrases are

> merely convenient cloaks for ignorance or sinister interest: they mean either that I hate the law to which I object and cannot tell

> why, or that I hate the law, and that the cause of my hatred is one which I find it incommodious to avow. If I say openly, I hate the law, *ergo*, it is not binding and ought to be disobeyed, no one will listen to me; but by calling my hate my conscience or my moral sense, I urge the same argument in another and more plausible form: I seem to assign a reason for my dislike, when in truth I have only given it a sounding and specious name.[121]

These considerations explain why Austin believed that anarchy is the practical effect of Blackstone's confusion of law and morality. If Austin was justified in fearing anarchy, he seems to have grossly exaggerated the extent to which Blackstone's conception of law would produce this state of affairs. To begin with, disobedience to established laws is probably much more widespread than Austin evidently believed to be the case. Most persons disobey some laws some of the time, without causing the dissolution of government and the war of all against all. Aside from this, the alleged confusion of law and morality may promote *obedience* to established laws. For the effect of this confusion may be to sanctify the *status quo*, by encouraging the idea that it embodies what ought to be. Blackstone himself, who was anything but a revolutionary, is a good example. He 'liked to identify the existing laws of England with laws as they always ought to be'.[122] This identification may well be mistaken, but the effect of it is certainly not disobedience and anarchy.

At any rate, Austin objected to the confusion of positive law and positive morality for the same reasons that he criticized the confusion of positive and divine or natural law. The focus of his critique was the statement of the Roman jurist Ulpian that law is the creature of justice. On the one hand, Austin claimed that this assertion involves a 'detestable abuse of articulate language'.[123] Justice is in fact the offspring of law, which is the standard of what is just or unjust. On the other hand, he criticized Ulpian's assertion on the utilitarian ground that its *effects* are mischievous. This idea encourages both jurors and judges to reach whatever decisions they wish rather than those required by law. For example:

> The veriest dolt who is placed in a jury box, the merest old woman who happens to be raised to the bench, will talk finely of equity or justice – the justice of the case, the equity of the case, the imperious demands of justice, the plain dictates of equity. He forgets that he is there to enforce *the law of the land*, else he does not administer

> that justice or that equity with which alone he is immediately concerned.[124]

Austin believed that several precedent-shattering decisions of Lord Mansfield, the great eighteenth-century British judge, illustrate this danger. He developed the novel rule that a merely moral obligation was sufficient consideration for a promise to be legally binding.[125] Austin did not object to this doctrine because it originated in an act of judicial legislation. Such law-making is both 'highly beneficial and . . . absolutely necessary'. Rather, he criticized the vagueness and indeterminateness of 'moral obligation'. The meaning of this term is so open-ended that it enables a judge to enforce 'whatever he pleases'. In fact, moral obligation is 'anything which we choose to call so . . . the precepts of positive morality are infinitely varying, and the will of God, whether indicated by utility or by a moral sense, is equally matter of dispute.'[126]

These criticisms seem to involve Austin in an inconsistency. For they appear to conflict with his justification, in an earlier portion of his book, of utilitarianism. His defence of it implies that the principle of utility is a very useful index to the tacit commands of God. Austin's critique of the confusion of law and morality assumes, it could be argued, that no index to these commands is very good. Even utilitarians apply the principle of utility differently. What appears pernicious to one person seems useful to another. As an index to the will of God, utility is as much a matter of dispute as the moral sense.

An evaluation of this criticism requires further clarification of Austin's thought. The basic question is his rationale for the uncertainty of some Divine laws and whether it conflicts with his defence of utilitarianism. In fact, several explanations of this uncertainty can be found in the pages of his book which criticize the confusion of law and morality. One reason is the lack of consensus within society about *the* proper index to the tacit commands of God. Since Austin's defence of the principle of utility presumes such disagreement, this argument is not a sign of any inconsistency on his part. A second reason is the insufficiency of the extant indices to the tacit commands of God, which include the principle of utility. Austin vacillates somewhat, however, in his estimations of the degree of its insufficiency.

The brunt of his remarks imply that utility is not a wholly insufficient index. He does not say that what appears pernicious to one person *will* appear beneficial to another, only that it *may*. Furthermore, he admitted that disobedience 'grounded on clear and definite prospects of good, is sometimes beneficial'.[127] This admission implies that utilitarian calculations *can* offer clear guidance about whether to disobey. To the extent that Austin takes *this* position, his critique of the confusion of law and morality is not inconsistent. For his justification of the principle of utility does not imply that it is a wholly sufficient index to God's tacit commands. In fact, Austin stressed that even this principle is imperfect and at times may provide only a 'glimmering light'.[128]

This interpretation of Austin does not imply that criticism of his internal inconsistency is entirely groundless. At the least it draws attention to an undeniable difference of emphasis in various sections of his book. On the one hand, his defence of the principle of utility tends to stress its superiority to other indices to the tacit commands of God. On the other hand, his critique of the confusion of the law as it is and as it ought to be tends to emphasize the limitations of the principle. In the course of driving this point home, Austin once or twice suggests that utility is no better than the moral sense, natural law, or other ethical standards. This suggestion is not only inconsistent with Austin's defence of utilitarianism. Aside from this, it adumbrates the ethical noncognitivism which strongly conditioned the thought of *some* later legal positivists such as Hans Kelsen.[129]

In any case, some of Austin's criticisms of the confusion of law and morality very definitely reflect a 'logic of consequences'. The confusion between divine and positive law, or positive law and positive morality, is undesirable in part because of its bad practical effects. Austin's negative reaction to natural law also reflects certain undeniably *political* preferences. They include a preference for order over disorder, peace instead of war, and reform rather than revolution. To say this is not to criticize Austin's values, which appear to me to be quite reasonable. Nevertheless, they are also highly political.

Austin's critique of the confusion of law and morality also indicates why he devoted so much space to a discussion of ethics. Proper understanding of the principle of utility is essential for choosing between some of the rival concepts of jurisprudence. Otherwise, students of this science might employ either defective interpretations of utility or unsatisfactory alternatives to it. An explanation and defence of utilitarianism is therefore a necessary and consistent step in the development of Austin's philosophy of positive law.

3

This conclusion suggests the possibility that Austin's utilitarianism may also have influenced other elements of his philosophy of law. His command conception of law, the nature of which has been explained, and his theory of sovereignty, are two important examples. After all, the ultimate basis of these axioms of his positivist jurisprudence is not readily apparent. It is therefore possible that his ethical and political theories had an impact. Determination of whether they did requires, at the outset, clarification of Austin's famous theory of sovereignty. A description and criticism of the most plausible extant explanations of it are also desirable. This critique indicates the need for another explanation, the details of which will be elaborated in the next section.

Austin believed that a sovereign is the foundation of the legal order of every independent political society. Each society of this kind has a sovereign whose will is the ultimate source of its positive laws. This supreme authority is a common and determinate human superior with two distinctive features. One is the 'positive mark' of receipt of *habitual* obedience from the *bulk* of a given society. The other is the 'negative mark' of the absence of habitual obedience to any other determinate human superior. To be independent a political society must have a superior not only of the first, but also the second, kind. As Austin points out, however, 'the party truly independent . . . is not the society, but the sovereign portion of the society'.[130]

Austin recognized that these marks of sovereignty are fallible tests of specific cases. It is impossible to specify with absolute precision how many people must obey if the *bulk* of the population obeys. The same is true of the length of time they must obey before their obedience can be described as *habitual*. The source of the difficulty, which pervades legal language, is 'the vagueness or indefiniteness of the terms in which the definition . . . is inevitably conceived.'[131] Despite this, Austin believed that this difficulty is not insuperable. The application of the tests for the identification of the sovereign in most societies is in general quite simple. It is not difficult as a rule to establish that the bulk of the population habitually obeys a common and determinate superior. 'Such . . . is the ordinary state of England, and of every independent society somewhat advanced in civilization.'[132]

This theory of sovereignty was the basis of Austin's classification of forms of government. His ideas on this subject assume that the government of any independent political society is the sovereign. A similar assumption also appears at many other places in Austin's writings. Despite this, he acknowledged that in certain independent political societies the government is *not* sovereign. The political systems of both the United States and Great Britain are examples. The sovereign in the United States is not the federal government, but the state governments considered as an aggregate. Austin defined these governments, however, as the body of citizens who elect the legislatures of the states. These persons are the real sovereign in the United States.[133]

Austin specifically rejected the notion that Parliament was the British sovereign. Rather, he argued that the Crown, the House of Lords, and the *electors* of the House of Commons were the sovereign in the United Kingdom.[134] In any event, he insisted that the sovereign possesses all political powers. Although it ordinarily does and should delegate a substantial number of these powers, they ultimately belong to this authority.[135] Austin also took the position that its powers are incapable of legal limitation. If the government is sovereign, then its powers cannot be limited by positive law. If the government is not sovereign, then the powers of the person or persons who are sovereign cannot be limited by positive law. It is for this reason that neither customary, international, nor constitutional law in the strict sense of the term are positive law. If they obligated legally the supreme authority, then this person or persons could not in fact be sovereign.[136]

Austin believed that this position will hold 'universally or without exception'.[137] Federal systems such as the American which have governments of limited power are only an apparent deviation from the rule, which is invariable. The sovereign in the United States is not the government, but the persons who elect the state legislatures which must ratify constitutional amendments. The power of these electors is supreme and incapable of limitation by positive law. The same is true of the power of the sovereign in any independent political society.

To say this is not to deny that the sovereign is subject to various and significant non-legal restraints. Divine law imposes ethical obligations on this supreme person or persons. Positive morality conditions the extent to which positive law is enforceable.[138] The exercise of sovereign power is checked by fear 'of rousing to active resistance the might which slumbers in the multitude'.[139] Austin's only point is that these restraints are not *legally* binding. The power of the real sovereign is incapable of *legal* limitation.

This stress on the illimitability of the supreme power is probably the most controversial feature of Austin's conception of sovereignty.

It is in any case an attribute of it which this study attempts to explain by the impact of utilitarian arguments. No such justification of the concept appears, however, in the pages of *The Province of Jurisprudence Determined*. The only *argument* that Austin adduced in support of his position had nothing to do with the *inexpediency* of limitations on the powers of the sovereign. Instead, he emphasized the *impossibility* or *incoherence* of such restraints. The idea that supreme power *can* be limited by positive law is 'a flat contradiction in terms'.[140]

Austin acknowledged that sovereigns have enacted laws attempting to limit or obligate themselves or their successors. He insisted, however, that these attempts were futile. Sovereigns *cannot* impose legally binding limitations or obligations on themselves or their successors for two reasons. To begin with, they may abrogate these restraints at their pleasure. 'Laws' that are subject to this contingency are not genuine laws. Aside from this, 'sovereigns' who were subject to legal sanctions for their actions would be 'in a state of subjection to a higher or superior sovereign'.[141] In other words, the person or persons liable to the sanction would not be the real sovereign. 'Laws' by which sovereigns attempt to bind themselves or their successors are not therefore positive laws imposing legal obligations. Rather, they are merely moral rules, principles, or maxims which sovereigns 'adopt as guides, or which they commend as guides to their successors in sovereign power'.[142] For the same reasons no one has legal rights 'against the Government itself'.[143]

The cogency of this argument depends on the necessity of a supreme power and on the definition of the term. If this power is necessary, and if it means that which is incapable of legal limitations, then the argument is irrefutable. To say that the supreme power is subject to such limitations is a contradiction in terms. It is a contradiction, however, only because of the way in which supreme power has been defined. The genuine question is, therefore, why this concept should be defined as legally unlimited power. Unfortunately, Austin gives no satisfactory response to this question. While he does attempt to demonstrate that the facts are compatible with his definition, he adduces no other justification of it. Rather, he spells out in great detail the implications of this basic axiom of his legal philosophy. In other words, he utilizes the 'geometrical' method which with Locke and Hobbes he so intensely admired. As a result, the basis of his conception of sovereignty is not apparent.

This uncertainty is a major problem in the interpretation of Austin.

Resolution of it depends upon an understanding of the basic purpose of his jurisprudence, which is not entirely clear. This fact helps to explain the lack of consensus among scholars about the rationale of his philosophy of law. Their diverse outlooks are evident from the writings of Julius Stone, W. L. Morison, and Eira Ruben. Their studies of Austin run the gamut of possible interpretations of his thought.[144]

Although Stone does not describe his position in precisely these terms, the essence of it is a view of Austin's conceptions of law and sovereignty as useful fictions. He supports this contention by the argument that Austin's science of jurisprudence is 'rational' rather than 'empirical'. His objective was *not* to explain actual or desirable political conditions. Rather, it was to develop a conceptual framework for understanding the *logical coherence* of any mature legal system. His goal was 'to suggest a framework for viewing the propositions of a legal order as a logically self-consistent system.' His elaborate apparatus of definitions and classifications was designed to reveal 'whether a particular proposition was a proposition of the law of a particular society'. His aim was logical testing and his work is 'a kind of paradigm of the approach to law in terms of logic'.[145]

This interpretation has a very important implication for the widespread tendency discussed at the outset of this chapter. The vast majority of Austin's critics object to his doctrines by showing *that*, and *how*, they conflict with the facts. Such criticisms assume that the purpose of his theories was to describe the facts. If Stone's interpretation is correct, this assumption is unfounded. To be sure, he admits that Austin's work is intermingled with empirical observations of actual legal systems.[146] To this extent, he bears some responsibility for the misinterpretations of his critics. Nevertheless, Stone insists that Austin's goal was *not* to formulate empirically valid generalizations about existing legal orders. His concept of the legally unlimited power of the sovereign is a prime example. This doctrine is

> not an assertion that such a sovereign is to be found, as a matter of political fact, in every actual society which enjoys a legal system. It is rather an assertion that such logical coherence as the propositions of a legal order may have is likely to be most easily and most fully seen if we arrange them *as if* they were commands of such a sovereign. . . . the Austinian sovereign is a formal postulate.[147]

This interpretation of Austin's conception of sovereignty is intelligent and original. The only question is whether it is accurate, which it does not seem to me to be. The evidence that Austin himself conceived of sovereignty as a purely formal postulate is minimal, while the evidence that he thought of it as a verifiable reality is substantial. Otherwise, he would not have attempted to identify in detail the American and British sovereigns. In fact, he felt this need so strongly that he stretched his conception of sovereignty to the breaking-point in order to satisfy it. If the electors of the state legislatures are the American sovereign, they do not fit very easily into the Austinian mould. The power to elect state legislators who will then ratify or reject amendments to the Constitution hardly seems to be the essence of sovereignty in the Austinian sense. The same can be said of the power of the British people to elect members of the House of Commons, a choice that they may exercise as infrequently as once every five years. 'Nothing is more certain,' Dicey writes, 'than that no English judge ever conceded, or, under the present constitution, can concede, that Parliament is in any legal sense a "trustee" for the electors. Of such a feigned "trust" the Courts know nothing.'[148]

The purpose of this section is not, however, to criticize Austin's conception of sovereignty. Rather, it is to demonstrate that he did not view sovereignty as a purely formal postulate. Stone's interpretation of Austin is also subject to other objections. Most of them were enumerated by W. L. Morison in a famous article that he published in 1958.[149] He described the basic weakness of Stone's position as its conflict with 'what the utilitarians regarded as the fundamental tenets of their jurisprudential school'. Morison cites the observation of Leslie Stephen that 'the strong point of Benthamism may . . . be summed up in two words. It meant reverence for facts. Knowledge was to be sought not by logical jugglery but by scrupulous observation and systematic appeals to experience.'[150]

This reverence for the facts pervades Austin's work. Evidence of it includes: his conception of the relationship between theory and practise; his careful analysis of the existence, sources, and forms of judicial legislation; his criticism of Hobbes' definition of 'independent political society';[151] and his interpretation of Bentham's relationship to the historical school of jurisprudence.[152] The testimony of John Stuart Mill provides additional confirmation of the empirical orientation of Austin's work. His course on jurisprudence was attended by Mill, who took copious notes of Austin's lectures. The foundation of his jurisprudence was, Mill claimed, 'legal institutions which exist, or have existed, among mankind, considered as actual facts'.[153]

These considerations are the basis of Morison's interpretation of Austin. His alleged objective was the establishment of an 'empirical' rather than a 'rational' science of law. The formulation of an empirical definition of law is an indispensable means for the achievement of this goal. Accordingly, this is the problem to which he 'devoted practically exclusive attention in the major work he did publish'. His conceptions of law and sovereignty are attempts, thus, to 'describe legal rules in strictly factual terms in order to make them identifiable in the social process'. This empirical approach constitutes his 'real contribution to legal philosophy'.[154]

Morison substantially broadened this interpretation of Austin in a book published in 1982.[155] This is evident from his novel argument that James Mill's *Elements of Political Economy* strongly influenced Austin's approach to the study of law. He allegedly viewed this work, which was published in 1821, as 'the very model of what an account of any social field should be like, and this applied to jurisprudence as much as anything else.'[156] Austin's commitment to this model derived largely, Morison contends, from his conversations with John Stuart Mill. He studied Roman law under Austin in the winter of 1821–2 and the two utilitarians developed a close friendship. Despite Mill's youth – he was only fifteen in 1821 – he supposedly impressed his father's notions of political economy upon Austin.

These notions included the conception of political economy as a science rather than an art. Austin also accepted Mill's view of this discipline as 'a behavioural science elaborated in laws of nature, not teleology'. These 'laws' would take the form of 'if-then' propositions describing necessary sequences of phenomena. A science of law analogous to political economy would *not*, thus, expound legal provisions. Rather, it would explain laws of nature that determine 'things' about these provisions 'wherever they appear, in any code . . . or . . . might ideally appear'. Morison argues that this is precisely what Austin sought to discuss.[157]

Morison contends that Austin particularly admired two aspects of Mill's conception of political economy. One was its character as an empirical science, the subject-matter of which consisted of 'patterns of observed mental and physical events'.[158] The other was its 'formalism' or 'logically systematic' character. Political economy was formalistic in that it analyzed particular events on the basis of their universal features. Morison stresses the importance, for this approach, of the five predicables of Aristotelian logic as explained by John Stuart Mill. The understanding of things in the real world requires analysis and classification of them in terms of their genus, species, differentia, propria, and accidentia. Morison argues that Austin not only believed that events may be analyzed on the basis of these categories, but tried to apply them to the analysis of law. Indeed, the primary thrust of his jurisprudence was the attempt 'to define the species law by its genus and its differentia, and to investigate what propria were exhibited by all systems of the legal species: what features necessarily accompany their being of the species law.'[159]

This interpretation of Austin's jurisprudence underlies Morison's evaluation of it. Although he is critical of many aspects of it, he lauds Austin's unique combination of empiricism and formalism. His ideas are in this respect preferable to Bentham's and fully warrant a ' "back to Austin" movement'.[160] This judgment reflects an interpretation of Austin that is subject, however, to a number of serious criticisms. To say this is not to deny Morison's very real achievements. He is the foremost living authority on Austin, the quality of his book and article is high, and his critique of Stone's position is cogent. Even so, his interpretation of Austin is flawed in several respects.

To begin with, it is highly unlikely that James Mill's conception of political economy was the model for Austin's jurisprudence. In the first place, whether Austin had even read Mill's *Elements of Political Economy* is uncertain. It is not among the collection of his books, for example, that Sarah Austin bequeathed to the Library of the Inner Temple. This collection did include, however, seven of the articles that Mill contributed to the Supplement to the Fifth Edition of the *Encyclopaedia Brittannica*.[161] In the second place, Austin's published and unpublished writings do not contain a single reference to James Mill. At least I have been unable to find any and Morison adduces none. The absence of such references contrasts sharply with Austin's generous praise of other thinkers whom he admired, like Hobbes and Bentham.[162] In the third place, John Stuart Mill's description of the relationship between his father and Austin is incompatible with Morison's interpretation of it. J. S. Mill wrote: 'He [Austin] was not, like Mr Grote, *to any extent* a pupil of my father.' (emphasis added). To be sure, the younger Mill pointed out that Austin had 'attained, by reading and thought, a considerable number of the same opinions [as James Mill], modified by his own very decided individuality of character'.[163] These opinions included tremendous admiration for the principles of classical political economy. It is one thing, however, to maintain that Mill and Austin were enthusiastic proponents of the 'dismal science'. It is a very different thing to argue that Austin used

Mill's account of political economy as the model for his jurisprudence.

Although this evidence does not conclusively disprove Morison's interpretation of Austin, it casts grave doubt upon it. A number of other considerations reinforce this scepticism. They include Austin's disdain for phrases such as the 'laws' of nature, or human nature, words that abound in the writings of James Mill. He had indeed maintained that the purpose of the science of political economy was to discover the 'laws' regulating the production, distribution, exchange and consumption of goods.[164] Austin would probably criticize this use of language as metaphorical, figurative, and harmful. At least he took precisely this position with respect to 'talk' of such things as the '*laws* observed by the lower animals; of *laws* regulating the growth or decay of vegetables; of *laws* determining the movements of inanimate bodies or masses.'[165] If it is improper to speak of the 'law' of gravity, then it would also be mistaken to write of the 'law' of supply and demand. Austin insisted that laws 'properly so-called' are commands and that the use of the term to refer to anything else is incorrect. He also felt that this mistake was widespread and had 'deluged' the fields of jurisprudence and morals with 'muddy speculation'.[166]

J. S. Mill's interpretation of Austin's jurisprudence is a final reason for doubting that political economy was his model. Mill's writings contain no trace of a suggestion that his father's ideas on this subject had the impact that Morison imputes to them. In fact, Mill advanced the very interpretation of Austin that Morison rejects. The essence of it is the notion that conceptual clarification was the basic objective of Austin's approach to law. The 'main problem' that he addressed was, Mill claimed, 'to give clearness, precision, and consistency to the juristical conceptions themselves. What Mr Austin has done towards this object, constitutes the great permanent worth of his speculations.'[167] Mill also sharply contrasted Austin's efforts in this direction with those of Sir Henry Maine. The purpose of his studies was to explain the causes of 'the various legal institutions which obtain, or have formerly obtained. . . . His book [*Ancient Law*] may be called a treatise on the action and reaction between the ideas prevalent among mankind, and their positive institutions.' Unlike Maine, the focus of Austin's jurisprudence was analysis of the 'organic structure' of legal systems.[168]

It is therefore most improbable that James Mill's approach to political economy influenced Austin's jurisprudence. The extent to which he tried to analyze law on the basis of the Aristotelian predicables is more difficult to judge. On the one hand, he attached even more importance to Aristotelian logic than to Roman law. Indeed, he viewed a familiarity with logic to be 'absolutely necessary' for the study of the moral sciences, a category that included law.[169] On the other hand, he questioned *both* the possibility and the value of defining legal terms *per genus et differentiam.*

> In truth, some of these terms will not admit of definition in the formal or regular manner. And as to the rest, to define them in that manner is utterly useless. For the terms which enter into the abridged and concise definition, need as much elucidation as the very expression which is defined.[170]

Morison's response to this passage is to argue that it should not be taken at face value. Rather, Austin was 'probably just retailing recollected Bentham. But then he proceeds to work on the opposite basis'.[171] If this interpretation is accurate, which is arguable, it is of limited value for understanding Austin's conception of law and sovereignty. It is one thing to try to define law in terms of the Aristotelian predicables. It is a very different thing to decide what the genus, species, differentia, propria, and accidentia of law are. This decision depends upon factors other than the categories themselves, which provide only a framework of analysis.

The question thus remains of the rationale of Austin's definition of law and sovereignty. Morison's interpretation implies – and with good reason – that Austin's empiricism was a factor. He clearly belongs to the long tradition of British thinkers who held that all knowledge is ultimately derived from experience. He was in this respect typical of the utilitarians, all of whom rejected the notion that 'truths external to the mind may be known by intuition or consciousness, independently of observation and experience'.[172] John Stuart Mill, for example, assailed this doctrine as 'the great intellectual support of false doctrines and bad institutions'.[173] Austin would take the same position and his empirical orientation probably influenced his conceptions of law and sovereignty. Even so, his actual approach to the problems of jurisprudence is not nearly as empirical as Morison suggests.

To begin with, Austin attributed a degree of certainty to his conceptions of law and sovereignty that is not possible for empirical generalizations. They are in principle capable of being confirmed or disconfirmed by study of the facts. Yet, Austin believed that the legally unlimited power of the sovereign holds true 'universally or without exception'.[174] The omnipotence of the sovereign is 'indisputable'. Its freedom from legal restraints is 'involved in the notion of sovereignty, as the properties of a circle are implied by the definition of the figure'.[175] In other words, no facts *could* disprove the existence of this power. The existence of sovereigns with legally limited power is *inconceivable* or *logically impossible*.

This position may well reflect the impact upon Austin of geometrical models of scientific inquiry. If ethics is to become a science, he claimed, its adepts must 'attend to the suggestions of Hobbes and of Locke, and . . . imitate the method so successfully pursued by geometers.'[176] Austin quotes several times Locke's statement that ethics is a science 'capable of demonstration'. Locke does not mean by 'demonstration', however, confirmation by the facts. Rather, he means logical deduction from 'self-evident propositions . . . as incontestable as those in mathematics'. He cites as an example the assertion that where there is no property, there is no injustice. This proposition is capable of demonstration 'as certain as any . . . in Euclid'. For it is necessarily implied by the definitions of property and injustice. Given those definitions, the truth of this proposition can be known as certainly 'as that a triangle has three angles equal to two right ones'.[177]

The similarity between this reasoning and Austin's defence of his conception of sovereignty is striking. Both he and Locke presumed that the truth of certain axioms of their systems can be known with as much certainty as the truth of the propositions of Euclidian geometry. This presumption reflects an approach that is also evident from Austin's attitude toward the facts of linguistic usage. Although he respected these facts and could use them for his own purposes, his elucidation of legal concepts was not dictated by them. Instead, he tended to distinguish between the common and the proper meanings or usages of terms. His comment upon expressions such as rights and duties *ex lege* or *ex lege immediate* is an example. He claimed that in many systems of positive law these phrases are not used, or consistently employed, with the meaning that is 'obviously the proper one'.[178] His classification of customary, constitutional, and international 'law' is a more famous example of the same tendency. He was well aware that they are often *called* law, but this fact did not *control* his analysis of them.[179] Otherwise, he would never have referred to them as law 'improperly so-called'.

Austin's insistence on the necessary generality of law reflects the same approach. He did not argue that law should be defined as general commands because this is how the word is ordinarily used. Rather, he maintained that general orders are the essence or nature of law '*properly* so-called'. Occasional or particular commands might sometimes be labelled 'laws'. Austin believed, however, that this fact is 'immaterial . . . with reference to the present purpose'. Despite what an occasional or particular command is called, 'its nature would be the same. It would not be a law or rule.'[180] In short, his conception of law is not an induction from the facts of linguistic usage. Instead, it appears to represent what he felt to be the 'true' definition of the term.

Finally, Austin generalized about the laws of societies of which he had little knowledge. They include not simply 'the scanty and crude systems of rude societies', but also some of 'the ampler and maturer systems of refined communities'.[181] While he admitted that he had studied with 'some accuracy' only the Roman law and the law of England,[182] he argued that 'it is only the systems of two or three nations which deserve attention'. Furthermore, he claimed that '[f]rom these . . . the rest may be presumed'.[183] In other words, he assumed that ample and mature legal systems *must* be similar. Only for this reason could he be so certain that 'a lawyer who has mastered the law which obtains in his own country, has mastered implicitly most of the substance of the law which obtains in any other community'.[184] He thus believed *independent of empirical inquiries* that the content of most laws of all systems *must* be the same. The basis of this conviction was not his careful study of the facts of actual legal systems. Rather, it was a certain conception of human nature, ethics, and politics.

Eira Ruben's quasi-Marxist interpretation of Austin is very different from that of either Stone or Morison. The purpose of her study is to unmask the ideological motivations of Austin's allegedly scientific jurisprudence. She portrays it as anything but a value-free or impartial approach to the study of law. Rather, its *raison d'être* was 'to defend the stability of a particular economic system and protect the interests of the middle class'.[185] His definition of sovereignty is, she claims, an obvious expression of these interests. This crucial element of his philosophy of law reflects an 'individualism in the economic order which is the basis on which middle-class interests are founded'.[186] Political motivations thus explain why Austin chose one definition of sovereignty rather than another. All-in-all, he 'collapses his notion of what the law is into his notion of what the law ought to be'.[187]

Although this interpretation of Austin is original and provocative, it rests almost entirely on unsubstantiated conjecture. To be sure,

Austin was an avid proponent of economic individualism. He also admired greatly the virtues of the middle-class. Still, Ruben adduces little evidence in support of her theory that Austin's philosophy of law was a rationalization of these opinions. In addition, the evidence that she does cite is unconvincing. If there is a case to be made for her interpretation of Austin, which is very unlikely, she does not make it.

Ruben's explanation of Austin's definition of sovereignty is a prime illustration of this weakness. She fails to answer the crucial question of *how* this definition protects economic individualism or middle-class interests. The question is crucial because the definition does not appear to have this effect and because Austin described it very differently. He classified sovereignty as one of the 'principles, notions, and distinctions' without which 'we cannot imagine coherently a system of law (or a system of law as evolved in a refined community)'.[188] Sovereignty is thus one of the conceptions that the legal system of *every* independent political society, regardless of its economic structure, 'implies'.[189] He also explained the legally unlimited powers of the sovereign as an indisputable and universal truth. While this position is quite clearly mistaken, Ruben presents no good reason for interpreting it as a cover for middle-class interests.

If Austin's conception of sovereignty had been a rationalization of economic individualism, the substance of it probably would have been quite different. In particular, he would have been likely to emphasize the limited rather than the unlimited powers of the sovereign. Such an emphasis would certainly have been a far more effective means to protect middle-class interests. For it would have hindered the enactment of the restrictions on freedom of contract which Austin strenuously opposed. Instead, he and the other utilitarians developed a theory of sovereignty that *upheld* the power of Parliament to enact *any* kind of legislation. To this extent, they forged a tool that was useful for *undermining* rather than *protecting* economic individualism. Although this was obviously not the purpose of their conception of sovereignty, it had this effect. Albert V. Dicey was therefore correct to point out that the development of this idea was one reason for the English collectivists' 'heavy debt . . . to the utilitarian reformers'.[190]

These criticisms imply that Ruben's interpretation of Austin's jurisprudence has little support in the facts. Her account of his conception of economic individualism is also subject to criticism. Although he was a staunch advocate of it, he did *not* view 'all' governmental interference in the economy as 'pernicious'.[191] He not only specifically criticized the maxim *laissez-faire* as 'plainly false and absurd',[192] but favoured a number of governmental programmes that restricted actual or possible economic activities. He thus maintained that, in some cases, 'the interference of the government, if not necessary, is expedient. It is often expedient, for example, that public roads, or other means of public transport, should be created by public resources; and . . . that government should provide their subjects with secular and religious instruction.'[193] In other words, Austin's position is not as extreme as Ruben represents it to be. To say this is not to imply that his economic individualism is satisfactory, which it does not appear to me to be. The point is, rather, that Ruben's description of it is not entirely accurate.

4

The literature about Austin thus contains various interpretations of his thought, all of which have certain limitations for understanding his conceptions of law and sovereignty. This consideration highlights the need for another explanation of these axioms of his jurisprudence. To say this is not to minimize the contributions of Stone and Morison, in particular, to an understanding of Austin. He no doubt felt that his notions of law and sovereignty are essential for a coherent understanding of actual legal systems. He also believed that these ideas denote phenomena which are empirically identifiable in past or present legal orders. This belief probably influenced his conceptions of law and sovereignty. The explanation to be advanced in this study does not rule out this possibility. The argument is only that a third factor is no less important and may even have had a greater impact upon him.

This consideration is his perception of the practical necessity for commands and sovereigns of legally unlimited powers. They are necessary, though not sufficient, conditions for the achievement of the utilitarian end of government. The effects of conceptions of law and sovereignty with a different content would impede this goal. Law 'properly so-called' must be defined in terms of commands or it will be an ineffective means to control behaviour. Coercion or the threat of sanctions is indispensable for this purpose. The same 'logic of consequences' could explain Austin's insistence on the legally unlimited power of the sovereign. In the absence of this power the general happiness could not be achieved. Although its existence does not guarantee this utilitarian end, the power is a necessary condition for its achievement.

The concept of sanction obviously played a crucial role in Austin's philosophy of law. While he recognized that the word had various meanings, he defined the term as 'any conditional evil annexed to a law to produce obedience and conformity to it'. Since he maintained that laws may be sanctioned by nullities, he acknowledged that this 'evil' need not consist of punishment in the strict sense of the term.[194] Even so, the conception of sanction developed by Austin definitely entailed suffering. In other words, it necessarily implied 'some pain which may be inflicted upon the wrong-doer whether he consent or not'. He insisted that in the 'last result, every obligation is sanctioned by suffering'.[195]

This analysis raises the question of the rationale of Austin's position that *every* obligation *is* sanctioned by suffering. Was this claim merely a tautology that spelled out the logical implications of his definitions of obligation and sanction? Or did it also reflect his belief that the threat of sanctions is indispensable for deterring illegal conduct? Since he *defined* legal obligation or duty as liability to a sanction,[196] his contention that *every* obligation *is* sanctioned by suffering is indeed a tautology. At the same time, his conviction of the practical necessity of sanctions strongly influenced his definition of obligation. At least he left no doubt of his opinion that 'men are held to their duties by the sanctions annexed to those duties. . . . Sanctions . . . counteract the motives or desires which prompt to a breach of duty, and they tend to excite the attention which the fulfillment of duty requires.'[197] While fear of punishment is not a completely effective deterrent, the likelihood of obedience varies directly with the magnitude and probability of incurring the threatened sanction. To be sure, an unwillingness to incur sanctions is not the only source of the disposition to obey the law. Nevertheless, 'the Sanction of Sanctions is always Punishment' and suffering is the 'ultimate sanction'.[198] Furthermore, the very *raison d'être* of law is the existence of evil or imperfection. In a very significant, but seldom cited passage, Austin writes that every law 'supposes an evil which it is designed to prevent or remedy. Law, like medicine, is a preventive or remedy of *evil*: and, if the world were free from evil, the notion and the name would be unknown.'[199] The very name and notion assume, in other words, that some or most people will not do what they ought to do without the threat of sanctions.

This justification of the necessity for sanctions was not, of course, in any way unique to Austin. For example, the basis of his argument is a view of human nature which Thomas Hobbes had specifically applied to law almost 200 years prior to Austin's lectures. Hobbes insisted that the fear of punishment is absolutely necessary to induce obedience to the law. 'Covenants, without the sword, are but words.' Indeed, he went so far as to say that 'excepting some generous natures', fear is 'the only thing, when there is appearance of profit or pleasure by breaking the laws, that makes men keep them.'[200] Some evidence indicates that this argument for the necessity of sanctions could have influenced Austin. At the least he praised highly Hobbes' 'masterly treatises on government'. No other writer except Bentham 'has uttered so many truths, at once new and important, concerning . . . the larger of the *necessary distinctions implied by positive law*'[201] (emphasis added).

Austin's attitude toward another of his predecessors provides additional evidence for this explanation of his conception of law. He not only admired Locke, but specifically praised his classification of law. Indeed Austin acknowledged the close similarity between this classification and his own.[202] He also repeatedly uses Locke's phrase of laws 'properly so-called', which occurs in a passage of great significance for this study. These words appear at the conclusion of his argument that *the power to punish is essential for the true nature of all law.*

Locke's exact words, which Austin fully quotes,[203] are these:

> For, since it would be utterly in vain to suppose a rule set to the free actions of man, without annexing to it some enforcement of good and evil to determine his will, we must, wherever we suppose a law, suppose also some reward or punishment annexed to that law. It would be in vain for one intelligent being to set a rule to the actions of another, if he had it not in his power to reward the compliance with, and punish deviation from his rule, by some good and evil, that is not the natural product and consequence of the action itself. For that, being a natural convenience or inconvenience, would operate of itself, without a law. This, if I mistake not, is the true nature of all law, properly so called.[204]

The logic of Locke's reasoning in this notable paragraph is of crucial importance. He not only asserts that the power to reward or punish is essential for inducing compliance with rules. He also argues that *because* this power is essential, it is involved in the true nature of *all* law 'properly so-called'. In other words, Locke draws the precise inference which is now being attributed to Austin.

Utilitarian considerations also had an impact upon Austin's theory of sovereignty. This notion implies that the obedience of the bulk of the population is a necessary condition for the existence of sovereign governments. Austin's explanation of this obedience weighted heavily popular perceptions of the *utility* of such governments. Although the habitual fear of sanctions is a reason for obedience to law, it is not the only one. The disposition to obey is 'partly generated . . . by a perception of the *utility* of justice; and by that love of general utility which is felt by all or most men more or less strongly.'[205] Austin indeed maintained that if the people were perfectly enlightened, their obedience would be based entirely upon utilitarian calculations.[206] Their reasoning would be that the effects of obedience on the general happiness were preferable to the effects of resistance. If the government were good, it would be an effective means to enlarge human happiness. If the government were bad, resistance to it would be a remedy worse than the disease.

Austin believed that the bulk of the people in every actual society were inadequately instructed. He therefore acknowledged that their habitual obedience is not explainable simply on utilitarian grounds. A majority of the population usually obeys the law for different reasons, which include the force of custom, or prejudice. Austin meant by the latter obedience which has 'no foundation whatever in the principle of general utility'.[207] Still, people also habitually obey for a reason which is 'bottomed' in this principle.[208] This factor is a perception of the expediency of political government, or a preference for any government rather than anarchy. In fact, this last consideration is the 'only cause of the habitual obedience in question, which is common to all societies, or nearly all societies'.[209] It was therefore the only factor that could be examined in detail in a treatise on general jurisprudence. A desire to avoid the bad effects of anarchy is also the only general cause of the permanence of political government.

Austin was less explicit about whether perceptions of utility explain the legally unlimited power of sovereigns. If this characteristic of sovereign power were evident to all persons, he would not have felt compelled to explain it at such length. Despite this, it is likely that Austin believed that the legally illimitable power of sovereigns was expedient. He probably assumed that the effects of the absence of this power would be practically disastrous, or at least pernicious. Although a sovereign of legally unlimited powers is not a *sufficient* condition for achievement of the utilitarian end of government, it is a *necessary* condition.

Like Hobbes, Austin believed that 'security, and the feeling of security . . . ought to be the principal end of . . . government and law.'[210]

He certainly could have also accepted Hobbes' argument that this security can only be achieved by a sovereign of legally unlimited powers. According to the seventeenth-century philosopher, such a 'great leviathan' is necessary to prevent anarchy. The effect of the absence of a common power to keep men in awe is the war of all against all. Without a 'mortal God' the life of man is 'solitary, poor, nasty, brutish, and short'. Moreover, the common power which is necessary to keep men in awe must have legally unlimited power. It must be 'as great, as possibly men can be imagined to make it'. While the state of man under such a sovereign is not free of incommodities, 'the consequences of the want of it, which is perpetual war of every man against his neighbour, are much worse'.[211]

Some evidence indicates that Austin accepted this argument. He praised the 'many truths' which Hobbes set forth about 'the necessary structure of supreme political government'.[212] Moreover, Austin quoted at some length three passages from his great predecessor for support of the view that the sovereign is incapable of legal limitation. One of the quotations develops the argument for a 'mortal God' based upon the *consequences* of its absence. Furthermore, Austin criticized Hobbes for his failure to derive the existence of government from a perception by the bulk of the governed of its 'great and obvious expediency'. Instead, he ascribes the origin of sovereignty and of independent political society to a 'fictitious agreement or covenant'.[213] Austin then makes this extremely important comment about Hobbes:

> He supposes, indeed, that the subjects are induced to make that agreement, by their perception of the expediency of government, and by their desire to escape from anarchy. But, placing his system immediately on that interposed figment, instead of resting it directly on the ultimate basis of utility, he often arrives at his conclusions in a sophistical and quibbling manner, though his *conclusions are commonly such as the principle of utility will warrant* (emphasis added).[214]

Aside from Locke and Hobbes, the other seminal British thinker whom Austin intensely admired was Bentham. Not surprisingly, he was highly critical of the attempt to place limits on the power of the sovereign. His conception of sovereignty is not, to be sure, identical with Austin's. Unlike the latter, Bentham admitted that the authority of the supreme governor *may* be limited by 'express convention'. To deny that possibility would be to say 'rather too much'.[215] In other words, Bentham did not share Austin's or Blackstone's view that the *existence* of legal limitations on the powers of the sovereign is *impossible*. While Bentham 'accepted that the sovereignty of the King in Parliament in Great Britain was subject to no legal limitations . . . from his earliest writings onwards [he] felt misgivings about the general doctrine [of sovereignty].'[216] These doubts did not extend, however, to the question of whether the powers of the sovereign *ought* to be limited by positive law. Bentham's response to this issue was unambiguous and uniform throughout his long life. His view was that all attempts to tie down the power of the sovereign are 'absurd and mischievous'.[217]

Limitations on the power of the sovereign are absurd for conceptual and linguistic reasons.[218] The effects of these restraints are mischievous because they contradict the principle of the greatest happiness. One bad effect would be to prevent beneficial changes in at least certain kinds of laws. The attempt to limit legislative power reflects only 'the old conceit of being wiser than all posterity . . . the old recipe for enabling the dead to chain down the living'.[219] Another pernicious result would be to empower the judges to enforce the limitations against the legislature. Bentham admitted that the consequences of judicial review might be desirable in particular cases, but on balance its effects would be bad. This practice involves the transfer of power 'from an assembly which the people have had *some* share, at least, in chusing, to a set of men in the choice of whom they have not the least imaginable share.'[220]

For these and other reasons Bentham concluded that no good purpose is served by trying to tie 'the hands of future legislators'.[221] A number of considerations provide the basis for believing that Austin may well have accepted this argument. He profoundly admired his great predecessor. The most fundamental reason for this 'profound veneration' was Bentham's contributions 'as a Jurist, or . . . the most original and inventive of all writers on Law.'[222] According to Sarah Austin,

> When we married, my husband had just been introduced to . . . [Bentham] and was an enthusiastic admirer, almost a worshipper, of him, *in consequence of those great works which remain*, and will remain, monuments of his original genius and acute mind – the 'Fragment on Government', the 'Defence of Usury', and the 'Principles of Morals and Legislation', more especially. *Concerning these, his opinion never altered*[223] (emphasis added).

Although Austin could have admired the first and third of these works without accepting Bentham's criticisms of limitations on sovereignty, this possiblity is highly unlikely.[224] The criticisms are part of a doctrine of sovereignty which is a central theme of *A Fragment on Government*. While Bentham says much less about this concept in *An Introduction to the Principles of Morals and Legislation*, he does not ignore it. In fact, he specifically criticizes the bad practical effects of limitations on the power of supreme representative assemblies.[225] If Austin very rarely employs such avowedly utilitarian arguments, one of his most obscure writings indicates his acceptance of one of them.

The reports that Austin and George C. Lewis wrote in their capacity as Royal Commissioners to Malta will be described in detail subsequently in this study. One of their papers consisted of an extended critique of the censorship that prevailed on the island. Although the Commissioners recommended its abolition, they defended its legality. Their argument was apparently a response to a not uncommon criticism of colonial censorship. Some critics argued that it was illegal because contrary to 'natural equity' or 'the fundamental principles of the British constitution'. The dicta of certain judges suggest, the Commissioners admitted, that no institution which is contrary to these principles may be introduced into or continued in a British colony. Austin and Lewis insisted that these dicta were not controlling. The ground on which they justified their insistence reflects the same fear of judicial supremacy evident in Bentham:

> But if these dicta were valid, any act of the Sovereign, however imperative and precise, would be placed at the mercy of subordinate judges. The phrase 'natural equity', or 'fundamental principles of the British Constitution', has no meaning generally agreed upon; and they therefore might easily accommodate the positive laws of the Sovereign to their real or pretended conceptions of its genuine import.[226]

5

This chapter has attempted to illuminate the relationship between John Austin's utilitarianism and his philosophy of law. While the assumption that they are unrelated is widespread in the literature about him, it is impossible to reconcile with a large body of evidence. This data establishes that his ethical and political theories probably influenced some elements of his legal philosophy. They include such basic components of it as his conceptions of law and sovereignty, the rationale for which is by no means apparent. The impact of utilitarian arguments constitute, it has been contended, one reason for his unshakable commitment to these ideas. At the least this possibility merits more consideration than it has hitherto received.

The validity of this interpretation cannot be proven with absolute certainty. Nor is it a complete explanation of Austin's conceptions of law and sovereignty. Factors other than utilitarian calculations could also have influenced him, and probably did. An explanation in terms of these calculations also raises its own problems. The most notable example is whether this account is consistent with Austin's stated justification of his conception of sovereignty. His argument was that the legally unlimited powers of this person or persons were a necessary truth, the denial of which is self-contradictory. This argument implies that demonstration of the inexpediency of limiting the sovereign's power is irrelevant and unnecessary, if not incoherent.

This implication may have influenced Austin's reluctance to justify his conception of sovereignty on utilitarian grounds. Nevertheless, he could have supported it on this basis without contradicting himself. This is evident from a defence of his position that he could have adduced in addition to the argument that he in fact developed. It would be that limitations on the sovereign's power would be undesirable *if* they were possible. Although this contention differs from his stated argument, the two are perfectly consistent with each other.

This book's partial explanation of Austin's conceptions of law and sovereignty also faces a second problem. It is his very real unwillingness explicitly to justify these conceptions on utilitarian grounds. This unwillingness does not necessarily mean, however, that he was not influenced by such considerations. He may have had his own reasons for not formally developing a utilitarian rationale for these ideas. One such consideration could have been his reluctance to become involved in what is obviously a highly controversial matter. Austin clearly did not want the study of jurisprudence to be burdened with debate about the worth of positive laws. Fear of its bad effects is one reason for the sharp division of labour which he urged between the sciences of jurisprudence and legislation. To be sure, he admitted that the teacher of jurisprudence in 'certain cases which do not try the passions . . . may, with advantage, offer opinions upon merits and demerits'.[227] This exception indicates, however, the reason for the rule. Opinions of the merits or demerits of positive law generally 'try the passions'. The very same conviction could explain Austin's unwillingness to justify his conceptions of law and sovereignty by utilitarian arguments.

At any rate, a partial explanation of these ideas on the basis of the impact of such factors is credible. Austin was deeply convinced of both the truth and importance of utilitarianism. It is difficult to understand how this conviction could fail to influence some basic concepts of his legal philosophy. Furthermore, he explicitly justified his separation of law and morals by arguments some of which are utilitarian. The impact of a similar line of reasoning on his conceptions of law and sovereignty would explain why he devoted so much space to an analysis of ethics. His discussion of the principle of utility is not, in any case, inconsistent with or unrelated to the rest of his book. Austin insisted that the sciences of jurisprudence and legislation are connected by 'numerous' and 'indissoluble' ties. Finally, his predecessors for whom he expressed the greatest admiration adduced partly utilitarian reasons for their concepts of law and/or sovereignty.

This explanation is not only important because it helps to explain the basis of Austin's conceptions of law and sovereignty. In addition to this, it facilitates understanding of the distinctiveness of his influential version of legal positivism. It must not be uncritically identified with the interpretations of subsequent jurists. They were not necessarily ardent exponents of utilitarianism, a description which exactly fits John Austin.

4 *Judicial legislation and legal positivism*

The custom of using simple labels for complex traditions of legal philosophy is no doubt too well-established to change.[1] The tenacity of the practice should not, however, obscure the imprecision which frequently results. Nothing illustrates the point better than 'legal positivism'. H. L. A. Hart has distinguished five meanings of the term 'bandied about in contemporary jurisprudence'. They include the idea that the legal order is a 'closed logical system'.[2] The implications for judicial reasoning are clear and familiar. Judges supposedly reach decisions by an impersonal process of logical deduction from established rules or principles. Social aims, moral standards, or political considerations have little if any impact. The business of courts is only to apply rather than to make the law. In one of its meanings, that is to say, 'positivism' denotes a well-known kind of legal formalism or mechanical jurisprudence. Those who use the word in this sense frequently cite the ideas of John Austin, or jurists whom he inspired, as the *pièce de résistance*.[3] After all, no one would deny that he was a legal positivist of the very first rank.

In the last decade or two this interpretation of Austin has been sharply challenged, most notably by W. L. Morison.[4] His article on the subject has been praised by H. L. A. Hart as correcting the erroneous impressions of earlier writers.[5] Hart has also added an oar or two of his own. In his words: 'Only an entire misconception of what analytical jurisprudence is and why he [Austin] thought it important has led to the view that he, or any other analyst, believed that the law was a closed logical system in which judges deduced their decisions from premises.' Austin not only recognized the existence of judicial legislation, but criticized the pretences by which it is obscured. He also 'berated . . . judges for legislating feebly and timidly'. If the responsibility for the conception of the judge as an automaton lies with any theorist, Hart claims, it is thinkers such as Blackstone and Montesquieu rather than Austin.[6]

Although these interpretations of Austin are on the right track, his ideas about judicial legislation merit a more comprehensive explanation than they have hitherto received. The purpose of this chapter is to fill this gap in the literature by explaining Austin's analysis of the nature, scope, value, and disadvantages of what he called 'judiciary law'. Fulfillment of this objective is desirable for a number of reasons. One such consideration is the need to understand precisely how mistaken any interpretation of Austinian positivism is, which attributes to it a blindness to the fact or utility of judge-made law. Yet, satisfaction of this need will also demonstrate that this mistake is understandable. For Austin was acutely conscious of what he felt to be the grave defects of judicial legislation. Indeed, his perception of these evils in large part explains his enthusiasm for codification. In sum, he had a foot in the camp of both the critics and admirers of the law that judges make. Although this straddling is not without its strengths, it accentuates the need carefully to sort out his actual thoughts on the matter.

Moreover, his analysis of judicial legislation is of substantial historical importance. Unlike his great predecessor Jeremy Bentham, Austin was by no means an unalterable opponent of judge-made law. In fact, his attitude was sufficiently *au courant* to adumbrate certain of the ideas developed in this century by the American legal realists. His analysis of general terms and the judicial process also foreshadowed, in a number of respects, H. L. A. Hart's discussion of the problem.[7] Austin was, in short, far ahead of his time. No other Anglo-American jurist with whose writings I am familiar had produced *by 1832* as penetrating an analysis of the law that judges make.

Finally, Austin's account of judicial law-making is valuable in its own right. Nor is its value limited to conceptual clarification. Although elucidation of legal concepts was the centre of his lectures, it did not mark the circumference. Significant portions of his work go beyond the confines of analytical jurisprudence strictly interpreted. Nothing illustrates the point better than his analysis of judicial legislation. On a normative and empirical as well as conceptual level, much of it is appealing even today. His explanation of the role which established legal rules do and should play in judicial decision-making is an illustration. It constitutes a plausible middle-of-the-road position between mechanical jurisprudence and an extreme form of rule-scepticism.

1

Austin's conception of positive law may be one reason for the low saliency of his analysis of judicial legislation. For this conception appears to imply that judges could not *make* law, which consists of the commands of the sovereign. The function of judges would seem to be only to enforce the will of this supreme and legally illimitable authority. Since Austin firmly believed in the existence of judicial legislation, this apparent implication of his notion of positive law obviously created a problem for him.

From a purely logical point of view Austin could have resolved this difficulty in at least four ways. One is by denying the existence of judicial legislation, a solution which he did not adopt. A second alternative is to argue that judges are the *de facto* sovereign. For it could be argued that they have the final say on *whether, how,* and *which* rules are enforced. Such an argument is the basis of certain famous American conceptions of law, most notably that of Oliver Wendell Holmes, Jr., and John Chipman Gray.[8] Although this line of thought can be viewed as an outgrowth of Austin's emphasis on the power to enforce, he never considered this possibility. For it involves substantial stretching of his notion of sovereignty and his view of the subordinate place of judges in the legal hierarchy. A third alternative is explicitly to alter the original definition of positive law so as to make it compatible with judge-made law. This course of action requires a change in a basic axiom of Austin's legal philosophy and was not adopted. The final possibility is to interpret his definition of positive law in such a way as to render it compatible with judicial legislation. This is the argument which he chose to present and which is not without its own problems. Yet to some extent they arise from a commendable desire not to sweep judge-made law under a definitional rug.

Austin's theory of sovereignty implies the existence of a pyramid of authority within an independent political society. This structure consists of the sovereign, various classes of political inferiors, and subjects. 'All political powers, actual and possible,' he claimed, 'reside actively or passively in the central authority; and all such powers residing in others are merely emanations from it.'[9] Despite this, Austin fully recognized that political subordinates in fact exercise 'some' of the powers of the sovereign. This development is 'rendered absolutely necessary, in every actual society, by innumerable causes'.[10] The powers of these ministers of the sovereign have included the power to *make* law, a power that they have exercised to a 'vast extent' in 'all countries'.[11] The laws made by colonial governments are one example of this phenomenon, while the judicial legislation of English courts of justice is a second.[12]

Although judges make law, they have no independent authority to legislate. Rather, Austin insisted that whatever power they have is delegated to them by the sovereign. This delegation of power may be either express or tacit. If the authorization is express, its existence is clear. If the delegation is tacit, its existence is to be inferred from the behaviour of the sovereign. The conduct which justifies the inference is the supreme commander's toleration of or acquiescence in judicial decisions. Despite the ability of the sovereign to reverse the rules made by a judge, the higher authority may decide not to exercise this power. In that case, 'its sovereign will "that his [the judge's] rules shall obtain as law" is clearly evinced by its conduct, though not by its express declaration.'[13]

Most commentators on Austin have criticized this attempt to squeeze judicial legislation into the pigeon-hole of commands of the sovereign. The reaction of Sir Henry Maine and John Chipman Gray is typical. To say that judge-made law is the tacit command of the sovereign is, they maintain, a 'mere artifice of speech', a 'straining of language',[14] a 'forced expression'.[15] Their dissatisfaction seems to me to be well-founded. The rules that judges make may be contrary to the will of the sovereign or its elected representatives. These rules may also be for problems about which the sovereign has no discernible will. Numerous cases of statutory interpretation richly illustrate the point.[16] Austin's argument also presupposes a conception of sovereignty that is the object of a century or more of criticism.[17]

If these objections are cogent, this fact is not a good reason for the relative neglect of Austin's analysis of judicial legislation. It is one thing to argue that his conception of the relationship between the sovereign and judges is unsatisfactory. It is another thing to infer *from this* that his analysis of judge-made law is unacceptable. The one does not follow from the other. While some of Austin's ideas about judicial legislation may be mistaken, they merit consideration and evaluation on their own.

2

Elucidation of Austin's conception of how judges make law requires an explanation of how they apply it. The resolution of disputes by the *application* of law is, in his eyes, the hallmark of *judicial* decision-making. Although he never formally defined 'judge', he implicitly conceived of such an official as a person who decides cases by applying the law. He recognized, to be sure, that judges can reach decisions without reference to old or new rules. Nonetheless, he apparently regarded such action as exceptional and in any case wholly indefensible. The dominant method by which courts reach decisions is through the application of law. The essence of this process is the classification of the facts, their subsumption under rules. Most cases do, and all cases should, involve the application of law in this sense.

The law which judges apply may be one of two types. One kind consists of *established* rules, the sources of which are statutes or precedents. The other type consists of *newly-created* rules. Judges legislate to the extent that the law which they apply consists of these rules. The vast majority of cases thus fall into two basic categories. In one kind judges only apply rather than create rules, while in others they make the rules which they then apply. Although the first sort of case does not require judicial *legislation*, Austin recognized that it may involve serious difficulties. In fact, his analysis of the problems which judges confront in such cases is highly perceptive. The factors which he isolated could be cited as evidence of large-scale creativity within the judicial process. They support, in short, the case for what Justice Holmes called the judge's 'sovereign prerogative of choice'.[18]

Three of these problems merit special attention. One is statutory interpretation, which Austin labelled either genuine or spurious. Since the latter is a species of judicial legislation, it will be explained subsequently. The object of the former is the *discovery* of the legislative *intent*, the primary index to which is the literal, grammatical, customary, or obvious meaning of words. In most cases the goal of this semantic quest is not difficult to achieve. As a rule the customary meaning of words is 'obvious or easily assignable'.[19] Yet, in some cases the problem is more formidable.

Austin in effect subdivided these difficult cases of statutory construction into two categories. Sometimes the customary meaning of the statutory language is indiscoverable or indicative of an indeterminate intent. Under these circumstances the judge must seek additional *indicia* of the legislative intent. They include the *ratio legis*, the history of the statute, or other relevant statutes. At other times the literal meaning of the words is discoverable, but conflicts with other indicators of the legislative intent. In these cases the judge should generally abide by the former. Otherwise, the statutory law would become as fallible a guide for conduct as judicial legislation. On rare occasions, however, the result of rigid adherence to the customary meaning of statutory language is manifestly contrary to the intent of the legislator. In this situation judges should reach the decision that is most consistent with the underlying purpose of the law. In short, the literal meanings of words are not an infallible guideline for statutory interpretation.[20]

A second difficulty which confronts judges who apply established rules is the determination of the *ratio decidendi* of a case. This problem has evoked considerable attention as well as controversy in recent years, and for understandable reasons. On the one hand, the need to determine the *ratio* seems crucial in a system of case-law. Most jurists would agree with Austin that the law which cases establish is not the particular decision itself, but the *ratio decidendi*. Only the latter can function as a general rule applicable to other cases. On the other hand, the ambiguity of this term is notorious. In the words of Arthur L. Goodhart, with 'the possible exception of . . . "malice", it is the most misleading expression in English law'.[21]

Two major problems are the definition and the determination of the *ratio*. Austin defined the term as the 'general reasons or principles of a judicial decision'.[22] This definition is, however, subject to two quite different interpretations. It could mean the psychologically decisive reasons for or causes of the decision. Some of the evidence tends to support this interpretation of Austin's thought.[23] The *ratio* may also be defined as the rule implied or imported by the decision. On balance Austin seems to have adopted this second interpretation of the term. The *ratio* is necessarily implied, he argued, by the judge's decision in a particular case. The crucial factor is not what the judge *says*, but what his decision *implies*. The latter must be decisive because the stated reasons for decisions may be too narrow or too broad. The arguments of the judge may be couched in terms which apply only to the instant case. These reasons cannot 'serve as a guide of conduct, or . . . be applied to the solution of subsequent cases'. At the other extreme, the rationale of the decision may go far beyond the precise issues raised by the case. Such *dicta*, or *obiter dictum*, are commonly 'extra-judicial, and . . . have no authority'. In addition to all of this, judicial opinions are often hastily written and inaccurately expressed. For these various reasons the *ratio* is the ground for decision regardless of whether it is explicitly stated as such.[24]

The problem then is how to determine *which* rule a decision implies. Austin described the procedure to be followed in this fashion: 'Looking at the *general reasons* alleged by the Court for its decisions, and *abstracting those reasons from the modifications which were suggested by the peculiarities of the cases*, we arrive at a *ground* or *principle* of decision, which will apply universally to cases of a class, and which, like a statute law, may serve as a rule of conduct.'[25] This formula implies that a rule which is the true *ratio decidendi* of a case must meet two requirements. At the least it must be broad enough to govern similar fact-situations in other cases. Otherwise the case could not serve as a precedent, since no two cases are precisely alike. Yet, the *ratio* must not be so broad that it is applicable to several *classes* of cases. If it were, then the judge would be legislating for some issues not before him and which he had no authority to resolve.

Austin's formula for determining the *ratio decidendi* thus assumes that every case establishes a *single* rule. While it may not be easy to discover, he believed that it was discoverable. The accuracy of this assumption is open to very serious question. In fact, the particular holding in a specific case can often be logically subsumed under different rules. Determination of which of these rules is 'the' *ratio* of the case requires judgments that are anything but mechanical. If some interpretations of a precedent are outrageous, the merit of others is highly debatable. No canons of logic provide an unambiguous test of the correctness of these interpretations, which are frequently the subject of spirited disagreement among judges and lawyers. They must choose between different possibilities, each of which may be more or less defensible. In the words of Herman Oliphant, a prominent legal realist, a student

> is told to seek the 'doctrine' or 'principle' of a case, but which of its welter of stairs shall he ascend and how high up shall he go? Is there some one step on some one stair which is *the* decision of the case within the meaning of the mandate *stare decisis*? . . . . Each precedent considered by a judge and student rests at the center of a vast and empty stadium. The angle and distance from which that case is to be viewed involves the choice of a seat. Which shall be chosen? Neither judge nor student can escape the fact that he can and must choose.[26]

To say this is in no way to deny that some choices are better than others. The only point is that the rules of logic do not provide the standards, or the only criteria, for such a judgment. In Felix Cohen's apt phraseology, 'Logic provides the springboard, but it does not guarantee the success of any particular dive'.[27] Austin was not totally unaware, however, of this possibility. In fact, it was the basis of another difficulty that he felt judges may face in the application of established law. They must sometimes choose between conflicting rules, each of which could be the basis of their decision. The facts of the instant case could be subsumed under any of these rules, from which different decisions are deducible. Austin believed that several factors are responsible for this type of hard case, including the indefiniteness of the applicable rule or rules. The essence of the class of cases which they were intended to govern is not marked with 'perfect exactness'. Each rule covers fact-situations analogous in some, but not all, respects to the instant case. The result is the competition of opposite analogies, which may indeed be severe. The larger the number of analogies, the greater is the judge's difficulty in choosing the rule that fits the facts.[28] A second source of the problem may be the inconsistency of several definite rules. The same fact situation has been classified differently on the basis of competing rules. The difficulty which this conflict creates is less common, however, than the problem for which indefiniteness is the cause.

The existence of these various dilemmas seems to vest considerable discretion or range of choice in judges. For this precise reason it could be argued that these hard cases necessitate judicial legislation. Cases which require a choice between competing rules or interpretations, each of which could be a reasonable basis of the decision, in effect create law. Although Austin teetered on the brink of this position, he never took the final plunge. He came close to it, however, because of his keen awareness of the vagueness or indefiniteness of general terms. He gave these examples: 'What can be more indefinite . . . than the expressions, *reasonable* time, *reasonable* notice, *reasonable* diligence? Than the line of demarcation which distinguishes libel and fair criticism; than that which constitutes a violation of copyright; than that degree of mental aberration which constitutes idiocy or lunacy?'[29]

Austin's analysis of this indefiniteness represents one of his most valuable contributions to jurisprudence. He stressed that the vagueness of terms creates difficulties not only in international law, but law 'strictly so-called'. While a rule and the facts to which it is to be applied may be known, 'the difficulty is in bringing the species under the rule; in determining not what the law is, or what the fact is, but whether the given law is applicable to the given fact.'[30] Moreover, cases involving the application of rules containing vague or imprecise words may be 'hotbeds of competing analogies. The indefiniteness is incorrigible. A discretion is left to the judge. Questions arising on them. . . . are hardly questions of interpretation or induction, for though the rule were explored and known as far as possible, doubt would remain.'[31]

These ideas do *not* imply that the application of *every* rule to a particular set of facts is uncertain. Austin would reject any such notion on the ground that how general terms apply to actual cases may be obvious. His explication of the 'negative mark' of sovereignty illustrates the rationale of his position. A necessary condition of being sovereign is receiving *habitual* obedience from the *bulk* of the population. *How long* or *how often* the people must obey, however, for their obedience to be 'habitual' is unclear. The exact proportion of the population that constitutes the 'bulk' of the people is also uncertain. The reason for this uncertainty is the indefiniteness of 'habitual' and 'bulk'.[32] Nevertheless, their application to specific cases may be clear. Often, for example, 'so large a proportion of the members [of an independent political society] obey the same superior, and the obedience of that proportion is so frequent and continued, that, without a moment's difficulty and without a moment's hesitation . . . we should say the *generality* of its members were in a *habit* of obedience . . . to a certain and *common* superior.' This was indeed the usual condition of England and of 'every independent society somewhat advanced in civilization'.[33]

Austin's development of these ideas means that he foreshadowed H. L. A. Hart's analysis of language and the judicial process. He distinguished between a general term's 'hard core of . . . settled meaning' and penumbra of vagueness.[34] General expressions must have standard instances to which they apply or they would be useless as a means of communication. If a particular fact-situation is readily classifiable on the basis of a rule's core of fixed meaning, it constitutes a 'plain case'. In these circumstances 'general terms seem to need no interpretation and . . . the recognition of instances seems unproblematic or "automatic" . . . there is general agreement in judgments as to the applicability of the classifying terms.' A hypothetical rule prohibiting motor vehicles in the park illustrates the argument. If anything is a motor vehicle, it is an automobile. The application of the rule to the case of a car is, thus, simple and obvious. This situation is only one example of the countless 'plain cases constantly recurring in similar contexts to which general expressions are clearly applicable'.[35]

While general terms have a core of settled meaning, they also have a fringe of 'open texture'. Accordingly, there is 'a limit, inherent in the nature of language, to the guidance which general language can provide'. Although application of the rule prohibiting motor vehicles in the park is obvious in some cases, it is very uncertain in others. Does it prohibit, for example, toy cars electrically propelled? In these 'hard cases' reasons exist 'both for and against our use of a general term, and no firm convention or general agreement dictates its use, or . . . its rejection by the person concerned to classify.' A judge who decides these kinds of cases has discretion and must choose between 'open alternatives'.[36]

While Austin adumbrated these dimensions of Hart's analysis, he was unwilling to say that judges necessarily make law even in hard cases. The reason for his unwillingness was his particular definition of judicial legislation, which he confined to the introduction of *new* rules. Since difficult cases may result in the application of *established* rules, they do not necessarily require judicial *legislation*. For in 'every judicial decision by which law is made, the *ratio decidendi* is a *new* ground or principle . . . *not previously law*.'[37]

This quotation nicely captures one of the ingredients in Austin's conception of *judicial* legislation. To say that judges make law means in part that they introduce *new* rules. Yet, he did not leave the matter at this. He also emphasized a number of important differences between direct and indirect, or judicial, law-making. An understanding of these distinctions is crucial for grasping his evaluation of the latter. For his appraisal of judicial legislation was strongly conditioned by his conception of its unique attributes.

A major difference between the two kinds of legislation is the varying goals of their respective authors. If a judge legislates, it is only for the purpose of deciding a particular case. 'He legislates *as properly judging*, and not *as properly legislating*.' Judicial law-making is for this reason indirect or oblique. Whatever rules a judge introduces are secondary to his primary function, which is to decide a case. The major purpose of the direct legislator is, however, to *make* rules. Statutory law is not designed to resolve a specific case, but is 'intended solely to serve as a rule of conduct'.[38]

A second difference between statutory and judge-made law is its form. The latter is embedded in concrete cases, from which it must be extracted. Judicial legislation exists nowhere in general or abstract form, while statutory law 'wears the form or shape of a . . . rule'. This fact is responsible for a third difference between the two kinds of law, which is the significance of the language of the legislator. The judge's actual words 'are rather faint traces from which the principle [of the case] may be conjectured, than a guide to be followed inflexibly in case their obvious meaning be perfectly certain.' While the language of a judge may not be even a clue to the *ratio decidendi* of the case, the words of a statute are crucial. The law that it establishes 'must be collected from the *terms* wherein the statute is expressed'.[39]

In any event, Austin fully understood that the law which judges apply is sometimes created rather than discovered. Indeed, he drove the point home in language which would gladden the heart of the most convinced rule-sceptic among the legal realists.[40] He censured 'the childish fiction employed by our judges, that judiciary or common law is not made by them, but is a miraculous something made by nobody, existing . . . from eternity, and merely *declared* from time to time by the judges.' Austin also claimed that judges make a large amount of law, the basis of which is 'their own conceptions of public policy or expediency'. Still further, he recognized that a modicum of judicial legislation is inevitable. No legislator can foresee every possible future case. A system of law which attempted to do so would be 'endless'.[41]

Austin not only believed in the existence of a substantial amount of judicial legislation. Aside from this, he argued that judges frequently attempt to conceal their law-making role. His exposé of what actually happens in this respect would once more be applauded by the legal realists. He insisted that judges frequently *introduce* rules under the guise of interpreting statutes or precedents. The new rule, 'thus disguised under the garb of an old one, is applied as law to new cases'. He explained this covert mode of judicial legislation on several grounds, one of which is the respect of the judges for the established law which they are emasculating. This attitude partially explains the use of fictions, which preserve the appearance of continuity with the past. A second factor is the desire to appease the admirers of the annulled rules, for which purpose fictions are also useful. They are analogous in this respect to 'those conventional, and not incommodious lies, through which much of the intercourse of polished society is habitually carried on'.[42] A third factor is 'constitutional jealousy', which 'would have forbidden the judges to assume and exercise *eo nomine* the power of legislation, but . . . allows them, on condition of proceeding bit by bit, to nibble away.'[43]

Whatever the reasons for it, judges use various pretexts in order to conceal their law-making. They sometimes argue, for example, that they are simply applying customary rules. 'For since the judicial legislator is properly acting judicially, and therefore abstains naturally from the shew [sic] of legislation, he apparently *applies* a *pre-existing rule*, instead of making and applying a new rule.'[44] Judges may also try to conceal their law-making by defending their decisions on grounds of equity, a term that came to signify fairness. This argument was 'consequently used by every innovating judge, who sought to cover his innovations by a specious and imposing name.'[45] Finally, judges frequently legislate under the guise of construing statutes. The process of 'spurious' interpretations *ex ratione legis* particularly interested Austin. The real basis of it, he argued, is *not* the accepted meaning of the words of a statute. Rather, it is the judge's conception of the language that the legislator ought to have used. This consideration underlies judicial restriction, or extension, of the unambiguous meaning of statutory language. The judge substitutes for this meaning his interpretation of the expressions which the legislator would, or should, have used in order to achieve his purposes. A large amount of judge-made law develops, Austin maintained, through this process.[46]

One example which Austin gave is the Statute of Frauds, enacted in 1677. According to Sir William Holdsworth, it is 'the most important of the few statutes of the seventeenth century which are concerned solely with the technical doctrines of English private law'. The stated purpose of the Statute, he writes, was to prevent many fraudulent practices which are commonly endeavoured to be upheld by perjury and subornation of perjury. For Holdsworth, 'most of its clauses are concerned with carrying out this object, by making written or other adequate evidence necessary for certain transactions'.[47] The Statute has been the subject, in any event, of an immense amount of litigation. Austin believed that the cases interpreting its provisions have generated judge-made law introduced on the occasion of 'pretended applications of the statute'. Such interpretation does not, however, deserve the name. In reality, it is 'a process of legislative amendment, or . . . correction'.[48]

3

This evidence supports the judgment of W.L. Morison that 'after all this, he [Austin] could hardly have anticipated that he himself would one day be regarded as the leading theoretical apologist for [the] . . . childish fiction [that judges do not make law].'[49] To appreciate his awareness of the existence of judicial legislation is, however, only part of the problem. Determination of how he evaluated it is another and much more complicated matter. On some occasions he warmly praised the law which judges make. For better or worse, such praise constitutes another similarity between Austinian and realistic jurisprudence. At other times he took a position which could not be more different from that of the legal realists. The internal consistency of these stances is an open question. The development of a satisfactory response to it requires further explanation of his evaluation of judge-made law.

A substantial number of considerations attest to Austin's approbation of judicial legislation. To begin with, he explictly distinguished his position from that of Jeremy Bentham. The latter could not have been more dissatisfied with the law that judges make. He condemned it with a legion of epithets of which the following are but samples. Judge-made law is a 'fictitious', 'bastard', and 'dog' law[50] which is 'disgraceful to men',[51] a 'shapeless heap of odds and ends',[52] and a 'wretched substitute to real and genuine law'.[53] A major reason for this condemnation of judicial legislation was Bentham's disapproval of the uncertainty that it generates. 'The grand utility of the law', he once wrote, 'is certainty: unwritten law does not – it cannot – possess this quality.'[54] The law that judges make is always after the fact and applicable only to a particular case. Sound legal reasons can usually be adduced, in a case involving interpretation of the common law, for a decision either way. Judicial power is therefore 'everywhere *arbitrary*, with the semblance of a set of rules to serve as a *screen* to it'.[55] The only remedy for this pernicious situation is a complete code of laws which would take from the judges *any* power to legislate. Under no circumstances would they introduce new rules, a power that belongs exclusively to the legislature.[56]

Despite his laudatory evaluation of legal certainty and enthusiasm for codification, Austin was critical of this categorical denunciation of judicial legislation. He was particularly bothered by the disrespectful connotations of the term 'judge-made law'. 'As I cannot concur with Mr Bentham, in his sweeping dislike of law made by judges,' Austin wrote, 'I cannot consent to mark or brand it with a name importing irreverence.' If judges only made law candidly, then they 'might do the business [of legislation] *better* than any of the sovereign Legislatures which have yet existed in the world.' For outside of their judicial function judges are 'the very best legislators possible, if they are enlightened as well as experienced lawyers'.[57]

Furthermore, Austin explained the existence of judicial legislation in almost every community on the basis of its necessity and 'obvious utility'. Beyond this, he *criticized* judges for their *reluctance* to legislate. He lashed out at their 'too great . . . respect for established rules,'[58] a point which constitutes another link between his work and that of the legal realists. As an example he cited the origin of the distinction between law and equity. It arose

> because the Judges of the Common Law Courts would not do what

> they ought to have done, namely to model their rules of law and of procedure to the growing exigencies of society, instead of stupidly and sulkily adhering to the old and barbarous usages. Equity, when it arose, has remained equally barbarous from the same cause.[59]

Accordingly, Austin was a strong advocate of more candid judicial legislation. Indeed, he imputed many of the evils of judge-made law to the covert mode in which it has been introduced.[60] He also assailed the 'timid, narrow, and piecemeal manner in which they [the judges] have legislated, and . . . under cover of vague and indeterminate phrases.'[61]

Austin appears to have regarded judicial legislation as necessary or desirable under three circumstances. In the first place, established rules may be too indefinite to function as the basis of decisions. Rules which involve degrees are the example *par excellence.* The judge who must apply them has no choice but to make law. In the second place, judicial legislation is desirable as a means to eliminate inconsistent rules. Although statutes also may reduce this defect in the *corpus juris,* the role of judge-made law is very important.[62] In the third place, it may be desirable as a means to adjust the law to socio-economic or other changes. No person who has considered the subject, Austin maintained, can believe that society could 'possibly have gone on if judges had not legislated'.[63] Their legislation has been imperative because of the 'negligence or the incapacity of the avowed legislator'.[64] Austin made no attempt to conceal his conviction that these evils were widespread.

> In almost every community, such has been the incapacity, or such the negligence, of the sovereign legislature, that unless the work of legislation had been performed mainly by subordinate judges, it would not have been performed at all, or would have been performed most ineffectually: with regard to a multitude of most important subjects, the society would have lived without law; and with regard to a multitude of others, the law would have remained in pristine barbarity.[65]

Unfortunately, Austin did not spell out in any detail the standards to be used by judges in deciding *what*, or *how*, to legislate. His few explicit remarks on this subject indicate that he would apply a utilitarian guideline, which is hardly surprising. In any case his theory of rule-utilitarianism described in the third chapter of this study provides a plausible model for judicial decisions. This is evident from Richard Wasserstrom's recent defence of what he calls the two-level procedure of justification. This doctrine holds that judges should decide cases on the basis of the norm that a decision is justifiable 'if and only if it is deducible from the legal rule whose introduction and employment can be shown to be more desirable than any other possible rule'.[66] This procedure is very similar to that involved in Austin's theory of rule-utilitarianism, a fact of which Wasserstrom is fully aware.[67] While Austin did not explicitly apply his theory to judicial decisions, the two-level procedure is a logical outgrowth of it.

4

Austin's analysis of judicial legislation has, in a number of respects, a very modern ring. They include his candid acknowledgment of the existence of judge-made law, his perceptive explanation of the pretexts by which it is obscured, and his praise of its utility. These dimensions of his philosophy of law also run deeply against the current of thought personified by Professor Ronald Dworkin, who is highly critical of many of the trends of modern legal theory. Nothing illustrates more clearly the differences between the two jurists than Dworkin's critique of the positivist doctrine of discretion.[68] A brief discussion of it is desirable in order to demonstrate the implications of Austin's position for contemporary jurisprudence.

Dworkin's critique reflects a particular interpretation of the positivists' conception of law. He describes it as the notion that the law of a community consists of a system of *rules*, which he sharply distinguishes from both *policies* and *principles*. His conception of rules appears to be similar to Roscoe Pound's definition of them as 'definite, detailed provisions for definite, detailed states of fact'.[69] Dworkin conceives of policies as the type of standard 'that sets out a goal to be reached, generally an improvement in some economic, political, or social feature of the community'. To argue for a decision on policy grounds is to justify it by claiming that it 'advances or protects some collective goal of the community as a whole'.[70] A principle is a standard that justifies a decision because it is 'a requirement of justice or fairness or some other dimension of morality'. Arguments from principle support a decision by showing that it 'respects or secures some individual or group right'. Principles differ from rules in that they do not *dictate* or *determine* the outcome of a specific case. Instead, a principle 'states a reason that argues in one direction, but does not necessitate a particular decision'.[71] Principles also have a dimension of weight or importance that rules lack.

Dworkin claims that the distinction between rules and principles is vital for understanding how judges decide hard cases in which no settled rule dictates a particular result. He imputes to positivism the notion that in these situations the judge has discretion in the strong sense of the term. To say that a judge has discretion may signify either the necessity for judgment in the application of a standard, or the unreviewability by a higher authority of an official's decision. Dworkin contrasts these 'weak' meanings of the term with the 'strong' sense of the word. An official has discretion in this last respect if he is 'simply not bound by standards set by the authority in question'.[72] Dworkin claims that this is what positivists mean when they say that the judge has discretion in deciding hard cases. Although a judge is not free in this situation to do whatever he pleases and may be subject to criticism, he is not obligated by any antecedent legal standard to reach a particular decision. Rather, he legislates and decides cases on the basis of some extra-legal standard or policy preference.

Dworkin criticizes this doctrine on various grounds, but his underlying argument seems to be that it is inaccurate. In fact, judges recognize an obligation to base their decision in hard cases upon the legal principle that seems to them to be the weightiest or most important. 'The rights thesis, in its descriptive aspect, holds that judicial decisions in hard cases are characteristically generated by principle not policy.'[73] The rights thesis also holds that there is a single right answer even to the hardest of hard cases. Of course, lawyers and judges often disagree about *which* principle should prevail and *what* the decision of the court should be. Still, established practices presume that legal questions have single right answers which judges are obligated to discover. The process of deciding even hard cases, thus, can 'sensibly be said to be aimed at discovering, rather than inventing, the rights of parties concerned, and . . . the political justification of the process depends upon the soundness of that characterization.'[74] If judges were to invent rather than to discover the rights of the parties, they would be legislating. In a democracy the elected representatives of the people, not judges, are supposed to make law. Judicial invention of new rights retrospectively would also mean that the law controlling the case is *ex post facto*. A decision based upon this kind of law would therefore be unfair or unjust to the parties.[75]

This critique raises a large number of issues, discussion of which is beyond the scope of this study. The question of whether Dworkin's interpretation of legal positivism is accurate is an important example. If Austin is a typical legal positivist, however, the answer to this question is 'no'. For he did not hold at least one of the core-doctrines that Dworkin attributes to this tradition of legal thought. Nothing in Austin's legal philosophy suggests that principles are not law or cannot obligate judges or other officials. Indeed he repeatedly emphasized that '*principles,* notions, and distinctions . . . are the subjects of general jurisprudence'[76] (emphasis added). Moreover, the kind of code that he favoured would consist of 'broad principles' that subordinate 'narrow principles under them'. Established law offers a 'rich mine of such examples'.[77] If the sovereign commanded these or other principles, the denial that they are law would conflict with a basic premise of Austin's positivist jurisprudence.[78] A fundamental component of it is, after all, the notion that positive law consists of the sovereign's tacit or express commands. Whether they take the form of rules, standards, principles or other types of generalizations is irrelevant to their status as law.

Another issue raised by Dworkin's critique is, how strongly do principles influence judges in deciding hard cases? Whatever the correct answer to this question is, Austin would certainly disagree with Dworkin's response to it. In particular, Austin would be likely to argue that considerations of public policy are much more influential than Dworkin acknowledged. Austin might even cite as evidence the very case – *Riggs* v. *Palmer*[79] – that Dworkin used to support his argument. Dworkin described the issue in the case to be whether 'an heir [Elmer Palmer] named in the will of his grandfather [Francis Palmer] could inherit under that will, even though he had murdered his grandfather to do so'.[80] A majority of the justices of the New York Court of Appeals held that the heir could not inherit under the will. The opinion of the Court justified this decision on several grounds, one of which involved an appeal to the principle that 'all laws as well as all contracts may be controlled in their operation and effect by general, fundamental maxims of the common law. No one shall be permitted to profit by his own fraud, or to take advantage of his own wrong, or to found any claim upon his own iniquity, or to acquire property by his own crime.'[81]

Dworkin claims that this reasoning supports his analysis of the significance of principles in hard cases. He fails to mention, however, that a dissenting justice also supported his decision by referring to a principle. Moreover, it reflects the very opposition to judicial policy-making that Dworkin claims substantiates his position. The essence of the principle was that judges are obligated to apply the rules enacted by the legislature for the alteration or revocation of a will.[82] Since the legislature had not enacted a rule permitting or requiring the alteration or revocation of a will under the circumstances presented by this case, Elmer Palmer must be permitted to inherit his grandfather's property. According to Justice Gray, 'a valid will must continue as a will always, unless revoked in the manner provided by the statutes.'[83] How wills may be revoked or altered is for the legislature rather than the courts to decide.

Austin would probably argue that in this case the judges had to choose between competing principles. Each of them was an acceptable rationale of conflicting decisions. The majority of the justices opted for the principle that no man shall profit from his own wrongdoing. They therefore held that Elmer Palmer was not entitled to inherit the property willed to him by his grandfather. Justice Gray chose the principle that the legislature should determine how valid wills are altered or revoked. Accordingly, he decided that Elmer was entitled to inherit. Austin would be likely to say that the choices of these judges consciously or unconsciously reflected a value judgment. It was that the *effects* of applying one of these principles were more *beneficial for the community* than the *effects* of applying the other. Austin might also maintain that Dworkin has imputed too much significance to the frequent judicial disavowal of policy-making. At least this inference may be drawn if Justice Holmes was warranted in arguing more than a century ago that

> in substance the growth of the law is legislative. And this in a deeper sense than that what the courts declare to have always been the law is in fact new. It is legislative in its grounds. The very considerations which judges most rarely mention, and always with an apology, are the secret root from which the law draws all the juices of life. I mean, of course, considerations of what is expedient for the community concerned. Every important principle which is developed by litigation is in fact and at bottom the result of more or less definitely understood views of public policy.[84]

This explanation of Austin's likely reaction to Dworkin's critique does not imply that his response to it would be completely negative. In fact, Austin shared Dworkin's dissatisfaction with the injustice that may result from the *ex post facto* character of judicial legislation.[85] Even so, Austin would distinguish more sharply than Dworkin between two different issues. One is the question of the *existence* of judicial legislation and policymaking, while the other is the issue of their *merits* or *demerits*. Austin would also emphasize that in our kind of legal system judicial legislation and policy-making are inevitable and, in many ways, beneficial.

5

This interpretation implies that Austin's evaluation of judge-made law was ambivalent. If at times he praised it highly, on other occasions he was very critical of it. His negative appraisal of judicial legislation is also more systematically developed than his approbation of it. Although he was displeased with Bentham's critique of this kind of law, Austin did not reject it entirely. Moreover, he was very sympathetic to his predecessor's prescription of codification as the remedy for the disadvantages of judicial legislation. To be sure, Austin implied that Bentham was guilty of 'overstating the degree of simplicity which can be given to the law'.[86] Nevertheless, both men argued that the ideal legal system would take the form of a code of laws.

A number of recurring themes in Austin's writings testify to his dissatisfaction with judicial legislation. The most notable example is his detailed explanation of its six disadvantages, the bulk of which he felt to be inherent in judiciary law. The first, second, third, and sixth of the evils to be explained clearly merit this description, and the fourth probably does. Austin thus believed that most of the problems of judicial law-making were insoluble *as long as this form of legislation exists*.

The six disadvantages are:

(1) The relative inaccessibility and unknowability of judicially created rules in comparison with a clearly worded statute. Judge-made law is virtually unknown, Austin claimed, to the bulk of the community. The only exceptions are a few extremely simple rules of the criminal law and contracts. The layman might as well be subject, thus, to the 'mere *arbitrium* of the tribunals, as to a system of law made by judicial decisions'. Most lawyers are not in a much better position. The knowledge of judge-made rules by even the most experienced members of the legal profession is imperfect.[87] A number of factors account for this defect of judiciary law, one of which is the 'covert mode in which it has been introduced'. A second factor is the enormous bulk of the documents in which judicial legislation has to be uncovered. A final cause is the determination of the *ratio decidendi* of a case, which is

'not uncommonly . . . delicate and difficult'.[88] The difficulty is proportionate to the number and complexity of the cases from which the *ratio* must be derived.

(2) The discovery of the *ratio* by no means ends the problems which confront the judge in a case law system. Besides this, he or she must decide precisely how much *weight* should be given to a precedent. Austin believed that no certain test exists for reaching this decision.

> Is it the *number* of decisions in which a rule has been followed, that makes it law binding on future judges? or is it the *elegantia* of the rule . . . or its consistency and harmony with the bulk of the legal system? Or is it the *reputation* of the judge or judges by whom the case or cases introducing the rule were decided?

Whether a precedent will be followed by future judges in analogous cases cannot for this reason be known with absolute certainty.[89]

(3) In addition to these disadvantages, the rule which a judge introduces is 'always an *ex post facto* law with respect to the particular case on which the point first arose'.[90] The understandable revulsion for such law is, according to John Chipman Gray, the major reason for the unwillingness to recognize the existence of judicial legislation.[91] Although Austin obviously did not share this reluctance, he was deeply troubled by the retroactive quality of judge-made law. It has in general all of the 'mischievous consequences' of *ex post facto* law.[92] This objection would not apply, of course, if the effect of the new rules which judges introduce were prospective rather than retrospective. Unfortunately, Austin did not consider this possibility.[93]

(4) The circumstances under which judges legislate, most notably the rush of judicial business, are far from ideal. As a result, they must make law without the calm deliberation and reflection which Austin believed wise legislation requires. To be sure, he recognized that rules made by appellate courts were an exception to this generalization. The law which they make may indeed be devised 'with as much care and foresight, perhaps, as any statute law'. Since most judicial legislation occurs on the appellate court level, this admission seems seriously to qualify Austin's criticism. Nevertheless, he insisted that the situation of judges does not 'render them the best of legislators, nor does it fit them preeminently for actual legislation'.[94]

(5) Judge-made rules are not only made in haste but tend to lack comprehensiveness. The major reason for this unfortunate tendency is, Austin claimed, the reluctance of judges to make rules that are

more inclusive than is necessary to decide the cases before them. If they make broader rules than this, these generalizations could always be disregarded in future cases as mere *dicta*. The effect of this judicial tendency is that

> the exigencies of society are provided for bit by bit, in the slowest and most inefficient manner, and the documents containing the law are swelled to an immense volume. In lieu of one comprehensive rule determining a *genus* of cases, there are many several and narrow rules severally and successively determining the various species which that *genus* includes.[95]

(6) A final disadvantage of judicial legislation is its bad effect on the symmetry of the *corpus juris*. If much of the law is judge-made, then the entire legal system is necessarily a 'monstrous chaos'. On the one hand, it will contain rules 'introduced bit by bit, and imbedded in a measureless heap of particular judicial decisions'. On the other hand, the system will have rules 'stuck by patches on the judiciary law, and imbedded in a measureless heap of occasional and supplemental statutes'.[96]

Austin's perception of these disadvantages of judicial legislation was no doubt strongly influenced by the actual evolution of English law. Albert V. Dicey described its development in these terms:

> English law, as it existed at the end of the eighteenth century, had in truth developed almost haphazard [sic], as the result of customs or modes of thought which had prevailed at different periods. The laws actually in existence had certainly not been enacted with a view to any one guiding principle. They had, indeed, for the most part never been 'enacted' (in the strict sense of that word) at all. They were, as they still indeed to a great extent are, the result of judicial legislation built up in the course of deciding particular cases. English law has in fact grown, rather than been made.[97]

Austin was convinced, at any rate, that a well-constructed code of laws was the most effective remedy for the ills of judicial legislation. His dissatisfaction with it is evident both from the kind of code that he advocated and his rationale for codification. A code in the modern sense is 'a body of law expressed in general *formulae* arranged systematically, and complete'.[98] It is 'a *complete* body of statute law' (emphasis added) that is designed to 'supersede all other law whatever'. Codified rules will be '*the only positive law* obtaining in the community'[99] (emphasis added). If this design is not wholly achievable, judicial legislation may be confined to 'narrow limits'.[100] Austin felt that a useful device for limiting the scope of judge-made law was to include within a code

> a perpetual provision for its amendment, on suggestions from the judges who are engaged in applying it, and who are in the best of all situations for observing its defects. By this means the growth of judiciary law explanatory of, and supplementary to, the code, cannot indeed be prevented altogether, but it may be kept within a moderate bulk, by being wrought into the code itself from time to time.[101]

Furthermore, the major reason that Austin adduced for a code is the inexpediency of judicial legislation. It has 'great defects' and 'monstrous evils', a mere enumeration of which is 'amply sufficient to demonstrate . . . that codification is expedient'. Other proof of its expediency is 'superfluous'. In fact, he maintained that *any* judicious and candid person would admit that a properly drawn statute is '*incomparably superior* to a rule of judiciary law'[102] (emphasis added). While no code can so condense and simplify the law that the bulk of the community may know much of it, rules may be drafted that at least lawyers could master. They would then be able to advise laymen 'beforehand [of] the legal effect of transactions in which they are about to engage'.[103]

Dissatisfaction with judicial legislation also conditioned Austin's proposal, in 1847, for the establishment of a Permanent Commission of Legislation.[104] To say this is not to suggest that his unhappiness with judge-made law was the only reason for his enthusiasm for this body. His conviction of the ineptitude of sovereign legislators also played a role, as did his fear of popular legislation. He evidently found the very idea of the latter to be 'alarming' and 'absurd'.[105] Nonetheless, Austin's belief in the disadvantages of judicial legislation also influenced his recommendation for the appointment of this Commission.

The members of this body would consist of an unspecified number of lawyers who were 'at once thoroughly versed in the sciences of jurisprudence and legislation, and in the particular system [of law] of the given community.'[106] The purpose of the Commission would be to help Parliament in the performance of its legislative business, by studying and reporting on bills submitted to either House. The Commission would indicate whether the objective of the proposed legislation was achieved by established laws. It would also suggest specific provisions by which the purpose of the bill could be best realized. Finally, the Commission would recommend forms and language by which the goal and provisions of the measure would be 'as definite and clear as possible'.[107]

Austin obviously believed that the appointment of this Commission would facilitate the task of codification. As such, his proposal for its establishment expressed his life-long desire to rationalize and to systematize English law. The Commission was necessary because of the 'frightful and accumulating chaos of the written and unwritten law'. The absence of this kind of body is responsible for judicial legislation, in England and 'all countries'. Judges have been forced to interpret statutory law in order to help the 'lame productions of the sovereign legislature'. The judge-made law that has resulted is 'bad in itself', and has derogated from 'the proper office of the sovereign authority'.[108]

The most fundamental reason for Austin's dissatisfaction with judicial legislation is, thus, the uncertainty that it fosters. This criticism is by no means the only ground on the basis of which judge-made law can be, and has been, attacked. The rules which judges make may create inequality before the law, by applying different standards to the same material facts. The enactment of new rules also belongs in a democratic society, it could be argued, to the elected representatives of the people. None of these criticisms is to be found in the lectures of John Austin. The great defect of judicial legislation as he perceived it is the uncertainty that this kind of law-making inspires. Positive law is, he believed, a guide for conduct or a means for controlling behaviour. The law that judges have made is difficult to find and to know and therefore to follow. The law that they will make is also not easy to predict. If judges do decide to change the rules of their predecessors, the law which they make is by definition *ex post facto*. To this extent, the uncertainty of judicial legislation is also a source of injustice.

This evaluation of the rules which judges make obviously presupposes that legal certainty is an extremely important value. For Austin, it was the most significant technical value of a legal system. He believed that laws may be appraised from two radically different perspectives, the technical and the ethical. Although he did not use this precise language, it corresponds to terms which he did employ.

From the ethical point of view, laws are good or bad depending on whether they promote the general happiness or good. From the technical point of view, laws are good or bad if they are 'well-arranged and expressed'. According to Austin, the achievement of the desired sort of arrangement and expression 'is incomparably more difficult than what may be styled the *ethical* [goal of legislation]. . . . it is far easier to conceive justly what would be useful law, than so to construct that same law that it may accomplish the design of the lawgiver.'[109] The satisfaction of this need requires, in any case, that the rules which are made offer clear guidance. Legal certainty in this sense was also for Austin a universally shared value. Thus he believed that the question of codification 'may be agitated with safety, because everybody must admit that Law ought to be known, whatever he may think of the provisions of which it ought to consist.'[110]

Other dimensions of Austin's thought also indicate the great importance that he imputed to legal certainty. This attitude underlies, for example, his highly negative evaluation of spurious interpretation of statutes. He insisted that the judge must as a rule abide by the literal meaning of statutory language. Of course, his dread of the uncertainty which loose construction would generate is not the only reason for his commitment to this norm. Another factor was his conception of the subordinate position of the judge in the legal chain of command. If he disregarded or defied the will of the sovereign legislature, then the will of the agent would be superior to that of the principal. Nevertheless, a no less fundamental reason for Austin's condemnation of spurious interpretation was the vast uncertainty it causes. This kind of indirect legislation lays *all* statute law, he argued, at the mercy of the courts. Such arbitrariness markedly reduces, if it does not utterly destroy, the certain guidance which statutory rules can and should provide.[111]

This judgment assumes that in most cases of statutory construction the intent of the law-maker is in fact discoverable. The accuracy of this assumption, in at least some cases, is dubious. John Chipman Gray was of the opinion, which was shared by some legal realists, that

> when a Legislature has had a real intention, one way or another, on a point, it is not once in a hundred times that any doubt arises as to what its intention was. . . . The fact is that the difficulties of so-called interpretation arise when the Legislature has had no meaning at all; when the question which is raised on the statute never occurred to it; when what the judges have to do is, not to determine what the Legislature did mean on a point which was

present to its mind, but to guess what it would have intended on a point not present to its mind, if the point had been present.[112]

Austin also condemned judicial legislation with respect to certain kinds of precedents. Once more, his criticism reflects the high priority which he attached to legal certainty. The introduction of a new rule is unjustified if it would interfere with 'interests and expectations which have grown up under established rules'. For judges lack power to indemnify the injured parties.[113]

Austin's critique of the equitable application of law provides additional evidence of his commitment to legal certainty. The decision-maker who utilizes this approach does not substitute a good for a bad rule. Rather, he 'allows the law to remain, and simply dispenses with it in specific cases'.[114] Austin vehemently assailed this practice. Jurors who refuse to enforce the law of the land in a particular case out of the belief that it is unjust or inequitable act improperly.[115] Nor will it do to argue that jurors judge only the facts of the case. 'Generally, and notoriously, the jury is judge of law as well as of fact.'[116]

Austin also excoriated judges who render decisions on the basis of their *le bon sens* or *l'equité* rather than the dictates of the law. Equitable decisions attempt to avoid the injustice which can result from strict compliance with the letter of even good laws. Precisely for this reason they have been endorsed by Aristotle, St Thomas Aquinas, Roscoe Pound, Jerome Frank, and many others. While they are not agreed on how frequently judges should apply law equitably rather than strictly, each of them approved of equitable application *to some degree*.[117] In contrast, John Austin was convinced that its effects are 'clearly mischievous'. The reason for his disapproval was his perception that the application of almost any rule is 'productive of some consequence which a good-natured judge would wish to avert'. He therefore argued that the judicial refusal to apply a good rule the particular application of which is inequitable would be disastrous. The effect would be the destruction of *any* rule to guide expectations and conduct. The process of equitable application renders all law 'utterly uncertain'.[118] Decisions reached in this manner introduce an unpredictability which 'would defeat all the ends of law, more than an army of robbers'. In a word, equitable application gravely threatens the 'security, and the feeling of security, which ought to be the principal end of political government and law'.[119]

Evaluation of this criticism requires a more detailed explication of the argument by which Austin justified it. His rationale is subject to several possible interpretations. Under one of them, cases in which equitable application is proper are indistinguishable from those in which it is improper. The justification of this mode of reaching decisions is the avoidance of an evil which characterizes the application of any rule. In fact, this process always has some particular painful effect which a benevolent judge would wish to avoid. If equitable application is justifiable in *any* case, it is for this reason justifiable in *every* case. On the other interpretation, this method of reaching decisions is bad because it is uncontrollable. To sanction its use in a few cases will open the floodgates. Little if any law would exist prior to decisions on the basis of which reliable expectations could be formed. The law of a great nation, to use John Chipman Gray's phrase, would indeed be utterly uncertain.

Regardless of which of these interpretations is correct, Austin's argument is unsatisfactory. It is possible (though not easy) to distinguish between cases in which the equitable application of law is proper and improper. One way to draw the distinction is in terms of the magnitude of the evil which results from the application of a rule which is on balance good. Austin's moral philosophy reflects just this kind of distinction. Although he was a rule-utilitarian, he recognized that in some extraordinary cases non-compliance with a good rule is justifiable. The specific consequences of such deviation may be so important 'that the evil of observing the rule might surpass the evil of breaking it. Looking at the reasons from which we had inferred the rule, it were absurd to think it inflexible.'[120] The same sort of reasoning furnishes a utilitarian justification for equitable application of law. This conclusion is also justifiable by an appeal to a higher law than positive law, an approach for which Austin had no sympathy. In any case, the history of common law adjudication indicates that equitable application of law is controllable. The actual extent of this mode of reaching decisions is difficult to gauge, but it no doubt exists. The result has not been, however, utter uncertainty. The reason for this may well be judicial awareness of the dire effects of a too frequent equitable application of law. Whatever the explanation, the effects which Austin projected are not borne out by the record.

6

The vast importance that Austin imputed to legal certainty was, in any event, the major reason for his condemnation of equitable application of law. The same value underlies his support of a type of codification that reduces judicial legislation to the minimum. His ideas in this respect could not be more different from those of the American legal realists. To be sure, most of them did not explain fully their opinion of the possibility and desirability of codes. It is therefore impossible to elucidate their reaction to Austin's analysis of codification with complete certainty. Nevertheless, it is highly likely that they would have disagreed with the ideas he developed on this subject. In particular, the realists would argue that not even the best code could, or should, eliminate judge-made law to the extent that Austin had desired.

This response may be inferred from the views that two leading realists – Jerome N. Frank and Karl N. Llewellyn – expressed about codification. Frank maintained that unchanging application of codes is 'impossible'.[121] European experience with allegedly gapless codes had, in his view, confirmed this judgment. He proffered several reasons for the failure of these efforts to construct unvarying bodies of law, one of which was the scope and rapidity of socio-economic change. He also observed that even the wisest legislators command a limited vision of the future:

> [T]he history of Continental law . . . [demonstrates that] a code cannot be stable, it must be adaptive. Even in a relatively static society, no one can foresee all future combinations of events. . . . Situations are bound to occur which the legislature never contemplated when enacting the statutes. Then the incompleteness of the code calls for judicial law-making.[122]

Frank also argued that a comprehensive, gapless code of laws would become a straightjacket, impeding necessary and useful changes. Since this result would be socially intolerable, judges would be forced to change and adapt the terms of the code surreptitiously. This practice would inevitably increase rather than decrease legal uncertainty. Judges would develop forced 'interpretations' of the code and obscure what they would actually be doing, which was to make law. Although this process may create the appearance of certainty, it actually 'increases legal contingency and doubt'.[123]

Despite these criticisms, Frank disclaimed an intent to reject every conceivable kind of code. He emphasized that his critical remarks should not be interpreted as a 'blanket indictment of wise codification which aims at simplicity and flexibility rather than completeness and finality'.[124] The sort of code that Frank advocated differed substantially, however, from the type that Austin favoured. This is evident from Frank's endorsement of the Swiss Civil Code. He portrayed it as seeking 'simplicity and flexibility, not detailed, complete regulation. It is "more like an outline of legal principles than a body of provisions purporting to regulate all legal relations." '[125] Indeed, he even stated that 'a code deliberately devised with reference to the desirability of growth and stated in terms of general guiding and flexible principles may some day prove to be the way out of some of the difficulties of legal administration in America.'[126]

This quite tentative assessment of the limited benefits of codification differs significantly from Llewellyn's position. Otherwise, he would not have expended such a vast amount of time and energy drafting the Uniform Commercial Code.[127] A conspicuous feature of the Code is the significant role that courts must play in the development of its provisions. This idea reflects Llewellyn's belief that ' "semi-permanent Acts must envisage and encourage development by the courts" ' – ' " [b]orderline, doubtful, or uncontemplated cases are inevitable." '[128] The Code therefore requires a liberal interpretation of its provisions:

> This Act is drawn to provide flexibility so that, since it is intended to be a semi-permanent piece of legislation, it will provide its own machinery for expansion of commercial practices. It is intended to make it possible for the law embodied in this Act to be developed by the courts in the light of unforeseen and new circumstances and practices.[129]

Of course, the Uniform Commercial Code was not intended to give courts *carte blanche* in interpreting its provisions. The proper construction of the Act ' "requires that its interpretation and application be limited to its reason. . . . The Act should be construed in accordance with its underlying purposes and policies." ' The Code was drafted in the hope that lawyers and judges would interpret and apply it in the 'Grand Style'.[130] This approach means that 'every current decision is to be tested against life-wisdom, and . . . the phrasing of the authorities which build our guiding structure of rules is to be tested and is at need to be vigorously recast in the new light of what each new case may suggest either about life-wisdom, or about a cleaner and more usable structure of doctrine.'[131]

Llewellyn contrasted the Grand Style with the Formal Style. The latter involves precisely the kind of approach that Austin advocated for applying the terms of a code. Under the Formal Style, 'the rules of law are to decide the cases; policy is for the legislature, not for the courts.' Judges who had perceived their function in this manner '*sought* to do their deciding without reference to much except the rules, *sought* to eliminate the impact of sense, as an intrusion.'[132]

Both Frank and Llewellyn rejected, thus, the kind of code that Austin favoured. Llewellyn, however, ascribed greater value to codification than did Frank. This difference reflects, among other things, their conflicting appraisals of the possibility and desirability of legal certainty. Llewellyn, for example, expressed the opinion that law, 'in the sense of decision, is in fact much more predictable, and hence more certain, than [Frank's] treatment would indicate. Llewellyn also maintained that 'even adventurous spirits want some footing to adventure from. That need is practical.'[133]

Unlike Llewellyn, Frank claimed that law 'always has been, is now, and will ever continue to be, largely vague and variable'.[134] Although he explained this certainty on different grounds at various stages of his career, he came to attribute it mainly to the inherently unpredictable reactions of judges or jurors to the facts of most cases. This fact-scepticism is the most basic reason why 'it is impossible, and will always be impossible . . . to predict future decisions in most (not all) law suits, not yet begun or not yet tried.' The fact-sceptics among the legal realists therefore argued that the attempt to increase substantially legal certainty was 'futile – and . . . indeed, may well work injustice'. Accordingly, the fact-sceptics did not pursue this course of action. Instead, their objective was 'increased judicial justice'.[135]

These ideas engendered Frank's and Llewellyn's difference of opinion on the subject of codification. Fact-scepticism implies the inevitability of a tremendous amount of legal uncertainty at the trial court level. A fact-sceptic could therefore entertain only the most limited expectations about the benefits of codification. For this reason, the distance between Frank and Llewellyn may have been as great as that between Llewellyn and Austin.

Even so, all of the realists would criticize Austin's expectations for codes as too optimistic. His support of codification assumes that a comprehensive set of legal rules can be drafted that will control or dictate the vast majority of judicial decisions. This assumption was unacceptable to the realists, who criticized it on various grounds. Arthur L. Corbin set the tone for others by emphasizing that 'however "well-settled" the rules may be, their application to life is always uncertain. A rule lives only in its application; apart from that, it is a dead, inert thing. A new and different application of the rule is the creation of a new rule.'[136] Corbin left no doubt of his conviction that new and different applications of established rules are inevitable. He therefore disputed the assumption that syllogistic reasoning on the basis of these rules can prevent the development of new rules. Of course, in

> a superficial aspect, the application of rules to cases may seem to be a deductive process; a pre-existing general rule is the major premise from which the judge arrives at a particular conclusion applicable to John Doe. In fact, however, the law in its growth and application is an inductive process. The supposed pre-existing rule is a mere assumption of the court. . . . [Y]ou can get out of a major premise all you put into it. . . . In all cases the judge must construct his own major premise, and this he does not find an easy matter.[137]

These ideas explain why Corbin was more pessimistic than Austin about the benefits of codification. Although Corbin acknowledged that it may increase legal certainty somewhat, he insisted that 'uncertainty remains. Society does not stay put; and if the code lags behind, it is no longer the governing law.'[138] The legal realists would also criticize Austin's evaluation of codification for a quite different reason. It is the conviction that the norm of stare decisis, properly understood, provides a sounder basis for decisions than the abstract rules of a code of law. The best expression of this point of view came from the pen of Herman Oliphant.[139] Despite his harsh indictment of legal scholarship for the transition from stare decisis to 'stare dictis', he extolled the spirit of the former. Stare decisis demonstrates thoughtfulness about consequences, cautiousness in considering only 'immediate problems', and carefulness in illuminating these difficulties 'from the glow of the prudence and insight which its own experimentation patiently forges'. Stare decisis affords us both the 'counsel of experience' and the 'latitude of trial and error.'[140] Thus,

> [w]ith eyes cleared of the old and broad abstractions which curtain our vision, we come to recognize more and more the eminent good sense in what courts are wont to do about disputes before them. . . . [T]he decision of a particular case by a thoughtful scholar is to be preferred to that by a poorly trained judge, but the decision of such a judge in a particular case is infinitely to be preferred to a decision of it preordained by some broad 'principle' laid down by the scholar when this and a host of other concrete cases had never even occurred to him.[141]

These attitudes explain why Oliphant described stare decisis as the 'greatest contribution of our common law and of our people to the art of human government'.[142] As such, his point of view illustrates what Llewellyn could have meant when he wrote, 'Still wholly within the tradition of our law, [the realists] strove to improve on that tradition.'[143] In contrast, Austin was, in a sense, outside the common law tradition. At least his commitment to the ideal of codification reflects dissatisfaction with the practices that Oliphant praised. Austin's attitude toward codification also embodies a belief in an *elegantia juris* that the realists did not share.

The realists would thus have disagreed with Austin about the extent to which a good code could and should eliminate judicial legislation. Since he believed that not even the best code could entirely eliminate judicial law-making, this difference is a matter of degree rather than fundamental principle. Furthermore, it is not as significant as it might at first appear. Despite his belief that a good code is both possible and desirable, Austin was uncertain that it would ever be enacted. His uncertainty reflected his keen appreciation of the 'vast difficulty of successful codification'.[144] The task was difficult for two reasons, one of which was the evil that necessarily attended the transition from one legal system to another. Whether a code could be produced that would adequately compensate for this disadvantage was, for Austin, an open question.[145] The other and more basic difficulty was the distinct possibility that a community would lack codifiers of the requisite ability. Austin's visionary conception of the rare and demanding qualifications that they must possess was the basis of his doubts. The persons who draft a code must be 'consummate' and 'enlightened practical lawyers' whose talents he described in these terms:

> It is pre-eminently necessary that they should possess clear and precise and ever-present conceptions of the fundamental principles and distinctions, and of the import of the leading expressions; that they should have constantly before their mind a map of the law as a whole; enabling it to subordinate the less general under the more general; to perceive the relations of the parts to one another; and thus to travel from general to particular and particular to general, and from a part to its relations to other parts, with readiness and ease: to subsume the particular under the general, and to analyse and translate the general into the particulars that it contains.[146]

These considerations explain Austin's reservations about the feasibility of codification. Although the idea of a code had tremendous appeal for him, he recognized that its practicality was a question of time, place, and circumstance. He also in effect took the stance that until we arrive at the promised land, a substantial amount of judge-made law is inevitable and expedient. Precisely for this reason, his very different assessments of judicial legislation are not contradictory.

While Austin never expressed his views in exactly these words, his actual position was that the utility of judge-made law varies in accordance with the kind of legal system in which it occurs. On the one hand, judiciary law would have little or no place in the ideal *corpus juris*, the foundation of which is a comprehensive code. This situation would be desirable because indirect legislation has substantial disadvantages. On the other hand, in a mixed system of statutory and common law judicial legislation is a necessary evil. To be sure, Austin sometimes emphasized its necessity or even utility, while at other times he stressed its drawbacks. Nevertheless, as a rule he argued that the benefits of judge-made law have outweighed its costs in 'almost every community'.[147] He also claimed that 'there is more . . . stability and coherency in judiciary law, than might, at the first blush, be imagined.'[148] In fact, he asserted that judicial respect for precedents is 'too great'.[149] Moreover, he took the position that judge-made rules are in practice less uncertain than statutory law. He emphasized not only that 'unless a statute be well made, it commonly is more uncertain than a rule of judiciary law,'[150] but that judicially created rules are in fact technically superior to existing statutory rules. Austin even stated that 'the law of every country which was made by judges has been far better made than . . . statutes enacted by the legislative.'[151] The technical superiority of judge-made rules is indeed the major reason for the sovereign's acquiescence in judicial legislation.[152] This situation is likely to continue until legislators are much better qualified than they have been in the past, a possibility he doubted would ever be realized.

Although Austin believed that the benefits of judicial legislation outweighed its costs in mixed legal systems, he was acutely conscious of its disadvantages. He was also convinced that in the best of all possible legal worlds the amount of judge-made law would be miniscule. The drafting and implementation of a comprehensive and ideal code of laws is difficult, but it is not impossible. The realists' disagreement with this notion reflects, in part, a differing understanding of the limitations of legal rules as a means to control or dictate judicial decisions. They also appraised somewhat differently than Austin the costs and benefits of judicial legislation. While he obviously was more conscious than many of the realists of what he believed to be the disadvantages of judge-made law, the practical significance of these differences is not immense. The Englishman and the Americans disagreed largely about the place of judicial legislation in a highly problematical future. They would have agreed that, in the meantime, judges will and should continue to make law. If Austin and the realists were to arise from the grave, they would therefore be likely to form a united front against Professor Dworkin's 'pre-Benthamite'[153] analysis of judicial decision-making.

7

The major purpose of this study is to explain John Austin's analysis of judicial legislation. The evidence is overwhelming that he was not ignorant of either its existence or utility. Such ignorance is also not evident in the work of Hans Kelsen, who is probably the most influential European legal positivist of this century.[154] The same can be said of H. L. A. Hart, whose importance for the philosophy of law needs no elaboration.[155] For these reasons the association of legal positivism with mechanical jurisprudence is, in all probability, unfounded. Proof of this point is, however, beyond the scope of this essay. It has only demonstrated that John Austin should not be tarred with the brush of legal formalism.

Of course, some qualification of this conclusion is necessary. Austin cannot be wholly exempt from all responsibility for the misinterpretation of his version of legal positivism. His conception of positive law seems to imply that judges *could* not legislate. He was also an ardent proponent of codification, which he partially justified by enumerating the grave disadvantages of 'judiciary law'. He was convinced that a well-constructed code would obviate most, if not all, of the law which judges make. To that extent, the legal order which he felt to be ideally desirable would approximate a closed logical system. This train of thought provides the basis, such as it is, for the interpretation of Austin as a proponent of 'mechanical jurisprudence'.

Even so, his analysis of judicial legislation is a notable achievement. On at least three levels – conceptual, descriptive, and prescriptive – it constitutes a substantial contribution to an important problem. Austin's conception of the differences between statutory law and the rules which judges make may be profitably scrutinized even today. His explanation of the difficulties which frequently characterize the application of established rules is full of insights. His analysis implies that judges must exercise a choice which, if it is not legislative, is far from mechanical. His account of the existence of judicial legislation, and the covert form which it often takes, was far ahead of his time. Over seventy years ago Roscoe Pound correctly pointed out that Austin's view of spurious interpretation 'deserves more attention than it has received. . . . in a time when we ought to have outgrown fictions, the pretended interpretation by virtue of which the law grows judicially, deserves to be so branded that no one shall be deceived.'[156] His explanation of the necessity for, and utility of, judge-made law is no less valuable. In many respects he clearly adumbrated positions which twentieth-century sociological and realistic jurists were subsequently to take. Moreover, Austin's far-sightedness in this regard was not fortuitous. Rather, it reflected his strong interest in the realities of law and the legal process. If he did not originate the phrase 'living law', for example, he certainly employed it.[157] He specifically referred in one passage to 'the *living* Roman Law or the Roman Law *administered and enforced by the tribunals*.'[158] He also mentioned at least twice the value of distinguishing 'living from dead law'.[159] At the same time, his appraisal of judicial legislation has a balance not always present in the work of more recent jurists. For the introduction of new rules by judges in the context of deciding cases *can* have serious disadvantages.

To say this is in no way to imply that Austin's analysis of judiciary law is the end-all or be-all. His reconciliation of judicial legislation with his conception of positive law is not notable for its success. The intent of the legislature may be much less discoverable than he believed it to be. The value of his formula for determining the *ratio decidendi* is subject to considerable doubt. His critique of equitable application of law is hyperbolical. The root of many of these problems may well be the extraordinary priority which he attached to legal certainty. On more than one occasion it skewed his vision of what is or ought to be the case. Furthermore, the utilitarian basis which he favoured for the rules which judges should make is also debatable. No one who accepts the criticisms of utilitarianism put forth by John Rawls, for example, could regard it as satisfactory.[160]

Despite this, Austin's perceptive analysis of judicial legislation stands in refreshing contrast to that of most nineteenth-century Anglo-American jurists. Indeed, the quality of his account was not superseded historically until the classic works of Justice Holmes[161] (if then). Moreover, Austin's discussion of judge-made law is not without relevance for our own time. He not only foreshadowed H. L. A. Hart's valuable distinction between the 'core of fixed meaning' and 'fringe of open texture' of general terms, but cogently explained why judges do and should have a large amount of discretion in hard cases. A contribution of this magnitude merits much greater attention than it has heretofore received.

5 *The reform of Malta*

John Austin was primarily a theorist rather than a man of action. Of course, this distinction is not absolute. Theorists are not disembodied spirits who never act, nor are men of action unintelligent beings who never think. Nevertheless, the distinction is useful for characterizing the general direction of a person's life. Austin's orientation was quite obviously to the field of theory rather than practice. His ideas also had little, if any, impact on the course of human events during his lifetime.

This generalization is subject to an important exception. Many of Austin's ideas did affect the organization and policies of the British colony of Malta. He was in a position to exert this influence because of his appointment in 1836 to a Royal Commission on Malta. The other Commissioner was George Cornewall Lewis, a bright young man who was only thirty at the time of his appointment. A former student and great admirer, if not disciple, of Austin, he subsequently had a notable career as a public servant and writer.[1] Lewis was definitely the junior partner, however, in the work of the Commissioners.[2] Their jointly signed reports and letters are, thus, reliable evidence of Austin's thought.

To say that the Commissioners influenced British policy toward Malta is not to imply that they had the power of Plato's philosopher kings. Nor is it to suggest that they even had as much power over Malta as James Mill exercised over India. As Examiner of India Correspondence for the East India Company from 1830 to 1836, Mill stood at the 'very centre of power and [was] in a position to carry into practice the principle of utility'.[3] Austin and Lewis were neither at the very centre of power nor in a position to carry into practice the principle of utility. They could only *recommend*, not *enact*, changes in the *status quo*. Even so, they could and did exercise a substantial amount of *influence* over British colonial policy toward Malta.

This influence is one reason for the importance of the reforms proposed by the Commissioners, only a limited number of which will be discussed in this chapter. Their recommendations are also important because of the light that they shed on Austin's political, social, and legal thought. His role as a Commissioner required him to express opinions on numerous subjects about which he wrote little, or nothing, elsewhere. They include freedom of the press, libel laws, trial by jury, terms of imprisonment and other details of a penal system, military government, and the role of natives in a colony such as Malta. Moreover, the reports and letters of the Commissioners illustrate how Austin applied general principles that are evident in his other works. Some examples are: his commitment to a Malthusian explanation of the misery of the bulk of the workers; his faith in popular education as *the* most effective remedy for this condition; and his belief in an informed public opinion as the primary deterrent to misgovernment.

The reports and letters of the Commissioners are important for another reason as well, which is their illumination of an important movement in nineteenth-century British life. Some of the recommendations of the Commissioners are almost 'text-book' applications of utilitarian principles. Others involved the expression of opinions that would have shocked at least Benthamite utilitarians. A number of the reforms that Austin advocated for Malta also contrast sharply with the changes urged by James Mill for India. Knowledge of Austin's reforms is therefore necessary in order to understand the diversity in the colonial policies of the utilitarians.[4]

The almost compulsive drive of Austin for the reform of Malta is a final reason for the importance of the Commissioners' labours. The very existence of this motive illustrates how false any interpretation of legal positivism is which attributes to its advocates a sterile indifference to questions of what ought to be. If Austin's interest in these issues was less evident than that of Jeremy Bentham, the reports of the Commissioners indicate that it still was very substantial.

1

Although the Commissioners did not explicitly make this classification, their reforms tend to fall into two broad categories. One set of recommendations concerned the structure and organization of the colonial government, while the other focussed on its policies. None of these proposals emerged, however, in a vacuum. Rather, the plans of Austin and Lewis for Malta were developed in a particular context and were subject to various constraints. An explanation of both the context and the constraints is therefore necessary if the reforms themselves are to be fully understood.[5]

British rule of Malta was a fortuitous consequence of the Napoleonic Wars. The fabled Knights Hospitallers of St John of Jerusalem had governed the Island from 1530 to 1798. Their reign was terminated by the forces of Napoleon, who regarded Malta as of 'priceless' value to the French.[6] The French occupation was unpopular with the Maltese, who revolted against their new rulers. Representatives of the Maltese people sought and received the assistance of the British. The result was a blockade of Malta which forced the French to withdraw in 1800.

Although the British assumed responsibility for the government of Malta, they did not originally intend to incorporate it into the Empire. This attitude persisted for several years despite the representations of certain of the Maltese to obtain 'His Britannic Majesty for our Sovereign'.[7] British authorities subsequently decided to accede to this request. Their decision received international recognition in 1815, under Article Seven of the Treaty of Paris.[8]

The primary basis of the decision of the British to incorporate Malta into the Empire was a perception of its great military value. The Island was governed as a Crown Colony, the distinctive characteristics of which were:

> (1) The maintenance of the original laws and institutions of the colony, instead of the grant of English law and the old representative system; (2) The concentration of power in the hands of the governor; (3) The strict control of the governor from a newly established colonial department in London, and government as far as possible under the prerogative without recourse to Parliament; (4) The maintenance by the Crown of the power of legislation by order in council.[9]

Malta's status as a Crown Colony meant, thus, that the structure of the colonial government was very autocratic. As such, it elicited periodic complaints from the Maltese. A petition to the Crown in 1811 illustrates the stated basis of their dissatisfaction.[10] The petitioners assailed the alleged despotism of Sir Alexander Ball, the Civil Commissioner of Malta, 1802–9. They also requested the re-establishment of the 'sacred' and 'ancient' rights of the Maltese people, the most important of which was a 'free representation of the People or "Consiglio Popolare" '. Other demands of the petitioners included the institution of independent tribunals, a free but not 'licentious' press, and trial by jury. In short, the protesters wanted a constitution which would unite the spirit of their 'ancient, free, and only legitimate government with that of the English Constitution.'[11]

Similar petitions were submitted to the British government in the next two decades. The agitation accelerated in the 1830s. It culminated in the submission to Parliament on 7 June 1836 of a petition signed by over 2,000 residents of Malta.[12] The petitioners assailed the 'ill-conducted' government of the Island, which was alleged to be 'preeminent' for its misrule. They protested against the large number of highly salaried officials, the absence of a truly representative assembly, and the weakness of the Council of Government established in 1835. The petitioners also requested a free press, popular education, and the abolition of the governmental monopoly of the supply of grain.[13]

Less than 2 per cent of the people of Malta signed this petition. Although an accurate estimate of the proportion of the population who shared the grievances of the petitioners is impossible, it was probably large. Austin and Lewis estimated that dissatisfaction with British rule was 'nearly universal'.[14] The response of the British government to this discontent was to appoint in 1836 a Royal Commission to Malta.[15] The motives of this decision are subject to conflicting interpretations, but the letter of William IV appointing the Commissioners specified two objectives for their study. One was to promote the happiness and prosperity of the Maltese, while the other was to strengthen the ties between Malta and Great Britain. The Commissioners could only achieve these goals if their inquiry had a very broad scope, which it in fact did. The King specifically empowered them to 'examine into . . . every . . . matter or thing in any way connected with the administration of the civil government, the principles and practices of the judicature, the civil and ecclesiastical establishments, the revenues, trade, and internal sources thereof.' William IV also instructed the Commissioners to recommend 'whether any and what changes are necessary . . . in the administration of affairs . . . in order to fulfil our gracious intentions, and to promote the happiness and prosperity of our Maltese subjects.'[16]

Despite this language, Austin and Lewis did not receive *carte blanche* from the British government. Lord Glenelg, the Colonial Secretary, cautioned them to do nothing which threatened the strategic importance of Malta for Great Britain. In his words,

> you will . . . in every part of your researches and proceedings, keep steadily in recollection the peculiar character which Malta has borne . . . and which it must continue to bear, as a Naval and Military Station of the highest importance. With the deepest solicitude for the interest and well-being of the Inhabitants at large, His

> Majesty is yet satisfied that even those objects cannot properly be consulted or pursued in any such manner as should impede or weaken the action of that Military Authority which must be exercised for the protection and defence of the Island.[17]

Glenelg stressed that this end is of such 'extreme national importance' that it must have priority over 'all other interests'.[18]

These instructions obviously limited the kind of changes that the Commissioners could propose. In particular, a substantial amount of self-government for Malta was out of the question. Even so, the Commission's agenda was broad. Glenelg specifically instructed Austin and Lewis to investigate eight problems. At the top of the list was the feasibility of a representative body to deal with the 'subordinate local affairs of the Island'. The second item was the prevailing system of censorship of the press. The other areas of investigation were the courts, public revenues, the Civil Establishment, exclusion of the Maltese from public employment, education, and the distress and poverty of the natives. The Colonial Secretary left no doubt of the importance which he attached to the beneficial solution of these problems.

> If for purposes European as well as British, it be found necessary to deny in their full extent to the Maltese People some of the advantages enjoyed by His Majesty's subjects in other parts of His dominion, this circumstance only increases the solicitude of the King that they should in other respects enjoy as many blessings, and in as large a measure, as it may be in the power of a wise and paternal government to provide.[19]

This letter expressed the genuine, if paternalistic, concern of Lord Glenelg for the well-being of the Maltese. The Commissioners shared his attitude. They became convinced, for example, that many of the grievances of the natives against British rule were well-founded. As they wrote to Lord Glenelg:

> At the time of our arrival in Malta, and for a considerable time before, the discontent of the Maltese at the abuses in the government of the island, was great and nearly universal; indeed, in the opinion of the local government, (though not in ours,) their discontent was such as to make it probable that it would break out in acts of violence . . . . *much of this discontent was well-founded.*[20] (emphasis added)

2

This sympathetic appraisal of the grievances of the Maltese informed all of the changes proposed by the Commissioners. They attempted to alleviate the discontent caused by the autocratic character of the colonial government by several reforms, including the appointment of a civilian as the head of the civil government. Austin and Lewis argued that the conduct of the government on civil rather than military principles was a matter of 'great importance'.[21] They justified their recommendation on various grounds, one of which was the inability of most military men to appreciate certain functions of civil government. An important example is the need for 'consulting the opinions and feelings of the governed, and in satisfying their reason before requiring their obedience'.[22] A second argument stressed the promises of the British government to the Maltese people at the outset of British rule of the Island. The Commissioners claimed that these commitments would induce a rational man to expect that the government would be conducted on as 'liberal and popular principles as might be consistent with its security'.[23] The same theme pervades a second letter from the Commissioners to Lord Glenelg, which contains this highly significant passage:

> The honour of the British government is tarnished to the eyes of foreigners, by its breach of its moral engagements towards the Maltese, and by the really barbarous condition in which the mass of them remain, notwithstanding their long subjection to the British crown. If it would efface the stain, it will fulfill its virtual contract with the people of Malta, so far as it can fulfill it consistently with their own interests; and by changing their military, despotic and ignorant, for a civil, popular, and enlightened government, will raise them to the elevated point in the scale of civilization and happiness, which, as subjects of the British crown, they would naturally occupy.[24]

This passage expresses attitudes that strongly conditioned the bulk of the Commissioners' reforms for Malta. The most important of these sentiments were: revulsion at the deplorable condition of the vast majority of the Maltese people; outrage against the failure of the British to fulfill their obligations to Malta; the spirit of 'uplift'; and a certain pride, if not *hubris*, in British civilization. The Maltese should naturally stand higher on the ladder of civilization than they now do *because* they are British subjects. The passage also reflects the profound faith of the Commissioners in progress, an indispensable requirement of which was the replacement of military rule by a civil, popular, and enlightened government.

The Commissioners believed that achievement of this goal required another change in the colonial government. The essence of it was a limited revision of the Council of Government, a subject to which Lord Glenelg attached considerable importance. Otherwise, he would not have placed it at the head of the list of topics on which he desired the Commissioners to report. At the same time, he restricted the kind of changes that they could recommend. He specifically ruled out, for example, a Council of Government similar to the General Assemblies of the transatlantic colonies. He claimed that such a body would not only be 'foreign to the spirit and incompatible with the situation of the Maltese people, but entirely hostile to the ends of good Government on the Island'. Nevertheless, he instructed the Commissioners to report on whether the subordinate local affairs of Malta should be placed under the 'inspection and control of the more wealthy and better instructed members of society, *in such a manner as without leading to hazardous results may yet secure general confidence*'[25] (emphasis added).

The underlined portions of this quotation indicate the difficulty of the assignment of the Commissioners. Proposals that had results which the British viewed as hazardous may well have been the only ones that would secure the confidence of the Maltese people. This dilemma may have contributed to the inability of the Commissioners to complete a report on the Council of Government. The drift of their thinking about changes in it is evident, in any case, from their correspondence with the Colonial Office. It includes a long, twenty-two-page letter to Lord Russell, who had become Colonial Secretary in 1839.[26]

The Commissioners adamantly opposed any broadening of the powers of the Council. They were especially critical of establishing a powerful *Consiglio Popolare* of that sort demanded by some critics of the colonial government. Such an institution would conflict with 'the purposes for which England occupies Malta, and would not permanently afford to the people of Malta the desired security against English misrule.' In particular, a *Consiglio Popolare* would be likely to make 'imprudent and disastrous uses . . . of its powers'.[27]

The Commissioners did not deny, however, that the failure to institute a *Consiglio Popolare* raised certain 'embarrassing difficulties'. These problems included the arguable claim that Great Britain had a moral obligation to establish such a council. The basis of this alleged duty was the promise of British authorities to establish a council with extensive powers. Certain declarations of representatives of the British government when it took control of the Island could be interpreted, the Commissioners admitted, to imply such a promise. Indeed, they emphasized that the bulk of the Maltese construed these statements in precisely this fashion.

The Commissioners could have resolved this problem by challenging the accuracy of this interpretation. In short, they could have denied that any promise to institute a *Consiglio Popolare* was ever made. Instead, they acknowledged that the declarations in question could be interpreted to imply a promise to establish a Popular Council. Austin and Lewis insisted, however, that this promise did not impose *a morally binding obligation* on the British. They justified this contention in classic utilitarian fashion:

> Moral obligations immediately arising from promises arise in the last result from general expediency; and since it would endanger the interests of the Empire and the special interests of Malta herself, a strict performance of the promise in question would not consist with that ultimate principle.[28]

In short, strict fulfilment of the promise was inexpedient and therefore not morally obligatory.

Austin and Lewis maintained that this reasoning was supported by the 'inflexible facts of the case'. They also claimed that its force would be readily admitted by the 'impartial' and 'reflecting'.[29] In short, they expressed the utmost confidence about the cogency of their argument. The Commissioners readily acknowledged, though, that the refusal of the British to establish a *Consiglio Popolare* would be highly unpopular among the Maltese. Still, Austin and Lewis emphasized the possibility of convincing at least the 'intelligent' classes of the inexpediency of a popular council. Until a majority of these persons see this institution in its 'true light', the refusal to establish a *Consiglio Popolare* 'will agitate the Maltese people and embarrass the British Government'.[30]

The Commissioners were also critical of *any* enlargement of the political or administrative powers of the established Council. In other words, they took the position that its powers should remain advisory and consultative. Austin described the views of himself and Lewis in these terms:

(1) that the advice of the Council shall be taken by the Gov. before any [legislative] . . . act be passed and promulgated by him: (2) that if the Council dissent from him, but he persist in passing the act, he shall record, and send to the Col. office, their and his reasons; (3) that if he pass and promulgate the act, notwithstanding their dissent, it shall be valid, (on his complying with that condition) until it be disallowed by the Home Government.[31]

The Council proposed by the Commissioners would exercise, thus, a purely 'moral influence' over the British Government.[32] It therefore fell well within the boundaries established by Lord Glenelg's instructions. In fact, his guidelines permitted a substantially more powerful Council than Austin and Lewis actually proposed. After all, he instructed them to consider whether the subordinate local affairs of Malta should be placed under the inspection *and* control of the wealthier and better-instructed classes. The Council proposed by Austin and Lewis had no such *control*. Indeed, Austin claimed that it would be less powerful than the *established* Council.[33] While this claim was erroneous, it indicates a desire on the part of at least Austin to recommend a Council that was *weaker* than the established Council.

Despite the Commissioners' refusal to recommend enlargement of the *powers* of the Council, they did propose expansion of its *representative basis*. To say this is not to imply, however, that they advocated an institution that would be representative by democratic standards. Rather, the Commissioners took the position that the Council should 'directly' or 'virtually' represent the 'property and intelligence of the island'.[34] Such a body would serve 'as a channel for communicating to the Home (and even the Local) Gov. the genuine opinions and wishes of the proprietary and intelligent classes'. This kind of assembly would create a medium through which these opinions and wishes 'can be made known, in an authentic and trustworthy manner, to the superior (or even the inferior) authority'.[35] The establishment of this Council would facilitate, thus, accurate communication of the views of the propertied and intelligent classes to both the Governor and the Colonial Office.

The Commissioners did not spell out the details of their proposal, which leaves a number of important questions unanswered. These unresolved problems include the form of representation, whether it would be direct or virtual; the qualifications for the suffrage, if direct representation were used; the precise basis of representation, or the selector of representatives, if members of the Council were not elected; and the number of persons who would sit on the Council.

The Commissioners were anything but vague about the moral obligation of the British government to establish this type of assembly. They insisted that it was essential in order to fulfill the general obligation of Great Britain to promote the interests of her colony. A representative Council would achieve this goal by giving to the Maltese an effective deterrent to English 'misrule'.[36] Austin left no doubt of his conviction of the absolute necessity of protecting the Maltese against 'ignorant and narrow-minded Governors'.[37] Aside from this, the Commissioners stressed that a revised Council would probably reach knowledgeable and prudent decisions. This probability will be strengthened, Austin wrote, by the report of the Commissioners. He was extremely anxious to make it a 'Code of Instruction' for the guidance of the Maltese. The report would be

> so framed as to put them on their guard against any considerable indiscretion; and judging from the change in their opinions which . . . we have already made by mere dint of dry reason . . . a large majority of the higher and middle classes will listen to the sober advice which we can contrive to insinuate in our Report.[38]

Although Austin acknowledged that the revised Council might be a source of 'some trouble' to Great Britain, he emphasized that it could not do 'any considerable harm'. He also pointed out that this body would cause far less difficulty than maintenance of the *status quo*.[39] Finally, the Commissioners argued that the British government was obligated by its promises to the Maltese to establish a more representative Council. If Great Britain were not obligated to strict performance of this commitment, she was 'bound to perform it *quam proxime*, or as nearly as the principle will allow'.[40]

The Commissioners recognized that their proposal was not an ideal solution for the defects of the established Council. Instead, Austin described it as 'the least inconvenient course which the great difficulties of [the case] will permit'.[41] The Commissioners were also not optimistic that their recommendation would be acceptable to either of the major parties. On the one hand, the Maltese were likely to view a Council of advisory powers only as an unsatisfactory alternative to a *Consiglio Popolare*.[42] On the other hand, the British might regard the revised Council as too powerful. Still, the Commissioners expressed the belief that these doubts would eventually be overcome:

> considering the solemnity and strength of the obligations by which the British Government is bound to the Maltese people, we think that any objection to *so moderate a concession*, which may be raised by any party in England, will yield to a fair statement of the entire case[43] (emphasis added).

The negative reaction by the British government to the proposal of the Commissioners confirmed their worse fears.[44] Moreover, Lord Russell did nothing to encourage them to finish their long delayed and never completed report on the Council.[45] Since their recommendation was unknown to the Maltese, the latter had no opportunity to react to it. If they had been familiar with it, their reaction probably would have been unfavourable. Two petitions to Parliament from Malta on 15 June and 23 June 1839 are the basis of this judgment.[46] The first petition was a general indictment of the Commission, the proposals of which did not meet in the 'slightest degree the wants of the population'. The petitioners particularly emphasized the failure of Austin and Lewis to recommend a Legislative Council with substantial powers. The petition stated that the Maltese people urgently needed a Council with authority to superintend the administration, to vote all taxes or supplies, and to introduce new laws. If it was not granted the power to propose such laws, 'on all other occasions of necessity, the faculty may be conceded to the . . . Assembly as the legitimate and natural organ of public opinion of making instance for the proposition of any specific law.'[47]

The completely negative attitude of these petitioners toward the Commission did not represent the views of all the Maltese. This is evident from the other petition, which expressed gratitude for some of the recommendations of the Commissioners. Nevertheless, even this petition advocated the establishment of a Council with substantial powers:

> Your petitioners most confidently expect to witness soon the adoption and establishment of a salutary and permanent system of government for these islands, grounded upon the advantage of a council or representative body, freely elected by the people and entrusted with the direction and protection of their local interests, so as that it may at any future period be effectually competent to promote the prosperity of these islands.[48]

The Commissioners were familiar with these petitions, which were submitted to Parliament almost a year prior to their letters to Lord Russell. This fact raises the question of why they did not propose as powerful a Council as Lord Glenelg authorized them to recommend. One reason was the conviction that it would abuse its powers, while another was the belief that such an assembly was unnecessary. Although the Commissioners fully acknowledged the existence of misgovernment on Malta, they attributed it largely to ignorance on the part of colonial officials of the needs and wishes of the educated Maltese. The Commissioners obviously believed that their revised Council would make the Governor aware of at least informed public opinion on Malta. This awareness would tend to deter him, the Commissioners assumed, from supporting unpopular and inexpedient laws or policies. If the Governor did endorse law or policies of this character, he would be overruled by the Colonial Office. Otherwise, unnecessary dissatisfaction with British rule on the Island would be fostered. This effect was not in the self-interest of Great Britain and would not be approved of by enlightened officials.

This explanation of British misrule on Malta is, however, at least partially inaccurate. It ignores a basic reason for colonial misrule, which is the priority that may be given to interests other than those of even educated natives. To say this is not to deny that ignorance of the effects of policies or laws, or the attitude of the people toward them, is one reason for colonial misrule. It is to say that this is not necessarily the only or most fundamental reason. Political power for natives was necessary not so much to inform and educate colonial rulers, as to check them. If the interests of the two parties conflicted, which would sometimes be the case, a Council with advisory powers might not have been an effective check.

This weakness of the Commissioners' proposal is not only important in and of itself. Besides this, it reflects a limitation of the colonial theories of utilitarians who were more sympathetic to democracy than Austin.[49] No one more eloquently defended than J. S. Mill, for example, the need for constitutional checks against rulers. He took the position, however, that these safeguards against misrule are not universally desirable. They are indispensable 'in England, and the other nations of modern Europe'.[50] Constitutional checks are also necessary in dependencies that consist of 'people of similar civilization to the ruling country; capable of, and ripe for, representative government'. These kinds of restraints are undesirable in countries such as India which 'are still at a great distance from that state'.[51] For societies in such a backward state of development, the obstacles to progress are so great that 'a ruler full of the spirit of improvement is warranted in the use of any expedients that will attain an end, perhaps otherwise unattainable.' These means include despotism, which is 'a legitimate mode of government in dealing with barbarians, provided the end be their improvement, and the means justified by actually effecting that end.'[52]

These ideas presume a substantial degree of ability and disinterestedness on the part of colonial rulers. This presumption may or may not be warranted, but it certainly is

> at odds with what utilitarian theory leads us to expect from unchecked governments; the whole point of the utilitarian advocacy of representative democracy was the underlying assumption that unless some check could be exercised by the ruled upon those who ruled them, there would be no hope of curbing the standing inclination of all governors to rule in their own rather than their subjects' interests.[53]

In any case, Austin's and Lewis's expectations about the beneficial effects of their proposal were grossly exaggerated. Indeed, their recommendation for limited revisions in the established Council of Government may be their least satisfactory reform for Malta. Their proposals for the Island represented, in general, substantial improvements in the public affairs of the colony. The very modest changes that they recommended for the Council do not, however, merit this evaluation. At the same time, the Maltese probably would have been better off if the British government had accepted the Commissioners' proposal. At least a larger number of them would have been represented on the Council of Government than had been the case previously. Implementation of the Commissioners' proposal also would not have endangered British rule on Malta. If the value of *this* effect is open to serious question, Austin and Lewis obviously were in no position to question it unless they resigned.

3

The other recommendations of the Commissioners were for changes in the policies of the colonial government. Their proposals included the suggestion of a number of changes in its employment practices, one of which was for the abolition of all sinecures. A second proposal was the 'systematic appointment of meritorious natives to superior offices'. The Commissioners justifiably regarded these changes as among the 'most useful reforms which could be introduced into Malta'.[54] The reforms also reflected the liberal and relatively enlightened character of most of the changes proposed by Austin and Lewis. In fact, their recommendation for employment of natives involved a kind of affirmative action policy for the Maltese.

Malta was part of an empire in which patronage played an important role in the appointment of colonial officials. One student of the subject has claimed that 'lax standards and indifference to the welfare of the colonies often prevailed in the choice of their officials. . . . When unfit men were given appointments overseas, the colonists suffered.'[55] Austin and Lewis were convinced that the Maltese had indeed suffered from these, and other, colonial policies. The stated objectives of their recommendations discussed in this section were to 'raise the condition of the natives; and to increase the efficiency and popularity of the Government, by diffusing amongst the public a belief in its wisdom and justice.'[56]

The abolition of needless offices would contribute to these ends by reducing taxation on Malta, which was a major source of discontent. 'We should have great difficulty', the Commissioners wrote to Lord Glenelg, 'in conveying to your Lordship an adequate sense of the vehement and universal dislike of taxation which exists in this island.'[57] This dissatisfaction mandated the reduction of taxation to the 'lowest amount consistent with the public service'. It was therefore essential to abolish 'every office appearing to be needless, and to diminish every salary appearing to be exorbitant'.[58]

This line of reasoning explains the large number of offices the abolition of which was recommended by Austin and Lewis. These offices, which were filled by Englishmen, included the highly paid positions of Chief Justice, Attorney-General, and Collector of Land Revenue. The Commissioners viewed these posts as sinecures, the existence of which was deeply resented by the Maltese. Moreover, Austin and Lewis urged the appointment of qualified natives to higher offices. Indeed, the Commissioners perceived no reason why almost all of the administrative positions 'should not be filled ultimately by natives of the island'.[59]

At any rate, the Commissioners recommended an affirmative action policy for the Maltese, who ought 'generally to be preferred to Englishmen'.[60] Austin and Lewis defended this preference on various grounds. They cited its efficacy as a means to increase the popularity of the colonial government; the competence of the Maltese to perform the duties of governmental office-holders; their greater familiarity than the English with the 'circumstances of the country . . . its laws, institutions, and usages'; and the superior ability of natives to Englishmen *who would come to Malta*. English office-holders have for the most part been persons who 'failed to advance their fortunes in England'.[61]

This last argument reflects a rather low opinion of the English residents of Malta. Lewis was even blunter than this in his personal correspondence. The 'scum' of England, he wrote, is 'poured into the colonies: briefless barristers, broke-down merchants, ruined debauchees, the offal of every calling and profession'.[62] If an Englishman is to 'preserve any vestige of sympathetic feelings towards his own countrymen as such, he should certainly never see them out of England.'[63]

Whether Austin shared these caustic opinions of his fellow-countrymen is not known. At any rate, the Commissioners' belief in the ability of the Maltese was quite different from that of some Englishmen.[64] The insistence of Austin and Lewis on the employment of natives also differed from the view which James Mill held with respect to India. He did not share 'the widely entertained opinion that the natives of India should be more largely employed in the business of government'. Rather, he took the position that the 'great concern of the people of India . . . was that the business of government should be well and cheaply performed . . . it was of little or no consequence who the people were who performed it.'[65] It was of little consequence, that is, as long as the people who performed it were competent. Mill left no doubt of his judgment that the people of India lacked this virtue. At the same time, he emphasized that 'intimate knowledge' of the natives was essential for the good government of the country. His solution to this problem was colonization, a policy the 'admirable effects' of which he extolled.[66] He particularly emphasized the value of the migration of 'English gentlemen' to India. He argued that it is impossible to envisage their settlement

> as proprietors of land, and as manufacturers, without perceiving how advantageously they would be situated for acquiring that knowledge of the natives, in which the [East India] Company's servants are proved to be so defective; and for giving that aid in the administration of justice, without which a good administration is not to be attained. Such men would be forced into an intimate intercourse with the natives, whence . . . an intimate knowledge would arise. They would have a local influence of great efficacy.[67]

This recommendation contrasts sharply with the reforms proposed by Austin and Lewis for Malta. They expressed no support for colonization and attached the greatest importance to the employment of natives by the colonial government. These differences may not be as significant, however, as they appear to be. The basis of Mill's views was his extremely low ranking of the Hindus on the 'scale of civilization', a scale on which the comparative position of nations may be 'accurately marked'.[68] Testimony of the ignorance of the Hindus and their low state of civilization is, he claimed, 'clear, concurring, and undeniable'.[69] Their actual condition is 'little removed from that of half-civilized nations'.[70] Their laws and institutions reflect one of the 'rudest and weakest states of the human mind'. Indeed, the Hindus were mentally and physically 'the most enslaved portion of the human race'.[71]

Austin and Lewis apparently accepted this assessment. They distinguished, however, the situation of the Hindus from that of the Maltese:

> If the moral and intellectual condition of the Maltese were as low as that of the Hindoos, it might be necessary that the civil government of the island should be mainly administered by Englishmen. But though the Maltese are not so advanced in civilization as we could desire, and as they would be if they had enjoyed a liberty of the press, and good institutions for education, yet they are an European and Christian community, and far superior in institutions, manners, science, and arts to the most advanced of the Asiatic nations. The system, therefore, which may be necessary in Hindostan, is altogether unjustifiable in Malta.[72]

Lord Glenelg did not fully accept, at any rate, the proposals of the Commissioners for the employment of natives. His reaction to their plans was in general, however, very positive.[73] His response was quite different from that of the opposition party in the House of Lords, which was controlled by the Tories. Frederick John Robinson, Earl of Ripon, was the leader of the assault on the Commission. On 3 May 1838 he introduced a motion for the return of the expenses incurred by the Commission.[74] He justified this motion by various arguments, some of which had as their focus the recommendations of the Commissioners discussed in this chapter. He strenuously denied that the positions which they wished to abolish were sinecures and ridiculed their proposal that natives should occupy all high offices.[75] Other members of the House of Lords criticized the failure of the Commissioners to consult the holders of the offices about the abolition of their positions. Lord Brougham, for example, asserted that the House of Commons would not abolish the 'place of a tide-waiter without making such an inquiry'.[76]

Spokesmen for the Government took a different, and much more reasonable, position. Lord Glenelg eloquently justified the need to expand the opportunities of the natives for governmental service. He emphasized the invidious distinctions between the English and the Maltese which the Commissioners had described. He expressed his abhorrence of the degradation and humiliation to which the natives had been subjected. He maintained that if the Commission had done nothing but end this 'unnatural and unjust distinction between the two races, that in itself would be a benefit of so much importance, as fully to compensate for its appointment'.[77]

Lord Glenelg also defended the Commissioners' recommendation for the abolition of sinecures. He criticized the principle that office-holders have a right to be consulted about the abolition of their positions. He emphasized that Malta was 'overloaded with expensive establishments . . . not adaptable to the wants of the country'.[78] Other spokesmen for the government documented the fact that the specific offices which the Commissioners wished to abolish were either sinecures, or jobs with exorbitant salaries.[79] Lord Glenelg also emphasized that the only persons with grievances were displaced office-holders who were 'naturally enough anxious to make out as strong a claim for compensation as they could'.[80]

The defenders of the Commission appear to have had much the better of this war of words in the House of Lords. Although the critics of the Commission may have been entirely sincere, they were probably motivated more by partisan political considerations than the disinterested effort to appraise the work of the Commissioners. The Melbourne administration was in political hot water because of its handling of the rebellion in Canada, which had taken place in 1837.[81] The opponents of the government may have attempted to exploit this situation by attacking another alleged weakness in its colonial policies. At any rate, the proposals of the Commissioners discussed in this chapter are among the most attractive of their plans for the reform of Malta. Sinecures existed in the colonial government which should have been, and were, abolished. The exclusion of the Maltese from higher governmental offices, which their taxes financed, was unjust and inexpedient. Awareness of this required both a sense of justice and a certain degree of cultural open-mindedness on the part of Austin and Lewis. To be sure, they did not believe that the vast majority of the natives were competent to fill higher offices. The immediate beneficiaries of the change in policy would be the middle class of Malta, which was a small proportion of the whole population. Still, the Commissioners recognized that at least some of the Maltese should be eligible for offices formerly held only by Englishmen.

4

Another significant set of changes urged by the Commissioners concerned the educational policies of the colonial government. Their recommendations in this area are not only important intrinsically, but as a symbol of their general approach to *social* reform. While they obviously did not view structural changes as insignificant, they attached more importance to modification of the attitudes and opinions of the Maltese. It is for this reason that the Commissioners accorded such vast significance to revision of the educational system. The priority that they attached to it also distinguishes their reforms for Malta from James Mill's plans for India. He claimed that it was necessary 'before education can operate to any great result, that the poverty of the people should be redressed; that their laws and government should operate beneficently'.[82] Unlike Mill, Austin and Lewis argued that education was a prerequisite for redressing the poverty of the people.

The Commissioners' educational reforms were strongly conditioned by the Malthusian lenses through which they perceived social problems. Thomas Robert Malthus published the second edition of his famous book in 1803.[83] Although he never has lacked critics, they did not include the utilitarians. On the contrary, a belief in the Malthusian theory of population was 'the most essential article of their faith, and marked the line of cleavage between the two wings of the Radical party'.[84] James Mill took the position, for example, that discovery of the 'best means of checking the progress of population, when it cannot go on unrestrained, without producing . . . most undesirable effects . . . is. . . . the most important practical problem to which the wisdom of the politician and moralist can be applied.'[85] John Stuart Mill indicated that Malthus's principle of population was a major element in the credo of the philosophic radicals. Although they were more optimistic than Malthus, they believed that the sole means of indefinitely improving human affairs was 'by securing full employment at high wages to the whole labouring population through a voluntary restriction of the increase of their numbers'.[86]

The ranks of true believers included John Austin. His commitment to Malthusian principles is evident from a close reading of *The Province of Jurisprudence Determined*. He fully recognized the 'present wretched condition of human society' and the 'unfavourable . . . outward circumstances wherein most men are placed'. He expressed the wish that the rewards of the masses were greater and that they could be relieved of their 'incessant drudgery'.[87] Nonetheless, Austin was critical of attempts to change these conditions through socialism or direct governmental assistance to the indigent. 'Social engineering' of this sort is not only harmful, but utterly unnecessary. The wages and labour of the workers depend 'upon their own will, and not upon the will of the rich. In the *true principle of population*, detected by the sagacity of Mr Malthus, they must look for the cause and the remedy of their penury and excessive toil.'[88]

The question, thus, was how to convince the people of the true cause of and actual remedy for their misery. Malthus himself stressed the value of popular education as a means to limit the growth of population. Its development will make the 'lower' classes of society aware of their 'dependence on themselves for the chief part of their happiness or misery'. It is therefore the duty of the government to educate the masses. Indeed, 'no government can approach to perfection that does not provide for the instruction of the people'.[89]

Austin fully accepted this rationale for popular education. The extent of his commitment to it is evident from his criticism of persons who expect 'magnificent results' from penal reform. 'An enlightened people were a better auxiliary to the judge', he claimed, 'than an army of policemen.'[90] The highly class-conscious language that he employed to drive the point home very clearly discloses his conception of the socially beneficial effects of education. Although a rational system of punishment is useful,

> nothing but *the diffusion of knowledge through the great mass of the people* will go to the root of the evil. Nothing but this will cure or alleviate the poverty which is the ordinary incentive to crime. Nothing but this will extirpate their prejudices, and correct their moral sentiments: will lay them under the restraints which are imposed by enlightened opinion, and which operate so potently on the higher and more cultivated classes.[91]

Austin not only extolled the benefits of popular education, but argued that financing of it was a responsibility of government. He insisted that support of education is 'one of the weightiest of the duties, which God has laid upon governments'. To diffuse knowledge among the people is no less incumbent upon governments than 'to protect their subjects from one another by a due administration of justice, or to defend them by a military force from the attacks of external enemies'. The cost of complete education of the workers is, after all, only a 'small fraction of the sums squandered in needless war'.[92]

The reforms proposed by the Commissioners were a logical application of these ideas. The educational system of Malta consisted of a small number of elementary schools, a Lyceum or preparatory school, and the University of Valetta. Austin and Lewis reacted negatively to elementary education on the island, which they criticized as 'small in quantity and bad in quality'.[93] The high rate of illiteracy among the Maltese was vivid evidence of how unsatisfactory the system was. In 1835 only a tiny proportion of the population could read or write, and by 1851 the figure was only 10 per cent.[94]

The Commissioners recommended several changes in order to reduce this widespread illiteracy, one of which was the expansion of the number of elementary schools. The other was the elimination of tuition, to be achieved by governmental financing of elementary education. Since England did not develop a system of free public elementary education until 1891, this proposal was bold. Implementation of it was also expensive. Governmental expenditures for education would have to be more than doubled, a course of action that the Commissioners were very reluctant to recommend. Nevertheless, they concluded that the reform of elementary education in Malta was important enough to justify this cost.

The immediate objective of free tuition was to insure that the entire population had rudimentary knowledge. Austin and Lewis argued that the Maltese youth of every class and background must have 'the most complete education which the resources of the country can afford'.[95] Free public education at the elementary level was a necessity if this objective were to be realized. The bulk of the people were too unenlightened to appreciate the 'manifold advantages of knowledge'. They were also so poor that the requirement of tuition would probably prevent them from educating their children.[96]

Although these ideas were not unusual for a utilitarian, the Commissioners' plans for public elementary education included a proposal that would have shocked either James Mill or Jeremy Bentham.[97] This recommendation was for religious instruction in the public schools, under the exclusive direction of the Catholic priests. Austin and Lewis even claimed that members of the clergy should have virtually unlimited access to the schools in order to instruct the children in the 'religion of their parents and country'.[98]

The basic reason for this provocative recommendation was not the Commissioners' sympathy for the Roman Catholic religion. Instead, it stemmed from their conviction that their reforms would be unsuccessful without the support of the Catholic church. The overwhelming bulk of the population of Malta consisted of persons who were 'ardent, almost fanatical, Roman Catholics'. One effect of this ardour was the seriousness with which the Maltese took the advice of the clergy, who exercised 'tremendous influence over all ranks of society'.[99] Indeed, Henry Seddall believed that the sizable contingent of priests on the Island were the 'real rulers in Malta'.[100]

In any event, the Malthusian outlook of the Commissioners was the most fundamental reason for their enthusiasm for popular education. Unemployment, low wages, and poverty were widespread on Malta. A twentieth-century historian has written that the 'pages of English history record the sufferings of the factory hand in the early years of the Industrial Revolution. . . . The sufferings of the Maltese agriculturist at the time of the Commission were as heart-rending and deplorable.'[101] Sarah Austin may have believed that the sufferings of the Maltese were more severe than those of the English workers. At the least she expressed the view that such 'a state of extreme and hopeless destitution can hardly be conceived'.[102]

The Commissioners shared this opinion.[103] They also emphasized the pernicious social consequences of the deplorable conditions of the agriculturists. Their necessitous circumstances forced most of them to pawn their effects, to beg, or to steal in order to survive. Theft was particularly widespread in periods of unemployment, when 'want is . . . more urgent and almost general'.[104] The problem became so severe, at times, that the farmers were compelled to guard their lands and gardens by both day and night. They were so afraid of theft that they even felt obliged to gather their crops prematurely.

The Commissioners believed that the underlying reason for these conditions was over-population. Their reports emphasized that popular education was the best solution to the problem. In particular, it will help to induce the Maltese people to change their perception of the reasons for their poverty, which are 'for the most part utterly mistaken'. They attribute it 'not to their own improvidence in multiplying their numbers beyond the demand for their labour, but to the acts or omissions of the Government'.[105] The actual root of the evil is the rapid growth of population, which fosters a large pool of workers for a relatively small number of jobs. The inevitable result is a pattern of low wages, poverty, and crime.[106]

This Malthusian point of view also underlies the Commissioners' negative reaction to certain proposals for the alleviation of the poverty of the Maltese. The problem itself was the subject of considerable discussion by contemporaries, who proposed various remedies for it. Some argued forcefully for large-scale emigration, organized and sponsored by the government. Others advocated governmental programs of public works which would employ substantial numbers of people.[107] Austin and Lewis were highly critical of both of these proposals. They assailed 'the futility of the schemes . . . which have been commended to the people by ignorant projectors and declaimers; as, for example, the emigration of the surplus population, or the employment of it at the expense of the government.'[108] These proposals are not genuine solutions to the problem of poverty and might in fact aggravate the evil.

At any rate, the educational reforms proposed by the Commissioners included several changes for the University of Valetta. Their most significant proposal was for the establishment of a Chair of Political Economy. At least nothing reveals as unmistakably as this recommendation the basis of Austin's belief in the social utility of education. The Commissioners recommended that the holder of the Chair should give lectures which would be open to all and held at night. Austin and Lewis insisted that the usefulness of a Chair on the subject of political economy can 'hardly be exaggerated'.[109] They supported this judgment by praising the utility of the Chair as a means to diffuse knowledge throughout the entire population. Its establishment would gradually familiarize the Maltese with the elementary and most important tenets of political economy, popular awareness of which would be immensely valuable. Consciousness of these truths would dispel the prejudices of the people that 'blind them to the causes of their poverty, and divert their attention from the only remedies for the evil'.[110]

The Commissioners also justified the utility of a Chair of Political Economy by a second argument. It reflected their conviction that popular education is one of the 'indisputable and important securities against misgovernment'.[111] The Chair would help to diffuse knowledge among the people and thereby enable them to evaluate intelligently the government's policies. An enlightened public opinion would thus be fostered that would deter the enactment of policies dictated by the 'presumptuous ignorance' of the government. If the elementary truths of the science of political economy had been generally understood by the Maltese, the economy of the island would have been saved from 'many of the evils which the ignorance of its former Governments inflicted upon them'. These ills include the government monopoly of corn, governmental intervention in the corn trade, long and complicated tariffs, and 'indiscriminate public charity to paupers of the lower classes . . . with the conversion of public offices into receptacles for paupers of the higher.'[112]

The Commissioners' educational reforms favourably impressed Lord Glenelg. He instructed Governor Bouverie to revise the 'whole of the existing establishments for public instruction, on the principles laid down in the Report of her Majesty's Commissioners'.[113] The reforms that Austin and Lewis proposed for elementary education are especially praiseworthy. Elimination of the high rate of illiteracy on Malta was a prerequisite of individual development, if not social progress. The widespread poverty on the Island meant that only the government had the resources to transform popular education into a reality.

The soundness of the reasoning by which the Commissioners justified their educational reforms is another matter. Their arguments presuppose an explanation of the poverty of the Maltese that may not be wholly accurate. At least Charles Price, a twentieth-century demographer, has criticized a Malthusian explanation of the misery of the Maltese people. A more influential factor than the growth of population was, he claims, the loss of certain valuable eighteenth-century resources. They included the substantial revenues of the Knights and the precipitous decline of the cotton trade. The social predicament of the Maltese was therefore a result

> not so much [of] the pressure exerted by a rapidly expanding population on slowly increasing resources as the pressure exerted by a dense population unexpectedly deprived of much of its former wealth. In short, a sudden change in economic circumstances was more important than the 'tendency' of population to increase faster than the means of subsistence.[114]

If this explanation is accurate, which it appears to be, the Commissioners' diagnosis of the distress of the Maltese was not entirely valid. Accordingly, the remedies that they prescribed to cure this distress were insufficient. While popular education might eventually check the rapid growth of the population, this tendency was not the only cause of the plight of the Maltese. Educational reforms were not therefore sufficient to alleviate their distress.

Aside from this, the Commissioners exaggerated the efficacy of their educational reforms as a means to check the growth of population. The prominent role that Austin and Lewis gave to Roman Catholic clergymen is the major reason for this flaw. It is highly unlikely that *they* would have stressed excessive population as the root of the problems of the Maltese. Indeed, the teachings of the clergy were apparently one reason for the large families which characterized the Island. Austin and Lewis did not explain how these teachings would change after the implementation of their reforms.

To take this position is not to criticize the Commissioners for proposing religious instruction by the Catholic clergy in elementary schools. This recommendation probably was necessary in order to ensure the successful implementation of the changes proposed by Austin and Lewis. Otherwise, parents might have been too distrustful of the system to send their children to the new schools. Also, the large number of priests on the Island might have encouraged this distrust in the absence of a provision for religious instruction. Even so, this feature of the Commissioners' plan would markedly reduce its effectiveness *as a means to limit the growth of population*.

This proposal also reflected the ambivalent attitude of Austin and Lewis toward the Roman Catholic church. On the one hand, they were convinced that its social effects had been pernicious. On the other hand, they opposed as counter-productive any direct attempt to wean the population from the 'superstitions which enfeeble their understanding and deprave their moral feelings'.[115] Rather, Austin and Lewis decided to attack this problem indirectly. As they wrote to Lord Glenelg,

> The only way of accomplishing the object is the diffusion of secular knowledge amongst them . . . [which would] at least, change them [the Maltese] from ignorant and bigoted, into instructed and liberal Catholics; and might ultimately incline them to give a candid consideration to the arguments in favour of protestantism.[116]

The Commissioners might say the same thing about the effects of their educational reforms on the growth of the population of Malta. Their implementation would ultimately 'incline' the Maltese to a 'candid consideration' of the evils of over-population. This expectation was much more modest, however, than the effects that the Commissioners predicted from the adoption of their reforms. To say this is not to deny that the reforms themselves were desirable or that over-population was a grave evil. Nor is it to disparage the genuine insights of the Commissioners into Malta's very severe social problems. Their explanation of the connections between poverty and crime on the Island is an example. Rather, the point of emphasis is simply that the impact of their educational reforms on the growth of population would not be as substantial as they claimed.

5

Educational change was not the only means by which the Commissioners attempted to reform the attitudes and opinions of the Maltese. Austin and Lewis pinned even more of their hopes on abolition of the prevailing system of censorship, for which they had little use. They did not propose, however, to lift all legal restrictions on publications in Malta. Instead, they recommended the enactment of a comprehensive law of criminal libel to replace the censorship. They also drafted the law, which they commented upon in a copious set of notes.[117] Their draft was eventually enacted into law on 15 March 1839.[118] It thus became part of their long-term legacy to Malta.

This law may be the single most important product of the Commissioners' labours for the purpose of understanding Austin's thought. The ordinance reflects certain of his ideas about law that are not evident from his other writings; it discloses how he applied several principles of his legal philosophy to concrete problems; and it illustrates the limitations of some of his ideas about law. The ordinance also illuminates his political thought by indicating how he weighed certain values, such as security for government and freedom of expression. Moreover, knowledge of the law is essential for understanding Austin's relationship to other nineteenth-century British utilitarians. He firmly believed in the utility, for both Malta and England, of a comprehensive law of *political* libel. This belief is symptomatic of the general tenor of his political thought, which was more conservative than that of Bentham or the Benthamites. Austin's attitude toward political, and several other, libels thus illustrates the important differences of opinion that are possible among utilitarians.

The censorship that antedated the proposals of the Commissioners was a classic example of governmental repression. Both the trade of a printer and the operation of a printing press required a licence from the government. The rules for granting licences were very restrictive. Any censure of Her Majesty's government or of any foreign government in amity with it, as well as any discussion of religion, was prohibited. No licences for printing had ever been issued and presses without licences had been confiscated. The effect of the censorship was not only to give the government an effective monopoly of printing, but to suppress the publication of printed writings on a wide range of subjects. They included politics, legislation, morality, and religion. In short, the censorship had been exercised with the 'greatest possible strictness' and in a 'jealous and exclusive spirit'.[119]

Austin and Lewis initially favoured liberalization rather than abolition of this system. They eventually concluded, however, that elimination of the censorship was vastly preferable to any mere reform of the *status quo*.[120] This judgment reflected their profound dissatisfaction with the established system, which they attacked on several grounds. To begin with, they claimed that it combined the evils of censorship and liberty of publication without the advantages of either.[121] Although the importation and publication of works printed abroad was permitted, the publication of domestically printed works by anyone but the government had been effectively suppressed. This suppression tended to undermine public confidence in the colonial government, by exposing it to 'groundless surmises and imputations'. Aside from this, the censorship prevented the diffusion of information which would have been 'most useful to Government and people'.[122] The established system was also responsible for 'much pernicious ignorance, and many mischievous prejudices'. The censorship thus prevented the popular enlightenment which the Commissioners felt to be imperative for the reform of Malta. Finally, they argued that continuation of the censorship was only possible by 'a dishonourable breach of the strong moral obligations [of the British government] to the defenceless people of Malta.'[123] The immediate basis of these obligations was not *expediency*. Rather, it was the *promises* of the British to govern Malta by means analogous to the popular institutions that once existed on the island, which included a free press.

Despite these criticisms of the censorship, the Commissioners expressed no doubt about its legality. In other words, they distinguished sharply between the law as it is and as it ought to be. Their writings reflect, in this respect, a basic principle of Austin's positivist legal philosophy. To be sure, the Commissioners admitted that the censorship had never been explicitly authorized by the British sovereign. Nevertheless, they defended its lawfulness by an argument developed by Austin in *The Province of Jurisprudence Determined*. He claimed that if the sovereign permits his ministers to enact or enforce certain rules, they are a tacit expression of his will. As such, these rules are as legally valid as the explicit commands of the sovereign.[124] Since the British sovereign has permitted the government of Malta to enforce the censorship, it is as lawful as it would have been if he had explicitly commanded it.

> Subject to the control of Parliament, the King in Council, or by his representative the Governor, is the sovereign legislator in Malta. The validity of unwritten law rests upon tacit significances of the sovereign legislator's will; and by permitting the exercise of the existing censorship, His Majesty has established it just as effectively as if he had created it by an express declaration of his pleasure.[125]

While the Commissioners acknowledged the legality of censorship, they were highly critical of it. They also ardently defended the utility of liberty of publication. Their arguments presuppose the traditional conception of this liberty as the absence of *prior restraints* on publication, a notion that had a very solid foundation in British legal theory and practice. In his *Commentaries on the Laws of England*, for example, Sir William Blackstone extolled the value of liberty of the press. He defined it, however, as 'laying no *previous* restraints upon publications, and not in freedom from censure for criminal matter when published'. He argued that 'every freeman has an undoubted right to lay what sentiments he pleases before the public; to forbid this, is to destroy the freedom of the press, but if he publishes what is improper, mischievous, or illegal, he must take the consequence of his own temerity.'[126]

Later scholars have accepted Blackstone's account as an accurate description of the law of England.[127] Indeed, the conception of freedom of the press as the absence of prior restraints was even shared by most seventeenth- and eighteenth-century libertarians.[128] At any rate, the Commissioners' adherence to this idea explains why they believed that their ordinance was perfectly compatible with liberty of publication. Since the restraints that it imposed were *subsequent* rather than *prior* to publication, it left individuals free to publish whatever they desired. Their legal responsibilities for *what* they published in no way restricted their freedom of publication, properly understood. The Commissioners' conception of liberty of the press is ironic, however, in at least one respect. For it means that they employed the same conception of this basic liberty as Sir William Blackstone, the *bête noire* of the utilitarians in general and Austin in particular.

The Commissioners defended the utility of liberty of the press for both the British and their Maltese subjects. Great Britain will benefit from this liberty because it will help to stabilize the political situation on Malta. Otherwise, the people of the Island will not be 'permanently tranquil, and His Majesty's Government will be annoyed by their complaints . . . in the House of Commons.'[129] Liberty of publishing will also tend to foster obedience to law, by reducing the ignorance of it which is prevalent 'in all classes'.[130] Finally, this reform would facilitate control by the Imperial government of its subordinate officials on Malta.

The Commissioners defended the utility of freedom of the press for the people of Malta on various grounds. This liberty would deter the colonial government from the enactment of bad policies, encourage the adoption of beneficial measures, spotlight the misconduct of colonial officials, and help to dispel the widespread ignorance of the Maltese.[131] The Commissioners ascribed the highest importance to this last effect of freedom of the press, which they felt to be indispensable for individual and social progress. Their view was that any 'considerable improvement in the physical and moral condition of the mass of the population must proceed from an antecedent improvement in their opinions, sentiments, and habits.'[132] Indeed, Austin and Lewis were so deeply convinced of the necessity of liberty of publication to achieve this end that they not only recommended abolition of the censorship. They proposed too a number of other steps to foster the *growth* of the press on Malta. These measures included abolition of the entire printing establishment of the government, the discontinuation of the Government Gazette, and governmental assistance to an independent newspaper in the form of advertisements and notices of official actions.[133]

Although the Commissioners enthusiastically defended liberty of publication, they did not regard it as an entirely unmixed blessing. From their point of view it was subject to 'abuses' and had certain 'evils'.[134] Of course, they insisted that the bad effects of this liberty were 'but as dust in the balance when weighed against its advantages'.[135] Still, Austin and Lewis perceived these evils to be more serious than this assertion implies. Otherwise, they would not have drafted a comprehensive criminal law of libel to deter alleged abuses of liberty of publication.

The ordinance itself prohibited the *publication*, or *contributions* to the publication, of certain kinds of *printed writings*. The particular writings that the law prohibited were in general similar to those banned by English law. While the Commissioners were critical of certain aspects of it, they felt that the law of England was the only model from which they could derive 'any considerable assistance'.[136] They explained their general attitude toward it in these terms:

> Having compared the English criminal law of libel with that of several other countries, we thought the English law incomparably the most rational, though open to obvious and generally admitted objections. Accordingly, the provisions of the Ordinance were framed by analogy to those of the English law. We selected such of these as appeared to be applicable in Malta, and adapted them . . . to the position and circumstances of the Island.[137]

This attitude helps to explain why the ordinance prohibited five political libels. The most serious of these offences was the publication of any printed writing tending to incite attempts to subvert Her Majesty's government, or acts tending to subvert it. The punishment for this crime was a term of imprisonment not to exceed twenty-four months, which was the longest sentence prescribed in the ordinance. A second political libel consisted of publications tending to incite the use, or threat, of violence to obstruct, or to attempt to obstruct, the administration of the laws. The purpose of this prohibition was to deter publications tending to incite acts that *weakened* the authority of the government, but did not *overthrow* it.[138] Violation of this provision of the law was punishable by a term of imprisonment not to exceed eighteen months.[139]

Although these libels imposed serious limitations on freedom of the press, the Commissioners took the position that these crimes permitted a wide range of political criticism. They pointed out that the law only prohibited inflammatory censure which tended to *incite* acts that *tended* to subvert, or weaken the authority of, the government. All other criticism was permitted as long as it did not have this effect. Even vituperation or ridicule was permissible, though the Commissioners indicated their strong disapproval of it as 'invariably mischievous'. They therefore expressed the paternalistic hope that the Maltese will 'show themselves worthy of the liberty which the Ordinance will introduce amongst them, by severely reprobating every such outbreak of malignant feeling or ignoble taste'.[140]

Whether the first and second political libels would in practice permit a wide range of political criticism is another matter. Nonetheless, the Commissioners expressed the fear that the bulk of the prohibitions of the entire law was 'open to the reproach of excessive laxity, rather than to that of excessive restrictiveness'.[141] If the criticisms developed later in this chapter are acceptable, this opinion says as much about the Commissioners as the law of libel which they drafted. In any case, they justified the wide range of political criticism which they perceived the law to permit on the ground that it would encourage peaceful and legal redress of grievances.[142]

The two offences that have been explained were the most serious of the political libels prohibited by the ordinance. The others were punishable by a term of imprisonment not to exceed twelve months. These crimes included the publication of any printed writing that censured or mentioned disrespectfully the King or Queen. The Commissioners justified this offence on these grounds:

> The prohibition is in keeping with the constitutional and legal maxim which supposes the King incapable of wrong; and is also in keeping with the practice of the Houses of Parliament, by which the acts of the King are ascribed to his ministers and servants. The direct censure in question is hardly consistent with the reverence which is due to the royal office and person; and the permitted criticism o[f] the King's ministers, and others in authority under him, is a sufficient check upon misgovernment.[143]

Another political libel prohibited untrue imputations of specific misconduct on the part of public officials. The truth of the imputation was a valid defence, thus, to the charge of libelling a *public official*. This offence was the only libel specified in the ordinance which permitted this defence. The Commissioners justified this exception on the ground that its benefits in this instance outweighed its disadvantages. Their argument was that true imputations of misconduct by public officials tend 'to prevent the recurrence of similar mischiefs'.[144]

The final political libel had a different focus than any of the others. This offence prohibited any publication that reviled, ridiculed, or insulted the head of a sovereign government, or anyone in high office under it, which was 'in amity' with Her Majesty's government. The publication of any writing that tended to incite subversive or violent acts against sovereign governments in amity with Her Majesty's government was also prohibited.[145]

This crime implied that the Maltese were freer to criticize their own government than many foreign governments. The Commissioners were aware of this anomaly, but stressed that the people of Malta did not view these prohibitions as 'unreasonably severe'.[146] Austin and Lewis also emphasized that the British government was obligated to protect its allies from the words, or acts, in question. They maintained too that the right of the Maltese to criticize British foreign policy is not of crucial importance:

> What is needed for the improvement of Malta (and even for the immediate satisfaction of the great majority of the Maltese) is not so much the freedom of commenting upon foreign politics, as the freedom of discussing political institutions of the island, the spirit and manner in which the Government is administered, the economical condition and interests of its inhabitants, and the opinions, sentiments, and habits prevalent amongst them.[147]

This passage is an excellent illustration of the Commissioners' rationale for freedom of the press. Despite their conviction that it was essential for the improvement of Malta, the question remains of *how much* freedom of political discussion the ordinance actually permitted. Austin and Lewis maintained that it allowed a wider range of political criticism than the law on-the-books of their own country. If Sir James Fitzjames Stephen's interpretation of English law is accurate, their contention was justified. His account implies that almost any persuasive criticism of government would be punishable as a seditious libel. The essence of this offence was the publication of any words or documents with a seditious intention, which included the intention 'to raise discontent or disaffection amongst Her Majesty's subjects, or to promote feelings of ill-will and hostility between different classes of Her Majesty's subjects.'[148] Since virtually any persuasive criticism of the government could be construed to have this intention, it was subject to prosecution as a seditious libel. The ordinance drafted by the Commissioners prohibited, however, a much narrower range of publications than this. They were therefore warranted in claiming that it permitted more freedom of political criticism than the English law that was on-the-books.

This does *not* mean that the ordinance would be *in practice* more permissive than the law of England. Indeed, the Commissioners expected that their law of libel 'will afford practically more protection to the government, and to the persons concerned in administering it', than the analogous provisions of the English law. The basis of this expectation was the belief that the ordinance corresponded to the dictates of Maltese public opinion and would therefore be enforced. Since the formal prohibitions of the English law of political libel lack this support, it is

> rarely enforced . . . even in regard to the political libels which call the most urgently for penal preventions and restraints. In consequence of its extending to cases which it ought not to embrace, there is an indisposition in the public, and even in the government, to enforce it in the cases which it justly includes. As is usual, the excessive rigour of the law leads to universal impunity; or, rather, to something which is more pernicious than universal impunity itself. The law is enforced rarely and capriciously, and, therefore, uselessly and vexatiously; whilst the great majority of offenders escape chastisement, though richly meriting the punishments which the law annexes to their offences.[149]

This passage is a very clear indication of the Commissioners' attitude toward the English law of political libel. Their outlook indicates that Austin's appraisal of its utility had changed substantially since 1824. His first publication was a critique of primogeniture in which he expressed disapproval of such laws. Although he did not explicitly mention England, he was quite obviously referring to it when he wrote that by 'the judge-made law of libel, which would probably obtain in such a country, any censure, merited or unmerited, upon any body or any thing, would, strictly speaking, be criminal: and so often as it was thought discreet to apply this handy instrument, censure upon the ruling few would be visited with appalling punishment.'[150] A long footnote toward the end of his article provides even clearer evidence that at this stage of his life Austin had no use for criminal laws of political libel. For one thing, he pointed out the inconsistent application of the English law. 'Of all the tools of the oligarchy, counting from Burke downward, who have employed their talents, great or small, in traducing the mass of mankind, not one, most certainly, has been punished as for libel on the people.'[151] For another thing, Austin praised the absence of legal restraints on the expression of political opinions in the United States. In this country, where the *people reign*, the partizans of the federalist or aristocratical faction have ever vented their spleen and abuse with perfect impunity. Whilst that faction was in authority, they passed a Libel Law, which the democratical party, on their accession to power, might have used as a weapon against their adversaries. But with the wisdom and magnanimity peculiar to popular counsels, they disdained the poor advantage; and one of the first acts of Mr Jefferson's glorious administration was, to repeal the odious Law, and *to permit that unbounded censure* of public men and measures which has ever since been exercised by writers of all parties[152] (emphasis added).

These ideas indicate that in 1824 Austin shared Jeremy Bentham's hostility toward the English law of political or seditious libel. The absence of this offence in the United States was one of the numerous reasons for his most favourable impression of the American republic. Bentham's praise of this aspect of American law reflected, if it did not reinforce, his profound conviction of the evils of seditious libel. To begin with, this crime is an indefinable offence which amounts in practice to 'the publishing, respecting a man in power, anything which he does not like'.[153] Aside from this, the law of libel as it stands is 'incompatible with English liberties'.[154] If it were 'half executed', the people 'remaining out of jail would not be enough to guard those that were in'.[155] If the law were fully and consistently enforced, English liberties would be destroyed and the government would be a 'despotism'.[156] The result would be the 'extirpation of the inhabitants . . . the conversion of all dwellings into jails'.[157] Furthermore, the law of political libel undermines essential restraints against misrule. The only way to prevent, remedy, or check misgovernment is by means that 'have a tendency to lower either the managing heads, or the system, or both, in the affection and estimation of the people. When this effect is produced to a high degree, it may be termed bringing them into hatred and contempt.'[158] Publications that have this effect are, however, subject to prosecution as seditious libels. Finally, this offence presupposes the 'sham' distinction between liberty and licence of the press. The latter is simply a term for 'every disclosure by the press of any abuse from the practice of which they [rulers] derive any advantage', while the former is 'only such disclosure as will occasion them no apprehension of inconvenience'.[159]

These criticisms underlie Bentham's strong commitment to freedom of the press. Yet, he did not claim that it should be completely exempt from legal liability for criticisms of public officials. Although no one should be subject to criminal prosecution for publishing seditious libels, defamation ought to be a civil cause of action. If 'false facts' are alleged in support of unjust imputations, 'the act of him who makes such false allegations not only ought to be regarded as pernicious, but ought to be, and is, consistently with justice and utility, punishable.'[160] Bentham elaborated upon the rationale of this position in this way:

> If you fail in the proof, you may be punished for the injury, by being obliged to pay money on that account to the individual injured: and it is right you should be so, if you had not before you a reasonable ground for believing the imputation: much more, if you are conscious of the falsity of it. In this there would be nothing but what is right: for though he is neither a vice-god, nor a magnate, the person is an individual, and an individual whom you have injured.[161]

While Bentham supported civil redress for defamatory libels of public officials, he restricted the scope of such actions in several respects. To begin with, he insisted that the truth of the imputation should be a defence against this cause of action. Moreover, he maintained that a defendant should be able 'to extract evidence from the person who is the subject of it [the libel], as he might from any other person at large'.[162] Finally, Bentham argued that proof of malice is necessary for recovery. In other words, he adumbrated to an incredible extent the doctrine developed in 1964 by the Supreme Court for libels of public officials. The Court specifically held that constitutional guarantees prohibit 'a public official from recovering damages for a defamatory falsehood relating to his official conduct unless he proves that the statement was made with "actual malice" – that is, with knowledge that it was false or with reckless disregard of whether it was false or not.'[163] Bentham's position was virtually identical to the Court's interpretation of the Constitution. He argued that a false assertion or insinuation against public functionaries should not be libellous unless it is 'the result of willful mendacity, accompanied with the consciousness of its falsity, or else with culpable rashness'.[164]

Bentham extolled, at any rate, the utility of freedom of the press. He viewed it as an indispensable security for good government and 'the foundation of all other liberties'.[165] He was also the author of the 'broadest statement on the scope of political expression that anyone had ever or could ever make'.[166] At the least, Bentham interpreted the liberty of the press and public association very broadly. The former consists of the 'security with which every man, be he of the one class or the other, may make known his complaints and remonstrances to the whole community'. The latter is the 'security with which malcontents may communicate their sentiments, concert their plans, and practice *every mode of opposition short of actual revolt*, before the executive power can be legally justified in disturbing them'[167] (emphasis added).

Bentham thus advocated a much greater liberty of publication than Austin believed, in 1837, to be desirable *for England*. His position on this issue was also much less libertarian than that of James Mill or John Stuart Mill.[168] These differences are not only significant because they indicate that Austin became more conservative than Bentham or either of the Mills. In addition, their disagreement vividly illustrates the wide differences of opinion that are possible among utilitarians, or that a single utilitarian may express at different stages of his life. Both Austin and Bentham took the classic utilitarian position that liberty is not an end-in-itself or intrinsically good. Rather, it must be evaluated on the basis of its efficacy as a means to advance general utility.[169] Their disagreement about the value of the liberty of the press as a means to achieve this end was, however, very great. Furthermore, Austin's evaluation of the utility of limitations on liberty of the press changed substantially in the course of his life.

These considerations illustrate how much the application of the principle of utility depends upon judgments of fact about which different persons, or the same person at different times, may reach different conclusions. To say this is not to suggest that these disparate conclusions are equally well-founded in the facts, which they may not be. Nor is it to imply that utilitarianism is an unsatisfactory ethical theory. The general principle which is *not* subject to different interpretations, at least as applied to some situations, is rare. The implication is, rather, that the principle of utility is subject to the same limitation in this regard as most other general principles.

6

Although the ordinance drafted by the Commissioners included five political libels, it also imposed criminal liability for the publication of certain non-political writings. One of these offences was blasphemous libel, or the publication of printed writings that reviled, ridiculed, or insulted an essential or basic doctrine of Christianity or any Christian church. The ordinance also banned this kind of censure of the government, discipline, rituals, or religious observances of any Christian church.[170] Despite this language, the underlying purpose of this libel was not to protect the Christian religion in general or *all* Christian churches from censure. Rather, it was to deter published insults of the Roman Catholic Church.

The Commissioners justified the utility of this libel on a number of different grounds. To begin with, they argued that the people of Malta fervently desired this protection. Almost all of them were ardent Catholics who would be profoundly 'wounded and offended by contemptuous attacks upon their religion'. Austin and Lewis also maintained that the British government was morally obligated to protect the Catholic Church on Malta from published insults. The basis of this obligation was its promise 'to protect the natives in the unmolested enjoyment of their religion'.[171] The Commissioners claimed, too, that 'whoever feels the reverence with which so awful a subject ought to be approached, will admit that religious doctrines ought to be protected from insult, although he may not admit that they ought to be protected from argument.' Besides this, Austin and Lewis maintained that this protection will facilitate achievement of the purpose which renders freedom of religious discussion 'useful' and 'desirable'. This objective is 'the advancement and diffusion of religious truth'.[172]

Although this libel appears to be very repressive, the Commissioners did not view it in this light. Instead, they argued that it would permit a large amount of freedom of religious discussion. In particular, the ordinance would permit 'serious' and 'decorous' published criticism of Christianity.[173] The Commissioners therefore argued that the ordinance was more permissive than the English law of blasphemous libel. If they were referring to the law which was on-the-books rather than the law which was enforced, their contention was well-founded.[174] At any rate, the Commissioners were critical of the prohibition of *any* published criticism of the Catholic religion. They argued that such a broad limitation would not only be counter-productive and unenforceable, but would expose the people of Malta to ridicule.[175]

The punishment for this offence was a term of imprisonment not to exceed twelve months. The same sanction was specified for the publication of any obscene writing,[176] the nature of which was not defined in either the ordinance or notes of the Commissioners. The ordinance also imposed criminal liability for the publication of any writing tending to incite 'unlawful violence to a person in a private capacity', or the property of such a person. Conviction of this libel was punishable by a term of imprisonment not to exceed eighteen months.[177]

The final libel was one of the most controversial of all of the offences prohibited by the ordinance. This crime consisted of the publication of any printed writing which *reviled*, *ridiculed*, *insulted*, or *censured* any person in a private capacity.[178] If the publication tended to defame a person, the offender was subject to a term of imprisonment not to exceed twelve months. The Commissioners defined defamation as the 'total or partial loss of good fame or reputation'.[179] If the publication tended only to wound or injure a person's feelings, the sanction was imprisonment for not more than six months.[180]

The extraordinary amount of protection that this libel provided is evident from numerous considerations, including the Commissioners' very broad interpretation of 'censure'. While neither the law nor their notes contained a definition of the term, they apparently interpreted its meaning to be equivalent to any kind of criticism. The Commissioners pointed out, for example, that published censures of persons in a private capacity would be libellous '*whatever . . . the nature or form of the censure*: whether the censure be serious or ironical; be express or implied; consist of an imputation of general misconduct, or of an imputation of misconduct in a specific instance or instances'[181] (emphasis added). Furthermore, the truth was no defence to a prosecution for this libel. Finally, it extended criminal liability to published censure of a person that injured his feelings without defaming him.

This libel would virtually prohibit, thus, *any* published criticism of a person in a private capacity. Persons in this capacity were therefore insulated from criticism to a much greater extent than were persons in a public capacity. Published criticisms of them were libellous only if the imputations of misconduct were false and specific, requirements that need not be satisfied to establish criminal liability for published censures of persons in a private capacity. Although the Commissioners were fully aware of these differences between the two libels, they claimed that the feelings and reputations of persons in a private capacity deserved the 'most jealous protection'.[182]

Austin and Lewis justified this position on various grounds. For one thing, the Maltese wanted the maximum possible protection for persons in a private capacity. For another thing, the effects of published criticisms on the feelings of persons in a public *and* private capacity were very different. The 'wound' inflicted by such censures on the former is 'comparatively slight',[183] while the damage to the feelings of persons in a private capacity is substantial. In addition, the ordinance's libel of a person in this capacity was 'scarcely more comprehensive than . . . the analogous provisions of the English Criminal Law'. The Commissioners also emphasized that the particular circumstances of Malta required strong protection for published censures of private persons. Libels of their private reputation 'would give intense pain to the injured persons. The liability to such attacks would keep the higher classes in continual anxiety.' The density of the population of the Island no doubt influenced the weight which Austin and Lewis attached to this 'conclusive consideration'.[184]

Finally, the Commissioners maintained that no countervailing good to the public outweighed these evil effects of published censure, true or false, of persons in a private capacity. This fact is the major reason why their rationale for allowing truth as a defence to an alleged libel of a public official did not apply, they argued, to libels of persons in a private capacity. Although the availability of the defence was a useful deterrent to misconduct by the former, it had no such effect on the latter. Unlike Bentham, the Commissioners claimed that persons would not be deterred from misconduct in their private lives by fear of the adverse reaction of public opinion. In fact, individuals tend to 'despise and defy so shallow and unfair a tribunal'. The source of the effective restraints on private misconduct is, rather, the law, the individual's religious and moral sentiments, and the 'opinion of the narrower public which is formed of his family and friends'.[185]

7

It is one thing to draft an ordinance that imposes criminal liability for the publication of certain printed writings. It is another thing to prescribe how the prohibitions of such a law are to be enforced. The very brief final chapter of the ordinance had as its focus this last problem. If this portion of the law reflected any single theme, it was the belief of the Commissioners that it was 'highly expedient that the Ordinance *should* be rigidly enforced'[186] (emphasis added). They were also convinced that it *would* be strictly enforced. The basis of this conviction was their belief that public opinion on Malta supported both the substantive prohibitions and the sanctions of the law. At least the Commissioners took this position for the political libels that they drafted. In their words:

> We have endeavoured to frame a law of political libel, which, owing to the nature of the offences embraced by it, and to the moderation of its penalties, the government would be enabled to enforce with the concurrence of public opinion. The publications embraced by these five sections . . . are manifestly mischievous to the public; whilst the highest penalties annexed to them are not immoderate, and may be mitigated by the court. It appears to us, therefore, that the law would be enforced with the concurrence of public opinion; and that the public would generally incline to aid in the enforcement of it.[187]

The Commissioners recommended various institutions and practices for the enforcement of the ordinance. Its most important provision in this respect was the vesting of exclusive jurisdiction to try cases of libel in her Majesty's Criminal Court.[188] As a result, no cases under the law would be tried by juries. The ordinance fundamentally differed in this respect from the English criminal law of libel. The right of a defendant in a libel case to a trial by jury long antedated the enactment of Fox's Libel Law in 1792. This statute firmly and unambiguously established, however, the power of juries in libel cases to give 'a general verdict of guilty or not guilty upon the whole matter put in issue upon . . . indictment and information.'[189] The exclusion of trial by jury from the ordinance would also have evoked the strong censure of Sir William Blackstone. He extolled the jury as the 'glory of the English law', and 'the most transcendent privilege which any subject can enjoy'.[190] Even Jeremy Bentham might have been displeased by the absence of jury trials in cases of libel. Of course, he was much more critical of this institution than Blackstone. Indeed, trial by jury in its traditional form would not exist in Bentham's ideal republic. Nevertheless, he believed that in actually existing states this institution was a necessary evil in criminal cases. For it furnishes the only available 'counter-force' to the temptation of judges to identify with the prosecution.[191]

Unlike England, trial by jury was of very recent origin in Malta. The institution was apparently introduced for the first time in 1829. At any rate, the Commissioners were well aware that their exclusion of this mode of trial would be controversial. They therefore justified its unavailability by various arguments, including the contention that no Maltese jury would try persons indicted for libel with 'due impartiality'.[192] Since jurors would be selected from a very small proportion of the population, they would be so familiar with the defendant that a fair trial would be impossible. Trials for libel would also be likely to involve highly emotional events that would evoke the prejudices of jurors.[193]

Austin and Lewis did not contend that Maltese judges would be totally impartial. Rather, the argument was that they would be 'likely to evince a greater degree of impartiality than would probably be shown by the best constituted jury'. On the one hand, jurors are not responsible to public opinion. If they are influenced by it, they are affected by the 'crude opinion of the cause which the public entertains at the moment of the trial'. On the other hand, judges are subject to public observation and criticism. They therefore are 'chiefly regardful of the sound opinion of the cause which the public will probably arrive at on calm and deliberate reflection'. Unlike jurors, judges are also subject to various checks on their decisions. These restraints include the publicity of the trial, the duty to articulate the reasons for their decisions, and the criticisms of a free press. The Commissioners expressed the hope that the 'pains . . . taken to explain the spirit of the Ordinance, would render it difficult for them [the judges] to warp the letter of it to purposes of injustice.'[194]

The notes of the Commissioners do not explain *how* they believed that Maltese jurors would be prejudiced. The files of the Colonial Office express, however, the fear of the Commissioners that jurors would be too lenient. 'We made this provision under a conviction', they wrote, 'that if offences against the law of libel were submitted to trial by jury, the restrictions imposed by the law upon the liberty of publication would be rendered nugatory in practice.'[195] Indeed, Austin and Lewis took the position that these restrictions would become so inoperative that the censorship would be restored.[196]

These criticisms raise the intriguing question of whether Austin believed that trial by jury in England was as objectionable as he thought it would have been in Malta. The answer to this question is not certain because the situation of Malta was obviously very different from that of England. No long-established tradition of trial by jury existed on the Island; the rate of illiteracy was much higher than it was in England; and the proportion of the population of Malta which would be eligible for jury service was much lower than it was in Austin's native country. The possibility of a fair trial would thus be arguably greater in the one country than in the other. It is therefore conceivable that Austin might have endorsed for England that which he censured on Malta. The chances are, however, that the Commissioner's objections to trial by jury reflect Austin's overall evaluation of this institution.

This interpretation draws support from numerous considerations, including the applicability of at least one of the Commissioners' criticisms of trial by jury on Malta to England. While a larger proportion of the English people were eligible for jury service than would have been the case in Malta, English jurors were no more responsible to public opinion than Maltese jurors would have been. The former were also as likely to be influenced by the 'crude opinion' of the case as the latter. Besides this, English judges were subject to at least as many checks as Maltese judges.

Furthermore, Austin specifically criticized trial by jury in *The Province of Jurisprudence Determined*. In particular, he was critical of jury lawlessness or nullification.[197] He also was well aware of the *de facto* power of juries to determine questions of both law and fact. In a vein rather similar to the position of the late Judge Jerome N. Frank,[198] Austin disputed the view that the jury judged only the facts. It is 'only necessary to look at the terms of the finding', he claimed, 'to see that this maxim is false. Generally, and *notoriously*, the jury is judge of law as well as of fact'[199] (emphasis added).

The evidence that Austin was critical of trial by jury in England as well as Malta is, thus, quite convincing. The most fundamental reason for his dissatisfaction with it was its tendency to defeat an end to which he attached the greatest importance. His commitment to the value of legal certainty could not have been stronger.[200] Achievement of this objective required strict enforcement of established law, of which Austin was also a staunch proponent. For him, trial by jury is objectionable because it tends to nullify such enforcement. Instead of enforcing the law, jurors tend to enforce their individual conceptions of fairness or justice.

Despite Austin's attitude toward strict enforcement and legal certainty, the ordinance vested a substantial amount of sentencing discretion in judges. The law only specified the maximum possible term of imprisonment for offenders and did not prescribe any minimum term. The Commissioners justified this omission on the ground that flexibility of sentencing was required by the 'incessant variations' in the population of the prison.[201] The ordinance also authorized judges to impose two punishments as alternatives to imprisonment alone. One was incarceration for less than the maximum *and* a fine, while the other was a fine.[202] The law specified that these sanctions must be 'equivalent' to the punishment which would be inflicted 'as of course', i.e., imprisonment.[203] The notes of the Commissioners set forth a purely hedonistic standard of equivalency. It was whether the pain caused by the alternative punishments was equivalent to the pain produced by imprisonment alone. This standard required, Austin and Lewis maintained, some flexibility in sentences available to the court. Imprisonment alone 'might occasionally produce a pain which would far exceed the suffering usually caused by it; and, consequently, which would far exceed the suffering intended by the law'.[204] One example was a person whose health was so poor that he would be destroyed by imprisonment, while another was an individual whose affairs would be ruined by such a punishment.

Despite this, the ordinance did not contain a schedule of fines. The Commissioners justified its absence on the ground that such a system 'falling equally on rich and poor, could hardly be contrived'. Indeed, it was for this reason that incarceration was to be the normal mode of punishment under the ordinance. Even so, Austin and Lewis did furnish a utilitarian guideline for the amount of the fine to be imposed. It should be 'proportioned to the pecuniary means probably possessed by the defendant; so that the pain from the substituted fine may equal the pain from the commuted imprisonment.' If the amount of the fine were the same for all offenders, then this punishment would be much less painful to a comparatively rich criminal than to a relatively poor one. The former might experience almost no inconvenience, while the latter would be subject to an 'incalculable weight of sufferings'.[205]

8

A full understanding of the ordinance requires an explanation of its strengths and weaknesses. Of course, right-minded men and women are unlikely to agree in their assessments of the law. The question of *whether*, or *how much*, liberty of publishing should be restricted to protect other values is highly debatable. The problem of freedom and its limitation is, after all, one of the great issues of politics and political theory. Still, even controversial assessments of the ordinance are preferable to none.

To begin with, some of the limitations that it imposed on liberty of publication were unduly repressive. The excessive amount of protection that the law furnished for the *feelings* of a person in a private capacity is a good example. The argument that this protection was no greater than that of the analogous provisions of English law does not appear to be well-founded. At least this contention presupposes an interpretation of the English law of libel which Lord Brougham rejected. The ordinance elicited a substantial amount of discussion in the House of Lords. None of the critics of the law assailed it more vigorously than Brougham. The former Lord Chancellor indicted the ordinance as 'full of the grossest, the most monstrous, and most incredible absurdities'.[206] He believed that such a 'mass of blunders . . . had never been known to modern legislation'.[207] The gravamen of his complaint was that the press was much less free after the enactment of the law than it had been under the censorship, which was 'ten times more harmless' than the ordinance.[208]

Brougham adduced various arguments to support this charge, one of which was the difference between the ordinance and the English law of defamatory libel. 'The homely language' of the latter 'merely extended', he claimed, 'to that which actually defamed, to that which lowered the estimation in which a man was held, to that whereby his reputation was tarnished, or his character damaged in the eyes of the public.'[209] In short, the English law of libel furnished no protection for the mere feelings of a person.

The ordinance is also open to the objection that judges would have a vast amount of discretion in the interpretation and application of its provisions, a power that is subject to abuse. This discretion is not only evident from the judges' wide range of choice in the sentencing of convicted offenders. In addition, it is apparent from the vagueness of certain key provisions of the ordinance. One example is the term 'tending to incite', a crucial element in the definition of the most serious political libels. Although the notes of the Commissioners attempted to clarify the meaning of this formula, they acknowledged that determination of the probability that a published writing will incite the specified mischief will depend on 'the particularities of the case; and since the particularities . . . cannot be anticipated by general provisions, the tendency of the publication will be a question of fact which the court will decide according to its discretion.'[210]

A second example of vague terminology is the libel for *obscene* publications. The Commissioners made no attempt to clarify the meaning of this term, the ambiguity of which is notorious. In fact, their notes contain no discussion whatsoever of this particular libel. A third example is the imprecision of the line that separates insults of the Christian religion from serious and decorous criticism of it. While language may be cited that is easily classifiable as the one or the other, borderline cases would certainly exist. The number of such cases is larger than usual because of the highly emotional character of much religious discussion. The classification of some words as insults or permissible criticism might therefore vary considerably among the judges.

In defence of the Commissioners, they candidly acknowledged that the leading notions and terms of a law of libel are 'extremely vague'.[211] They maintained, however, that this vagueness was not a valid reason for criticism of the ordinance. They pointed out, for example, that their notes to the law imparted to its leading ideas and words 'the degree of precision of which they are susceptible'.[212] Although the Commissioners did not specify *how much* precision was possible, they must have believed that it was large. Otherwise, they would have been unlikely to write thirty-seven pages of notes attempting to clarify the terminology of the law.

This argument raises the question of the extent to which the notes of the Commissioners actually reduced the 'extreme vagueness' of the leading notions and terms of their law of libel. If the criticisms of it that have been explained are satisfactory, their efforts in this direction were far from being entirely successful. Their lack of success is also indicative of a broader weakness in Austin's philosophy of law. While he recognized that even the best code would contain an irreducible element of vagueness, he thought that the amount of it would be very limited. His draft of the ordinance implies that a greater degree of vagueness than he expected is probable. Either codification would not be as effective a tool to reduce legal uncertainty as he anticipated, or he and Lewis were very inept legislative draughtsmen. Finally, there is no guarantee that the judges who had to construe and apply the law would be bound by the Commissioners' interpretation of it.

The Commissioners emphatically denied, in any case, the likelihood that the judges would abuse their powers. To be sure, Austin and Lewis admitted that the substantial amount of judicial discretion *might* be abused in certain cases. They included prosecutions for libels upon the Christian religion, persons in a private capacity, and the person or persons at the head of or in high office under governments in amity with the British government. The Commissioners denied, however, the *probability* that judges would abuse their powers. Austin and Lewis justified their position on these grounds:

> Every law of libel is open to a similar objection, in consequence of the vagueness with which it is inevitably expressed. In the next place, every prosecution for an offence against the Ordinance will be instituted by the Government; and the Government is not only checked by the public opinion of England and Malta, but has little

> inducement to abuse its powers in cases of offences against the provisions in question. Probably, therefore, it will rarely prosecute an offender against any of these provisions, who shall not have offended against the spirit as well as the letter of the law.[213]

These arguments are not very convincing. The capacity of public opinion *in England* to check prosecutions or convictions for alleged libels *in Malta* is remote at best. Although the possibility for Maltese public opinion to check prosecutorial or judicial power is greater, it is not likely to be very great. Public opinion can be a powerful restraint upon a government which is elected by and accountable to the people, or a significant portion of them. The government of Malta was not, however, of this type. The assumption that it would have little or no inducement to abuse its powers is also subject to very serious question. Prosecutors and judges are, after all, a part of the establishment. Their judgment that critics of the regime should be prosecuted or convicted may not be entirely disinterested. In fact, this decision may be consciously or unconsciously influenced by the consideration that the criticism was unflattering, embarrassing, or otherwise damaging to those in power. To this extent, persons may be prosecuted or convicted not so much for violating the law as for offending the high and the mighty. William Wickwar has drawn this lesson from his study of the English law of political libel, and it is applicable to Malta as well. According to Wickwar:

> The English law of State libel . . . was too sweeping to draw any certain line between liberty and licentiousness. The administration of that law was exceedingly uncertain, and . . . became still more so as time went on. One thing was certain, and that was that that law sprang from the natural dislike of opposition which has been common to almost all who have ever ruled.[214]

If the rulers of Malta shared this dislike, the tilt of the ordinance toward the prosecution put them in a strong position to enforce it. One example of this bias is the provision that indictments need not specify the prohibitions of the ordinance that were allegedly violated.[215] A second example is the absence of trial by jury. At least it was the view of Lord Brougham that this mode of trial was essential for securing a free press. He asserted that if 'he had wished for the abolition of the liberty of the press, he would require no readier means of attaining that object than the abolition of jury trial in libel cases.'[216]

Brougham emphasized that since all cases under the ordinance would be tried by a judge removable by the Crown, 'the very evil would exist which formed the great objection to a censorship'.[217] This consideration was one reason for his contention that the ordinance in effect restored the censorship on the pretence of abolishing it.

Although Brougham's criticisms are hyperbolical, none of the arguments by which the Commissioners defended the absence of trial by jury is convincing. Of course, it is difficult to know with certainty how jury trials would have functioned on Malta in 1839. Even so, at least some evidence does not support the conclusion drawn by the Commissioners. In 1832 the Chief Justice of Malta delivered an address in which he maintained that denial of the ability of the natives of Malta to serve as jurors was a 'calumny'. According to Sir John Stoddart, the verdicts rendered since trial by jury was introduced in 1829 'have been as satisfactory . . . as any equal number of verdicts taken indiscriminately in any Court in England, ever were to English judges or to the English public.'[218] Indeed, even Austin and Lewis did not criticize the verdicts which juries had reached on Malta since 1829. If these verdicts had been outrageous, the Commissioners certainly would have emphasized that fact. Instead, they argued that the number of cases tried by juries was insufficient to provide a sound basis for evaluating this mode of trial.

These criticisms indicate that the ordinance did not permit as much liberty of publication as was desirable. Although it is difficult to be certain how much liberty would have been acceptable to the British government, the Commissioners could have appealed to English legal *practice* in order to justify a more permissive ordinance if they had been inclined to do so. The infrequent enforcement of the English law of political libel could have been cited as a reason for a very narrow definition of these offences. A much narrower libel of a person in a private capacity than the ordinance prescribed also could have been justified by an appeal to English law. Then, too, the Commissioners could have defended trial by jury on the basis of English practice.

These possibilities raise the question of why the Commissioners did not draft a more permissive ordinance. Their unwillingness to do so may have been influenced by two considerations, one of which was their ascription of more importance to security for certain values than to liberty of publication. It is for this reason that the ordinance illuminates Austin's political thought, or at least hierarchy of political values. Laws of libel inescapably reflect a weighing of the competing values which they are designed to protect. The law of libel drafted by the Commissioners is no exception. Although Austin believed that liberty of publication was important, he also felt that it was not as important as certain other values. If the exercise of this liberty threatened these values, limitations on it were therefore justifiable.

Another factor may also have affected the kind of ordinance that the Commissioners drafted. This consideration was the tension, if not incompatibility, between the different objectives that they entertained for it. The law that they drafted was designed both to eliminate the evils of the established system *and* 'to a great extent . . . accomplish the purposes of the censorship'.[219] The Commissioners argued, for example, that under the ordinance the Catholic Church will receive 'a more ample protection than it derives from the Government monopoly and censorship'.[220] Unlike the censorship, the law of libel protected the Church from published libels imported into Malta. To the degree that a law of libel achieves the same purposes as the censorship, however, it is subject to the same criticisms. If the one is pernicious, which the Commissioners insisted it was, then so is the other. They were no more able than anyone else, in short, both to have their cake and eat it too.

These criticisms do *not* imply, however, that the ordinance was wholly undesirable. In fact, it represented a substantial improvement over the censorship. If the law did not permit as much liberty of publication as was desirable, it permitted a vastly greater amount than existed under the censorship. Its abolition was bound to increase the amount and variety of published criticism and discussion of public officials, politics, religion, economics, morality, and other matters. Moreover, a number of the strictly penal provisions of the ordinance are enlightened. The maximum terms of imprisonment that it authorized were vastly shorter, for example, than those which were *possible* under the English law of libel. Lord Campbell testified in 1843 that a judgment, 'though unjust, would not be erroneous whereby for the Offence of Libel the Defendant should be sentenced to Twenty Years Imprisonment'.[221] According to Lord Brougham, an even longer sentence was legally possible. 'It would be no Error upon the Record', he testified, if 'Forty Years Imprisonment were to be given for a Libel.'[222] Although in practice such obviously unjust sentences were not in fact imposed, the Commissioners were wise to draft a law under which such draconian punishments were impossible. If their recommendations were accepted by those who enforced the law, the likelihood of lengthy incarceration before trial would also be reduced.

No fair evaluation of the ordinance can disregard, either, the imposing difficulties that the Commissioners faced. The political context in which they operated limited to some extent the kind of law that they could draft, if it were to stand any chance of adoption. Also, some of the conditions on Malta were not conducive to the maximization of liberty of publication. The density of the population, its inexperience with the operation of an uncensored press, the absence of religious pluralism, and the demands of the Maltese clergy for heavy restraints on the press are some of the most important examples. While the latter expressed approval of liberty of publication, they insisted that ' "every printed attack, direct or indirect, upon the Catholic, Apostolic, Roman Religion, as determined by the sacred canons of the Church . . . be prohibited under the severest penalties." '[223] Nor can the relatively brief period of time which the Commissioners had to draft a law on a very complex subject be ignored. The lack of a statutory model of a comprehensive law of libel in the English language is important, too. It meant that the Commissioners had to start virtually from 'scratch', which is not easy. It is obviously much easier, also, to criticize a statute than it is to draft one. In fact, the difficulty of the task that the Commissioners faced was admitted even by Lord Brougham. Despite his savage critique of the ordinance, he concluded his discussion of it by pointing out that this

> was the first time, that there had been any attempt to make a code of the libel laws. It was easy to pick holes in the first step, but it was not so easy to take the first step itself: and he gave the full benefit of that observation to the Commissioners, who had succeeded moderately, though only moderately in their first attempt, which it was impossible could have been absolutely perfect.[224]

These judgments imply that the ordinance was a praiseworthy step, under the circumstances, in the right direction. It was also a course of action that took some courage for the Commissioners to recommend. At least their recommendation subjected them to criticism in high places. The Duke of Wellington, for example, bitterly assailed their proposal. He attacked the introduction of liberty of publication in Malta as 'wholly unnecessary', 'greatly unbecoming', 'dangerous', 'fraught with evil', and 'disgraceful'.[225] The 'Iron Duke' could not have been blunter in explaining the rationale of British control of Malta. It is an English settlement 'the business of which must be carried on for the safety of this country *and for nothing else*'[226] (emphasis added). If he is correct, 'we might as well think of planting a free press on the fore deck of the admiral's flagship in the Mediterranean, or in the casernes of the batteries of Gibraltar, or in the camp of Sir John Colborne in Canada, as of establishing it in Malta.'[227]

The Duke of Wellington was probably not the only British political figure who held these views. The Prime Minister – Lord Melbourne – asserted that 'persons of great weight, influence, and power, viewed this matter with very considerable alarm'.[228] Commissioners who felt this 'alarm' would never have recommended abolition of the censorship, which was a desirable course of action. As such, it typified most of the recommendations of the Commissioners for the reform of Malta. Despite the limitations of some of their proposals, their recommendations constituted a comprehensive, carefully designed, and beneficial programme of reform.

6 *A defence of the British Constitution*

No informed scholar would deny the importance of John Austin for the development of English jurisprudence and the philosophy of law. It is therefore not surprising that this dimension of his thought is the subject of extensive critical discussion. At the same time, the various ideas that he developed on other topics have received very little scholarly attention, which is surprising. Although his views on these matters are not as significant as his legal philosophy, they deserve closer examination than they have traditionally received. These ideas include not only the changes that he proposed for Malta, but his opposition to the reform of Parliament.

Unlike his philosophy of law, some of Austin's political ideas changed drastically in the course of his life. Nothing illustrates the point better than his evaluation of the British aristocracy and the need for parliamentary reform. In 1819 he expressed his intention to be an ardent preacher of the gospel of Benthamism.[1] In 1824 he published his first article and denounced primogeniture for, among other things, its support of the British aristocracy.[2] His last publication was *A Plea for the Constitution*, a pamphlet that appeared in 1859.[3] It involved a defence of aristocratic power that would have aroused either Jeremy Bentham or James Mill from the slumbers of death, if that were possible. The same is true of Austin's praise of the 'matchless union of order and liberty' of the present 'incomparable Constitution', *any* reform of which he opposed.[4] Indeed, he extolled its virtues in terms which Edmund Burke, William Paley, and Sir William Blackstone would applaud.[5]

Austin's critique of reform is not important because it is remarkably cogent, a virtue that it does not possess. Instead, his pamphlet is significant for a number of other reasons. To begin with, it is a good statement of the 'worst-case' scenario for the effects of reform. At least this was the reaction of John Stuart Mill to *A Plea for the Constitution*. Despite his disagreement with Austin's conclusions, Mill praised his pamphlet as an exposition by

> probably the most intellectual man who is an enemy to further reform [of] . . . the specific evils to be apprehended from it. Who-

> ever points out the rocks and shoals with which our course is beset, does us a service which may be all the greater because we are not terrified thereby into renouncing the voyage.[6]

Mill went on to say that every plan of reform 'ought to stand his [Austin's] test; ought to show, either that it does not tend to produce the evils dreaded by him, or that its tendency to do so can be counteracted.'[7]

Moreover, *A Plea for the Constitution* adumbrates objections to parliamentary reform of much better known Victorian critics of democracy than Austin. The list includes such major figures as James Fitzjames Stephen, Sir Henry Maine, Albert V. Dicey, and Robert Lowe.[8] The substantial extent to which Lowe followed in Austin's footsteps is especially striking and important. Lowe was, after all, the author of 'the most comprehensive case against democracy expressed in the House of the Commons in the nineteenth century'[9] and 'the embodiment of classical liberalism'.[10] His rejection of *a priori* reasoning, his appeal to experience, and his reliance upon expediency have a very Austinian tone.[11] The same is true of his arguments that reform of the suffrage will impede progress, foster corruption, emasculate the executive, encourage protectionism, lower the quality of legislators, and begin the irreversible slide down the 'slippery slope' to complete democracy.[12]

Finally, *A Plea for the Constitution* is a very clear illustration of the substantial political differences that are possible among utilitarians. To be sure, it has been argued that this pamphlet reflects Austin's rejection of the principle of utility.[13] This interpretation of his thought cannot, however, be substantiated. In the first place, his criticisms of parliamentary reform are variations of the argument that its effects would be pernicious. In the second place, he explicitly uses 'public utility' as his standard of judgment on at least six occasions.[14] In the third place, he refers to it as the 'ultimate' principle or test.[15] Finally, John Stuart Mill wrote that Austin 'never ceased to be an utilitarian'.[16]

Austin was not the only British utilitarian, at any rate, who rejected democratic reform of the Constitution. William Paley criticized it on utilitarian grounds in 1785,[17] a precedent followed eighty years later by Robert Lowe. While Lowe evidently did not adopt a utilitarian *moral* philosophy,[18] he insisted on the need to decide *political* questions on utilitarian grounds.[19] Accordingly, he argued that the issue of reform of the franchise should not be 'decided *a priori*, or on what a gentleman can evolve from the depths of his inner consciousness. It is a question of practical experience of the working of our laws. . . . Government does not deal with justice – it deals with expediency.'[20] Lowe's speeches leave no doubt of his implacable conviction that democratic changes in the franchise were inexpedient.

The political outlook of Paley and Lowe contrasts sharply with the attitudes of the Benthamites. Although Bentham himself was not a democrat for much of his long life, he eventually became an avid proponent of radical democratic reform.[21] James Mill and the philosophic radicals took the same position.[22] The differences between them and figures such as Paley or Lowe raise the question of the relationship between utilitarianism and democracy. Did the Benthamites, or opponents of democratic reform, draw the logical conclusion from utilitarian premises? Or is the principle of utility logically consistent with either democratic or non-democratic forms of government? How much guidance does general utility furnish for political practice? Of course, these very large issues cannot be comprehensively explored in this chapter. Nonetheless, it will shed some light upon them.

1

Although the reform of Parliament was not as heated an issue in the 1850s as it had been in the early 1830s, a certain amount of discussion of the subject was 'in the air'. Asa Briggs maintains that its survival as an issue in the period from 1852 to 1865 is 'best explained in terms of a delicately balanced situation within the House of Commons rather than in terms of sustained pressure from outside or of the persistent attraction of a fundamental theory'. He argues that the 'reform bills of ministers were less triumphant vindications of principle than useful political manoeuvres which had the special advantage of being very unlikely to come off.'[23] Whatever the reasons for it, the government had introduced modest reform bills in 1852 and 1854. Sarah Austin may have been referring to these measures when she described the 'severe blow' that various schemes of parliamentary reform gave the respect her husband wished to feel for 'eminent public men'.[24] Austin was so upset with these proposals that he overcame his habitual reluctance to express his ideas in print. The specific incentive for his literary efforts was a book by Henry George Grey, the third Earl Grey, on the subject of the reform of Parliament.[25] He was by no means an advocate of extensive democratic changes, but he did favour modest reform of Parliament. He even went so far as to say that the people have become more qualified to exercise political rights than they were in 1832.[26]

Grey thus expressed a more sympathetic attitude toward parliamentary reform than was acceptable to Austin. This fact may explain his enthusiastic reaction to an invitation to review Grey's book, a request to which he 'immediately consented'.[27] Although he completed the review, it was not accepted for publication. He then decided to publish a portion of the review in the form of a pamphlet.[28]

Austin divided his pamphlet into two general sections, the first and shortest of which consisted of a laudatory interpretation of the British constitution. The other and much longer part of the work was a critique of parliamentary reform, a phrase that covered a large number of proposals. They included extension of the suffrage, the redistribution of seats on a more equal basis, and the elimination of electoral bribery or coercion. While Austin touched upon most of these matters, he tended to focus on various proposals for extension of the suffrage. Since he believed that *any* enlargement of it would ultimately result in universal suffrage, he was as much opposed to the one as to the other.

Austin could have based his critique of extension of the suffrage on the argument that it would be intrinsically unjust. Instead, he chose to attack this reform on the basis of its inexpediency. He described his utilitarian argument in these terms:

> the consequences which I anticipate from any Parliamentary Reform are all . . . mischievous. . . . There are many imaginable reforms of the present representative system, which, by clearing it of its so-called anomalies, would render it more *symmetrical*. But, as brought to the test of *public utility*, (or, as tried by the sum of its effects on the general good of the country), our present Constitution is the least imperfect of positive political institutions: nor would all the partial improvements of which it is susceptible compensate the evil of reforming it without some urgent necessity.[29]

This statement implies that the British constitution had at least some imperfections. Austin also acknowledged the possibility that an 'urgent necessity' could justify the reform of Parliament. This qualification is the only exception to his otherwise inflexible opposition to *any* parliamentary reform. His position on this issue was indeed so rigid that the classification of him as a conservative is subject to question. At least this inference may be drawn from F. J. C. Hearnshaw's conception of conservatism as involving a belief in 'cautious or evolutionary reform'.[30] He sharply distinguished this principle from rigid opposition to *all* change. 'No persons are less true to the conservative genius than the reactionaries or "diehards" who resist all alteration whatsoever without ever inquiring into the causes that have led to its demand.'[31] By the end of his life Austin may have been just such a person. He was adamantly opposed to '*any* Parliamentary Reform', he did not inquire into the causes that led to the demands for change, and he expressed some doubt about the utility of the Reform Act of 1832.[32]

At the same time, the classification of Austin as a reactionary has its own problems. The most basic one is the inaccuracy of any label that imputes to him a resistance to 'all alteration whatsoever'. Despite his opposition to any reform of Parliament, he was a proponent of reform of 'our subordinate political institutions'.[33] *A Plea for the Constitution* was, at any rate, an unqualified defence of a suffrage that had not changed in twenty-seven years. Fewer than 500,000 persons had the right to vote prior to 1832. The Reform Act extended the suffrage to slightly over 800,000 adult males. The electors of the House of Commons thus formed one-thirtieth of the population and about one-seventh of adult males.[34] The Reform Act also reduced, but by no means eliminated, disparities in population between electoral districts. Norman Gash has pointed out that thirty-one boroughs had 300 or fewer electors, while twenty-nine boroughs had electorates of over 2,000 persons.[35]

Despite these gross inequalities, Austin insisted that any attempt to reduce them would be pernicious. One of its worst effects, he claimed, would be to disturb the equilibrium of power within Parliament. Bentham regarded this alleged balance as a fable that should be left to 'Mother Goose and Mother Blackstone',[36] but Austin was a staunch admirer of it. He believed that each of the three branches of the sovereign Parliament had a substantial amount of power, a situation which extension of the suffrage would alter for the worse. Its bad effects include the establishment of the virtual supremacy of the House of Commons, the emasculation of the Cabinet, and the destruction of free government in Great Britain. A government is free, Austin maintained, if it permits its subjects a 'large measure of *useful* liberty, or a large measure of *that* liberty which consists with the purposes of political society'. The British government is in this sense the 'freest of all governments past and present'.[37] A major reason for the existence of this freedom is the balance of power within Parliament. The Crown and the House of Lords not only restrain the temerity of the lower chamber, but prevent it from 'erecting the tyranny over subject bodies and individuals which it would impose upon them if it were virtually sovereign'.[38]

A second bad effect of extension of the suffrage would be to destroy the political aristocracy that ruled Great Britain. The word 'aristocracy' signified, Austin maintained, either a form of government or 'a class elevated by political privileges . . . or . . . social influence, springing from birth or wealth, or any cause whatever.'[39] Since the bulk of the members of Parliament belong to elevated classes, they are aristocrats in this sense of the term. The Head of State and the Peers obviously fall into this category, but it also includes most of the members of the House of Commons. These 'independent gentlemen' belong to the class of landed gentry and possess inherited or acquired wealth. They constitute, along with the members of the House of Lords, a *political* aristocracy because 'they are specially called upon by station and fortune, to devote themselves to the business of the nation'.[40]

Austin claimed that these political aristocrats were the best possible rulers. If the suffrage were extended, they would be replaced by workers or members of the middle class. The result of this change would be disastrous for the nation as a whole. Mastery of the difficult art of statesmanship required leisure, which only the men of independent wealth who made up the political aristocracy possessed. The knowledge of politics held by persons who must work for a living is necessarily 'superficial'.[41] They also completely lacked the capacity to legislate intelligently, which only the political aristocracy possessed. These considerations explain why Austin

> regarded with a sort of horror all schemes for placing the business of legislation in the hands of large bodies of men. He had followed step by step the progress of the great minds by which systems of law had been, through ages, slowly and painfully elaborated; and the project of submitting these highest products of the human intellect, or the difficult problems they deal with, to the judgment and the handling of uneducated masses, seemed to him a return towards barbarism. He, least of all men, was likely to be dazzled or attracted by wealth or rank; but he valued them on public grounds, as providing for their possessors the highest sort of education, and the leisure and opportunity to apply that education to the general

> culture of the human mind, – especially to the difficult sciences of legislation and government. The idea of popular legislation was to him as alarming as it was absurd.[42]

Mastery of the difficult science of legislation was not the only virtue of the political aristocrats. In addition, they have demonstrated a remarkable capacity to compromise. This virtue is essential, Austin claimed, for political stability and social happiness. Very few nations have ever had this ability to any large extent. Only the people of England have possessed the amount of it that is essential for 'enduring free government'. Their mastery of the art of compromise explains the longevity of the British constitution, which is 'perhaps the most wonderful of all the phenomena presented by the history of political institutions'. The capacity of the various branches of Parliament to compromise their differences is due mainly to the superior *breeding* of the vast majority of the members of the House of Commons.[43]

This factor is responsible for other valuable traits that Austin attributed to the political aristocrats. These virtues include self-possession, insight into human nature, and the ability to deal with men. He insisted that these traits are essential for statesmen in a 'free and Parliamentary country'.[44] Aside from this, the political aristocrats are naturally restrained by public opinion and the sentiment of 'gentlemanly honour'. Accordingly, the political morality of these men is of the highest possible quality. Their economic self-sufficiency also fosters a political independence that is very advantageous for the nation as a whole. This is evident from the conduct of the political aristocracy in the House of Commons. Unlike the situation in many other countries, Austin stressed, English statesmen have no special legal privileges which distinguish them from other commoners. Nevertheless, the landed gentry

> possessed the influence (all the greater for not being invidious) which belongs to a natural aristocracy. To *their* presence in the House of Commons we may attribute the weight and dignity acquired by that assembly; and its ability to rescue our Parliamentary Government from the fate of the analogous institutions in the rest of Western Europe.[45]

If the suffrage were extended, the political morality of the bulk of the members of Parliament would sharply deteriorate. Austin claimed that one of the worst effects would be a geometric increase in political corruption. Democratic reforms would also foster the most sinister form of this evil, which is political patronage. Extension of the suffrage has had precisely this effect, he claimed, in the United States. He thus reached the same conclusion as Robert Lowe. He visited America in 1856 and was apparently 'shocked by much that he saw. There seemed an utter absence of distinction, a complete lack of a leisured class, a wide range of corrupt institutions, and an anxiety to kowtow to the multitudes.'[46] Austin maintained, at any rate, that the effects of an extension of the suffrage in the United Kingdom would be much worse than in the United States. For the class of persons with little or no property is much larger in the former than the latter.[47]

Extension of the suffrage would cause the political morality of members of Parliament to deteriorate in other ways as well. Glibness and flattery of the masses would become the standard for election to Parliament. Representatives would probably be required to make pledges to their constituents, the dislike of which Austin shared with other nineteenth-century thinkers such as John Stuart Mill.[48] Austin also believed that the character of the nation as a whole would deteriorate if Parliament were reformed. Individuals would not be motivated to acquire superior ability and a 'nicer political morality', virtues that Members of Parliament would no longer personify.[49]

A third bad effect of extension of the suffrage would be to impede, if not to halt completely, progress. Austin's faith in the very real possibility of improving the human condition was a permanent element of his thought. His belief in progress strongly conditioned, for example, the reforms that he and George Cornewall Lewis proposed for Malta. Austin was convinced, however, that human betterment is by no means inevitable. Rather, it requires certain policies which extension of the suffrage will undermine.

To the extent that Austin utilized this argument, his pamphlet reflected a widespread fear of Victorian critics of democracy. No one described more vividly than Sir Henry Maine the alleged conflict between this form of government and progress. In 1885 he wrote:

> The delusion that Democracy . . . is a progressive form of government, lies deep in the convictions of a particular political school; but there can be no delusion grosser. It receives no countenance either from experience or from probability. . . . It seems . . . quite certain that, if for four centuries there had been a very widely extended franchise and a very large electoral body in this country, there would have been no reformation of religion, no change of

> dynasty, no toleration of Dissent, not even an accurate Calendar. The threshing-machine, the power-loom, the spinning-jenny, and possibly the steam engine, would have been prohibited. Even in our day, vaccination is in the utmost danger, and . . . generally . . . the gradual establishment of the masses in power is of the blackest omen for all legislation founded on scientific opinion.[50]

Maine believed that this kind of legislation could only be the product of intelligent and well-educated minorities. Robert Lowe, the 'last and by far the most effective opponent of any attempt to alter the settlement of 1832',[51] took a similar position. Despite his critical attitude toward democratic reform, he insisted in 1865 that he remained a Liberal. The basis of this claim was his belief that the happiness and prosperity of mankind could be 'enormously augmented'. This amelioration of the human estate would only occur, however, if it were recognized that 'by pure and clear intelligence alone can the cause of true progress be prompted'. It was precisely for this reason that Lowe so strenuously opposed, as did Austin, any attempt to 'subvert the existing order of things, and to transfer power from the hands of property and intelligence, and to place it in the hands of men whose whole life is necessarily occupied in daily struggles for existence'.[52] Since the political economy of these men is not that of Adam Smith, they advocate protectionist and other policies that undermine prosperity.

Austin's pamphlet reflected a similar conviction of the incompatibility between progress and extension of the suffrage. He defended his position by several arguments, including the contention that this change would stop legal or administrative reform. Moreover, both the sovereign government and subordinate political institutions would be 'ruthlessly torn in pieces by the hands of presumptuous incapacity'.[53] Austin argued that this effect would be most pronounced under universal suffrage. This 'radical' and 'destructive' change[54] would enfranchise large numbers of persons who are both poor and ignorant. This ignorance is apparent from the socialist biases of the workers, which Austin greatly feared. He distinguished between two meanings of socialism, neither of which he supported with much if any evidence. The word may denote a particular kind of social theory. Socialism in this sense means the control of the economy by a joint stock company 'consisting of the entire population . . . worked for the equal benefit of all, under the supreme direction of some narrower body'. Socialism also signifies 'an habitual disposition to insubordination and revolt: whether it comes from an addiction to social theories, from a thirst for pillage, from a wanton love of disorder and ravage, from the envy and hate of superiorities . . . or from any other cause.'[55]

Despite his acknowledgement that the workers are not theoretical socialists, Austin claimed that they fully shared the mischievous prejudices of which socialist and communist theories are an elaborate rationalization. Most workers believe that their wages depend upon the will of their employers, that the prices of goods reflect the desires of sellers, and that the interests of capital and labour necessarily conflict. Some of the most popular leaders of the workers, Austin contended, demonstrate the same 'astounding ignorance'.[56]

Both the workers and their leaders ignore, thus, the truths of the 'inestimable science of political economy'.[57] Their ignorance would have disastrous effects if they had political power. Socialist prejudices would form the basis of bills passed by the House of Commons. Thoughtless interferences with the 'natural arrangements' of society would become widespread,[58] as would pernicious restrictions on freedom of contract. Laws would probably be enacted that would establish minimum wages, or maximum hours of work. This probability immensely disturbed Austin. Indeed he condemned factory legislation as unconditionally as John Bright and the Manchester School. While Austin's opposition to state intervention was not dependent upon the religious outlook that heavily influenced Bright, he would strongly endorse the notion that 'all legislative interference with labour market, all attempts of Government to fix the wages of industry, all interference of a third party between employers and employed, are unjustifiable in principle and mischievous in their results.'[59]

Austin's hostility to factory legislation reflected a conception of the relationship between progress and contractual freedom to which Sir Henry Maine gave classic expression. His celebrated dictum was that the 'movement of the progressive societies has hitherto been . . . *from Status to Contract.*'[60] Paternalistic social legislation was objectionable because it would make rights or obligations depend upon position or status rather than voluntary agreements. In any case, Austin did not oppose laws establishing minimum wages or maximum hours of work simply because they limited freedom. All laws by definition have this effect. Rather, he believed that these restrictions were undesirable because they were inexpedient. He was also convinced that a reformed House of Commons would make a bad situation worse by saddling the affluent classes with the entire burden of taxation. The end-result of these harmful measures would be the destruction of the finances and prosperity of the nation. Legislation enacted by a democratic Parliament would also inspire a counter-revolution led by the proprietary classes. Although their revolt would probably succeed, the price of success would be high.[61]

Austin's pamphlet reflected, thus, profound fear of the economic stupidity of workers and their leaders, their ignorance of or opposition to the 'laws' of political economy. The proper remedy for this evil was not extension of the suffrage, which would only aggravate the problem. Rather, it was the prescription to which Austin adhered throughout his life. The long and short of it was 'the diffusion of sound political and economical principles amongst the body of the people; or, at the least, amongst such a number of the more intelligent of them as would suffice to form an authority for the safe guidance of the rest.' At the same time, he cautioned that intelligence and knowledge alone are insufficient electoral qualifications. His argument was that the 'grossest improvidence, with the grossest disregard for the interests of others, too often go hand-in-hand with intellectual gifts and acquirements.' The true requirements for political power 'especially in an age prone to revolutionary experiments, are sober good sense and care for the public interests; and nothing indicates with less uncertainty the possession of these qualities, than the possession of acquired, and even of inherited property.'[62]

Austin was deeply disturbed, at any rate, by a problem that was of little moment to an earlier generation of Benthamite utilitarians. Although they believed firmly in the principles of political economy, they were also ardent proponents of an extended suffrage. The possibility that a democratically elected Parliament would enact laws that were unsound economically was not, for them, a cause for concern. At least James Mill attempted to defuse anxiety on this count in his *Essay on Government*. His view was that the opinions of the class of people below the middle rank

> are formed, and their minds are directed by that intelligent, that virtuous rank, who come the most immediately in contact with them . . . to whom they fly for advice and assistance in all their numerous difficulties, upon whom they feel an immediate and daily dependence, in health and in sickness, in infancy and in old age, to whom their children look up as models for their imitation, whose opinions they hear daily repeated, and account in their honour to

> adopt. There can be no doubt that the middle rank, which gives to science, to art, and to legislation itself their most distinguished ornaments, and is the chief source of all that has exalted and refined human nature, is that portion of the community of which, if the basis of Representation were ever so far extended, the opinion would ultimately decide. Of the people beneath them a vast majority would be sure to be guided by their advice and example.[63]

It was less certain in 1859 than it was in 1820 that the 'lower orders' would in fact be guided by the advice and example of the 'middle rank'. This fact raises the question of how Mill would have reacted to a conflict between universal suffrage and political economy if he had perceived it to exist. Would he have given priority to his economic principles or his political preferences? Would he have agreed with the uneasy compromises worked out by John Stuart Mill? Or would James Mill have taken a position more similar to that of Austin or Robert Lowe? At any rate, Austin perceived a fork in the road that earlier utilitarians such as James Mill did not have to confront.

A final bad effect that Austin imputed to even limited extension of the suffrage was destruction of the sentiment of constitutionality. He conceived of this phenomenon as a *feeling* of attachment, or a positive *attitude*, of the people toward the constitution. This sentiment is not the result of a reasoned evaluation of the governmental system as an effective means to achieve a desired end. Instead, the sentiment is the effect of love and veneration of the constitution '*in and for itself*'.[64] The basis of this feeling is, thus, authority and habit rather than a rational calculation of the expediency of the established order. In short, the sentiment of constitutionality is similar to what Burke meant by 'prejudice'.[65]

A limited extension of the suffrage would undermine this sentiment, Austin believed, because such a change would foster additional revisions. The cumulative effect of these changes would be to destroy the reverence of the people for the constitution. They would view it in purely instrumental terms as a means to an end, rather than as an end in itself. The reform of Parliament would thereby destroy an attitude which Austin felt to be of immense utility. A stable government is, he argued, a necessary condition of good government and of progress. Stability is impossible in the absence of the sentiment of constitutionality, which is the 'strongest bond' of 'political union'. It is also the only feeling or opinion which the bulk of a people can share. The principle of utility cannot fulfill this essential function of unifying the people behind their government. The result of applying this standard to a government is not consensus, but an 'invincible diversity', of opinions.[66] A population which consisted only of self-conscious utilitarians would therefore disagree about whether their constitution was desirable.

Austin believed that the utility of the sentiment of constitutionality was evident from British, American, and French experience. The pervasiveness and strength of this feeling explains, he argued, the remarkable success of the English people in the reform of their constitution. They have wisely refused to venture on the 'ocean' of 'purely speculative innovations.' Instead, Englishmen have attempted to change their institutions gradually and peacefully. Their approach contrasts starkly with that of Americans. Austin claimed that their political behaviour demonstrates anything but reverence for the fundamentals of their various constitutions, which are subject to continual revisions. Americans frequently do not utilize constitutional amendments for this purpose, but exercise the 'sacred right' of insurrection. Under the influence of the 'absurd' and 'anarchical' notion of natural law, they all too often resort to Vigilante Committees or Lynch Law. Americans also tend to disregard the formalities essential to preserve the dignity of political leaders. Presidential receptions, for example, are attended by guests of the humbler classes with no sense of the need for even 'simple forms'.[67] The end-result is the lack of any profound or intense reverence by the American people for their government.

France has suffered even more deeply than the United States, Austin maintained, from the absence of the sentiment of constitutionality. The lack of this feeling is the ultimate reason for the inability of the French people to establish a free and stable government since 1789. French reformers utilized theories of natural rights and popular sovereignty which involved 'stupendous absurdities'.[68] The French constitution makers would have faced formidable problems even if they had relied upon the much more sensible notions of public utility.

> A government adapted to so complicated a thing as the situation of a great country, is a work for generations; and the creation of such a government in pursuance of a plan, would suppose on the part of its authors a range of intelligence more than human.[69]

2

These criticisms indicate how far Austin had departed, by the end of his life, from the political theories of Bentham, James Mill, and the philosophic radicals. To be sure, he retained vestiges of loyalty to his Benthamite heritage. He viewed himself as a utilitarian, he attempted to judge parliamentary reform on the basis of its public utility, and he had only contempt for natural rights. Even so, many of the ideas that he expressed would have shocked an earlier generation of Benthamites. They would not have believed that an erstwhile disciple of Bentham could defend the political aristocracy, reject an instrumentalist approach to constitutional evaluation, deny the possibility of creating the government of a great country in accordance with a plan, and oppose *any* reform of Parliament.

The changes in Austin's thought are indeed so profound that consideration of this question is imperative. What experiences that he underwent, if any, influenced the development of his inflexible opposition to Parliamentary reform? Although no absolutely certain answer to this question is possible, his residence in Europe had a strong impact upon the evolution of his 'turn to the right'. The ways in which his residence in Germany in 1827 and 1828 influenced his thought were described in an earlier chapter. The time that he spent in Germany and France from 1840 to 1848 evidently had an even stronger influence upon him. To be sure, precise calculation of *how much* this experience affected his political thought is impossible. Nevertheless, his residence in Europe and especially his direct observation of the French Revolution of 1848 had a strong impact. It reinforced opinions that he already held, confirmed tentative changes in his thought, and suggested new ideas. His reaction to the uprisings in Paris also had an effect of a quite different nature. It was to spur what has been described as John Stuart Mill's 'declaration of independence' from his mentor.[70] While this description may be hyperbolical, Mill expressed surprise at the extent of his disagreement with Austin. This is evident from a letter that Mill wrote Sarah Austin in March 1848: 'I never thought I should have differed from him [John Austin] so widely in feeling on any public event as it appears I do on this [the French Revolution of 1848].'[71]

Austin's residence in Europe had a number of quite specific effects on his political outlook. To begin with, it gave him a comparative view of British politics. He claimed in 1859 that this perspective particularly qualified him to appreciate the value of the British constitution. As he put it:

> By my reverence for Mr Bentham as a writer on law and legislation, I was naturally led (being then young) to accept his political opinions without sufficient examination. I have since dissented from many of his views of law. . . . Even before the Reform of 1832, I had rejected his *radical* politics. . . . I have since resided in Germany and France, and studied and observed their political institutions and condition; and I therefore am better qualified than most of my countrymen, to appreciate the matchless union of order and liberty for which we are indebted to our present incomparable Constitution.[72]

Moreover, Austin's observations of European politics influenced his attitude toward revolution. In particular, his opposition to it became more unqualified than it had been earlier in his life. To say this is not to deny that he always feared the anarchical effects of this drastic course of action. This fear was the basis of his contention that 'obedience to established government is enjoined generally by the Deity'.[73] Still, in 1832 he argued that revolution is justifiable on utilitarian grounds in exceptional cases.[74] He also took the position that the failure to recognize this was one of the two 'capital errors' in Hobbes' political works. He inculcated 'too absolutely the religious obligation of obedience to present or established government' and insisted 'unduly upon the evils of rebellion and strife'.[75]

The opinion of revolution that Austin subsequently developed was quite different from this. The French Revolution of 1848 appears to have strongly influenced the change in his outlook. According at least to Sarah Austin, 'it was from earnest observation of what passed in that country, that he became confirmed in his opinion of the difficulty, if not the impossibility, of reconstructing a society which has once been completely shattered.'[76] Austin's observation of French politics also influenced his opposition to revolution for another reason. It was his association of revolutionary movements with radical ideologies of which he could not have been more critical. Karl Marx and Friedrich Engels wrote in 1848 that a 'spectre is haunting Europe – the spectre of Communism. All the Powers of old Europe have entered into a holy alliance to exorcise this spectre.'[77] This same spectre haunted Austin and he insisted that his apprehensions were 'anything but fanciful'.[78] His reaction to the French Revolution of 1848 clearly indicates the major source of his worries. He expressed the most concern with the allegedly 'socialist' bent of the revolutionaries. His view was that

> it is important to recollect that the present revolutionary tendencies are social rather than political – aiming at equality of possessions, or an equal distribution of national revenue, rather than the mere establishment of democratical constitutions. *This is the alarming feature in the present condition of France*[79] (emphasis added).

Of course, this characteristic of the situation in France was not the only aspect of it that upset Austin. The unfamiliar spectacle of armed men roaming the streets, shouting revolutionary slogans, building barricades, and breaking up meetings must have bothered him. The same is true of the necessity that he and his wife felt to leave Paris and to return to England, a move that evidently entailed a 'serious pecuniary loss'.[80] The effect of the uprisings on close friends of the Austins such as M. Guizot, who fled to England out of fear for his life, were also upsetting. Besides this, Austin dreaded the possibility of war between France and England. He left no doubt of his hope that 'we shall not engage in a war for the vague purpose of crushing the revolutionary spirit, of from resentment and alarm at the foolish provocations which may be reasonably expected from the future Governments of France.' He supported this opposition to an aggressive war by several arguments, one of which was that it 'would spread the revolutionary spirit, instead of crushing it'.[81] Even so, he was most alarmed by the socialist objectives of the Parisian workers who sparked the Revolution.

The reason for his alarm was not simply fear of what might happen in Europe. He was no less apprehensive about the possibility of socialist or communist revolutions in England. To be sure, he acknowledged that in this country 'Socialist opinions and feelings have not as yet a definite shape; they are rather dispositions or tendencies than distinct theories or *formulas*.' Still, he expressed the view that socialism probably had more appeal for the English than for the French. His reasoning was that 'in consequence of the vast inequalities of our social positions, these [socialist] dispositions, though yet latent, are probably more strong and general than in France; for, in this last country, a large proportion of the people are small landowners, and have a visible and cogent motive to respect the properties of the rich.'[82]

Austin found support for this interpretation in certain allegedly 'socialist' tendencies in England, including the 'clamour' for tenant-rights, i.e., 'a partial confiscation of the Irish landlord's property, or, what comes to the same thing, a partial release of the tenant from his engagements and liabilities'. He also cited the 'language held by Lord Ashley and others of our ignorant humanitarians – language calculated to persuade the workmen that their privations and severe labour are caused by the selfishness of their masters'.[83]

Another effect of Austin's residence in Europe was to persuade him of, or to reinforce his belief in, the great value of a respected aristocracy. He wrote to John Stuart Mill in 1844 that, 'If you come here [France] and study the effect of revolutions, I think that you will agree with me in deprecating for the other countries the *regime* of *parvenus*. Without a class of *gentlemen*, diffusing gentlemanly feelings, there can be no good government or good morality.'[84] A letter in 1846 from Sarah Austin to Macvey Napier, the editor of the *Edinburgh Review*, elaborated on this theme. The purpose of the letter was to convince Napier to accept a proposal of John Austin for an article on the French Revolution of 1789. His study, which was never completed, was intended to apply the lessons of this momentous event to contemporary societies, especially England. One inference that he drew was the necessity for 'an enlightened and progressive aristocracy'. If such a body had existed in France, then it might have avoided 'all the horrors of the Revolution'. The absence of a respected aristocracy in contemporary France is also responsible for many evils. They include the lack of any effective counterweight to individual self-seeking in all of the 'points and details of life'. The existence of an aristocracy is perfectly compatible with, if it is not a requirement of, progress. In fact, *le fond de la pensée* of Austin's article was the idea that ' "ancient and revered institutions are not inconsistent with new ideas, and not unsusceptible of progress, and that therefore there is no excuse for violence." '[85]

The French Revolution of 1848 reinforced Austin's conviction of the necessity for a progressive aristocracy. Although he attributed the uprisings largely to the condition and attitudes of the workers, he did not neglect to criticize the king and the upper classes. He expressed the opinion that if Louis Philippe 'had been a *gentleman*, and had consulted the interests of the country instead of his blind greediness to aggrandize himself and his family, he might . . . have governed

France easily.' Instead, he 'alienated the only body upon which his Government could rest – viz., the middle classes, of whom the National Guard is mainly composed. . . . So much for the safety of a Government, which, in a civilized country, relies upon soldiers as against its subjects.'[86] Austin also had harsh words for the upper classes. Most of them

> are morally or intellectually a more complete *canaille* than the great majority of the lower. Some don't care for the well-being of the people, think them destined to a miserable and servile condition, and would keep them down by force or terror; others, with better dispositions, won't give themselves the trouble to master social questions, diffuse opinions which lead the people to anarchical courses, or would give the people an education confined to sectarian religion which has no tendency to enlighten them and to raise their condition.[87]

The last sentence of this quotation is a clue to the final effect of Austin's residence in Germany and France. The essence of it was the reinforcement of his life-long commitment to a particular prescription for the ills of the people. It is most definitely not the expansion of political democracy. Rather,

> The only remedy is the education of the people, especially the diffusing amongst them a knowledge of the natural causes which determine the distribution of the products of labour and capital. This knowledge, if diffused amongst them, would cut up revolutionary tendencies by the roots; for this last revolution has proved what I always believed, that they arise from popular ignorance, and not from popular envy.[88]

3

These ideas support Austin's claim, in 1859, that his 'actual political faith has not been adopted recently and has not been adopted lightly.'[89] If he had not reached his ultimate political destination by 1848, he had travelled most of the way toward it. The inflexible opposition to even limited extension of the suffrage that he eventually developed means, at any rate, that the course of British history since 1859 would have been a tremendous disappointment to him. The Reform Acts of 1867 and 1884 substantially expanded the electorate.

The Representation of the People Act of 1918 established virtually universal male suffrage. The Equal Franchise Act of 1928 granted the vote to women on the same basis as men. The Representation of the People Act of 1948 completed 'the progress of the British people towards a full and complete democracy begun by the Great Reform Bill of 1832'.[90] In short, the reforms of which Austin so profoundly disapproved have become a reality.

While this historical development does not itself disprove Austin's indictment of extension of the suffrage, his arguments are subject to a number of very serious criticisms. To begin with, certain of his predictions of the effects of extension of the suffrage were inaccurate. His calculation of the truly revolutionary behaviour of reformed Parliaments is one example. A second is his prophecy that reform would vest the leadership of Parliament in the hands of workers or the lower middle-class. The inaccuracy of this forecast is evident from W.L. Guttsman's careful analysis of the class structure of Cabinets from 1886 to 1955.[91] His study confirms in a sense the theory of Walter Bagehot that England is one of the 'deferential nations'. He held that the numerical majority is 'ready, is eager to delegate its power of choosing its ruler to a certain select minority. It abdicates in favour of its *elite*, and consents to obey whoever that *elite* may confide in.'[92] Guttsman's study indicates that while representation of the aristocracy has been reduced, it has by no means been eliminated.[93] This development has not, however, resulted in the predominance in the Cabinet of representatives of the workers or lower middle-class. To the extent that the aristocracy has lost representation in the Cabinet, it has tended to be replaced by the middle-class.

To be sure, it could be argued that this development was not foreseeable in 1859. This argument is unwarranted, however, in the light of the reactions of some of Austin's contemporaries to extension of the suffrage. Unlike him, they predicted that even universal suffrage would not deprive either the wealthy or well-born of political influence. A. V. Dicey wrote in 1867, for example, that universal suffrage would not disenfranchise the more affluent classes. He stressed that the 'influence of a minority is always considerable, and the influence of a rich minority could never be insignificant'.[94] With characteristic lucidity Leslie Stephen expressed a similar theme. 'Wealth and rank and social estimation', he argued, 'will always produce an effect which no legislation can neutralize.'[95]

Another prediction of Austin's that turned out to be inaccurate was his projection of a diminution of the power of the Cabinet if the suffrage were extended. Although the accuracy of some of his calcultations is no doubt uncertain or debatable, this prophecy is not one of them. Whatever the effects of parliamentary reform were, they did not include reduction in the Cabinet's power. Another nineteenth-century British lawyer and critic of democratic reform was more prophetic in this regard than Austin. Sir Henry Maine wrote in 1885 that a reformed House of Commons would probably abandon most of its legislative power to the Cabinet.[96] To be sure, the

> power of the House of Commons over legislation, including constitutional legislation, might seem at first sight to be complete and unqualified. Nevertheless . . . it some time ago surrendered the initiative in legislation, and it is now more and more surrendering the conduct of it, to the so-called Ministers of the Crown.[97]

These criticisms do not mean that Austin was an entirely inept calculator of the effects of extension of the suffrage. Indeed, in some respects he was quite prophetic. He correctly foresaw that gradual extensions of the suffrage would culminate in universal suffrage, and that the powers of the House of Lords would be reduced. He also discerned some of the legislative tendencies of a reformed Parliament. They include the enactment of high rates of taxation on inherited or acquired wealth, the development of the various policies associated with the 'welfare state', and the nationalization of some industries. Finally, reformed Parliaments have imposed the very restrictions on freedom of contract to which Austin was adamantly opposed.

Moreover, it is entirely possible that other developments that Austin predicted may take place at some point in the future. Socialism in its classical form may become a reality, and the monarchy or House of Lords may be abolished. If these developments do indeed occur, they are unlikely to be accompanied by the revolutionary chaos which Austin foresaw. His prediction of this dire turn of events reflected a number of misunderstandings on his part. The most important one was his distorted perception of the revolutionary fervour of the bulk of English workers and their leaders. At least Asa Briggs claims, in his study of the period from 1851 to 1867, that the

> English working class was not revolutionary, although for a moment it seemed as though it might become so; the trade unions were not the cells of socialist conspirators either in the provinces or in London. Nor were they shock troops. . . . The workers . . . de-

> manded their rights and secured them, but even when they were provoked they never flirted with the thought of 'a really bloody encounter with the ruling powers'.[98]

Austin's very different perception of the workers' revolutionary élan was the product of various factors. The most basic of them may have been his erroneous assumption that English workers held the same attitudes as the Parisian mobs whom he detested. If the development of a comparative perspective is usually a *broadening* experience, in Austin's case it had the opposite effect of *narrowing* his political outlook. He also failed to appreciate the social and political fragmentation of the disenfranchised. Although he recognized that the aristocracy was politically divided, he perceived other classes as highly unified. His analysis contrasts unfavourably, in this respect, with that of Dicey. He stressed, at least in 1867, that the so-called working class is, like all others, 'notoriously broken into divisions'.[99] 'Take . . . any class of Englishmen,' he wrote,

> from the highest to the lowest, and it will be found to mix, by imperceptible degrees, with the class below it. Who can say where the upper class ends, or where the middle class begins? Who, again, can draw a line which shall accurately divide working men from small tradesmen? Yet if there exist a class or order, it is the class of workmen. To those who see this class from without, and from a distance, it appears, no doubt, much more of a class or order than it really is; because its subdivisions escape notice.[100]

Austin's critique of extension of the suffrage is unsatisfactory, at any rate, in several other respects as well. They include the lack of a solid factual basis for his completely uncritical endorsement of the political aristocracy. If the nobility had mastered the art of statesmanship to the extent that he claimed, this virtue should be evident in the House of Lords. Statesmanship was not a conspicuous trait of most members of the upper chamber as viewed by Walter Bagehot, who was anything but an ardent democrat. While he believed in the great value of a good second house, he was critical of the House of Lords. One reason for his dissatisfaction with it was his impression of the mediocre quality of most of its members. The House of Lords

> may contain – it almost always has contained, it almost always will contain – extraordinary men. But its average born law-makers

> cannot be extraordinary. Being a set of eldest sons picked out by chance and history, it cannot be very wise.[101]

If some of the landed gentry who served in the House of Commons were very able men, others do not appear to merit this characterization. Such was at least the view of John Stuart Mill. He agreed with Austin that there was an art of statesmanship for the mastery of which leisure was a *necessary* condition. Mill argued, however, that it was not a *sufficient* condition. He felt that this fact was confirmed by the low quality of many Members of Parliament.[102] He pointed out that it is difficult to find a sufficient number of statesmen to form a cabinet, much less a legislature. The difficulty would not have existed if a high proportion of the landed gentry in the House of Commons had mastered the art of statesmanship. A recent historian of the Cabinet has in effect confirmed the accuracy of Mill's judgment. John Mackintosh writes of the period between 1832 and 1868: 'Yet the supply of front-bench talent was never plentiful. Out of 658 members only some 200 spoke or made any verbal contribution during the average session and few of these had the energy, persistence or weight for Cabinet office.'[103]

The extent to which the political aristocrats whom Austin extolled used their power to care for the public interest is also open to serious question. At the least their very substantial power was not always exercised for this laudable objective. Bagehot not only criticized the *ability* of most members of the House of Lords, but the *ends* for which they used their power. As large landowners they revised legislation 'exclusively according to the supposed interests, the predominant feelings, the inheritied opinions, of that class.' He also expressed the view that these interests had undue weight in the House of Commons. The lower chamber 'leans too much' to the opinions of the landed gentry. 'Half the boroughs in England', he wrote, 'are represented by considerable landowners, and when rent is in question . . . they think more of themselves than of those who send them.' [104]

A final weakness in Austin's critique of parliamentary reform is its lack of balance. He criticized *all* of the effects of this change as pernicious, a judgment that is too extreme to be tenable. His wholly negative appraisal of the restrictions on freedom of contract likely to be enacted by a reformed Parliament is an example. His evaluation demonstrated little awareness of the practical need for at least some of these measures as a means to improve the weak bargaining position of workers or tenant-farmers. The practical effect for them of unlimited contractual freedom was virtual exploitation by management or landlords. Such was the opinion, at least, of T. H. Green. He supported the kind of limitations on freedom of contract which Austin criticized. Green noted in 1881 that the competition for farms and jobs was so severe that 'freedom of contract is little more than a name. The peasant farmer is scarcely more free to contract with his landlord than is a starving labourer to bargain for good wages with a master who offers him work.' Green did not deny the importance of upholding contracts, but he did insist that it is no less a 'prime business of government . . . to provide against contracts being made, which, from the helplessness of one of the parties to them, instead of being a security for freedom, become an instrument of disguised oppression.'[105]

If these criticisms are warranted, Austin's critique of extension of the suffrage is not convincing. To say this is not to imply, however, that his case against it is without value. In the first place, some of his predictions of the effects of this reform turned out to be accurate. In the second place, his pamphlet is a good statement of the possible dangers of parliamentary reform. If most of the evils that he foresaw were not realized, he 'marked some of the dangers to be avoided'.[106] Finally, the 'sentiment of constitutionality' may well be a requirement of stable government. John Stuart Mill expressed the point in these terms:

> Until mankind are much more improved than there is any present hope of, even good political institutions cannot dispense with the support afforded by traditional sentiment. . . . An attachment resting on authority and habit to the existing Constitution 'in and for itself', is . . . in the existing state of the human mind, an almost indispensable condition of the stability of free government; which has the greatest difficulty in taking firm root among any people whose misfortune it is, never to have had institutions capable of inspiring such an attachment.[107]

4

Although Austin's arguments against extension of the suffrage are not bereft of insights, his overall indictment of this course of action was not warranted. The criticisms to which his arguments are subject also imply that his case against parliamentary reform is unsatisfactory from a utilitarian point of view. Despite his genuine commitment to the standard of public utility, his application of it lacked a solid basis in the facts. He also failed to support his case by the kind of dispassionate cost-benefit analysis that is the hallmark of a utilitarian approach. For he presumed that extension of the suffrage had only costs and no benefits, which was not the case. One of its benefits would be to allay the resentment, which could be destabilizing, that the disenfranchised might otherwise feel. Leslie Stephen expressed the point very well in a defence of parliamentary reform published in 1867. He pointed out that exclusion of workers from the suffrage 'tends directly and energetically to increase that profound division of classes which is one of the great evils of the time, and which may some day result in the very catastrophe most dreaded.'[108]

This consideration also indicates the weakness of Austin's pamphlet from a conservative point of view. Preservation of the essentials of the established order required a more flexible attitude toward parliamentary reform than he expressed. As George Brodrick wrote in 1867 in criticism of Robert Lowe's utilitarian arguments against reform:

> The vitality of all political organisms is in proportion to their capacity of adaptation to altered conditions of existence. . . . If the stability of our own Constitution has been the marvel of modern times, it is chiefly because it has grown with the growth, strengthened with the strength, and expanded with the expansive energies of the English people. We are now entering, with the rest of Europe, consciously or unconsciously, upon a new order of things . . . in which, come what may, Labour must henceforth occupy a far higher position than heretofore. Not to recognise the rise of this irresistible power by a timely extension of our representative system, is to break the spell which has preserved its identity through the vicissitudes of six centuries; and, with it, to imperil the destiny of constitutional government.[109]

Austin's critique of extension of the suffrage *may* also be subject to another objection. It is his choice of what may be the wrong standard as the basis for his evaluation of parliamentary reform. Although the effects of a change must be considered, this criticism implies that they should be measured on the scales of *justice* rather than *public utility*. An alteration in the *status quo* that was inexpedient might be just, in which case it would be warranted. The abolition of slavery is only one of the many examples that the author of this criticism might cite. To claim that this change was inexpedient and therefore unwarranted is thus an unsatisfactory argument. The contention that extension of the suffrage is inexpedient and therefore unjustified could merit the same criticism.

Determination of the soundness of this criticism raises fundamental issues of political philosophy, the resolution of which is beyond the scope of this study. Austin's arguments against parliamentary reform are subject, at any rate, to the criticism that they do not satisfy the standard he attempted to apply. While the principle of public utility is subject to various applications, some of them are much better grounded than others. It is one thing to *claim* that this standard required opposition to extension of the suffrage. It is another thing to *establish* that this change was in fact inexpedient. If the criticisms described in this chapter are well-founded, Austin failed to establish what he set out to prove.

7 *Conclusion*

The purpose of this book is to facilitate understanding of a limited number of John Austin's ideas. If there is a single key to understanding his thought, it is his unshakable commitment to utilitarianism. In spite of the substantial amounts of unhappiness in his own life, he never wavered in his intellectual loyalty to the paramount 'end' that he stipulated in 1824: '[A]ccumulation, *like every thing else*, is subordinate to the great end, happiness'[1] (emphasis added). His utilitarianism even influenced certain axioms of his legal philosophy. They include his conceptions of law, sovereignty, and jurisprudence. Utilitarian considerations also affected his sharp contrast between the law as it is and the law as it ought to be.

Despite Austin's unwavering commitment to the principle of utility, his application of it to certain issues changed dramatically in the course of his life. The turn-about in his appraisal of parliamentary reform and laws of political libel was, for example, truly remarkable. The conservative views that he eventually developed on these subjects could not be more different from the ideas of Bentham, James Mill, and the philosophic radicals. The different attitudes of these men and Austin indicate that Elie Halévy understated the conflict among the utilitarians. He speculated that, 'Had they ever been faced by a revolutionary crisis, the supporters of the principle of utility could not have avoided splitting into two extreme factions, some heading straight for equalitarian communism, and others becoming apologists of the hereditary and traditionalistic principle.'[2] The differences that developed between Austin and other Benthamites demonstrate that a revolutionary crisis was not necessary for utilitarians to take widely divergent positions. The existence of these conflicts also supports the interpretation of Alan Ryan that there was 'no such thing . . . as *the* utilitarian view of the proper role of government and the best mode of its fulfilling that role.'[3] Nevertheless, throughout his life Austin judged customs, institutions, laws, and policies on the basis of his perception of their effects on the general happiness.

Austin's achievements as a thinker vary, at any rate, in accordance with the different intellectual roles that he played. He was not only a philosopher of law, but an ethicist, colonial reformer, and political partisan. This study reinforces the conventional opinion that his legal philosophy represents his greatest contribution. It had a profound impact upon English jurisprudence and legal positivism, it foreshadowed certain developments in twentieth-century American legal thought, and it may be read profitably even today. Of course, this judgment does not imply that he was as great a legal philosopher as either Hobbes or Bentham. Even so, Austin's contributions to jurisprudence were substantial.

While Austin's legal philosophy constitutes his greatest achievement, it is not his only one. To begin with, he contributed significantly to the development of utilitarian ethical theory. His specific contribution was 'to work out with some care a mode in which the utilitarian principle could be coupled with reliance on moral rules.'[4] Aside from this, his accomplishments as a Royal Commissioner to Malta were varied and substantial. He not only demonstrated a laudable concern for the well-being of the natives of the Island. Beyond this, he and George Cornewall Lewis developed a coherent, practical, and beneficial programme of reform for the ills of Malta.

At the same time, this programme reflected the limitations of Austin's standard prescription for social evils. His habitual response to them was advocacy of '*the diffusion of knowledge through the great mass of the people*'.[5] Although this policy was desirable, it was not the cure-all that he represented it to be. Moreover, the content of the knowledge that he wished to diffuse included a number of debatable economic and social principles. Finally, his iron-clad commitment to this panacea illustrates the paradoxical quality of his thought. On the one hand, his legal philosophy reflects the 'tough minded' attitude of the typical legal positivist. On the other hand, his social philosophy embodies an almost utopian faith in the immense benefits of 'enlightenment'.

Austin was less successful as a political partisan than in any of his other intellectual roles. While *A Plea for the Constitution* is important, it failed to achieve its purpose of demonstrating that parliamentary reform was inexpedient. Austin's four articles are more difficult to evaluate. On the one hand, they tend to be polemical, unduly long, and somewhat repetitious. They also confirm John Stuart Mill's judgment that Austin 'spoilt much of his work for ordinary use by overlabouring it'.[6] On the other hand, the policies that Austin advocated in these writings tend to be enlightened and prophetic. At least his opposition to primogeniture and entails, his critique of the unlimited liability of joint stock companies, and his support of free trade merit this characterization. If he was not on the side of the angels in all matters, he tended to represent the views of the illuminati in his articles.

This assessment of Austin implies that he was not a truly seminal thinker. He was also not a very productive writer. His output was much smaller, for example, than that of Bentham, James Mill, or John Stuart Mill. Admittedly, Austin's failure to realize more fully his very great potential was not entirely his own fault. Furthermore, to some extent it reflected his laudable commitment to the maximum possible clarity and precision. Nevertheless, his limited achievements were influenced to some degree by certain flaws of his character. At the very least he could have made much better use than he did of the vast amount of free time he enjoyed in the final twenty-five years of his life.

Even so, the quality of some of Austin's achievements was very high indeed. These accomplishments reflected his rare ability for conceptual clarification, his intolerance of cant, his sense of realism, and his commitment to the good of society as he understood it. While some of his writing was laboured, he tended to write lucidly and could be eloquent. These virtues explain why his very best writings may be profitably scrutinized even today. If he is not a thinker of the very first rank, in short, he is an important and instructive thinker.

Notes

References to John Austin's works have been abbreviated throughout the Notes:

'DPW'	'Disposition of Property by Will – Primogeniture', *Westminster Review*, II (1824), 503.
LJ	*Lectures on Jurisprudence or the Philosophy of Positive Law*, ed. Robert Campbell, 2 vols, 5th edition, 1885.
PC	*A Plea for the Constitution*, 2nd edition, 1859.
PJP	*The Province of Jurisprudence Determined and The Uses of the Study of Jurisprudence*, with Introduction by H.L.A. Hart, 1954.

The Province of Jurisprudence Determined was based on the first ten lectures of the course in jurisprudence that Austin taught at the University of London 1829–33. The book was originally published in 1832 and was not reprinted during his lifetime. It was published in 1861 as the first volume of Sarah Austin's edition of her husband's *Lectures on Jurisprudence*. The two other volumes, which included the remainder of the lectures in John Austin's course, were originally published in 1863.

In the Notes, years within brackets signify the original date of publication of a book or the edition of it utilized in this study.

Introduction

1 For valuable studies of Austin's legal philosophy, see below, Note 33.
2 H.L.A. Hart, *The Concept of Law* (1961), pp. 18–76.
3 Ronald Dworkin, *Taking Rights Seriously* (1977), pp. 17–19.
4 As quoted by John Stuart Mill, review of *LJ*, *Edinburgh Review*, CXVIII (1863), 223.
5 Austin, *PJD*, p. 370.
6 Mill, review of *LJ*, p. 222.
7 *Biographical Studies*, ed. R.H. Hutton (2nd edn, 1889), p. 236.
8 Henry Maine, *Lectures on the Early History of Institutions* [7th edn, 1914] (1966), p. 343.

9 For discussion of the nature of legal positivism, see H.L.A. Hart, 'Legal Positivism', *Encyclopedia of Philosophy*, ed. Paul Edwards (1967), IV, 418; Roberto Ago, 'Positive Law and International Law', *American Journal of International Law*, LI (1957), 691; Samuel I. Shuman, *Legal Positivism: Its scope and limitations* (1963); Neil MacCormick, *H.L.A. Hart* (1981); Joseph Raz, *The Authority of Law: Essays on law and morality* (1979); Robert S. Summers, 'The *New* Analytical Jurists', *New York University Law Review*, LXI (1966), 861; and Richard Tur, 'Positivism, Principles and Rules', in *Perspectives in Jurisprudence*, ed. Elspeth Attwooll (1977), p. 42.

10 Hans Kelsen, *General Theory of Law and State*, trans. Anders Wedberg (1961), p. 114.

11 MacCormick, *H.L.A. Hart*, p. 6.

12 Hart, 'Legal Positivism', p. 419.

13 Summers, 'The *New* Analytical Jurists', p. 890.

14 See Hans Kelsen, 'The Pure Theory of Law and Analytical Jurisprudence', *Harvard Law Review*, LV (1941), 44, and Hart, *The Concept of Law*, pp. vii–viii.

15 See Kelsen, *General Theory of Law and State*, pp. xiii–xvi, 18–21, and Hart, 'Positivism and the Separation of Law and Morals', *Harvard Law Review*, LXXI (1958), 593.

16 Letter from Lord Brougham to Sarah Austin, 27 November 1860, in Janet Ross, *Three Generations of English Women: Memoirs and correspondence of Susannah Taylor, Sarah Austin, and Lady Duff Gordon* (rev. edn, 1893), p. 371 (hereafter cited as *Three Generations*).

17 Review of *PJD*, *Edinburgh Review*, CCXXXII (1861), 243.

18 Review of *LJ*, *Westminster Review*, LXXX (1863), 112.

19 Review of *LJ*, *North American Review*, C (1865), 246.

20 'The Study of Jurisprudence', *Law Magazine and Review*, V (1879–80), 388, 386. For a study of Dicey which emphasizes Austin's impact on him, see Richard A. Cosgrove, *The Rule of Law: Albert Venn Dicey, Victorian jurist* (1980).

21 T.E. Holland, *The Elements of Jurisprudence* (11th edn, 1910), pp. vi–vii.

22 Hart, 'Introduction', in Austin, *PJD*, p. xvi.

23 C.K. Allen, *Law in the Making* (7th edn, 1964), p. 7.

24 See Jeremy Bentham, *Of Laws in General*, ed. H.L.A. Hart (1970).

25 H.L.A. Hart, *Essays on Bentham: Studies in jurisprudence and political theory* (1982), p. 108.

26 H.L.A. Hart, 'Bentham on Sovereignty', in *Jeremy Bentham: Ten critical essays*, ed. Bhikhu Parekh (1974), p. 145.

27 Maine, *Lectures*, pp. 343–4. For similar opinions, see Mill, review of *LJ*, p. 223, and Leslie Stephen, *The Life of Sir James Fitzjames Stephen* (1895), p. 60.

28 Kelsen, *General Theory of Law and State*, p. xv.

29 See Mark DeWolfe Howe, *Justice Oliver Wendell Holmes: The shaping years, 1841–1870* (1957), p. 194; 'The Law Magazine and Review', *American Law Review*, VI (1872), in *Harvard Law Review*, XLIV (1930–31), 788; and John Chipman Gray, *The Nature and Sources of Law* [rev edn, 1921] (1963). For an outstanding study that emphasizes the impact of Austin

upon Holmes, see H.L. Pohlman, *Justice Oliver Wendell Holmes & Utilitarian Jurisprudence* (1984). Unfortunately, Pohlman's book was published too late in 1984 to be discussed in the text.

30 See above, pp. 119–22, and W.E. Rumble, 'The Legal Positivism of John Austin and the Realist Movement in American Jurisprudence', *Cornell Law Review*, LXVI (1981), 986.

31 Dworkin, 'The Model of Rules', *University of Chicago Law Review*, XXXV (1967), 17. Also, see Dworkin, *Taking Rights Seriously*.

32 See W.L. Morison, *John Austin* (1982).

33 For an excellent bibliography of Austin, see H.L.A. Hart, 'Bibliographical Note', in Austin, *PJD*, pp. xix–xxi. Noteworthy studies of Austin since 1954 include Morison, *John Austin*; Morison, 'Some Myth about Positivism', *Yale Law Journal*, LXVIII (1958), 212; Enid M. Campbell, 'John Austin and Jurisprudence in nineteenth-century England' (unpublished PhD dissertation, Duke University, 1958); Herbert Morris, 'Verbal Disputes and the Legal Philosophy of John Austin', *UCLA Law Review*, VII (1959), 27; Julius Stone, *Legal System and Lawyers' Reasonings* (1964); D. Gerber, 'A Note on Woody on Dewey on Austin', *Ethics*, LXXIX (1969), 303; Mark Francis, 'The Nineteenth-Century Theory of Sovereignty and Thomas Hobbes', *History of Political Thought*, I (1980), 517; Gerhard Maher, 'Analytical Philosophy and Austin's Philosophy of Law', *Archiv für Rechts- und Sozialphilosophie*, LXIV (1978), 401; Eira Ruben, 'John Austin's Political Pamphlets 1824–1859', in *Perspectives in Jurisprudence*, ed. Elspeth Attwooll, p. 20; and Alan R. White, 'Austin as a Philosophical Analyst', *Archiv für Rechts- und Sozialphilosophie*, LXIV (1978), 379.

34 Hart, *PJD*, p. xviii.

35 Review of *PJD*, *Tait's Edinburgh Magazine*, II (1832), 346.

36 Letter of John Stuart Mill to John Pringle Nichol, 14 October 1834, in *The Earlier Letters of John Stuart Mill, 1812–1848*, ed. Francis E. Mineka (1963), p. 236.

37 Review of *LJ Edinburgh Review*, CXVIII (1863), 228.

38 Richard Wasserstrom, *The Judicial Decision: Toward a theory of legal justification* (1961), p. 119.

39 John Austin, *PC* (2nd edn, 1859).

40 See 'DPW', 503; 'Joint Stock Companies', *Parliamentary History and Review* (1826), p. 709; review of *The National System of Political Economy*, by Frederic List, *Edinburgh Review*, LXXV (1842), 515; and 'Centralization', *Edinburgh Review*, LXXXV (1847), 221.

41 See Donald Winch, *Classical Political Economy and Colonies* (1965).

42 For the reports of the Commissioners, see 'Copies or Extracts of Reports of the Commissioners appointed to inquire into the Affairs of the Island of Malta and of Correspondence thereupon', in *Parliamentary Papers*, XXIX (1837–8) (two parts), and 'Copies or Extracts of Reports . . .', *Parliamentary Papers*, XVII (1839).

43 Albert V. LaFerla, *British Malta* (1938), I, 160.

44 Although this statement was true when it was written, it is no longer true. See Lotte Hamburger and Joseph Hamburger, *Troubled Lives: John and Sarah Austin* (1984). Since the text of my book had been set prior to the

publication of the Hamburgers' work, which I had not read, I do not refer to it in my account of Austin's life.

II *Austin's life and its relationship to his thought*

1 Sarah Austin, 'Preface', in John Austin, *LJ*, I, p. 2 (hereafter cited as 'Preface').
2 Gordon Waterfield, *Lucie Duff Gordon in England, South Africa and Egypt* (1937), p. 48. Sarah Austin bequeathed her husband's substantial library on jurisprudence to the Inner Temple, 'Preface', p. ix. Unfortunately, all but one of these volumes were destroyed during World War II.
3 Richard A. Cosgrove, *The Rule of Law: Albert Venn Dicey, Victorian Jurist* (1980).
4 For the necessary correction of this statement, see note 44, above. Besides Lotte Hamburger and Joseph Hamburger, *Troubled Lives: John and Sarah Austin* (1984), see these accounts of Austin's life: 'Preface', pp. 1–21; Waterfield, *Lucie Duff Gordon*; W.L. Morison, *John Austin* (1982), pp. 7–63; and A.D.E. Lewis, 'John Austin (1790–1859): Pupil of Bentham', *Bentham Newsletter*, II (1979), 19.
5 Asa Briggs, *The Making of Modern England, 1783–1867: Age of Improvement* (1965), p. 1 (published in the UK as *The Age of Improvement*, vol. 8, *The History of England* [1959]).
6 J.H. Plumb, *England in the Eighteenth Century* (1972), p. 214.
7 G. Kitson Clark, *The Making of Victorian England* [1962] (1974), p. 39.
8 Kitson Clark, p. 5.
9 Austin's praise of the middle class may be found in 'DPW', p. 508. For a study of him that claims that his jurisprudence is a rationalization of middle-class interests, see Eira Ruben, 'John Austin's Political Pamphlets 1824–1859', in *Perspectives in Jurisprudence* (1977), ed. Elspeth Attwooll, p. 20. For discussions of Ruben's interpretation of Austin, see Morison, *John Austin*, pp. 122–32, and above, pp. 98–100.
10 Kitson Clark, p. 6.
11 Janet Ross, *Three Generations of English Women: Memoirs and correspondence of Susannah Taylor, Sarah Austin, and Lady Duff Gordon* (rev. edn, 1893), p. 88 (hereafter cited as *Three Generations*).
12 Ibid.
13 Ross, p. 89.
14 *Autobiography of John Stuart Mill* (1924), p. 52.
15 Mill, *Autobiography*, p. 55.
16 'The Dream of Life', *Poems* (1876), p. 426.
17 Mill, *Autobiography*, p. 54.
18 A Mr Summer, as quoted in *Dictionary of National Biography* I (1917), 734.
19 Ibid.
20 Waterfield, *Lucie Duff Gordon*, p. 12.
21 Waterfield, p. 13.
22 Ibid.
23 'John Austin and the Analytical Jurists', in *The Social and Political Ideas*

of Some Representative Thinkers of the Age of Reaction and Reconstruction 1815–65, ed. F.J.C. Hearnshaw (1949), p. 163.

24 *LJ*, I, p. 3.
25 *Oxford English Dictionary* (1933), VIII, p. 599.
26 *PJD*, pp. 128, 294.
27 *PJD*, p. 186, and above, pp. 170–71.
28 *PJD*, p. 185.
29 *PJD*, p. 53.
30 Letter from John Austin and George C. Lewis to Lord Glenelg, 3 July 1837, Colonial Office Records, 158/114.
31 Sir William Holdsworth, *A History of English Law* (1938), XII, p. 77.
32 As quoted by Sir William Erle in a letter to Janet Duff Gordon, in Janet Ross, *The Fourth Generation: Reminiscences* (1912), p. 73.
33 Edwin W. Patterson, *Jurisprudence: Men and ideas of the law* (1953), p. 84.
34 *LJ*, I, p. 4.
35 Waterfield, *Lucie Duff Gordon*, pp. 25–9.
36 *Victorian England: Portrait of an age* (2nd edn, 1964), p. 3.
37 See the accounts of her life and achievements in the *Dictionary of National Biography*, I (1973), 742, and *The Athenaeum*, 2077, 17 August 1867, p. 209.
38 As quoted by Sarah Austin in a letter to M. Guizot, 31 December 1860, in Ross, *Three Generations*, p. 373.
39 For discussion of her efforts, see 'Preface', pp. 21–30.
40 *The Times*, 12 August 1867, p. 10.
41 A. Bain, *James Mill: A biography* (1882), p. 332.
42 Bain, p. 337.
43 John Roach, *Social Reform in England 1780–1880* (1978), p. 23.
44 Roach, pp. 23, 60.
45 *Autobiography of John Stuart Mill*, p. 72.
46 William Thomas, *The Philosophic Radicals: Nine studies in theory and practice, 1817–1841* (1979), p. 96.
47 Mill, *Autobiography*, p. 76.
48 Mill, pp. 73, 74.
49 Thomas, *The Philosophic Radicals*, p. 4. For other studies of the philosophic radicals, see Elie Halévy, *The Growth of Philosophic Radicalism*, trans. Mary Morris [1928]; (1955), and Joseph Hamburger, *Intellectuals in Politics: John Stuart Mill and the Philosophic Radicals* (1965).
50 Austin, *PC*, p. vi.
51 For an interpretation of Austin that emphasizes Mill's influence upon him, see Morison, *John Austin*. His analysis is subject, however, to the criticisms explained above, pp. 94–8.
52 Mill, *Autobiography*, p. 52.
53 Letter from Sarah Austin to M. Guizot, 18 December 1861, in Ross, *Three Generations*, p. 381.
54 Letter from John Austin to Jeremy Bentham, 20 July 1819, University College, London, Ogden MS 62 (2).
55 Ibid.
56 A.V. Dicey, *Lectures on the Relation between Law and Public Opinion in*

England during the Nineteenth Century [2nd edn, 1914] (1952) p. 149.
57 'DPW', p. 503.
58 Frederick Pollock, *The Land Laws* (1883), pp. 56–7.
59 F.M.L. Thompson, *English Landed Society in the Nineteenth Century* (1963), p. 69.
60 'Disposal of Property by Will – Entails – French Law of Succession', *Edinburgh Review*, XL (July 1824), 350.
61 *Edinburgh Review*, pp. 355, 358, 360–61.
62 *Edinburgh Review*, p. 374.
63 *The Works of Jeremy Bentham*, ed. John Bowring [1838–43] (1962), III, p. 442.
64 James Mill, 'Essay on Government', in *Utilitarian Logic and Politics: James Mill's 'Essay on Government', Macaulay's critique and the ensuing debate*, ed. Jack Lively and John Rees (1978), pp. 60–61. Mill's essay was first published in 1820.
65 *Utilitarian Logic and Politics*, p. 61.
66 For the relationship between the *Westminster Review* and the Benthamites, see *Autobiography of John Stuart Mill*, pp. 63–70, and George L. Nesbitt, *Benthamite Reviewing: The first twelve years of the 'Westminster Review' 1824–1836* (1934).
67 'DPW', p. 507.
68 'DPW', p. 509.
69 'Inheritance', *The New Encyclopedia Britannica: Macropedia* (15th edn, 1983), IX, 589.
70 'DPW', p. 547.
71 'DPW', p. 546.
72 'DPW', p. 512.
73 Ibid.
74 Ibid.
75 'DPW', p. 548.
76 'DPW', pp. 548–9.
77 'DPW', p. 549.
78 'DPW', p. 548.
79 'DPW', p. 508.
80 'DPW', p. 553.
81 'DPW', p. 531.
82 'DPW', pp. 549–50.
83 'DPW', p. 550.
84 Ibid.
85 *The Works of Jeremy Bentham*, IV, p. 564.
86 'DPW', p. 550.
87 Austin, 'Joint Stock Companies', *Parliamentary History and Review* (1826), p. 709 (hereafter cited as 'JSC').
88 H.A. Shannon, 'The Coming of General Limited Liability', *Economic History: A Supplement to the Economic Journal*, II (January 1931), 267.
89 Peter Mathias, *The First Industrial Nation: An economic history of Britain 1700–1914* (1969), p. 162.
90 'JSC', p. 719.
91 'JSC', pp. 711, 720.

92 'JSC', p. 720.
93 'JSC', p. 718.
94 'JSC', p. 727.
95 See Shannon, in *Economic History*, pp. 278, 282–91.
96 'JSC', p. 723. For Bentham's similar views on this problem, see *The Works of Jeremy Bentham*, III, p. 3.
97 For Bentham's economic writings, see *Jeremy Bentham's Economic Writings*, ed. W. Stark, 3 vols. (1952–4).
98 See *The Works of Jeremy Bentham*, II, pp. 496, 501, 510, 523, and Jeremy Bentham, *A Comment on the Commentaries and A Fragment on Government*, ed. J.H. Burns and H.L.A. Hart (1977), pp. 62–3.
99 See Jeremy Bentham, *An Introduction to the Principles of Morals and Legislation*, ed. J.H. Burns and H.L.A. Hart (1970), pp. 11, 25, 74.
100 See *An Introduction*, p. 294, and Bentham, *A Comment on the Commentaries*, pp. 429–31, 484–92.
101 See Mary Peter Mack, *Jeremy Bentham: An odyssey of ideas 1748–1792* (1962), pp. 74–6. Although Bentham was a severe critic of Blackstone, Austin had even less use than his mentor for the learned commentator. Bentham's basic criticisms of Blackstone were the 'antipathy to reformation' and the 'universal inaccuracy and confusion' which pervaded his work (*A Fragment on Government*, p. 394). Despite this, Bentham admired Blackstone's style of writing, his arrangement of the elements of jurisprudence, and several other features of his work (*A Fragment*, pp. 413, 415 and 420). Austin was critical even of Blackstone's literary style. See Austin, *LJ*, I, p. 69. He did praise, however, Blackstone's account of the origins and history of English courts of equity (*LJ*, II, p. 615).
102 See Mack, *Jeremy Bentham*, pp. 66, 67; *The Works of Jeremy Bentham*, IV, p. 498; III, p. 206.
103 See Halévy, *The Growth of Philosophic Radicalism*, p. 149, and *The Works of Jeremy Bentham*, I, pp. 180–81, and IV, pp. 455, 456.
104 *PJD*, p. 260 n. 23, p. 279 n. 25.
105 *PJD*, p. 68.
106 'DPW', p. 516.
107 'DPW', p. 509.
108 *Autobiography of John Stuart Mill*, pp. 45, 76, 55.
109 Letter from Sarah Austin to M. Guizot, 18 December 1861, in Ross, *Three Generations*, p. 382. For the relationship between Bentham and James Mill, see Bain, *James Mill*, pp. 136, 461.
110 James Steintrager, *Bentham* (1977), p. 94.
111 Waterfield, *Lucie Duff Gordon*, p. 38.
112 J.R. Dinwiddy, 'Bentham's Transition to Political Radicalism, 1809–10', *Journal of the History of Ideas*, XXXVI (1975), 683.
113 See above, pp. 25–6.
114 *PJD*, p. 191.
115 *LJ*, I, p. 420.
116 *LJ*, I, pp. 420–21.
117 *LJ*, I, pp. 90–91.
118 *LJ*, I, pp. 218–9.
119 *LJ*, I, p. 234.

120 *LJ*, II, p. 654.
121 *LJ*, II, p. 692.
122 *LJ*, II, p. 690.
123 *LJ*, II, p. 765.
124 *LJ*, II, pp. 882–3.
125 H.L.A. Hart, *Essays on Bentham: Studies in jurisprudence and political theory* (1982), p. 1.
126 See above, p. 74.
127 See Hart, *Essays on Bentham*, pp. 222–7, and J.H. Burns, 'Bentham on Sovereignty: An exploration', in *Bentham and Legal Theory*, ed. M.H. James (1973), p. 133.
128 *PC*, p. vi.
129 Ross, *The Fourth Generation*, p. 21.
130 'John Austin', *Dictionary of National Biography*, I (1917), p. 737.
131 Sarah Austin, 'Preface', p. 4.
132 As quoted by Gordon Waterfield, *Lucie Duff Gordon*, p. 121.
133 Sarah Austin, 'Preface', p. 4.
134 *Three Generations*, p. 91.
135 Sarah Austin, 'Preface', p. 5.
136 'Preface', p. 9.
137 H. Hale Bellot, *University College, London: 1826–1926* (1929), p. 47.
138 *Statement by the Council of the University of London explanatory of the Nature and Objects of the Institution* (1827), pp. 15–16.
139 As quoted by Bellot, *University College, London*, p. 97.
140 See *LJ*.
141 [Lord Brougham], 'John Austin', *Law Magazine Review* (1860), p. 165.
142 *The Life of Sir James Fitzjames Stephen* (1895), p. 60.
143 Bellot, p. 30.
144 J.H. Burns, *Jeremy Bentham and University College* (1962), p. 3.
145 Bellot, p. 12.
146 Burns, p. 3.
147 Bellot, p. 97.
148 Brougham, 'John Austin', pp. 166, 169. This praise may represent, at least to some extent, Brougham's attempt to atone for his savage indictment of Austin's reforms for Malta. See above, pp. 160, 185–6, 188–90.
149 Bellot, pp. 97–8.
150 *The Fourth Generation*, p. 22.
151 Stephen, *The Life of Sir James Fitzjames Stephen*, p. 60.
152 Letter from James Stephen to Macvey Napier, 27 July 1842, in *Selection from the Correspondence of the late Macvey Napier, Esq*, ed. Macvey Napier (1879), p. 399.
153 Letter from T.B. Macaulay to Macvey Napier, 14 July 1842, in *Selections from the Correspondence*, p. 395.
154 Letter to Sarah Austin, 22 May 1842, in *The Earlier Letters of John Stuart Mill 1812–1848*, ed. Francis E. Mineka (1963), p. 521.
155 Letter to Mr Senior, 7 February 1851, in Harriet Grote, *The Personal Life of George Grote* (1873), p. 200.
156 Letter from John Stuart Mill to Janet Duff Gordon (n.d.), in Ross, *The Fourth Generation*, p. 74.

157 Mill, *Autobiography*, p. 53.
158 Sarah Austin, 'Preface', p. 6.
159 Andreas B. Schwarz, 'John Austin and the German Jurisprudence of his Time', *Politica* I (1934), 182.
160 Schwarz, p. 180.
161 Letter from John Austin to George Grote, 9 December 1827, in Ross, *Three Generations*, p. 69.
162 *LJ*, II, p. 714.
163 Schwarz, p. 186.
164 *LJ*, II, p. 714.
165 Letter from John Austin to George Grote, as note 161 above.
166 *PJD*, p. 188.
167 Ibid.
168 *LJ*, I, p. 58.
169 *LJ*, I, p. 44.
170 'Report from the Select Committee on Legal Education, together with Minutes of Evidence', *Parliamentary Papers,* X (1846), 492 (hereafter cited as 'Report . . . on Legal Education').
171 'Report . . . on Legal Education', p. 493.
172 Mill, *Autobiography*, p. 124.
173 Mill, p. 125.
174 Letter from John Austin to Leonard Horner, 30 October 1828, University College, London, College Correspondence 583.
175 *James Mill: A biography*, p. 329.
176 For the list of Austin's students, see Bellot, *University College, London*, pp. 187–8.
177 *Report from the Council*, *Annual General Meeting of Proprietors*, 24 February 1830, p. 11.
178 Letter from Sarah Austin to Susan Reeve, 12 April 1830, in Ross, *Three Generations*, p. 80.
179 Letter of John Austin, 5 November 1830, University College, London, College Correspondence, p. 28.
180 Letter from John Austin to Leonard Horner, 12 November 1830, University College, London, College Correspondence, p. 29.
181 Bellot, *University College, London*, p. 176.
182 Bellot, p. 99.
183 Sarah Austin wrote in several places that her husband delivered his last lecture in June 1832. See *LJ*, I, p. 9, and II, pp. 898, 917. The bulk of the evidence indicates, however, that this date is incorrect. On 2 February 1833 John Stuart Mill wrote to Thomas Carlyle that 'the Austins are in their usual state – Austin lecturing to six or seven persons only, but those of a *kind* he likes'. *The Earlier Letters of John Stuart Mill 1812–1848*, p. 141. On 9 March 1833 Mill again wrote to Carlyle that Austin 'is lecturing to fit audience though few, & will . . . very probably go to live either at Berlin or at Bonn. He is still subject to his fits of illness'. *The Earlier Letters*, p. 147; see also p. 51 n. 2, and Bellot, p. 99.
184 Bellot, p. 99.
185 Sarah Austin, 'Preface', p. 6.

186 Letter of John Austin, 28 November 1829, University College, London, College Correspondence, p. 24.
187 Sarah Austin, 'Preface', pp. 6–7.
188 Brougham, 'John Austin', p. 166.
189 Letter of Nassau W. Senior to John Austin, 1829, Nassau W. Senior Papers, C 64, National Library of Wales.
190 Review of *LJ*, *Edinburgh Review*, CXVIII (1863), 227.
191 Letter from John Stuart Mill to Sarah Austin, 7 August 1830, in *The Earlier Letters of John Stuart Mill 1812–1848*, p. 52.
192 Austin, *LJ*, I, p. 32.
193 *LJ*, I, p. 31.
194 Review of *PJD*, *The Athenaeum*, 4 May 1861, p. 592.
195 *LJ*, I, p. 467.
196 *LJ*, I, p. 58.
197 *LJ*, I, p. 468.
198 Holdsworth, *A History of English Law*, XII, p. 88.
199 Holdsworth, pp. 77–78.
200 'Report . . . on Legal Education,' p. 498.
201 'Report . . .', p. 480.
202 'Report . . .', p. 481.
203 'Report . . .', p. 526.
204 C.H.S. Fifoot, *Judge and Jurist in the Reign of Victoria* (1959), p. 23.
205 As quoted by Fifoot, p. 23.
206 Sir William Holdsworth, *Some Makers of English Law* (1938), p. 257.
207 Bellot, *University College, London*, p. 175.
208 Sarah Austin, 'Preface', p. 9.
209 Letter from Sarah Austin to Susan Reeve, 12 April 1831, in Ross, *Three Generations*, p. 83.
210 Sarah Austin, 'Preface', p. 10.
211 Review of *PJD*, *Westminster Review*, XVIII (1833), 249.
212 Review of *PJD*, *The Times*, 9 August 1832.
213 Review of *PJD*, *Law Magazine Review*, VII (1832), 313.
214 *Law Magazine Review*, VII, 298.
215 *Law Magazine Review*, VII, 313.
216 Ibid.
217 Leon Radzinowicz, *A History of English Criminal Law and its Administration from 1750: Grappling for control* (1968), IV, p. 310.
218 Radzinowicz, p. 310 n. 21.
219 Radzinowicz, p. 310.
220 Letter of John Stuart Mill to Thomas Carlyle, 2 August 1833, in *The Earlier Letters of John Stuart Mill 1812–1848*, p. 169.
221 Brougham, 'John Austin', p. 167.
222 Sarah Austin, 'Preface', p. 10.
223 Ibid.
224 Brougham, p. 167.
225 Mill, *The Earlier Letters*, p. 170.
226 Sarah Austin, 'Preface', pp. 11, 12.
227 'Preface', p. 12.
228 'Report . . . on Legal Education', p. 504.

229 Sarah Austin, 'Preface', p. 16.
230 Letter of John Austin to Sir William Erle, 1844, in Ross, *Three Generations*, p. 201.
231 Letter of Sarah Austin to M. Guizot, 17 March 1857, in *Three Generations*, p. 325.
232 As quoted by Ross, *Three Generations*, p. vii.
233 Letter from Sarah Austin to Victor Cousin, 5 June 1842, *Three Generations*, p. 177.
234 Letter from Sarah Austin to M. Guizot, 21 January 1850, *Three Generations*, p. 244.
235 Sarah Austin, 'Preface', p. 12.
236 Waterfield, *Lucie Duff Gordon*, p. 65.
237 Sarah Austin, 'Preface', p. 13.
238 Letter from Sarah Austin to Dr Sciortino, 10 May 1839, in Ross, *Three Generations*, pp. 147–8.
239 Review of *The National System of Political Economy* by Frederic List, *Edinburgh Review*, LXXV (1842), 515 (hereafter cited as *Review*).
240 Donald Read, *Cobden and Bright: A Victorian political partnership* (1967), pp. 239–40.
241 Austin, *Review*, pp. 516, 520 and 519.
242 *PJD*, p. 66.
243 Roach, *Social Reform in England 1780–1880*, p. 66.
244 Austin, *PJD*, p. 72.
245 See Read, *Cobden and Bright*, pp. 30–32, 71, 103, 110 and 210.
246 Dicey, *Lectures on the Relation between Law and Public Opinion . . .*, p. 445n.
247 Letter from John Austin to John Stuart Mill, 27 June 1842, on file at the London School of Economics & Political Science.
248 Ibid.
249 *Review*, p. 523.
250 *Review*, p. 553.
251 *Review*, pp. 527–8.
252 As quoted by Read, *Cobden and Bright*, p. 238.
253 *Review*, pp. 529, 550, 541, and 544.
254 'Centralization', *Edinburgh Review*, LXXXV (1847), 221.
255 'Centralization', pp. 230. 231.
256 'Centralization', p. 239.
257 'Centralization', pp. 232, 233.
258 'Centralization', p. 234.
259 'Centralization', p. 250.
260 Ibid.
261 'Centralization', p. 254.
262 *LJ*, II, p. 841.
263 As quoted by Cosgrove, *The Rule of Law*, p. 247.
264 Dicey, *Lectures on the Relation between Law and Public Opinion . . .*, p. 310.
265 Dicey, p. 305.
266 *PJD*, pp. 281–2n.
267 Sarah Austin, 'Preface', p. 15.

268 *Lucie Duff Gordon*, p. 113.
269 For a useful collection of Comte's writings, see *Auguste Comte and Positivism: The essential writings*, ed. Gertrud Lenzer (1975).
270 As quoted by Roberto Ago, 'Positive Law and International Law', *American Journal of International Law*, LI (1957), 696 n.15.
271 Letter from John Austin to John Stuart Mill, 25 December 1844, Yale University Library.
272 Ibid.
273 Ibid.
274 Alfred Cobban, *A History of Modern France: From the First Empire to the Second Empire, 1799–1871* (2nd edn, 1965) II, p. 109.
275 Letter from Sarah Austin to Lord Brougham, 1857, University College, London, Brougham MSS, 26, 525.
276 John Austin, letter to John Stuart Mill.
277 Letter from Sarah Austin to M. Guizot, 17 March 1857, in Ross, *Three Generations*, p. 324.
278 Letter from Sarah Austin to M. Guizot, 1 January 1860, in *Three Generations*, p. 360.
279 Hermann Ludwig Heinrich Pückler-Muskau, *Tour in England, Ireland and France, in the years 1826, 1827, 1828 and 1829*, trans. Sarah Austin (1833), and *Tour in Germany, Holland and England, in the years 1826, 1827 and 1828*, trans. Sarah Austin (1832).
280 Waterfield, *Lucie Duff Gordon*, pp. 51–2.
281 See, for example, Waterfield, *Lucie Duff Gordon*, pp. 54–5, 58–9, 60.
282 Letter from Sarah Austin to M. Guizot, 1 January 1860, in Ross, *Three Generations*, p. 360.
283 *PC*.
284 'Preface', p. 21.
285 'Preface', pp. 22, 23.
286 Letter from Sarah Austin to M. Guizot, 1 December 1860, in Ross, *Three Generations*, p. 373.
287 'Preface', p. 21.
288 Letter from Sarah Austin to Lord Brougham, 11 June 1862, on file at University College, London, Brougham MSS, 26, 541.
289 Letter from Sarah Austin to Lord Brougham, 19 October 1857, Brougham MSS, 26, 524.
290 Letter from Sarah Austin to M. Guizot, 17 March 1857, in Ross, *Three Generations*, p. 326.
291 Letter from Sarah Austin to Lord Brougham, 11 June 1865, Brougham MSS, 38, 601.
292 *James Mill: A biography*, p. 422.

III *Divine law, utilitarian ethics, and positivist jurisprudence*

1 A draft of this chapter, which has been thoroughly revised for publication in this book, was published in the *American Journal of Jurisprudence*, XXIV (1980), 139–80.
2 Two important and very different interpretations of Austin may be found in W.L. Morison, *John Austin* (1982), and Julius Stone, *Legal System and*

Lawyers' Reasonings (1964), pp. 63–97.

3 John Austin, *PJD*, pp. 365–6.

4 *Lectures on the Early History of Institutions* [7th edn, 1914] (1966), p. 368.

5 *Studies in History and Jurisprudence* (1901), p. 613.

6 *The Nature and Sources of the Law* [rev. edn, 1921] (1963), p. 304. Gray somewhat qualified, however, this criticism. Since 'the doctrines of morality are largely . . . a most important source from which the judges draw and ought to draw the rules which make the Law, the true theory of morals comes properly within the purview of Jurisprudence; and I cannot, therefore, blame Austin, as some do, for dealing with the foundations of morality in his treatise' (pp. 143–4).

7 *Legal Theory* (5th edn, 1967), p. 258. For a similar interpretation of Austin, see R.A. Eastwood and G.W. Keeton, *The Austinian Theories of Law and Sovereignty* (1929). The view that Austin's utilitarian ethics are unrelated to his jurisprudence is not universal. See Sir William Holdsworth, *Some Makers of English Law* (1938), pp. 259–60.

8 See H.L.A. Hart, *The Concept of Law* (1961), pp. 26–76.

9 See *The Concept of Law*, pp. vii, 203–07, and Hart, 'Positivism and the Separation of Law and Morals', *Harvard Law Review*, LXXI (1958), 593.

10 *The Concept of Law*, pp. 26–76.

11 For Kelsen's view of the relationship between his work and Austin's, see his *General Theory of Law and State*, trans. Anders Wedberg (1961), pp. xv–xvi, and 'The Pure Theory of Law and Analytical Jurisprudence', *Harvard Law Review*, LV (1941), 44. According to Kelsen, 'The orientation of the pure theory of law is in principle the same as that of so-called analytical jurisprudence. Like John Austin . . . the pure theory seeks to attain its results exclusively by an analysis of positive law. . . . Where they differ, they do so beause the pure theory of law tries to carry on the method of analytical jurisprudence more consistently than Austin and his followers.' *General Theory of Law and State*, p. xv. Kelsen does not attempt to justify this claim, however, by reference to the impact of Austin's utilitarianism on his jurisprudence.

12 To say this is not to imply that Hobbes was a full-fledged utilitarian, which was not the case. He believed that promises rather than utility were the ultimate basis of political obligation. See Brian Barry, 'Warrender and his Critics', in *Hobbes and Rousseau: A collection of critical essays*, ed. Maurice Cranston and Richard S. Peters (1972), pp. 64–5. Still, there are utilitarian elements in Hobbes' political philosophy. See above, pp. 103–4. For his conceptions of law and sovereignty, which are very similar to Austin's, see Hobbes, *Leviathan: or the Matter, Forme and Power of a Commonwealth Ecclesiastical and Civil*, ed. Michael Oakeshott (1962); and *A Dialogue between a Philosopher and a Student of the Common Laws of England*, ed. Joseph Cropsey (1971). If Hobbes modifies some of his ideas in this last book, he still defines law in terms of the commands of the sovereign (*A Dialogue*, p. 71). He also maintains that the power of the sovereign cannot be limited by human laws (p. 76).

x 13 For a very lucid account of some of the different versions of utilitarianism, see J.J.C. Smart and Bernard Williams, *Utilitarianism for and against* (1973), pp. 3–7.

14 *PJD*, p. 75.
15 For a different interpretation, see Ernest Albee, *A History of English Utilitarianism* (1902), pp. 52–54.
16 John Locke, *An Essay Concerning Human Understanding*, ed. A.C. Fraser (1894), I, p. 67.
17 Locke, pp. 340–41, 64, 475, 476, 476–8.
18 See Leslie Stephen, *History of English Thought in the Eighteenth Century* (3rd edn, 1902), II, pp. 106, 121–5.
19 Jerome B. Schneewind, *Sidgwick's Ethics and Victorian Moral Philosophy* (1977), p. 122.
20 Elie Halévy, *The Growth of Philosophic Radicalism*, trans. Mary Morris (1955), p. 23.
21 *The Works of William Paley, D.D.* (1837), I, pp. 27, 12, 41, 42.
22 *The Works*, pp. 36, 46.
23 *The Works*, pp. 48, 51.
24 For Bentham's views on these subjects, see *An Introduction to the Principles of Morals and Legislation*, ed. J.H. Burns and H.L.A. Hart (1970), pp. 11, 38, 13, 100, 120 n. 2, and Jeremy Bentham, *A Comment on the Commentaries and a Fragment on Government*, ed. J.H. Burns and H.L.A. Hart (1977), pp. 444–5. The similarity between these ideas and Austin's is evident from *PJD*, pp. 105, 127–8, 294, 109, 310 and 61.
25 See Bentham, *An Introduction to the Principles of Morals and Legislation*, pp. 31–2, and John Stuart Mill, *Utilitarianism with Critical Essays*, ed. Samuel Gorovitz (1971), pp. 27–8.
26 Whether Austin actually believed what he wrote is a nice question, to which there is no certain answer. At any rate, his expressed views differ sharply from those of the Benthamites. According to Elie Halévy, 'the orthodox Utilitarian school, which . . . grew up in London around Bentham and James Mill, was radically irreligious, and endeavoured to prove that belief in God was not only a childish superstition, but a dangerous error.' *A History of the English People in the Nineteenth Century: England in 1815*, trans. E.I. Watkin and D.A. Barker (1961), p. 417. For Leslie Stephen, 'Utilitarianism, the Utilitarians clearly recognised, logically implies the rejection of all theology.' *The English Utilitarians* (1950), II, p. 348.
27 *PJD*, pp. 34, 42.
28 *PJD*, pp. 34–5.
29 *PJD*, pp. 35–6.
30 *PJD*, p. 96.
31 *PJD*, p. 128.
32 *PJD*, p. 99.
33 *Contemporary Utilitarianism*, ed. Michael D. Bayles (1968), p. 7.
34 *PJD*, p. 47.
35 *PJD*, p. 49.
36 *PJD*, pp. 39–40.
37 *PJD*, p. 41.
38 Ibid.
39 *PJD*, p. 40.
40 *PJD*, pp. 79, 75.

41 *PJD*, pp. 72, 282–3 n. 25.
42 *PJD*, p. 73.
43 *PJD*, pp. 61–2.
44 *PJD*, p. 105.
45 *PJD*, p. 294.
46 *PJD*, pp. 106–8.
47 *PJD*, pp. 108–9.
48 *PJD*, p. 294.
49 *PJD*, p. 13.
50 *PJD*, p. 14.
51 *PJD*, p. 24.
52 *PJD*, p. 21.
53 *PJD*, p. 32.
54 *PJD*, p. 126.
55 *PJD*, p. 33.
56 *PJD*, p. 365.
57 *PJD*, p. 367.
58 *PJD*, pp. 367–8.
59 *LJ*, II, p. 1030.
60 *PJD*, p. 369.
61 *LJ*, I, p. 448.
62 *PJD*, p. 370.
63 Jeremy Bentham, *Of Laws in General*, ed. H.L.A. Hart (1970), pp. 76a, 156.
64 *LJ*, II, p. 712.
65 *LJ*, I, p. 419, and II, p. 712.
66 *LJ*, I, p. 49.
67 Bentham, *An Introduction to the Principles of Morals and Legislation*, p. 295.
68 *PJD*, p. 366 n.35.
69 This book is in the library of the Honourable Society of the Inner Temple, London. I am indebted to Mr Wallace Breem, Librarian, for his help in deciphering Austin's almost illegible handwriting.
70 *Second Statement by the Council of the University of London Explanatory of the Plan of Instruction* (1828).
71 *PJD*, p. 366.
72 See H.L.A. Hart, 'Positivism and the Separation of Law and Morals', 601 n. 25.
73 For Kelsen's conception of the subjectivity of ethical judgments, see *General Theory of Law and State*, pp. xvi, 6.
74 *PJD*, p. 6.
75 *PJD*, p. 372.
76 *PJD*, p. 184.
77 *LJ*, II, p. 1048.
78 *LJ*, I, p. 485.
79 Ibid.
80 Letter from Sarah Austin to M. Guizot, 3 January 1862, in Janet Ross, *Three Generations of English Women* (rev. edn, 1893), p. 384.
81 Preface, *LJ*, I, p. 16.

82 *PJD*, pp. 55–6.
83 *PJD*, p. 57.
84 *PJD*, pp. 4, 6, 6–7, and 7.
85 *PJD*, p. 59.
86 Kelsen views the general theory of law as a 'structural analysis of positive law rather than . . . a psychological or economic explanation of its conditions, or a moral or political evaluation of its ends'. *General Theory of Law and State*, p. xiv. The aim of the general theory is 'to enable the jurist concerned with a particular legal order, the lawyer, the judge, the legislator, or the law-teacher, to understand and to describe as exactly as possible his own positive law'. This aim is achieved by a comparative analysis of different legal orders which 'furnishes the fundamental concepts by which the positive law of a definite legal community can be described' (p. xiii). According to Kelsen, it is as necessary to separate the pure science of law from natural science as it is from politics and morals. 'The behaviour of the individuals as it actually is, is determined by laws of nature according to the principle of causality. This is natural reality. And in so far as sociology deals with this reality as determined by causal laws, sociology is a branch of natural science' (p. xiv). For Kelsen's analysis of the sociological elements in Austin's analytical jurisprudence, see *General Theory*, p. 171. To say that Kelsen distinguished the pure science of law from the sociology of law is not to suggest that he regards the latter as unimportant. One of its most significant and promising tasks is explanation of how ideologies influence the creation and application of law. See Kelsen, 'The Pure Theory of Law and Analytical Jurisprudence', *Harvard Law Review*, LV (1941), 44.
87 *The Works of Jeremy Bentham*, ed. John Bowring [1838–43] (1962), IX, pp. 2, 5; and I, pp. 240, 255, 254.
88 *PJD*, pp. 185, 187.
89 *PJD*, p. 7. Austin took the position, in this context, that his lengthy discussion of ethics is probably not 'precisely in keeping with the subject and scope of . . . [his] course'. 'If I am guilty of this departure . . .', he went on to write, 'the absorbing interest of the purpose which leads me from my proper path, will excuse, to indulgent readers, my offence against rigorous logic'. On balance, however, he claimed that his discourse on ethics was consistent with jurisprudence as he conceived it.
90 See W.D. Hudson, *Modern Moral Philosophy* (1970), p. 1, and Bayles, *Contemporary Utilitarianism*, p. 1.
91 *PJD*, pp. 4, 103.
92 *PJD*, p. 7.
93 *PJD*, pp. 5–6.
94 For good discussions of this aspect of legal positivism, see R.W.M. Dias, *Jurisprudence* (4th edn, 1976), pp. 451–7; H.L.A. Hart, *The Concept of Law,* pp. 195–207; Hart, *Essays on Bentham: Jurisprudence and political theory* (1982), p. 28; and Hart, 'Positivism and the Separation of Law and Morals'.
95 Kelsen appears to justify his distinction between law and morals, for example, on several other grounds. One is linguistic usage, while another is the social facts that this usage reflects. The most important of these

realities is the 'specific social technique' of law, i.e., its provision of sanctions.

96 *PJD*, p. 159.
97 *PJD*, pp. 160–1.
98 *LJ*, II, p. 754.
99 *LJ*, II, p. 746.
100 *LJ*, II, p. 754.
101 Ibid.
102 *LJ*, II, p. 746.
103 *PJD*, p. 184.
104 *Commentaries on the Laws of England in Four Books* [1765–9] (19th edn, 1870), I, pp. 27–8.
105 *Commentaries*, pp. 28–9.
106 *PJD*, p. 185.
107 *LJ*, I, p. 388, and *PJD*, p. 187.
108 *PJD*, p. 297 n. 28.
109 *PJD*, p. 185.
110 *LJ*, II, p. 764.
111 *PJD*, p. 53.
112 Ibid.
113 *PJD*, p. 54.
114 *PJD*, p. 277 n. 25.
115 *PJD*, p. 186.
116 *PJD*, p. 54.
117 *PJD*, p. 186.
118 *PJD*, pp. 54, 55.
119 *LJ*, II, p. 552.
120 *PC*, pp. 39, 40, 41.
121 *PJD*, p. 186.
122 Daniel J. Boorstin, *The Mysterious Science of the Law* (1958), p. 60. For Blackstone's uncritical glorification of English law, see Blackstone, *Commentaries on the Laws of England*, I, pp. 91–2, 102, 111–12, 164, 200.
123 *PJD*, p. 190.
124 Ibid.
125 See Sir William Holdsworth, *A History of English Law* (n.d.), VIII, pp. 27–8.
126 *PJD*, pp. 191, 190–91.
127 *PJD*, p. 186.
128 *PJD*, p. 46; also see p. 84.
129 See above, note 73.
130 *PJD*, p. 194.
131 *PJD*, p. 207.
132 *PJD*, p. 203.
133 *PJD*, p. 251.
134 *PJD*, pp. 230–31.
135 *PJD*, pp. 225–6.
136 *PJD*, pp. 30–32, 262.
137 *PJD*, p. 254.
138 Austin censured, for example, the tendency of legislators to forget that

positive laws which conflict with positive moral rules 'may be superfluous or impotent, and therefore may lead to nothing but purely gratuitous vexation. . . . the moral or the religious sentiments of the community may already suppress the practice as completely as it can be . . . or that, if the practice is favoured by those moral or religious sentiments the strongest possible fear which legal pains can inspire may be mastered by a stronger fear of other and conflicting sanctions.' *PJD*, p. 162.

139 *PJD*, p. 25.
140 *PJD*, p. 254.
141 *PJD*, p. 255.
142 Ibid.
143 *LJ*, II, p. 789.
144 See Julius Stone, *Legal System and Lawyers' Reasonings* (1964); W.L Morison, 'Some Myth about Positivism', *Yale Law Journal*, LXVIII (1958), 212; W.L. Morison, *John Austin* (1982); and Eira Ruben, 'John Austin's Political Pamphlets 1824–1859', in *Perspectives in Jurisprudence*, ed. Elspeth Attwooll, p. 20.
145 Stone, *Legal System*, pp. 72–3, 74, 90, 68.
146 Stone, p. 66.
147 Stone, p. 73.
148 *Introduction to the Study of the Law of the Constitution* (8th edn, 1920), p. 29. Dicey added, however, that 'in a political sense the electors are the most important part of, we may even say are actually, the sovereign power, since their will is under the present constitution sure to obtain ultimate obedience.'
149 Morison, 'Some Myth about Positivism', p. 212.
150 Morison, p. 219.
151 *PJD*, pp. 49–50, 243, 191, 30–33, 213.
152 *LJ*, II, p. 679.
153 Review of *LJ*, *Edinburgh Review*, CXVIII (1863), 224.
154 Morison, 'Some Myth About Positivism', pp. 223, 221, 232.
155 *John Austin*.
156 *John Austin*, p. 48.
157 *John Austin*, pp. 47, 10.
158 *John Austin*, p. 1.
159 Ibid.
160 *John Austin*, p. 142.
161 See *LJ*, I, p. x.
162 See, for example, *PJD*, pp. 213, 260 n. 23, 113 n. 279 n. 25.
163 *Autobiography of John Stuart Mill* (1924), p. 52.
164 James Mill, *Elements of Political Economy* (3rd edn, 1826), reprinted in *James Mill: Selected economic writings*, ed. Donald Winch (1966), p. 211.
165 *PJD*, p. 12.
166 *PJD*, p. 13.
167 Review of *LJ*, *Edinburgh Review*, CXVIII (1863), 227.
168 *Edinburgh Review*, p. 224.
169 *PJD*, pp. 378, 386.
170 *PJD*, pp. 370–71.
171 Morison, *John Austin*, p. 60.

172 *Autobiography of John Stuart Mill*, p. 158.
173 Ibid.
174 *PJD*, p. 254.
175 'Centralization', *Edinburgh Review*, LXXXV (1847), 222.
176 *PJD*, pp. 77–8.
177 Locke, *An Essay Concerning Human Understanding*, II, p. 208. Geometrical models also had a tremendous impact upon the thought of Thomas Hobbes, whom Austin deeply admired. According to Hobbes, geometry is 'the only science that it hath pleased God hitherto to bestow on mankind'. *Leviathan*, p. 36. Knowledge of fact is important, but it is not scientific knowledge. The latter consists only of '*knowledge of the consequence of one affirmation to another*' (p. 69). Truth is the 'right ordering of names in our affirmations' (p. 36).
178 *LJ*, II, p. 894.
179 Gerhard Maher develops this point in his excellent article, 'Analytical Philosophy and Austin's Philosophy of Law', *Archiv für Rechts- und Sozialphilosophie*, LXIV (1978), 410.
180 *PJD*, pp. 20–21.
181 *PJD*, p. 365.
182 *LJ*, I, p. 33.
183 *PJD*, p. 373.
184 *PJD*, p. 383.
185 Ruben, 'John Austin's Political Pamphlets', p. 38.
186 Ruben, p. 37.
187 Ibid.
188 *PJD*, p. 367.
189 *PJD*, p. 368.
190 *Lectures on the Relation between Law and Public Opinion in England during the Nineteenth Century* [2nd edn, 1914](1952), p. 303.
191 Ruben, 'John Austin's Political Pamphlets', p. 31.
192 'Centralization', *Edinburgh Review*, LXXXV (1847), 241.
193 Review of *The National System of Political Economy*, by Frederic List, *Edinburgh Review*, LXXV (1842), 527–8.
194 *LJ*, I, pp. 507, 505, 507.
195 *LJ*, I, p. 456.
196 *PJD*, p. 18.
197 *LJ*, I, p. 469.
198 *LJ*, I, pp. 405 n. 61, 456.
199 *PJD*, p. 85.
200 Hobbes, *Leviathan*, pp. 129, 221.
201 *PJD*, pp. 260 n. 23, 279 n. 25.
202 *PJD*, pp. 164–5.
203 *PJD*, pp. 165–71.
204 Locke, *An Essay Concerning Human Understanding*, I, pp. 474–5.
205 *LJ*, I, p. 450.
206 *PJD*, pp. 296–8.
207 *PJD*, p. 299.
208 *PJD*, p. 300.
209 *PJD*, p. 301.

210 *LJ*, II, p. 577.
211 Hobbes, *Leviathan*, pp. 100, 157.
212 *PJD*, p. 279 n. 25.
213 *PJD*, pp. 275, 278 n. 25.
214 *PJD*, p. 278 n. 25.
215 Bentham, *A Fragment on Government*, pp. 484, 489.
216 *Essays on Bentham: Studies in jurisprudence and political theory* (1982), p. 223.
217 *Bentham's Handbook of Political Fallacies*, ed. Harold A. Larrabee (1971), p. 66.
218 Bentham, *A Fragment*, pp. 486, 487, 494–7.
219 *The Works of Jeremy Bentham*, ed. John Bowring [1838–43]; (1962), IX, p. 119; II, p. 494.
220 *A Fragment*, p. 488.
221 *Bentham's Handbook of Political Fallacies*, p. 54.
222 Letter from Sarah Austin to M. Guizot, 18 December 1861, in Janet Ross, *Three Generations*, p. 382.
223 Ross, *Three Generations*, p. 381.
224 Austin did criticize Bentham for his alleged neglect of the negative test of sovereignty. *PJD*, p. 212. For a criticism of this objection, see H.L.A. Hart, 'Bentham on Sovereignty', in *Jeremy Bentham: Ten critical essays*, ed. Bhikhu Parekh (1974), p. 148.
226 If the limitations are strictly construed, Bentham argued, the effect is to prohibit 'the making of the most necessary laws, perhaps even of all laws'. *An Introduction to the Principles of Morals and Legislation*, p. 309. If the limitations are liberally interpreted, then they express 'no more than if each man were to say, *Your laws shall become* ipso facto *void, as often as they contain anything which is not to my mind*' (p. 309). According to J.H. Burns, Bentham's criticisms of attempts to limit by fundamental laws the competence of supreme legislative bodies 'gained in strength and vehemence with the passing years'. 'Bentham on Sovereignty: An exploration', in *Bentham and Legal Theory* (1973), ed. M.H. James, p. 146. It was precisely in the last years of his life, when this vehemence was strongest, that Austin met Bentham and became his disciple.
226 'Copies or Extracts of Reports of the Commissioners appointed to inquire into the Affairs of Malta and of Correspondence thereupon', *Parliamentary Papers*, XXIX (pt 1) (1837–8), p. 10.
227 *PJD*, p. 374.

IV *Judicial legislation and legal positivism*

1 An early draft of this chapter, which has been substantially revised for publication in this book, was published in *University of Western Australia Law Review*, XIII (1977), 77.
2 H.L.A. Hart, 'Positivism and the Separation of Law and Morals', *Harvard Law Review*, LXXI (1958), 602 n. 25. Also, see Hart, 'Legal Positivism', *Encyclopedia of Philosophy*, IV (1967), 418.
3 See George W. Paton, *A Textbook of Jurisprudence*, ed. G.W. Paton and David P. Derham, (4th edn, 1972), pp. 9–10.

4 W.L. Morison, 'Some Myth about Positivism', *Yale Law Journal*, VIII (1958), 212.
5 *The Concept of Law* (1961), p. 237.
6 Hart, 'Positivism and the Separation of Law and Morals', pp. 608, 609, 610.
7 For a study of the relationship between Austin and the legal realists, see Rumble, 'The Legal Positivism of John Austin and the Realist Movement in American Jurisprudence', *Cornell Law Review*, LXVI (June, 1981), 986.
8 Holmes emphasized as early as 1872 that 'it must be remembered, as is clear from numerous instances of judicial interpretation of statutes in England and of constitutions in this country, that in a civilized state it is not the will of the sovereign that makes lawyers' law, even when that is its source, but what a body of subjects, namely, the judges, *by whom it is enforced* (emphasis added), *say* is his will. The judges have other motives for decision, outside their own arbitrary will, besides the commands of their sovereign. . . . The only question for the lawyer is, how will the judges act?' 'The Law Magazine and Review', *American Law Review*, VI (1872), 593, in *Harvard Law Review*, XLIV (1930–31), 789–90. This idea was the basis of Holmes' famous predictive conception of law, his fullest exposition of which may be found in 'The Path of the Law', an address that he delivered in 1897. See *The Mind and Faith of Justice Holmes: His speeches, essays, letters and judicial opinions*, ed. Max Lerner (1943), pp. 71–89. For Gray's views, see his *The Nature and Sources of the Law* [rev. edn, 1921] (1963).
9 'Centralization', *Edinburgh Review*, LXXXV (1847), 225.
10 *LJ*, I, p. 244.
11 'Centralization', 225.
12 Ibid.
13 *PJD*, p. 32.
14 Sir Henry Sumner Maine, *Lectures on the Early History of Institutions* [7th edn, 1914] (1966), pp. 364, 365.
15 Gray, *The Nature and Sources of the Law*, p. 85.
16 The interpretation of the Mann Act, the so-called 'White Slave Traffic Act', is an excellent example. For a fascinating analysis of this development, see Edward H. Levi, *An Introduction to Legal Reasoning* (1948), pp. 27–57. For a recent example of judicial acrobatics in the interpretation of statutes, see *United Steelworkers of America* v. *Weber*, 433 US 193 (1979).
17 See, among others, Maine, *Lectures*; James Bryce, *Studies in History and Jurisprudence* (1901), and Hart, *The Concept of Law* (1961), pp. 49–76.
18 *Collected Legal Papers* [1920] (1952), p. 239.
19 *LJ*, II, pp. 624, 990.
20 *LJ*, II, pp. 624, 625 and 990.
21 'Determining the Ratio Decidendi of a Case', *Yale Law Journal*, XL (1930), 162.
22 *LJ*, II, p. 627.
23 *LJ*, II, p. 625.
24 *LJ*, II, pp. 623, 622.

25 *LJ*, II, p. 622.
26 'A Return to Stare Decisis', *American Bar Association Journal*, XIV (1928), 73.
27 Felix S. Cohen, *Ethical Systems and Legal Ideals: An essay on the foundations of legal criticism* (1959), p. 35.
28 *LJ*, II, pp. 998, 999.
29 *PJD*, p. 207.
30 Ibid.
31 *LJ*, II, 1001 n. 20.
32 *PJD*, pp. 202–03.
33 *PJD*, p. 203.
34 H.L.A. Hart, 'Positivism and the Separation of Law and Morals', p. 607.
35 H.L.A. Hart, *The Concept of Law*, p. 123.
36 Hart, *The Concept of Law*, pp. 123, 123–4, 124.
37 *LJ*, II, p. 628.
38 *LJ*, II, pp. 621, 622.
39 *LJ*, II, pp. 622, 630, 628.
40 According to the late Karl N. Llewellyn, a characteristic mark of the realist movement is 'a distrust of the theory that traditional prescriptive rule-formulations are *the* heavily operative factor in producing court decisions'. *Jurisprudence: Realism in theory and practice* (1962), p. 56. This distrust is the essence of rule-scepticism, which is a matter of degree. Although all of the legal realists distrusted the theory that established rules had a decisive impact on judicial decisions, some were more distrustful than others. Individual realists also changed their minds about how much of an impact these rules had. For a good discussion of the evolution of Jerome Frank's thought on this problem, see J. Mitchell Rosenberg, *Jerome Frank: Jurist and philosopher* (1970), pp. 48–83. Llewellyn's *emphasis* on rule-scepticism also changed substantially in the course of his life, if the degree of his scepticism did not change. This seems to me to be evident from a comparison of the text of his *The Bramble Bush: On our law and its study* (1960), which was first published in 1930, and the Foreword to it (pp. 7–10), which he wrote in 1950. For a discussion of the ideas of the legal realists, see my *American Legal Realism: Skepticism, reform, and the judicial process* (1968). For a different interpretation of legal realism, see William Twining, *Karl Llewellyn and the Realist Movement* (1973).
41 *LJ*, II, pp. 634, 539, 665.
42 *LJ*, II, pp. 531, 610.
43 *LJ*, II, p. 613.
44 *LJ*, II, p. 537.
45 *LJ*, II, p. 557.
46 *LJ*, II, p. 635.
47 William Holdsworth, *A History of English Law* (1924), VI, pp. 379, 384.
48 *LJ*, II, pp. 635, 629.
49 Morison, 'Some Myth about Positivism', p. 215.
50 *The Works of Jeremy Bentham*, ed. John Bowring [1838–43] (1962), IX, p. 8; V, pp. 236, 235.
51 *The Works*, III, p. 206.

52 *The Works*, IV, p. 459.
53 *The Works*, IX, p. 8.
54 *The Works*, III, p. 206.
55 *The Works*, IV, p. 460.
56 *The Works*, III, p. 210.
57 *LJ*, II, pp. 532, 533, 651.
58 *LJ*, II, pp. 612, 646.
59 *LJ*, II, p. 647.
60 *LJ*, II, p. 613.
61 *PJD*, p. 191.
62 *LJ*, II, p. 1000.
63 *PJD*, p. 191. This point constitutes another and very strong analogy between the point of view of Austin and the legal realists. See Llewellyn, *Jurisprudence: Realism in theory and practice*, pp. 55, 72.
64 *PJD*, p. 191.
65 *LJ*, II, p. 612.
66 *The Judicial Decision: Toward a theory of legal justification* (1961), p. 138.
67 *The Judicial Decision*, pp. 119–20.
68 See Ronald Dworkin, *Taking Rights Seriously* (1977), pp. 31–9.
69 *An Introduction to the Philosophy of Law* (rev. edn, 1954), p. 56.
70 Dworkin, *Taking Rights Seriously*, pp. 22, 82.
71 Dworkin, pp. 22, 82, 26.
72 Dworkin, p. 32.
73 Dworkin, pp. 96–7.
74 Dworkin, p. 280.
75 Dworkin, pp. 84–8.
76 *PJD*, p. 367.
77 *LJ*, II, p. 1046.
78 This argument is developed by Joseph Raz, 'Legal Principles and the Limits of Law', in *Ronald Dworkin and Contemporary Jurisprudence*, ed. Marshall Cohen (1983), p. 75.
79 *Riggs* v. *Palmer*, 115 NY 506 (1889).
80 Dworkin, *Taking Rights Seriously*, p. 23.
81 *Riggs* v. *Palmer*, 506, 511.
82 *Riggs* v. *Palmer*, pp. 515–16.
83 *Riggs* v. *Palmer*, p. 517.
84 *The Common Law*, ed. Mark DeWolfe Howe [1881]; (1963), pp. 31–2.
85 See above, p. 128.
86 *LJ*, II, p. 654.
87 *LJ*, II, pp. 653, 652.
88 *LJ*, II, pp. 613, 650.
89 *LJ*, II, p. 655.
90 *LJ*, I, p. 487.
91 Gray, *The Nature and Sources of the Law*, p. 100. Although Gray felt this unwillingness to be natural, he also regarded it as unreasonable. His position was that practically 'in its application to actual affairs, for most of the laity, the Law, except for a few crude notions of the equity involved in some of its general principles, is all *ex post facto*. When a man marries, or enters into a partnership, or buys a piece of land, or engages in any other

transaction, he has the vaguest possible idea of the Law governing the situation, and with our complicated system of Jurisprudence, it is impossible it should be otherwise. . . . Now the Law of which a man has no knowledge is the same to him as if it did not exist' (p. 100).

92 *LJ*, II, p. 652.

93 For a discussion of this possibility, see B.H. Levy, 'Realist Jurisprudence and Prospective Overruling', *University of Pennsylvania Law Review*, CIX (1960), 1.

94 *LJ*, II, p. 651.

95 *LJ*, II, p. 658.

96 *LJ*, II, p. 660.

97 *Lectures on the Relation between Law & Public Opinion in England during the Nineteenth Century* (2nd edn, 1914), pp. 134–5.

98 *LJ*, II, p. 1026.

99 *LJ*, II, pp. 672, 636, 649.

100 *LJ*, II, p. 1028.

101 *LJ*, II, p. 675.

102 *LJ*, II, pp. 666, 660, 662, 663, 661.

103 *LJ*, II, p. 653.

104 'Centralization', *Edinburgh Review*, LXXXV (1847), 257.

105 'Preface', *LJ*, I, p. 20.

106 *LJ*, II, p. 613.

107 'Centralization', 257.

108 'Centralization', pp. 258, 257.

109 *LJ*, II, pp. 663, 660.

110 *PJD*, pp. 374–5.

111 *LJ*, II, p. 625.

112 Gray, *The Nature and Sources of the Law*, pp. 172–3. For analysis of statutory construction from the perspective of legal realism, see these articles by Max Radin: 'The Theory of Judicial Decision: Or how judges think', *American Bar Association Journal*, XI (1925), 357; 'Statutory Interpretation', *Harvard Law Review*, XLIII (1930), 863; 'Realism in Statutory Interpretation and Elsewhere', *California Law Review*, XXIII (1935), 156; 'A Short Way with Statutes', *Harvard Law Review*, LVI (1942), 388. Also, see Joseph W. Bingham, 'What is the Law?' *Michigan Law Review*, XI (1912), 1, 24; J. Frank, *Courts on Trial: Myth and Reality in American Justice* (1949), pp. 292–309; and K.N. Llewellyn, *The Common Law Tradition: Deciding Appeals* (1960), pp. 521–35.

113 *LJ*, II, pp. 646, 647.

114 *LJ*, II, p. 581.

115 *PJD*, p. 190.

116 *LJ*, II, p. 588.

117 See *The Basic Works of Aristotle*, ed. Richard McKeon (1941), pp. 1020, 1372; *The Political Ideas of St Thomas Aquinas: Representative selections*, ed. Dino Bigongiari (1953), pp. 75–7; R. Pound, 'The Scope and Purpose of Sociological Jurisprudence', *Harvard Law Review*, XXV (1912), 515; R. Pound, *An Introduction to the Philosophy of Law* (rev. edn, 1954), pp. 63–71; and Jerome Frank, *Law and the Modern Mind* [1930]; (1949).

118 *LJ*, II, pp. 581, 582.

119 *LJ*, II, pp. 620, 577.
120 *PJD*, p. 53.
121 Frank, *Law and the Modern Mind*, p. 190.
122 Frank, p. 189.
123 Frank, p. 191.
124 Frank, p. 192n*.
125 Frank, p. 192.
126 Frank, p. 311.
127 For an excellent discussion of Llewellyn and the Uniform Commercial Code, see Twining, *Karl Llewellyn and the Realist Movement*, pp. 270–340. Although the Code was the product of a collaborative effort, 'there is no doubt that Llewellyn was easily the most important single figure' (p. 271).
128 As quoted by Twining, pp. 304, 322.
129 S. Williston, as quoted by Twining, pp. 322–3.
130 Twining, pp. 323, 312.
131 Llewellyn, *Jurisprudence*, p. 217.
132 Karl N. Llewellyn, *The Common Law Tradition: Deciding Appeals* (1960), pp. 38, 5.
133 Llewellyn, *Jurisprudence*, pp. 107, 108.
134 Frank, *Law and the Modern Mind*, p. 6.
135 Frank, p. ix.
136 Arthur L. Corbin, 'The Law and the Judges', *Yale Review*, III (1914), 239.
137 Ibid.
138 Corbin, p. 245.
139 Herman Oliphant, 'A Return to Stare Decisis', *American Bar Association Journal*, XIV (1928), 71, 159.
140 Oliphant, pp. 162, 75.
141 Oliphant, p. 159.
142 Oliphant, p. 162.
143 Llewellyn, *Jurisprudence*, p. 57.
144 *LJ*, II, p. 662.
145 Ibid.
146 *LJ*, II, pp. 1092–3.
147 *LJ*, II, p. 612.
148 *LJ*, II, p. 647.
149 *LJ*, II, p. 646.
150 *LJ*, II, p. 661.
151 *PJD*, p. 191.
152 *LJ*, II, p. 612.
153 See Neil MacCormick, 'Dworkin as Pre-Benthamite', in *Ronald Dworkin and Contemporary Jurisprudence*, ed. Marshall Cohen (1983), p. 182.
154 See his *General Theory of Law and State*, trans. Anders Wedburg (1961), pp. 134–5, 149–50.
155 See Hart, *The Concept of Law*, pp. 121–50.
156 Pound, 'Spurious Interpretation', *Columbia Law Review*, VII (1907), 380–81.
157 For an influential modern statement of the concept, see Louis D.

Brandeis, 'The Living Law', in *The Curse of Bigness: Miscellaneous Papers of Louis D. Brandeis*, ed. Osmond K. Fraenkel (1935), p. 316. This essay was an address delivered before the Chicago Bar Association in 1915. For Pound's famous distinction between the law in books and the law in action, see his 'The Need of a Sociological Jurisprudence', *Green Bag*, XIX (1907), 607; 'Law in Books and Law in Action', *American Law Review*, XLIV (1910), 12; and 'The Causes of Popular Dissatisfaction with the Administration of Justice', *American Law Review*, XL (1906), 729.

158 *LJ*, II, p. 604.

159 *LJ*, II, pp. 1040, 1048.

160 See John Rawls, *A Theory of Justice* (1971).

161 See Holmes, 'The Law Magazine and Review', and Oliver Wendell Holmes, *Collected Legal Papers* (1920).

V *The reform of Malta*

The following abbreviations, or abbreviated titles, will be used below:

PP, for Parliamentary Papers of the Imperial Parliament.

CO, for Colonial Office Records at the Public Records Office, London.

PD, for Hansard's Parliamentary Debates.

RC, for Copies or Extracts of Reports of the Commissioners appointed to inquire into the affairs of the Island of Malta and of Correspondence thereupon.

Draft, for Draft of an Ordinance for abolishing the Censorship, and for providing against Abuses of the consequent Liberty of Publishing, *CO* 158/115, pp. 76–80.

Notes, for Notes on the Draft of the Ordinance for abolishing the Censorship, and for providing against Abuses of the consequent Liberty of Publishing, *CO* 158/115, pp. 80–117.

Remarks, for Remarks [of the Commissioners] on the objections to the Ordinance for granting a Free Press to Malta [no date], *CO* 158/115.

1 Lewis's best known work is probably his *Remarks on the Use and Abuse of Some Political Terms* [1832] (1970). For his views on colonial problems, see his *An Essay on the Government of Dependencies*, ed. C.P. Lucas [1841] (1891). An informative account of his life and achievements may be found in Charles F. Mullett, 'Introductory Essay', in Lewis, *Remarks on the Use and Abuse*, pp. 1–64.

2 Austin was fifteen years older than Lewis, who had attended his lectures at the University of London in 1830. Lewis's respect for Austin was so great that it approximated to hero worship. At the least he expressed the greatest admiration for his mentor, of whose talent and knowledge he had the 'highest opinion'. *Letters of the Right Hon. Sir George Cornewall Lewis, Bart., to Various Friends*, ed. Gilbert Frankland Lewis (1870), p. 57 [hereafter cited as Letters].

'No living person is so competent . . . ,' Lewis wrote of Austin in 1843, 'to instruct the world upon ethical and legal subjects' (p. 132). This admiration strongly influenced Lewis's decision to accept the appointment as a Commissioner to Malta. He doubted that he would have gone to the Island 'as the colleague of any other person [than Austin] if the appointment were offered . . . on the most unobjectionable terms.' Lewis wrote that he would 'never lose the opportunity of serving [Austin] . . . in any way in [his] power' (p. 56). Finally, he expressed the opinion that his views 'mainly coincided' with Austin's (p. 57). Although it is impossible to be certain, this evidence indicates the likelihood that if Austin and Lewis disagreed about what to recommend for Malta, the views of Austin would have prevailed.

For a significant analysis of the relationship between Austin and Lewis, see Walter Bagehot, *Biographical Studies*, ed. R.H. Hutton (2nd edn, 1889), pp. 235–8.

3 Eric Stokes, *The English Utilitarians and India* (1959), p. 48.

4 For studies of the colonial policies of the utilitarians, see Stokes, *The English Utilitarians and India*, and Donald Winch, *Classical Political Economy and Colonies* (1965).

5 For histories of various phases of British rule of Malta, see C. Willis Dixon, *The Colonial Administrations of Sir Thomas Maitland* (1939); Edith Dobie, *Malta's Road to Independence* (1967); William Hardman, *A History of Malta during the Period of the French and British Occupations, 1798–1815*, ed. J. Holland Rose (1909); Albert V. LaFerla, *British Malta* (1938), I; Henry Seddall, *Malta: Past and Present: A history of Malta from the days of the Phoenicians to the present time* (1870); and Harrison Smith, *Britain in Malta: Constitutional development of Malta in the nineteenth century* (1953), I.

6 As quoted by Hardman, *A History of Malta*, p. 8.

7 As quoted by Hardman, p. 204.

8 Hardman, p. 533.

9 Martin Wight, *The Development of the Legislative Council 1606–1945* (1946), p. 47.

10 See Hardman, *A History of Malta*, pp. 509–11.

11 Hardman, p. 510. Whether the Maltese people ever had the kind of *Consiglio Popolare* advocated in this petition, and others, is a matter of debate. For the typical views of a Maltese patriot, see George Mitrovich, *The Cause of the People of Malta; now before Parliament* (1836). A Royal Commission to Malta reported in 1812, however, that 'at no period of their history did the Maltese ever possess the slightest pretension or right to a deliberative and legislative assembly.' Quoted by Hardman, *A History of Malta*, p. 517. The Commissioners maintained that the actual *Consiglio Popolare* was 'simply an assembly of the people summond by order of the Crown for the nomination of certain jurats of the *Università*, which nomination was afterwards submitted to the Sovereign for his approbation' (p. 518). This finding may have been conditioned by the Commissioners' adamant opposition to the establishment of a powerful Council on Malta. If it were instituted, they argued, every 'chimerical project that folly, ignorance, or ambition can frame will be brought forward and discussed. The fury of superstition and the influence of priesthood will be set in motion. . . . it will be the focus of sedition . . . paralysing all the efforts of government' (pp. 522–3).

12 *PD*, XXXIV (1836), p. 161.

13 *PD*, XXXIV, pp. 161–3.
14 Letter of Austin and Lewis to Lord Glenelg, 28 December 1838, *CO* 158/115.
15 The reasons for the appointment of Austin and Lewis as Commissioners are unclear. James Fitzjames Stephen's friendship with and respect for Austin could have been, however, a crucial factor. Stephen was the legendary Permanent Under-Secretary of the Colonial Office from 1836 to 1847. In this capacity he exercised a strong influence over colonial affairs and 'strove with considerable success to make the government of the colonies more efficient and more responsive to the needs and wishes of the peoples concerned.' Paul Knaplund, *The British Empire 1815–1939* (1941), p. 6. Also see Paul Knaplund, *James Stephen and the British Colonial System 1813–1847* (1953). Although it is unclear whether Stephen recommended Austin's appointment as a Royal Commissioner, the Under-Secretary thought highly of him. Stephen once wrote to Macvey Napier, for example, that Austin 'enjoys, and deservedly, a very high and yet a peculiar reputation. I have a great attachment to him. He is, in the best sense of the word, a philosopher, an earnest and humble lover of wisdom. . . . I know not anywhere a larger minded man.' Letter of James Stephen to Macvey Napier, 21 May 1842, in *Selection from the Correspondence of the late Macvey Napier, Esq* (1879), p. 392.
16 *RC*, *PP*, XXIX pt 1 (1837–8), p. 4.
17 Letter from Lord Glenelg to the Commissioners, 16 September 1836, *CO* 158/113.
18 Ibid.
19 Ibid.
20 Letter of Austin and Lewis to Lord Glenelg, 28 December 1836, *CO* 158/115. The discontent of the Maltese no doubt explains their exhuberant reaction to the arrival of the Commissioners on Malta. According to Lewis, 'We found ourselves . . . much to our surprise, floating down the full tide of popularity. We made a sort of triumphal entry (of course against our will) into the town. . . . The people evidently thought, or were told, that we came out with a Maltese Magna Charta in our pockets . . . the chief complainants . . . seemed to think that we had merely to give a grind or two, and out would come a whole code of laws already made.' Letter of Lewis to E.W. Head, 5 November 1836, in *Letters*, p. 66.
21 Letter of Austin and Lewis to Lord Glenelg, 3 July 1837, *CO* 158/114.
22 Ibid. The Commissioners did not give any examples of Governors of Malta who failed to appreciate this need. Austin and Lewis may well have had in mind Sir Thomas Maitland, the Governor of Malta 1813–24. His autocratic regime was strongly criticized by Lewis, who castigated Maitland as 'an ape of Bonaparte'. Maitland not only copied the Frenchman's mistaken principles, but coupled them with a 'brutality and coarseness of deportment which Bonaparte had not'. The Governor's system of driving and kicking mankind into obedience was 'in the long run, mischievous and absurd.' Letter of Lewis to his father, 6 December 1836, in *Letters*, p. 69. Among other things, it perpetuated the ignorance and moral degradation of the Maltese. Such are the effects, Lewis wrote, of a

'paternal, military despotism, which rules people by keeping them in ignorance and dependence' (p. 82).

23 Letter of Austin and Lewis to Lord Glenelg, 3 July 1837, *CO* 158/114.

24 Letter of Austin and Lewis to Lord Glenelg, 1 September 1837, *CO* 158/14.

25 Letter of Lord Glenelg to Austin and Lewis, 16 September 1836, *CO* 158/113.

26 *CO* 158/118 [hereafter cited as First Letter]. On 27 May 1840, Austin also wrote a follow-up letter on this subject to James Stephen, *CO* 158/118 [hereafter cited as Second Letter].

27 First Letter, pp. 8, 5.

28 First Letter, p. 4.

29 Ibid.

30 First Letter, p. 6.

31 Second Letter.

32 First Letter, p. 11.

33 Second Letter.

34 First Letter, pp. 8–9.

35 Second Letter.

36 First Letter, p. 9.

37 Second Letter.

38 Ibid.

39 Ibid.

40 First Letter, p. 10. The Commissioners did not specify the precise author and date of the promise in question. Austin and Lewis may have had in mind the declaration by Sir Charles Cameron, in 1801, that 'His Majesty grants you [the Maltese] full protection, and the enjoyment of all your dearest rights.' At least this specific utterance was strongly emphasized by George Mitrovich, who used it as the basis of his contention that the British had promised the Maltese to establish a *Consiglio Popolare*. See Mitrovich, *The Cause of the People of Malta*, pp. iii, 9. His interpretation of Cameron's statement presumes that the right to a *Consiglio Popolare* was one of the dearest rights of the Maltese people. Mitrovich's argument also presumes that this body, if it existed, had substantial political and legislative powers. The truth of either presumption is uncertain.

41 Second Letter.

42 First Letter, pp. 6, 7, 5.

43 First Letter, pp. 12–13. The underlined portions of this quotation raise the question of whether the Commissioners desired more sweeping changes in the Council of Government than they recommended to Lord Russell. The possibility that they did cannot be dismissed out-of-hand. Austin and Lewis may have believed that anything but a very limited concession stood no chance of being accepted by the Colonial Office, which was a quite realistic calculation. If it was entertained by the Commissioners, this fact could have strongly influenced the substance of their recommendation. They may have concluded that the proposal of the sort of far-reaching changes which they believed to be desirable was futile. Accordingly, it could be argued that they tailored their recommendation to maximize the likelihood of its acceptance.

This interpretation of the proposal of the Commissioners cannot be conclusively disproven. Nevertheless, it seems to me to be less plausible than the acceptance of their recommendation at its face value. No evidence exists to corroborate the theory that they actually desired a stronger Council than they recommended to Lord Russell. Lewis also specifically endorsed this kind of Council for all colonies whose prospects for independence were remote. He argued that no institutions should be established in these dependencies which would 'probably tempt the people to aim at practical independence'. *An Essay on the Government of Dependencies*, ed. C.P. Lucas (1891), p. 31. Instead, colonies of this type should be governed by 'subjecting the governor (or other head of the local subordinate government) to the control of a council representing the opinions and feelings of the more intelligent portion of the people, but not possessing any legislative or administrative powers strictly so called' (pp. 312–3). This was precisely the kind of Council that the Commissioners recommended to Lord Russell.

44 The response of the government might have been quite different if Lord Glenelg had still held office. He had resigned as Colonial Secretary, however, in February of 1839. Lord Russell held the position in 1840 and was much less sympathetic to the cause of colonial reform on Malta than Lord Glenelg. In any event the official explanation of the government's decision not to accept the recommendations of the Commissioners adds up to less than a page and is not very convincing. Mr Vernon Smith, the Parliamentary Under-Secretary for the Colonies, dismissed the letter of Austin and Lewis as 'nothing more than an explanation of the causes which have hitherto delayed, and which are still to delay indefinitely, the final report'. The failure to complete the report would not be 'much cause for regret'. The basis of this judgement was the belief that the plan of the Commissioners would be 'impracticable to execute'. Smith also emphasized that no one will be pleased with their 'scheme'. *CO* 158/118.

The comments of Lord John Russell are equally brief. He began by expressing his inability to find any reasonable explanation of why the letter of the Commissioners had not been sent 'long ago'. He indicated that no additional public expenses should be incurred in preparation of the report. He argued that a report in 1842 of what was advisable in 1836 would lead to no 'good end'. He therefore concluded that the Commissioners should be released from any additional labours in preparation of their report. *CO* 158/118. He subsequently wrote them that they 'should use their own discretion about reporting further'. 13 June 1840, *CO* 158/118.

These comments are an unsatisfactory justification of the decision of the government for a number of reasons. For one thing, neither Smith nor Russell addressed the carefully developed arguments of Austin and Lewis for their proposals. For another thing, the criticisms of both officials raise more questions than they answer. Smith did not indicate why the innovation of Austin and Lewis would be impracticable to implement, which it does not appear to be. The Parliamentary Under-Secretary also failed to explain why this concession would not satisfy the

British government. Lord Russell did not explain why a report in 1842 of what was advisable in 1836 would serve no good end. His judgment might have been warranted if circumstances on Malta had radically changed from 1836 to 1840, or promised to change drastically by 1842. I am not aware of any such changes, none of which was cited by Lord Russell.

45 The Commissioners justified their decision to delay preparation of their report on several grounds, one of which was that the delay was involuntary and unavoidable. The preparation of the report posed serious difficulties, including uncertainty about the topics to be investigated and the details or principles of their recommendations (First Letter, p. 15). A second reason was the deliberate choice of the Commissioners to wait until they had developed detailed knowledge of conditions on Malta. Such an understanding was essential if they were to reach 'just' and 'safe' conclusions about the 'doubtful' and 'dangerous' problems that they had to resolve (pp. 17–18). A third reason for the delay was their desire to observe the effects of the abolition of censorship on Malta (pp. 18–19). None of these reasons seems to me to be a very persuasive explanation of the Commissioners' decision to postpone, much less not to complete, their report. A more compelling factor may have been their conviction that a report on representative institutions in Malta was 'too hot too handle', though this opinion is speculative.

46 The petitions may be found in *PP*, XXIX (1846), pp. 124, 127.

47 *PP*, XXIX, pp. 125, 126.

48 *PP*, XXIX, p. 127. The reaction of the Commissioners to the petitions was predictable. They were highly critical of the first petition, which they contrasted unfavourably with the second petition. See Letter of Austin to James Stephen, 18 July 1839, *CO* 158/118, and Letter of Austin and Lewis to the Marquis of Normanby, 19 July 1839, *CO* 158/118.

49 Bentham is an exception, though not a consistent one, to this generalization. He alternated between 'emphasis on the drawbacks of colonial rule and awareness of the opportunities presented by the existence of Britain's overseas possessions'. Winch, *Classical Political Economy and Colonies*, pp. 25–6. Despite this ambivalence, at times Bentham condemned colonies in the strongest possible terms. See *The Works of Jeremy Bentham*, ed. John Bowring [1838–43] (1962), II, p. 548; III, pp. 53, 55, 56; IV, p. 416. For the ideas of James Mill, see Stokes, *The English Utilitarians and India*, and 'Colony', in Supplement to the 4th, 5th and 6th editions of the *Encyclopedia Britannica*, III, (1824), p. 257.

50 John Stuart Mill, *A System of Logic Ratiocinative and Inductive: Being a Connected View of the Principles of Evidence and the Methods of Scientific Investigation*, ed. J.M. Robson (1974), p. 893.

51 John Stuart Mill, 'Considerations on Representative Government' in *Essays on Politics and Society*, ed. J.M. Robson [1861] (1977), p. 562.

52 John Stuart Mill, *On Liberty*, ed. David Spitz [1859] (1975), p. 11.

53 Alan Ryan, 'Utilitarianism and Bureaucracy: The views of J.S. Mill', in *Studies in the Growth of Nineteenth-Century Government*, ed. Gillian Sutherland (1972), p. 43.

54 *RC* (pt II), *PP*, XXIX (1837–8), p. 25. The Commissioners ranked only their proposals for liberty of the press, education, and government

charities as of greater importance than the recommendations discussed in this section.

55 Knaplund, *The British Empire 1815–1939*, pp. 46–7.
56 *RC* (pt II), *PP*, XXIX, p. 25.
57 *RC* (pt I), *PP*, XXIX, p. 69.
58 *PP*, XXIX, p. 70.
59 *RC* (pt II), *PP*, , p. 24.
60 *PP*, XXIX, p. 21.
61 *PP*, XXIX, pp. 22, 23.
62 Letter of Lewis to E.W. Head, 3 October 1837, in *Letters*, p. 90.
63 Letter of Lewis to his father, 6 December 1836, in *Letters*, p. 71.
64 See, for example, Seddall, *Malta: Past and Present*, pp. 284, 294–5.
65 Stokes, *The English Utilitarians and India*, pp. 64–5.
66 James Mill, *The History of British India*, abridged by William Thomas (1975), p. 573. This work was originally published in 1817, in six volumes; a second edition was published in 1820.
67 *The History of British India*, p. 551.
68 *The History of British India*, p. 228.
69 *The History of British India*, p. 213.
70 *The History of British India*, p. 231.
71 *The History of British India*, pp. 233, 237.
72 *RC* (pt II), *PP*, XXIX (1837–8), p. 23.
73 *PP*, XXIX, p. 28.
74 *PD*, XLII (1838), p. 799.
75 *PD*, XLVIII (1839), pp. 931, 930.
76 *PD*, XLVII (1839), p. 227.
77 *PD*, XLII (1838), p. 811.
78 *PD*, XLII, p. 810.
79 See the speeches in defence of the Commission by Lord Glenelg and the Lord Chancellor, *PD*, XLVIII (1839), pp. 942–50, 950–53.
80 *PD*, XLVIII, p. 946.
81 See David Cecil, *Melbourne* (1954), p. 350.
82 Mill, *The History of British India*, p. 580.
83 See Thomas Robert Malthus, *An Essay on the Principle of Population: Text, sources, and background criticism*, ed. Philip Appleman (1976), and William Petersen, *Malthus* (1979).
84 Leslie Stephen, *The English Utilitarians*, 3 vols [1900] (1950), II, p. 138.
85 'Colony' in Supplement to the 4th, 5th and 6th editions of the *Encyclopedia Britannica*, III (1824), p. 261.
86 *Autobiography of John Stuart Mill* (1960), p. 74.
87 *PJD*, p. 114 n. 4, and p. 68.
88 *PJD*, p. 68.
89 Malthus, *An Essay on the Principle of Population*, p. 137.
90 *PJD*, p. 70.
91 *PJD*, p. 71.
92 *PJD*, p. 72.
93 *RC* (pt II), *PP*, XXIX (1837–8), p. 42.
94 Charles A. Price, *Malta and the Maltese: A study in nineteenth century migration* (1954), p. 20.

95 *RC* (pt II), *PP*, XXIX, pp. 42, 44.
96 *PP*, XXIX, p. 42.
97 For the ideas of the utilitarianism about education, see Brian Simon, *Studies in the History of Education 1780–1870* (1960); *James and John Stuart Mill on Education*, ed. F.A. Cavenagh (1931); and Francis W. Garforth, *John Stuart Mill's Theory of Education* (1979).
98 *RC* (pt II), *PP*, XXIX, p. 42.
99 Price, *Malta and the Maltese*, pp. 17, 18.
100 Seddall, *Malta: Past and Present*, p. 299.
101 LaFerla, *British Malta*, pp. 161–2.
102 Letter of Sarah Austin to Nassau W. Senior, 12 January 1837, in Janet Ross, *Three Generations of English Women* (rev. edn, 1893), p. 131.
103 *RC* (pt I), *PP*, XXIX, pp. 33–4.
104 *RC* (pt III), *PP*, XVII (1839), p. 9.
105 *RC* (pt I), *PP*, XXIX, p. 54.
106 Lewis's letters were even more candid than the reports and letters of the Commissioners in emphasizing overpopulation as the root of the evils on Malta. See, for example, *Letters*, pp. 76, 68, 84. At times he became so depressed that he doubted whether anything could be done to alleviate the problems of the Maltese. Their real grievance 'lies beyond the reach of commissioners and governments, viz. the excessive population of the island' (p. 64). A government can do no more to arrest this evil than it can 'control the winds' (p. 64).
107 See Price, *Malta and the Maltese*, pp. 38–9.
108 Letter of Austin and Lewis to Lord Glenelg, 1 September 1837, *CO* 158/114.
109 *RC* (pt II), *PP*, XXIX, p. 47.
110 *PP*, XXIX, p. 48.
111 *RC* (pt III), *PP*, XVII (1839), p. 40.
112 *RC* (pt II), *PP*, XXIX, p. 48.
113 *PP*, XXIX, p. 57. Lord Glenelg qualified this instruction by asserting that the educational system should be revised 'at as early a period as the state of the finances of your government, and a regard for other demands on the local treasury, may permit' (p. 57).
114 Price, *Malta and the Maltese*, p. 186.
115 Letter of Austin and Lewis to Lord Glenelg, 20 February 1838, *CO* 158/115.
116 Ibid.
117 The notes of the Commissioners were more than seven times longer than the ordinance itself, which was a little more than four pages long. They attempted to draft a law, the provisions of which would be 'as few and concise as possible,' expressed 'in terms sufficiently extensive to include all the cases embraced by its purposes.' Letter from John Austin and George Cornewall Lewis to Lord Glenelg, December 1838, in *CO* 158/115, p. 74. The Commissioners believed that more detailed provisions than they drafted would 'overload' the ordinance. They also took the position that their notes would impart to the major notions and terms of the law 'the degree of precision of which they are susceptible'. They felt that their notes 'will naturally be nearly equivalent to authentic

interpretations of the law . . . proceeding directly from the legislator' (p. 75). Lord Brougham was highly critical of this presumption, as well as the quality of the notes. See *PD*, XLVII (1839), p. 644.

118 The Commissioners filed their initial draft of the ordinance with the Colonial Office on 10 March 1837. Since a copy of this draft has not been preserved, *whether* and *how* it differed from the final draft is unknown. The reasons for the substantial delay in the enactment of the Commissioners' initial draft of the Ordinance into law are also unknown. It is likely, however, that opposition to the proposed law was a major factor. According to Lord Melbourne 'there were many different opinions on this subject . . . persons of great weight, influence, and power, viewed this matter with very considerable alarm. . . . the views so taken . . . by many influential persons were sufficient to justify Government . . . for the delays which had taken place, for not having hurried the matter, for the procrastinations which had been made matter of charge against them'. *PD*, XLII (1838), p. 817. Lord Glenelg evidently viewed the abolition of censorship more favourably than many others. See his letter to Governor Bouverie, 27 November 1837, *RC* (pt I), *PP*, XXIX (1837–8), p. 26, and *PD*, XLVII (1839), pp. 655–64.

119 Report on Liberty of Printing and Publishing, *RC* (pt I), *PP*, XXIX, pp. 8, 9.

120 Letter of the Commissioners to Lord Glenelg, 1 September 1837, *CO* 158/114.

121 *RC* (pt I), *PP*, XXIX, p. 12.

122 *PP*, XXIX, pp. 11, 12.

123 *Remarks*.

124 *PJD*, pp. 31–2.

125 *RC* (pt I), *PP*, XXIX, p. 10.

126 *Commentaries on the Laws of England in Four Books* [*1765–9*] (19th edn, 1870), IV, p. 113.

127 See Sir James Fitzjames Stephen, *A History of the Criminal Law of England* (1883), II, pp. 348–9.

128 See Leonard W. Levy, *Freedom of Speech and Press in Early American History: Legacy of suppression* (1963).

129 Letter of the Commissioners to Lord Glenelg, 10 March 1837, *CO* 158/113.

130 *RC* (pt I), *PP*, XXIX, p. 12.

131 Ibid.

132 Letter of the Commissioners to Lord Glenelg, 1 September 1837, *CO* 158/114.

133 See *RC* (pt I), *PP*, XXIX, pp. 19–20.

134 *RC* (pt III), PP, XVII (1839), p. 80.

135 Letter of the Commissioners to Lord Glenelg, 1 September 1837, *CO* 158/114.

136 Letter of the Commissioners to Lord Glenelg, 10 March 1837, *CO* 158/113.

137 *Remarks*.

138 *Notes*, pp. 90–91.

139 *Draft*, c. III, sec. II.

140 *Notes*, pp. 98, 99.
141 *Remarks*.
142 *Notes*, p. 98.
143 *Notes*, p. 95.
144 *Notes*, p. 97.
145 *Draft*, c. III, sec. V.
146 *Remarks*.
147 Letter of the Commissioners to Lord Glenelg, 1 September 1837, *CO* 158/14.
148 Stephen, *A History of the Criminal Law of England*, II, p. 299 n.
149 *Notes*, pp. 98, 97–8.
150 'DPW', p. 548.
151 'DPW', p. 551 n.
152 Ibid.
153 *The Works of Jeremy Bentham* [1838–43] (1962), ed. John Bowring (hereafter cited as *Works*), I, p. 466.
154 *Works*, V, p. 66.
155 *Works*, IV, p. 393 n.
156 *Works*, V, p. 66.
157 *Works*, VIII, p. 538.
158 *Bentham's Handbook of Political Fallacies*, ed. Harold A. Larrabee (1971), p. 106.
159 *Bentham's Handbook*, p. 180.
160 *Bentham's Handbook*, p. 114.
161 *Works*, IX, p. 38.
162 *Works*, II, p. 279.
163 *New York Times Co* v. *Sullivan*, 376 US 254, 279–80 (1964).
164 *Works*, II, p. 279.
165 *Bentham's Handbook of Political Fallacies*, p. 158.
166 Levy, *Freedom of Speech*, p. 171.
167 Jeremy Bentham, *A Comment on the Commentaries and A Fragment on Government*, ed. J.H. Burns and H.L.A. Hart (1977), p. 485.
168 See 'Liberty of the Press', *Encyclopedia Britannica*, (8th ed, 1857), XIII, p. 360, and John Stuart Mill, *On Liberty*, ed. David Spitz (1975).
169 See *PJD*, pp. 187, 269–70; Bentham, *Works*, II, pp. 505, 506; and Douglas G. Long, *Bentham on Liberty: Jeremy Bentham's idea of liberty in relation to his utilitarianism* (1977).
170 *Draft*, c. III, sec. VI.
171 *Remarks*.
172 *Notes*, p. 99.
173 Ibid.
174 See Stephen, *A History of the Criminal Law of England*, II, pp. 474, 475.
175 *Notes*, p. 99.
176 *Draft*, c. III, sec. VII.
177 *Draft*, c. III, sec. IX.
178 *Draft*, sec. VIII.
179 *Notes*, p. 100.
180 *Draft*, c. III, sec. VIII.
181 *Notes*, p. 100.

182 *Notes*, p. 109. At least Lewis believed that in England as well as Malta, 'with regard to private libels in a criminal proceeding, the truth should in no case be permitted to be a defence'. *Report from the Select Committee of the House of Lords Appointed to Consider the Law of Defamation and Libel and to Report thereon to the House, with the Minutes of Evidence* (1843), p. 57.
183 *Notes*, p. 103.
184 *Remarks*.
185 *Notes*, pp. 102, 103.
186 *Notes*, p. 115.
187 *Notes*, p. 90.
188 *Draft*, c. V, sec. I.
189 Great Britain, Statutes at Large, 32 Geo. III, c. 60 (1792).
190 Blackstone, *Commentaries on the Laws of England*, III, p. 294.
191 *Works*, II, 119.
192 *Notes*, p. 109.
193 *Notes*, pp. 109, 110.
194 *Notes*, p. 110.
195 Letter of the Commissioners to Lord Glenelg, 11 January 1838, *CO* 158/115.
196 Letter of the Commissioners to the Marquis of Normanby, 19 July 1839, *CO* 158/118.
197 *PJD*, p. 190.
198 See Jerome Frank, *Law and the Modern Mind* (1963), pp. 183–99, 327–35, and Frank, *Courts on Trial: Myth and reality in American justice* (1949), pp. 108–45.
199 *LJ*, II, p. 588.
200 *LJ*, II, p. 577.
201 *Notes*, pp. 116, 117.
202 *Draft*, c. V, sec. II.
203 Ibid.
204 *Notes*, p. 117.
205 Ibid.
206 *PD*, XLVII (1839), p. 225.
207 *PD*, XLVII, p. 643.
208 *PD*, XLVII, p. 314. Brougham voiced these harsh charges during a period of his career in which he 'attacked the Ministry [of Lord Melbourne] on every occasion'. Frances Hawes, *Henry Brougham* (n.d.), p. 270. The character of his attacks induced even a sympathetic biographer to conclude that Brougham was 'obviously not quite sane' (p. 271). Although his overall denunciation of the ordinance seems to me far wide of the mark, some of his criticisms of it were anything but crazy.
209 *PD*, XLVII (1839), p. 646.
210 *Notes*, p. 92.
211 Letter of John Austin and George Cornewall Lewis to Lord Glenelg, December 1838, *CO* 158/115, p. 74.
212 Ibid.
213 *Remarks*.
214 William H. Wickwar, *The Struggle for Freedom of the Press* (1928), p. 28.

215 *Notes*, p. 114.
216 *PD*, LXVII (1839), p. 654.
217 *PD*, LXVII, p. 645.
218 *Trial by Jury: The Third Annual Address Delivered on Occasion of Opening a Commission Issued under the Law for Establishing at Malta a Modified Trial by Jury in Certain Criminal Cases* (1832), p. 58.
219 Letter of the Commissioners to Lord Glenelg, 28 December 1838, *CO* 158/115.
220 *RC* (pt I), *PP*, XXIX, p. 15.
221 *Report from the Select Committee of the House of Lords appointed to consider the Law of Defamation and Libel and to report thereon to the House; with the Minutes of Evidence taken before the Committee* (1843), p. 178.
222 *Report from the Select Committee*, p. 5.
223 As quoted by Albert V. LaFerla, *British Malta*, I, p. 165. The Pope and the Archbishop of Malta were adamantly opposed even to the abolition of the censorship. See pp. 150 note 1, 164, 165 note 1, 166.
224 *PD*, XLVII (1839), p. 677.
225 *PD*, XLII (1838), pp. 814, 815, 816.
226 *PD*, XLII, pp. 815–16.
227 *PD*, XLII, p. 814.
228 *PD*, XLII, p. 817.

VI *A defence of the British Constitution*

1 Letter from John Austin to Jeremy Bentham, 20 July 1819, University College, London, Ogden MS 62.
2 'DPW', 503.
3 *PC*.
4 *PC*, pp. vi, 16.
5 See *Edmund Burke: Selected Writings and Speeches*, ed. Peter J. Stanlis (1968), pp. 328–36; Edmund Burke, *Reflections on the Revolution in France*, ed. Thomas H.D. Mahoney (1955), p. 290; *The Works of William Paley* (1837), I, pp. 398–9; and Sir William Blackstone, *Commentaries on the Laws of England in Four Books* [1765–69] (19th edn, 1870), I, pp. 92, 200, 164.
6 'Recent Writers on Reform', in *Essays on Politics and Culture*, ed. Gertrude Himmelfarb (1963), p. 335. Mill's essay was first published in 1859.
7 Ibid.
8 See Sir James Fitzjames Stephen, *Liberty, Equality and Fraternity*, ed. R.J. White [1873] (1967); Sir Henry Sumner Maine, *Popular Government* [1885] (1976); A.V. Dicey, *Lectures on the Relation between Law and Public Opinion in England during the Nineteenth Century* [2nd edn, 1914] (1952); and Robert Lowe, *Speeches and Letters on Reform* (2nd edn, 1867).
9 Asa Briggs, *Victorian People: A reassessment of persons and themes 1851–67* (rev. edn, 1972), p. 236.
10 James Winter, *Robert Lowe* (1976), p. xii.
11 See Lowe, *Speeches and Letters*, pp. 4, 5, 32, 66, 84–5.

12 See Lowe, *Speeches and Letters*, pp. 60, 74, 153, 90–91, 149, 151, and Winter, *Robert Lowe*, p. 221.
13 See Eira Ruben, 'John Austin's Political Pamphlets 1824–1859', in *Perspectives in Jurisprudence*, ed. Elspeth Attwooll (1977), pp. 25, 28–9.
14 *PC*, pp. iii, 15, 29, 34, 36, 37.
15 *PC*, p. 37.
16 *Autobiography of John Stuart Mill* (1924), p. 125.
17 Paley, *Works*, I, pp. 341, 368, 370.
18 According to Lowe, the question is 'not whether the utilitarian theory of morals is right, but whether the extension of the franchise is a moral or a political question. If moral, it is to be judged by motives; if political, by results.' If the extension of the suffrage is a political question, which he obviously believed that it was, the proper answer to it 'has nothing to do with the defects or merits of any ethical system whatever'. Review of *Essays on Reform* (1867) and *Questions for a Reformed Parliament* (1867), in *London Quarterly Review*, CCXLV (July, 1867), 129. The fact that Lowe did not accept a utilitarian moral philosophy is evident from his claim that 'the best government is that which confers the greatest benefits on its citizens. The best man is he who acts from the best motives. The test of the one is political, of the other moral. The one must be judged by *a posteriori* empirical considerations, the other by *a priori* principle' (p. 130). No utilitarian could accept this conception of the best man.
19 Ibid.
20 *Speeches and Letters on Reform*, p. 85.
21 For discussion of the evolution of Bentham's attitude toward democracy, see above, p. 25.
22 See *Utilitarian Logic and Politics: James Mill's 'Essay on Government', Macaulay's critique and the ensuing debate*, ed. Jack Lively and John Rees (1978); William Thomas, *The Philosophic Radicals: Nine studies in theory and practice 1817–1841* (1979); Joseph Hamburger, *James Mill and the Art of Revolution* (1963); and Joseph Hamburger, *Intellectuals in Politics: John Stuart Mill and the philosophic radicals* (1965).
23 Briggs, *Victorian People*, p. 90.
24 *LJ*, I, p. 18.
25 *Parliamentary Government Considered with Reference to a Reform of Parliament: An essay* (1858).
26 *Parliamentary Government*, p. 112.
27 Sarah Austin, 'Preface', p. 20.
28 *PC*, p. iv.
29 *PC*, pp. iii–iv.
30 F.J.C. Hearnshaw, *Conservatism in England: An analytical, historical and political survey* (1933), p. 26.
31 Ibid.
32 *PC*, pp. 16, 29.
33 *PC*, p. 17.
34 Norman Gash, *Politics in the Age of Peel: A study in the technique of parliamentary representation, 1830–1850* (1971), p. 89.
35 Gash, *Politics in the Age of Peel*, p. 77.
36 *The Works of Jeremy Bentham*, ed. John Bowring [1838–43] (1962), III, p. 450.

37 *PC*, pp. 14–15, 15.
38 *PC*, p. 5.
39 *PC*, p. 10n.
40 *PC*, p. 12.
41 *PC*, p. 13.
42 *LJ*, I, p. 20.
43 *PC*, p. 7.
44 *PC*, p. 13.
45 *PC*, p. 12n.
46 Briggs, *Victorian People*, p. 246.
47 *PC*, p. 32.
48 See his 'Considerations on Representative Government' in John Stuart Mill, *Essays on Politics and Society*, ed. J.M. Robson [1861] (1977), pp. 504–12.
49 *PC*, p. 25.
50 Maine, *Popular Government*, pp. 111–12.
51 Dicey, *Lectures on the Relation between Law and Public Opinion*, p. 253.
52 Lowe, *Speeches and Letters on Reform*, p. 61.
53 *PC*, p. 17.
54 Ibid.
55 *PC*, pp. 19, 20n.
56 *PC*, p. 19.
57 *PJD*, p. 66.
58 *PC*, p. 19.
59 As quoted by Asa Briggs, *Victorian People*, p. 210.
60 *Ancient Law: Its connection with the early history of society and its relation to modern ideas* [1861] (1970), p. 165.
61 *PC*, p. 21.
62 *PC*, pp. 21, 22, 21.
63 *Utilitarian Logic and Politics*, p. 94.
64 *PC*, p. 37.
65 Burke, *Reflections on the Revolution*, pp. 98–9.
66 *PC*, pp. 42, 37.
67 *PC*, pp. 38, 39.
68 *PC*, p. 40.
69 *PC*, p. 41.
70 F.B. Smith, 'The View from Britain I: "Tumults Abroad, Stability at Home" ', in *Intellectuals and Revolution: Socialism and the experience of 1848*, ed. Eugene Kamenka and F.B. Smith (1979), p. 101.
71 Letter of John Stuart Mill to Sarah Austin, March 1848, in *The Earlier Letters of John Stuart Mill 1812–1848*, ed. Francis E. Mineka (1963), p. 73. For Mill's detailed reaction to the French Revolution of 1848, see his review of Lord Brougham's 'Letter to the Marquess of Lansdowne, KG, Lord President of the Council, on the late Revolution in France', in *Westminster Review*, L (April 1849), 1.
72 *PC*, p. vi.
73 *PJD*, p. 53.
74 *PJD*, pp. 53, 186. Austin's argument was that 'so momentous . . . is the difference between a bad and a good government, that *if it would lead to a*

good one, resistance to a bad one would be useful. The anarchy attending the transition were an extensive, but a passing evil: The good which would follow the transition were extensive and lasting. The peculiar good would outweigh the generic evil: The good which would crown the change in the insulated and eccentric case, would more than compensate the evil which is inseparable from rebellion' (p. 53). He also expressed the view that resistance may be justifiable on grounds of utility in a subsequent passage (p. 186).

75 *PJD*, p. 277.
76 *LJ*, I, p. 18.
77 *The Marx-Engels Reader*, ed. Robert C. Tucker (2nd edn, 1978), p. 473.
78 Letter from John Austin to the Editor of *The Times*, 27 February 1848, in *The Times*, 1 March 1848, p. 6 (hereafter cited as Letter to *The Times*).
79 Ibid.
80 *LJ*, I, p. 18.
81 Letter to *The Times*.
82 Ibid.
83 Ibid.
84 Letter from John Austin to John Stuart Mill, 25 December 1844, in Yale University Library.
85 *Selection from the Correspondence of the late Macvey Napier, Esquire*, ed. Macvey Napier (1879), pp. 528, 529. Mrs Austin was quoting M. Guizot.
86 Letter to *The Times*.
87 Ibid.
88 Ibid.
89 *PC*, p. vi.
90 Chuter Ede, as quoted by Robert L. Schuyler and Corinne C. Weston, *British Constitutional History since 1832* (1957), p. 78.
91 *The British Political Élite* (1963).
92 *The English Constitution* [1867] (1928), p. 235.
93 Guttsman, *The British Political Élite*, p. 78.
94 'The Balance of Classes', in *Essays on Reform* (1867), p. 70.
95 'On the Choice of Representatives by Popular Constituencies', *Essays on Reform*, p. 113.
96 Maine, *Popular Government*, p. 109.
97 Maine, *Popular Government*, p. 129.
98 Briggs, *Victorian People*, p. 196.
99 Dicey, *Essays on Reform*, p. 74.
100 Dicey, *Essays on Reform*, p. 82.
101 Bagehot, *The English Constitution*, p. 104.
102 Mill, 'Recent Writers on Reform', in *Essays on Politics and Culture*, p. 339.
103 John P. Mackintosh, *The British Cabinet* (1962), p. 101.
104 Bagehot, *The English Constitution*, pp. 102, 144, 144–5.
105 'Liberal Legislation and Freedom of Contract', in *The Political Theory of T.H. Green*, ed. John R. Rodman [1881] (1964), pp. 67, 67–8.
106 Mill, 'Recent Writers on Reform', p. 346.
107 Ibid.
108 'On the Choice of Representatives by Popular Constituencies', in *A Plea*

for Democracy: An edited selection from the 1867 essays on reform and questions for a reformed Parliament, ed. W.L. Guttsman (1967), p. 91.

109 G.C. Brodrick, 'The Utilitarian Argument against Reform as stated by Mr Lowe', in *A Plea for Democracy*, pp. 32–3.

VII *Conclusion*

1 'DPW', 509.

2 *The Growth of Philosophic Radicalism*, trans. Mary Morris [1928] (1955), p. 53.

3 'Utilitarianism and Bureaucracy: The views of J.S. Mill', in *Studies in the Growth of Nineteenth-century Government*, ed. Gillian Sutherland (1972), p. 37.

4 Jerome B. Schneewind, *Sidgwick's Ethics and Victorian Moral Philosophy* (1977), p. 153.

5 *PJD*, p. 71.

6 *Autobiography of John Stuart Mill*, p. 53.

Selected bibliography

This bibliography lists all of the works cited in this study as well as a few other important books or articles. Years within brackets signify the original date of publication of a book or the edition of it utilized in this study.

Articles, chapters in books, or contributions to periodicals

R. Ago, 'Positive Law and International Law', *American Journal of International Law*, LI (1957), 691.

'Charles Austin', *Dictionary of National Biography*, I (1917), 733.

[J. Austin], 'Disposition of Property by Will–Primogeniture', *Westminster Review*, II (1824), 503.

——, 'Joint-Stock Companies', *Parliamentary History and Review* (1826), p.709.

——, Review of *The National System of Political Economy*, by Frederic List, *Edinburgh Review*, LXXV (1842), 515.

——, 'Centralization', *Edinburgh Review*, LXXXV (1847), 221.

J. Austin, Letter, *The Times*, 1 March 1848, p.6.

S. Austin, 'Preface', in John Austin, *Lectures on Jurisprudence or The Philosophy of Positive Law*, I (5th ed; 1885).

'Sarah Austin', *Dictionary of National Biography*, I (1973), 742.

'Sarah Austin', *The Times*, 12 August 1867.

'Sarah Austin', *The Athenaeum*, 17 August 1867, p. 209.

W. Bagehot, 'Sir George Cornewall Lewis', in *Biographical Studies*, ed. R.H. Hutton (2nd edn, 1889).

B. Barry, 'Warrender and His Critics', in *Hobbes and Rousseau: A collection of critical essays*, ed. Maurice Cranston and Richard S. Peters (1972).

G.C. Brodrick, 'The Utilitarian Argument against Reform as stated by Mr Lowe', in *A Plea for Democracy: An edited selection from the 1867 essays on reform and questions for a reformed Parliament*, ed. W.L. Guttsman (1967).

[Lord Brougham], 'John Austin', *Law Magazine Review* (1860), p. 164.

J.H. Burns, 'Bentham and the French Revolution', *Transactions of the Royal Historical Society*, XVI (1965), 95.

——, 'Bentham on Sovereignty: An exploration', in *Bentham and Legal Theory*, ed. M.H. James (1973), p.133.

——, 'Dreams and Destinations: Jeremy Bentham in 1828', *Bentham Newsletter*, I (1978), 21.

A. Corbin, 'The Law and the Judges', *Yale Review*, III (1914), 234.

R. Cross, 'Blackstone v. Bentham', *Law Quarterly Review*, XCII (1976), 516.

J. Dewey, 'Austin's Theory of Sovereignty', *Political Science Quarterly*, IX (1894), 31.

A. Dicey, 'The Study of Jurisprudence', *Law Magazine and Review*, V (1879–80), 383.

——, 'The Balance of Classes', in *Essays on Reform* (1867).

J.R. Dinwiddy, 'Bentham's Transition to Political Radicalism, 1809–10', *Journal of the History of Ideas*, XXXVI (1975), 683.

R. Dworkin, 'The Model of Rules', *University of Chicago Law Review*, XXXV (1967), 14.

M. Francis, 'The Nineteenth-Century Theory of Sovereignty and Thomas Hobbes', *History of Political Thought*, I (1980), 517.

D. Gerber, 'A Note on Woody on Dewey on Austin', *Ethics*, LXXIX (1969), 303.

——, 'The Consistency of Legal Positivism and Legal Realism', *Personalist*, LII (1971), 557.

A. Goodhart, 'Determining the Ratio Decidendi of a Case', *Yale Law Journal*, XL (1930), 161.

L.C.B. Gower, 'English Legal Training: A critical survey', *Modern Law Review*, XIII (1950), 137.

T.H. Green, 'Liberal Legislation and Freedom of Contract', in *The Political Theory of T.H. Green*, ed. John Rodman (1964).

H.L.A. Hart, 'Analytical Jurisprudence in the mid-20th Century: A reply to Professor Bodenheimer', *University of Pennsylvania Law Review*, CV (1957), 953.

——, 'Positivism and the Separation of Law and Morals', *Harvard Law Review*, LXXI (1958), 593.

——, 'Introduction', in *The Province of Jurisprudence Determined* (1954).

——, 'Legal Positivism', *Encyclopedia of Philosophy*, vol. 4 (1967), 418.

——, 'John Austin', *Encyclopedia Britannica*, II (15th edn, 1974), 380.

——, 'Bentham on Sovereignty' in *Jeremy Bentham: Ten critical essays*, ed. Bhikhu Parekh (1974).

F.J.C. Hearnshaw, 'John Austin and the Analytical Jurists', in *The Social and Political Ideas of Some Representative Thinkers of the Age of Reaction and Reconstruction 1815–65* (1949).

O.W. Holmes, 'The Law Magazine and Review', *American Law Review*, VI (1872), 593.

'Inheritance', *Encyclopedia Britannica: Macropedia* (15th edn, 1983), vol. 9, p.585.

H. Kelsen, 'The Pure Theory of Law and Analytical Jurisprudence', *Harvard Law Review*, LV (1941), 44.

H. Lee, 'The Development of the Malta Constitution 1813—1849', *Melita Historica*, I (1952).

B. Levy, 'Realist Jurisprudence and Prospective Overruling', *University of Pennsylvania Law Review*, CIX (1960), 1.

A.D.E. Lewis, 'John Austin (1790–1859): Pupil of Bentham', *Bentham Newsletter*, II (1979), 19.

J. Lewis, 'John Austin's Concept of "Having a Legal Obligation": A defense and reassessment in the face of some recent analytical jurisprudence', *Western Ontario Law Review*, XIV (1975), 51.

[R. Lowe], Review of *Essays on Reform* (1867) and *Questions for a Reformed Parliament* (1867), *London Quarterly Review*, CCXLV (1867), 128.

N. MacCormick, 'Dworkin as Pre-Benthamite', in *Ronald Dworkin and Contemporary Jurisprudence*, ed. Marshall Cohen (1983).
G. Maher, 'Analytical Philosophy and Austin's Philosophy of Law', *Archiv für Rechts-und Sozialphilosophie*, LXIV (1978), 401.
W. Markby, 'Analytical Jurisprudence', *Law Magazine and Review*, I (1875–6), 617.
F.M. Maxwell, 'Austin's Jurisprudence and its Latest Critic', *Law Magazine and Review*, X (1884–5), 167.
[R. McCulloch], 'Disposal of Property by Will–Entails–French Law of Succession', *Edinburgh Review*, XL (1824), 350.
James Mill, 'Colony', Supplement to *The Fourth, Fifth, and Sixth Editions of the Encyclopedia Britannica*, vol. 3 (1824).
——, 'Liberty of the Press', *Encyclopedia Britannica*, vol. 13 (8th edn, 1857).
——, 'Essay on Government', in *Utilitarian Logic and Politics*, ed. Jack Lively and John Rees (1978).
[J.S. Mill], Review of Austin's *The Province of Jurisprudence Determined*, *Tait's Edinburgh Magazine*, II (1832), 343.
——, Review of *Letter to the Marquess of Lansdowne*, KG, *Lord President of the Council, on the Late Revolution in France*, by Lord Brougham, *Westminster Review*, L (1849), 1.
——, 'Recent Writers on Reform', in *Essays on Politics and Culture*, ed. Gertrude Himmelfarb [1859] (1963).
——, Review of *Lectures on Jurisprudence*, by John Austin, *Edinburgh Review*, CXVII (1863), 222.
W.L. Morison, 'Some Myth about Positivism', *Yale Law Journal*, LXVIII (1958), 212.
H. Morris, 'Verbal Disputes and the Legal Philosophy of John Austin', *UCLA Law Review*, VII (1959), 27.
C. Nino, 'Dworkin and Legal Positivism', *Mind*, LXXXIX (1980), 519.
H. Oliphant, 'A Return to Stare Decisis', *American Bar Association Journal*, XIV (1928), 71, 159.
F. Pollock, 'Law and Command', *Law Magazine and Review*, I (1872), 189.
R. Pound, 'The Causes of Popular Dissatisfaction with the Administration of Justice', *American Law Review*, XL (1906), 729.
——, 'Spurious Interpretation', *Columbia Law Review*, VII (1907), 379.
——, 'The Need of a Sociological Jurisprudence', *Green Bag*, XIX (1907), 607.
——, 'Law in Books and Law in Action', *American Law Review*, XLIV (1910), 12.
——, 'The Scope and Purpose of Sociological Jurisprudence', *Harvard Law Review*, XXV (1912), 489.
M. Radin, 'The Theory of Judicial Decision: Or how Judges think', *American Bar Association Journal*, XI (1925), 357.
——, 'Statutory Interpretation', *Harvard Law Review*, XLIII (1930), 863.
——, 'Realism in Statutory Interpretation and Elsewhere', *California Law Review*, XXIII (1935), 156.
——, 'A Short Way with Statutes', *Harvard Law Review*, LVI (1942), 388.
J. Raz, 'Legal Principles and the Limits of Law', in *Ronald Dworkin and Contemporary Jurisprudence*, ed. Marshall Cohen (1983).
Reviews of *The Province of Jurisprudence Determined:*

The Times, 9 August 1832.
Law Magazine Review, VII (1832), 298.
Westminster Review, XVIII (1833), 237.
Athenaeum, 4 May 1861, p.592.
North American Review, C (1865), 246.
Review of *Lectures on Jurisprudence, Westminster Review*, LXXX (1863), 252.
E. Ruben, 'John Austin's Political Pamphlets 1824–1859', in *Perspectives in Jurisprudence*, ed. Elspeth Attwooll (1977).
W. Rumble, 'The Legal Positivism of John Austin and the Realist Movement in American Jurisprudence', *Cornell Law Review*, LXVI (1981), 986.
A. Ryan, 'Utilitarianism and Bureaucracy: the views of J.S. Mill', in *Studies in the Growth of Nineteenth-Century Government*, ed. Gillian Sutherland (1972).
A. Schwarz, 'John Austin and the German Jurisprudence of his Time', *Politica*, I (1934), 178.
H.A. Shannon, 'The Coming of General Limited Liability', *Economic History: A supplement to the economic journal*, II (1931), 267.
F.B. Smith, 'The View from Britain I: "Tumults Abroad, Stability at Home" ', in *Intellectuals and Revolution: Socialism and the experience of 1848*, ed. Eugene Kamenka and F.B. Smith (1979).
[J. Stephen], Review of *The Province of Jurisprudence Determined, Edinburgh Review*, CCXXIX (1861), 233.
L. Stephen, 'On the Choice of Representatives by Popular Constituencies', in *Essays on Reform* (1867).
R. Summers, 'The *New* Analytical Jurists', *New York University Law Review*, LXI (1966), 861.
R. Tur, 'Positivism, Principles and Rules', in *Perspectives in Jurisprudence*, ed. Elspeth Attwooll (1977).
A. White, 'Austin as a Philosophical Analyst', *Archiv für Rechtsund Sozialphilosophie*, LXIV (1978), 379.

Books, dissertations, and pamphlets

Albee, Ernest, *A History of English Utilitarianism* (1902).
Allen, Sir Carleton K., *Law in the Making* (7th edn, 1964).
Austin, John, *The Province of Jurisprudence Determined and the Uses of the Study of Jurisprudence* (1954).
——, *A Plea for the Constitution* (2nd edn, 1859).
——, *Lectures on Jurisprudence or the Philosophy of Positive Law*, ed. Robert Campbell, 2 vols, [1863] (5th edn, 1885).
Autobiography of John Stuart Mill (1924).
Bagehot, Walter, *The English Constitution* [1867] (1928).
——, *Biographical Studies*, ed. R.H. Hutton, (2nd edn, 1889).
Bahmueller, Charles F., *The National Charity Company: Jeremy Bentham's silent revolution* (1981).
Bain, Alexander, *James Mill: A biography* (1882).
Bayles, Michael D. (ed.), *Contemporary Utilitarianism* (1968).
Bellot, H. Hale, *University College, London: 1826–1926* (1929).

Bentham, Jeremy, *An Introduction to the Principles of Morals and Legislation*, ed. J.H. Burns and H.L.A. Hart (1970).
——, *Of Laws in General*, ed. H.L.A. Hart (1970).
——, *A Comment on the Commentaries and A Fragment on Government*, ed. J.H. Burns and H.L.A. Hart (1977).
Bigongiari, Dino (ed.), *The Political Ideas of St Thomas Aquinas: Representative selections* (1953).
Blackstone, Sir William, *Commentaries on the Laws of England*, 4 vols [1765–9] (19th edn, 1870).
Boorstin, Daniel J., *The Mysterious Science of the Law* (1958).
Bowring, John (ed.), *The Works of Jeremy Bentham*, 11 vols [1838–43] (1962).
Briggs, Asa, *The Making of Modern England 1783–1867: The age of improvement* (1965; in the UK, 1959, as *The Age of Improvement*, vol. 8).
——, *Victorian People: A reassessment of persons and themes 1851–67* (rev. edn, 1972).
Bryce, James, *Studies in History and Jurisprudence* (1901).
Buckland, W.W., *Some Reflections on Jurisprudence* (1949).
Burke, Edmund, *Reflections on the Revolution in France*, ed. Thomas H.D. Mahoney (1955).
Burns, J.H., *Jeremy Bentham and University College* (1962).
Campbell, Enid M., 'John Austin and Jurisprudence in nineteenth-century England' (unpublished PhD dissertation, Duke University, 1958).
Cavenagh, F.A. (ed.), *James and John Stuart Mill on Education* (1931).
Cecil, David, *Melbourne* (1954).
Cobban, Alfred, *A History of Modern France: From the First Empire to the Second Empire, 1799–1871*, vol. 2, 2nd edn (1965).
Clark, G. Kitson, *The Making of Victorian England* (1974).
Cohen, Felix S., *Ethical Systems and Legal Ideals: An essay on the foundations of legal criticism* [1933] (1959).
Cohen, Marshall (ed.), *Ronald Dworkin and Contemporary Jurisprudence* (1983).
Cosgrove, Richard A., *The Rule of Law: Albert Venn Dicey, Victorian jurist* (1980).
Dias, R.W.M., *Jurisprudence* (4th edn, 1976).
Dicey, Albert V., *Lectures on the Relation between Law & Public Opinion in England during the Nineteenth Century* [2nd edn, 1914] (1952).
——, *Introduction to the study of the Law of the Constitution* (8th edn, 1920).
Dixon, C. Willis, *The Colonial Administrations of Sir Thomas Maitland* (1939).
Dobie, Edith, *Malta's Road to Independence* (1967).
Dworkin, Ronald, *Taking Rights Seriously* (1977).
Eastwood, R.A., and Keeton, G.W., *The Austinian Theories of Law and Sovereignty* (1929).
Essays on Reform (1867).
Fifoot, C.H.S., *Judge and Jurist in the Reign of Victoria* (1959).
Fraenkel, Osmond K. (ed.), *The Curse of Bigness: Miscellaneous papers of Louis D. Brandeis* (1935).
Frank, Jerome, *Law and the Modern Mind* [1930] (1949).
——, *Law and the Modern Mind* [1930] (1963).
——, *Courts on Trial: Myth and reality in American justice* (1949).

Friedmann, Wolfgang, *Legal Theory* (5th edn, 1967).
Fuller, Lon L., *The Law in Quest of Itself* [1940] (1966).
——, *The Morality of Law* (rev. edn, 1969).
Garforth, Francis W., *John Stuart Mill's Theory of Education* (1979).
Gash, Norman, *Politics in the Age of Peel: A study in the technique of parliamentary representation, 1830–1850* (1953; 1971).
Gray, John C., *The Nature and Sources of Law* [rev. edn, 1921] (1963).
Grey, Henry George, *Parliamentary Government Considered with Reference to a Reform of Parliament: An essay* (1858).
Grote, Harriet, *The Personal Life of George Grote* (1873).
Guttsman, W.L., *The British Political Elite* (1963).
——, (ed.), *A Plea for Democracy: An edited selection from the 1867 essays on reform and questions for a reformed Parliament* (1967).
Hacker, P.M.S. and Ras, Joseph (eds.), *Law, Morality, and Society: Essays in honour of H.L.A. Hart* (1977).
Halévy, Elie, *The Growth of Philosophic Radicalism*, trans. Mary Morris (1928; new edn, 1955).
——, *A History of the English People in the Nineteenth Century*, trans. E.I. Watkin and D.A. Barker, 6 vols (1961).
Hamburger, Joseph, *James Mill and the Art of Revolution* (1963).
——, *Intellectuals in Politics: John Stuart Mill and the philosophic radicals* (1965).
Hanbury, H.G., *The Vinerian Chair and Legal Education* (1958).
Hardman, William, *A History of Malta during the Period of the French and British Occupations, 1798–1815*, ed. J. Holland Rose (1909).
Hart, H.L.A., *The Concept of Law* (1961).
——, *Essays on Bentham: Studies in jurisprudence and political theory* (1982).
——, *Essays in Jurisprudence and Philosophy* (1983).
Hawes, Frances, *Henry Brougham* (n.d.).
Hearnshaw, F.J.C., *Conservatism in England: An analytical, historical and political survey* (1933).
Himmelfarb, Gertrude, *Victorian Minds* (1968).
Hobbes, Thomas, *Leviathan: or the Matter, Forme and Power of a Commonwealth Ecclesiastical and Civil*, ed. Michael Oakeshott (1962).
——, *A Dialogue between a Philosopher and a Student of the Common Laws of England*, ed. Joseph Cropsey (1971).
Holdsworth, Sir William, *A History of English Law*, 16 vols (1922–71).
——, *Some Makers of English Law* (1938).
Holland, Thomas E., *The Elements of Jurisprudence* (11th edn, 1910).
Holmes, Oliver W., *Collected Legal Papers* [1920] (1952).
——, *The Common Law*, ed. Mark DeWolfe Howe [1881] (1963).
Howe, Mark DeWolfe, *Justice Oliver Wendell Holmes: The shaping years, 1841–1870* (1957).
——, *Justice Oliver Wendell Holmes: The proving years, 1870–1882* (1963).
Hudson, W.D., *Modern Moral Philosophy* (1970).
Hume, L.J., *Bentham and Bureaucracy* (1981).
James, M.H. (ed.), *Bentham and Legal Theory* (1973).
Keeton, George W. and Schwarzenberger, Georg (eds.), *Jeremy Bentham and the Law: A symposium* (1948).

Kelsen, Hans, *General Theory of Law and State*, trans. Anders Wedberg (1961).
Knaplund, Paul, *The British Empire 1815–1939* (1941).
——, *James Stephen and the British Colonial System 1813–1847* (1953).
LaFerla, Albert V., *British Malta*, vol. 1 (1938).
Larrabee, Harold A. (ed.), *Bentham's Handbook of Political Fallacies* (1971).
LeMahieu, D.L., *The Mind of William Paley: A philosopher and his age* (1976).
Lenzer, Gertrud (ed.), *Auguste Comte and Positivism: The essential writings* (1975).
Lerner, Max (ed.), *The Mind and Faith of Justice Holmes: His speeches, essays, letters and judicial opinions* (1943).
Levi, Edward H., *An Introduction to Legal Reasoning* (1948).
Levy, Leonard W., *Freedom of Speech and Press in Early American History: Legacy of suppression* (1963).
Lewis, George C., *Remarks on the Use and Abuse of Some Political Terms* [1832] (1970).
——, *An Essay on the Government of Dependencies*, ed. C.P. Lucas (1891).
Lewis, Gilbert F. (ed.), *Letters of the Right Hon. Sir George Cornewall Lewis, Bart., to various friends* (1870).
List, Frederic, *National System of Political Economy*, trans. G.A. Matile [1856] (1974).
Lively, Jack, and Rees, John (eds.), *Utilitarian Logic and Politics: James Mill's 'Essay on Government', Macaulay's critique and the ensuing debate* (1978).
Llewellyn, Karl N., *The Bramble Bush: On our law and its study* (1960).
——, *The Common Law Tradition: Deciding appeals* (1960).
——, *Jurisprudence: Realism in theory and practice* (1962).
Locke, John, *An Essay Concerning Human Understanding*, ed. A.C. Fraser, 2 vols (1894).
Long, Douglas G., *Bentham on Liberty: Jeremy Bentham's Idea of Liberty in Relation to His Utilitarianism* (1977).
Lowe, Robert, *Speeches and Letters on Reform* (2nd edn, 1867).
MacCormick, Neil, *H.L.A. Hart* (1981).
Mack, Mary Peter, *Jeremy Bentham: An Odyssey of Ideas 1748–1792* (1962).
McKeon, Richard (ed.), *The Basic Works of Aristotle* (1941).
Mackintosh, John P., *The British Cabinet* (1962).
Maine, Sir Henry Sumner, *Ancient Law: Its connection with the early history of society and its relation to modern ideas* [1861] (1970).
——, *Popular Government* [1885] (1976).
——, *Lectures on the Early History of Institutions* [7th edn, 1914] (1966).
Malthus, Thomas R., *An Essay on the Principle of Population: Text, sources, and background criticism*, ed. Philip Appleman (1976).
Mathias, Peter, *The First Industrial Nation: An economic history of Britain 1700–1914* (1969).
Mill, James, *The History of British India*, 6 vols (2nd edn, 1820).
——, *The History of British India*, abridged by William Thomas (1975).
——, *Elements of Political Economy* (3rd edn, 1826), in *James Mill: Selected economic writings*, ed. Donald Winch (1966).
Mill, John Stuart, *A System of Logic Ratiocinative and Inductive: Being a connected view of the principles of evidence and the methods of scientific*

investigation, ed. J.M. Robson (1974).
——, *On Liberty*, ed. David Spitz [1859] (1975).
——, *Considerations on Representative Government*, in *Essays on Politics and Society*, ed. J.M. Robson [1861] (1977).
——, *Utilitarianism with Critical Essays*, ed. Samuel Gorovitz (1971).
Mineka, Francis E. (ed.), *The Earlier Letters of John Stuart Mill, 1812–1848* (1963).
Mitrovich, George, *The Cause of the People of Malta; Now before Parliament* (1836).
Morison, W.L., *John Austin* (1982).
Morrell, W.P., *British Colonial Policy in the Age of Peel and Russell* (1930).
Moultrie, John, *Poems* (1876).
Napier, Macvey (ed.), *Selection from the Correspondence of the late Macvey Napier Esquire* (1879).
Nesbitt, George L., *Benthamite Reviewing: The First Twelve Years of the 'Westminster Review' 1824–1836* (1934).
Parekh, Bhikhu (ed.), *Jeremy Bentham: Ten critical essays* (1974).
Paton, George W., *A Textbook of Jurisprudence*, ed. G.W. Paton and David P. Derham (4th edn, 1972).
Patterson, Edwin W., *Jurisprudence: Men and ideas of the Law* (1953).
Petersen, William, *Malthus* (1979).
Plumb, J.H., *England in the Eighteenth Century* (1972).
Pollock, Frederick, *The Land Laws* (1883).
Posner, Richard, *The Economics of Justice* (1983).
Pound, Roscoe, *An Introduction to the Philosophy of Law* (rev. edn, 1954).
Price, Charles A., *Malta and the Maltese: A Study in Nineteenth Century Migration* (1954).
Puckler-Muskau, Hermann, *Tour in Germany, Holland, and England, in the Years 1826, 1827, and 1828*, trans. Sarah Austin (1832).
——, *Tour in England, Ireland, and France, in the Years 1826, 1827, 1828, and 1829*, trans. Sarah Austin (1833).
Radzinowicz, Leon, *A History of English Criminal Law and its Administration from 1750: Grappling for control*, vol. 4 (1968).
Rawls, John, *A Theory of Justice* (1971).
Raz, Joseph, *The Authority of Law: Essays on law and morality* (1979).
Read, Donald, *Cobden and Bright: A Victorian political partnership* (1967).
Report from the Council, Annual General Meeting of Proprietors [of the University of London] (1830).
Roach, John, *Social Reform in England 1780–1880* (1978).
Rosenberg, J. Mitchell, *Jerome Frank: Jurist and philosopher* (1970).
Rosenblum, Nancy L., *Bentham's Theory of the Modern State* (1978).
Ross, Janet, *Three Generations of English Women: Memoirs and correspondence of Susannah Taylor, Sarah Austin and Lady Duff Gordon* (rev. edn, 1893).
——, *The Fourth Generation: Reminiscences* (1912).
Rumble, Wilfrid E., *American Legal Realism: Skepticism, reform, and the judicial process* (1968).
Salmond, John, *Jurisprudence*, ed. Glanville L. Williams (10th edn, 1947).
Schneewind, Jerome B., *Sidgwick's Ethics and Victorian Moral Philosophy* (1977).

Schuyler, Robert L., and Weston, Corinne C., *British Constitutional History since 1832* (1957).

Second Statement by the Council of the University of London Explanatory of the Plan of Instruction (1828).

Seddall, Henry, *Malta: Past and Present: A history of Malta from the days of the Phoenicians to the present time* (1870).

Shuman, Samuel I., *Legal Positivism: Its scope and limitations* (1963).

Sidgwick, Henry, *The Methods of Ethics* [7th edn, 1907] (1981).

Siebert, Fredrick, *Freedom of the Press in England 1476–1776: The rise and decline of government control* (1952).

Simon, Brian, *Studies in the History of Education 1780–1870* (1960).

Simon, W.M., *European Positivism in the Nineteenth Century: An essay in intellectual history* (1963).

Smart, J.J.C., and Williams, Bernard, *Utilitarianism for and against* (1973).

Smith, Harrison, *Britain in Malta: Constitutional development of Malta in the nineteenth century*, I (1953).

Stanlis, Peter J. (ed.), *Edmund Burke: Selected writings and speeches* (1968).

Statement by the Council of the University of London Explanatory of the Nature and Objects of the Institution (1827).

Stark, Werner (ed.), *Jeremy Bentham's Economic Writings*, 3 vols (1952–4).

Steintrager, James, *Bentham* (1977).

Stephen, James F., *Liberty, Equality, and Fraternity*, ed. R.J. White [1873] (1967).

——, *A History of the Criminal Law of England*, 3 vols (1883).

Stephen, Leslie, *The Life of Sir James Fitzjames Stephen* (1895).

——, *The English Utilitarians*, 3 vols [1900] (1950).

——, *History of English Thought in the Eighteenth Century*, 2 vols (3rd edn, 1902).

Stoddart, Sir John, *Trial by Jury: The Third Annual Address delivered on occasion of opening a commission issued under the law for establishing at Malta a modified trial by jury in certain criminal cases* (1832).

Stokes, Eric, *The English Utilitarians and India* (1959).

Stone, Julius, *Legal System and Lawyers' Reasonings* (1964).

Summers, Robert, *Instrumentalism and American Legal Theory* (1982).

Thomas, William, *The Philosophic Radicals: Nine studies in theory and practice, 1817–1841* (1979).

Thompson, F.M.L., *English Landed Society in the Nineteenth Century* (1963).

Tucker, Robert C. (ed.), *The Marx-Engels Reader* (2nd edn, 1978).

Twining, William, *Karl Llewellyn and the Realist Movement* (1973).

Wasserstrom, Richard, *The Judicial Decision: Toward a theory of legal justification* (1961).

Waterfield, Gordon, *Lucie Duff Gordon in England, South Africa, and Egypt* (1937).

Wickwar, William H., *The Struggle for Freedom of the Press* (1928).

Wight, Martin, *The Development of the Legislative Council 1606–1945* (1946).

Winch, Donald, *Classical Political Economy and Colonies (1965).*

——, (ed.), *James Mill: Selected economic writings* (1966).

Winter, James, *Robert Lowe* (1976).

The Works of William Paley, D.D., 5 vols (1837).

Young, G.M., *Victorian England: Portrait of an age* [2nd edn, 1953] (1964).

Collections of manuscripts

British Library of Political and Economic Science, Papers of J.S. Mill and Helen Taylor.
National Library of Wales, Nassau W. Senior Papers.
University College, London, Brougham MSS.
University College, London, Chadwick MSS.
University College, London, College Correspondence.
Unversity College, London, Ogden MSS.
Yale University Library, John Stuart Mill Papers.

Public documents and cases

Great Britain, *Hansard's Parliamentary Debates*, vols. 34 (1836), 42 (1838), 47 (1839) and 48 (1839).
Great Britain, *Parliamentary Papers*, vol. 29 (1837–8). 'Copies or Extracts of Reports of the Commissioners appointed to inquire into the Affairs of the Island of Malta and of Correspondence thereupon'. Two parts.
Great Britain, *Parliamentary Papers*, vol. 17 (1839). 'Copies or Extracts of Reports of the Commissioners appointed to inquire into the Affairs of the Island of Malta and of Correspondence thereupon'.
Great Britain, *Parliamentary Papers*, vol. 10 (1846). 'Report from the Select Committee on Legal Education, together with Minutes of Evidence'.
Great Britain. 'Report from the Select Committee of the House of Lords appointed to consider the Law of Defamation and Libel and to report thereon to the House; with Minutes of Evidence taken before the Committee (1843)'.
Great Britain. Public Record Office. Colonial Office Records 158/113–115, 118.
Great Britain. Statutes at Large, 32 Geo. III, c. 60 (1792).
New York Times Co. v. *Sullivan*, 376 US 254 (1964).
Riggs v. *Palmer*, 115 NY 506 (1889).
United Steel Workers of America v. *Weber*, 443 US 193 (1979).

Index

John Austin's name has been abbreviated to JA throughout the Index. References to his life or thought are indexed under the appropriate category, i.e. authority, codification, etc.

Ago, Roberto, 222, 232, 262
Albee, Ernest, 233, 265
Allen, Carleton Kemp, 4, 7, 265
America, United States of, 22, 89, 92, 175–7, 200, 205; constitution and libel of public officials, 175–7; JA's attitude toward, 175–6, 205; sovereign in, 92
anarchy: fear of, as basis of obedience, 103; JA's disapproval of, 82–3, 85, 104
Aquinas, St Thomas, 133
aristocracy, 19, 211, 213; JA's attitude toward, 20, 193, 198, 199, 206, 209
Aristotle, 133
articles, importance of JA's, 7, 219–20
Austin, Alfred, 11; Charles, 11, 24; George, 11; Joseph, 11
Austin, Anne, 10
Austin, Jonathan, 10–12
Austin, Sarah, 9, 12–15, 27–8, 41, 45–7, 53–8, 77, 94, 105, 164, 195, 206, 207, 209, 221, 222, 223, 225, 227, 228, 229, 230, 231, 232, 235, 240, 253, 258, 259, 260, 262; affair with Prince Puckler-Muskau, 55; Bentham, JA's view of, 105; edits JA's *Lecture on Jurisprudence*, 56–7; French Revolution of 1848 and JA, 207; lack of success of JA, 45–6; life with JA, 57; reform of Parliament, opposition to of JA, 195; publication of *The Province of Jurisprudence Determined*, her role in, 40; relationship to JA, 15, 54–5, 56–7; secures payment for JA's services on Malta, 46–7; utilitarian basis of JA's jurisprudence, her view of, 77
authority: ethical, need for, 69–70; JA's attitude toward, 12–14

Bagehot, Walter, 260, 263, 265; criticisms of House of Lords, 213–4; England as one of the 'deferential nations', 211; praise of JA's jurisprudence, 2
Bahmueller, Charles F., 265
Bain, Alexander, 16, 34, 58–9, 225, 265
Ball, Sir Alexander, 146
Barry, Brian, 233, 262
Bayles, Michael D., 236, 265
Bellot, H. Hale, 35, 228, 229, 230, 265
Bentham, Jeremy: 2–5, 15–19, 22, 24–6, 29, 30, 32, 52, 60, 64–5, 74, 75, 79, 83, 92, 94, 96, 102, 105, 106, 110, 121, 127, 145, 163, 168, 176–8, 181, 182, 193, 195, 197, 206, 207, 218–19, 220, 222, 225, 227, 234, 235, 240, 255, 257, 258, 265; USA, praise of, 22, 176; aristocracy, critique of, 19; Blackstone, criticism of, 227; *A Comment on the Commentaries and A Fragment on Government*, 106, 227, 234, 240, 265; compared to JA, 16, 17–18, 24–6, 64–5, 74, 75; Comte, Auguste, similarities to, 54; free press, conception and praise of, 176–8; *An Introduction to the Principles of Morals and Legistlation*, 75, 106, 227, 234, 235, 240, 265–6; judicial legislation, critique of, 121; judicial review, view of, 105; jury, attitude toward, 182; *Of Laws in General*, 4, 222, 235; parliamentary reform, support of, 195; political or seditious libels, criticisms of, 176; neologisms, use of, 74; utilitarianism of, 60, 64–5; sovereign power, inexpediency of limits on, 104–6; University of London, contributions to, 29; *and see* libel, liberty of publication, Maine, Mill (J.S.), and utilitarians
Benthamite or Benthamites, 6, 7, 11, 18, 24, 29, 30, 41, 52, 64, 141, 145, 168, 195, 203, 206, 218, 226, 234
Bentinck, Sir William, 12
Bergbohm, Karl, 53
Bigongiari, Dino, 266
Bingham, Joseph W., 244
Bingham, Peregrine, 18
Blackstone, Sir William, 81–3, 85, 105, 170–71, 182, 193, 227, 237, 256, 257, 266; *Commentaries on the Laws of England*, 81–2, 170, 237, 254, 256, 257; JA's criticisms of, 24, 81–2, 84–5, 227; jury, trial by, 182; law, conception of, 81–2; liberty of the press, 170
Bonaparte, Napoleon, 146, 248
Boorstin, Daniel J., 237, 266
Bouverie, Sir Henry F., 166, 254
Brandeis, Louis D., 245
Briggs, Asa, 195, 212–3, 224, 257, 258, 259, 266
Bright, John, 48, 202
British Constitution, 46, 106, 146, 193–217 *passim*
British government – see Great Britain
British Library of Political and Economic Science, 271
Brodrick, George, 216, 260, 262
Brougham, Henry, 3, 27, 29–30, 36, 38–9, 42, 56, 160, 185–6, 188–91, 222, 228, 230, 232, 259, 262, 271;

Commissioners' reforms for Malta, criticisms of, 160, 185–6, 191, 253, 256; Inns of Court, dissatisfaction with, 38–9; JA, praise of, 3–4, 27, 30, 36, 228; jury, trial by, defence of, 188–9
Bryce, James, 60, 241, 266
Buckland, W.W., 266
Buller, Charles, 34
Burke, Edmund, 78, 175, 193, 204, 257, 259, 266
Burns, J.H., 29, 228, 240, 262, 266

Cabinet, British, 197, 211, 212, 214
Cameron, Sir Charles, 249
Campbell, Enid, M., 223, 266
Campbell, Lord, 190
Carlyle, Thomas, 230
Cavenagh, F.A., 266
Cecil, David, 252, 266
censorship, 7, 169–70, 206
centralization, 6, 50–2
Chadwick, Edwin, 34, 271
character, JA's, 12, 44–5, 58–9
Clark, G. Kitson, 10, 224, 266
Cobban, Alfred, 54, 232, 266
Cobden, Richard, 48, 49
Codification: JA's conception and opinion of, 24, 110, 127, 129–30, 132, 139–40, 141; legal realists, opinion of, 135–9; place of judicial legislation in, 130, 134–5, 141–1
Cohen, Felix, 115, 242, 266
Cohen, Marshall, 266
Colborne, Sir John, 192
Colonial Office, 150, 152, 155, 183, 248, 249, 254
competition of opposite analogies, 116
Comte, Auguste, 53–4, 232
conservatism, 197, 216
Consiglio Popolare, 146, 150, 151, 153, 247, 249
constitutional law, 89, 97
Corbin, Arthur L., 137–8, 245, 262
Corn Laws, 47, 49
Cosgrove, Richard A., 9, 222, 224, 231, 266
Cousin, Victor, 231
Criminal Law Commission, 42–3
Cross, Rupert, 262
Crown, 22, 23, 89, 146, 173, 189, 198, 212
Crown Colony, 146
customary law, 89, 97

defamation, 180
democracy, 200–1
Dewey, John, 262
Dias, R.W.M., 236, 266
Dicey, Albert V., 4, 9, 18, 39, 48, 52, 92, 99, 129, 194, 211, 213, 222, 225, 231, 257, 259, 260, 263, 266; attitudes of lawyers to legal education, explanation of, 39; English working class, subdivisions of, 213; JA's article on free trade, criticism of, 48; JA's conception of the British sovereign, critique of, 92, 238; JA's jurisprudence, praise of, 4; judicial legislation, 129; socialism and omnipotence of Parliament, 52, 99; universal suffrage, effect of, 211
Dinwiddy, J.R., 25, 227, 263
discretion, judicial, 116, 123–7, 143, 184–5, 186–8
Divine law, 65–6, 68, 79–82, 84, 86–7, 89
Dixon, C. Willis, 247, 266
Dobie, Edith, 247, 266
Dworkin, Ronald, 1, 5, 123–7, 221, 223, 243, 263, 266

Eastwood, R.A., 233, 266
Ede, Chuter, 260
education, popular: JA's conception of as cure for social ills and misgovernment, 7, 34, 48, 145, 162–3, 165, 169, 171, 210, 219
empiricism, JA's, 92–3, 96–8
enforcement of law, 82, 181–5
Engels, Friedrich, 207
England, 9–10, 19, 21, 27, 33, 34, 39, 46, 47, 49, 54, 77, 81, 88, 117, 155, 157–8, 160, 163, 164, 172, 173, 178, 183, 184, 187, 205, 208, 211, 213, 214, 216
English law, lawyers: 22, 37, 39, 44, 81, 85, 120; JA's dissatisfaction with, 24, 33, 37, 98, 131; primogeniture, 20
entails – *see* primogeniture
Equal Franchise Act of 1928, 211
equity, 121–2; JA's criticisms of, 85–6, 106, 133; JA's experience, as draftsman of, 14
Erle, Sir William, 225, 231
ethical noncognitivism, 87
ethical theories, JA's, 62–71, 86–7
ethics and legislation, sciences of, 60, 65, 76, 84, 97
Europe, effect on JA's political thought of residence in, 34, 206–10
Expositor and Censor of law, 26
ex post facto law, 124, 126, 128, 131, 243

Fifoot, C.H.S., 39, 230, 266
Fox's Libel Law (1792), 182
Fraenkel, Osmond K., 266
France, 12, 19, 46, 205–10
Francis, Mark, 223, 263
Frank, Jerome N.,: 133, 244, 245, 256, 266; codification, critique of, 135–6, 137; fact-scepticism of, 137; juries, power of, 184; legal certainty, analysis of, 137
free discussion, 13, 17
free government, JA's conception of, 197–8

free press: Blackstone's conception of, 170–1; change in JA's attitude toward, 178; JA's conception of, 170; need for trial by jury to protect, 188–9; utility of on Malta, 171–2, 174; *and see* liberty of publication
free trade, JA's analysis of, 6, 7, 47–50, 219–20
freedom of contract, JA's support of, 202, 214–5
French Revolution of 1848, JA's reaction to, 54, 206–10
Friedmann, Wolfgang, 60, 266
Fuller, Lon L., 267

Garforth, Francis W., 253, 267
Gash, Norman, 197, 258, 267
Geldart, Dr, 38
generality of law, JA's conception of, 97–8
general terms, JA's analysis of indefiniteness of, 116–7; H.L.A. Hart's discussion of, 117–8
geometrical models, 97
Gerber, D., 223, 263
German Customs Union, 47
Germany, 47, 206–10; impact upon JA of his visit to in 1827–8, 31–4
Glenelg, Lord (Charles Grant), 147, 150, 152, 155, 157, 159, 160, 166, 167, 225, 247, 248, 249, 250, 252, 253, 254, 255, 256, 257
Goodhart, Arthur L., 114, 263
government, utilitarian end of, 70–1, 103
Government Gazette, 171
Gower, L.C.B., 263
Gray, John Chipman: 5, 60, 111, 128, 134, 222, 233, 241, 243, 244, 267; intention of legislature, difficulty of discovering, 132–3; JA's conception of judge-made law, criticism of, 112
Gray, Justice, 126
Great Britain, 10, 12, 49, 51, 89, 92, 105, 147, 150–1, 153, 155, 171, 197–8, 256, 271
Green, T.H, 215, 263
Grey, Henry George, 195–6, 267
Grote, George, 29, 32, 94, 229
Grote, Harriet, 30, 228, 267
Guizot, François, 45, 53–4, 56, 208, 225, 227, 231, 232, 235, 240, 260
Guttsman, W.L., 211, 260, 267

Hacker, P.M.S., 267
Halévy, Elie, 218, 225, 227, 234, 267
Hamburger, Joseph, 223, 224, 225, 258, 267
Hamburger, Lotti, 223, 224
Hanbury, H.G., 267
hard cases, 116, 118, 124, 125
Hardman, William, 247, 267
Hart, H.L.A., 1, 3, 4, 61, 110, 142–3, 221, 222, 223, 228, 233, 236, 240, 241, 242, 245, 263, 267; comments on JA, 4, 62, 109, 141; general terms, meaning of, 117–8; legal positivism, 109
Hawes, Frances, 256, 261
Head, E.W., 252
Hearnshaw, F.J.C., 12, 197, 225, 258, 263, 267
Himmelfarb, Gertrude, 267
Hobbes, Thomas, 3, 24, 32, 62, 74, 84, 90, 92, 94, 97, 103, 219, 239, 267; JA's attitude toward, 53, 83, 102, 104, 207; necessity for coercion and sanctions, 101–2; need for sovereign of unlimited power, 104; utilitarianism of, 233
Holdsworth, Sir William, 38, 39, 120, 225, 230, 233, 237, 242, 267
Holland, Thomas E., 4, 222, 267
Holmes, Oliver Wendell, 5, 111, 113, 126, 142, 223, 241, 246, 263, 267
Horner, Leonard, 229
House of Commons, 89, 92, 194, 195, 197–9, 202, 212, 214
House of Lords, 89, 159–60, 186, 198, 212–4
Howe, Mark DeWolfe, 222, 267
Hudson, W.D., 236, 267
human nature, JA's conception of, 69, 73, 79, 98
Hume, David, 30
Hume, L.J., 267
Hutton, R.H., 221

Inner Temple, 43, 94
Inns of Court, 38
international law, JA's conception of, 81, 89, 97, 116
interpretation of law, genuine or spurious, 113, 120, 132, 142

James, M.H., 267
Jefferson, Thomas, 51, 176
joint-stock companies: JA's defence of limited liability of partners in, 6, 7, 22–4, 219
judicial decision-making, JA's conception of, 112–3
judicial legislation: 5, 26, 92; assessment of JA's analysis of, 139–43; extent and forms of, 119–20; JA's conception of, 111–12, 118–9; JA's criticisms of Bentham's views of, 121; JA's dissatisfaction with, 127–34, 140–1; place of in a code, 130, 139–40; utility of, 109, 121–3, 140–1; *and see* 109–43
judicial policy-making, 123–7
jurisprudence: analytical, 3–5, 61, 109–10; English, 4, 5, 36, 193, 219; European, 5; general, 37, 72–5; German, 32, 46; JA's lectures on, 34–7, 75, 110; legislation, relationship to, 76, 78, 107, 108; links to ethical theories, 78–80, 236; mechanical, 109, 110, 141;

particular, 37, 72–3; science of, 60, 76, 130; *and see* Kelsen, H.
jury, 146, 188–9; trial by, JA's criticisms of, 85, 133, 182–4

Keeton, George W., 233, 267
Kelsen, Hans: 3, 62, 87, 222, 236, 263, 268; comparison of his conception of jurisprudence and JA's, 5, 78–9, 233; general theory of law, 236; judicial legislation, view of, 141; noncognitivism of, 76, 235
Knaplund, Paul, 248, 251, 268

La Ferla, Albert V., 223, 247, 253, 257, 268
laissez-faire, 100
Langdell, Christopher Columbus, 29
Larrabee, Harold A., 268
law, 75, 94, 96; basis of JA's conception of, 60–2, 69, 100–2, 106–8; JA's command conception of, 24, 71–2, 88, 96, 100; properly so-called, 71–2, 98, 100, 102; of things and persons, 8, 9, 73; strictly so-called, 116; *and see* jurisprudence, legal obligation, positive law
Lectures on Jurisprudence or the Philosophy of Positive Law (JA), 3, 4, 25, 57, 221, 222, 223, 224, 225, 227, 228, 229, 230, 231, 235, 237, 238, 239, 241, 242, 243, 244, 245, 246, 256, 257, 258, 259, 260, 265
legal certainty, JA's commitment to, 24, 131–5, 142, 184
legal education, 14, 38–9, 43–4
legal formalism, 109
legal obligation, JA's conception of, 72, 101; and sanctions, 101–2; *and see* law, positive law
legal positivism: association with mechanical jurisprudence and legal formalism, 109, 141; comparison of JA's and Kelsen's versions of, 5, 62, 76, 78–81, 87; Dworkin's critique of, 123–7; H.L.A. Hart's conception of, 109; JA's contributions to, 3, 76, 108, 219; judge-made law, implications for, 110, 141; nature of, 2–3, 80–1; reform of law, 145, 169–70; relationship to Comte's positivism, 53, separation of law and morals, 76, 80–1; studies of, 222
legal realism, 110, 132, 244; and codification, 135–42; compared to JA's legal philosophy, 119, 120, 121, 142; rule-scepticism of, 242
legislation: Permanent Commission of, Austin's notion of, 130–1; popular, JA's opposition to, 130, 198–9, 203; science of, 76, 130
LeMahieu, D.L., 268
Lenzer, Gertrud, 268
Lerner, Max, 268
Levi, Edward H., 241, 268
Levy, B.H., 244, 263
Levy, Leonard W., 254, 255, 268
Lewis, A.D.E., 224, 263
Lewis, George Cornewall, 7, 13, 34, 35, 39, 46, 106, 144–92 *passim*, 200, 216, 219, 225, 246, 247, 248, 249, 250, 251, 252, 253, 255, 256, 269
Lewis, J., 263
libel: JA's and Lewis's draft of criminal law of for Malta, 6, 7, 145, 253, 254; English law of, 168–89 *passim*; political, JA's attitude toward, 168, 175–6, 218; Bentham's criticisms of, 176
liberty, JA's conception of, 178, 197
liberty of publication: JA's support of, 170–1, 190; Bentham's defence of, 176; Duke of Wellington's criticisms of, 191–2; utilitarians' attitude toward, 190
Lincoln's Inn, 27
linguistic usage, JA's attitude toward, 97–8, 113–4
List, Frederic, 47–9, 223, 231, 239, 268; *National System of Political Economy*, 47
Lively, Jack, 268
living law, JA's conception of, 142
Llewellyn, Karl N., 135, 136–7, 139, 242, 243, 244, 245, 268
Locke, John; 32, 64, 69, 90, 104, 234, 238, 268; conception and classification of law, 102; comparison with JA, 97, 102; utilitarianism of, 63
Long, Douglas, G., 255, 268
Lowe, Robert, 204, 257, 259, 263, 268; America, negative reaction to, 200; Parliament, utilitarian opposition to reform of, 194–5, 258; progress and the suffrage, 201
Louis-Philippe, 54, 209
lynch law, 205

Macaulay, Thomas Babington, 30, 228
MacCormick, Neil, 222, 245, 264, 268
McCulloch, Ramsay, 19–20, 264
Mack, Mary Peter, 227, 268
McKeon, Richard, 268
Mackintosh, John, 214, 260, 268
Maher, Gerhard, 223, 239, 263
Maine, Sir Henry: 60, 95, 194, 221, 222, 241, 257, 259, 260; comparison of JA and Bentham, 5; democracy, critique of, 200–1; JA's conception of judge-made law, critique of, 112; parliamentary reform expands power of Cabinet, 212; progress and contractual freedom, 202
Maitland, Sir Thomas, 248
Malta, 7, 8, 12, 46–7, 106, 193, 200, 246, 247, 248, 250, 251, 255, 257; British

rule of, 145–7, 154; Catholicism, support for by people of, 164; censorship on, 168–70; Council of Government on, 147, 150, 151–6; free press, value for, 171; military significance of, 146, 147–8; overpopulation on, 164–5; poverty of people of, 164; *and see* 144–92
Malthus, Thomas Robert, 16, 24, 161–2, 252, 268; impact on JA, 34, 145, 162, 164–5
Manchester School, 48, 202
Mansfield, William M., 1st Earl of, 86
Markby, W., 264
Marx, Karl, 48, 207
Mathias, Peter, 22, 226, 268
Maxwell, F.M., 264
Melbourne, Viscount, 160, 192, 254, 256
middle class, 10, 21, 98–100, 198, 203–4, 210, 211
military, service of JA in the, 12–13
Mill, James: 15–17, 19, 24, 29, 58, 93–5, 144–5, 158–9, 161, 163, 178, 193, 195, 203–4, 206, 218, 220, 226, 227, 234, 238, 251, 252, 264, 268; aristocracy, critique of, 19; comparison with JA, 16–17, 93–5; East India Co., association with, 144; education and poverty in India, 161; incompetence of Indians for self-government, 158–9; Malthusian views of, 161; middle class, praise of, 203–4; philosophic radicals, impact upon, 16; reforms for India, 145; reform of Parliament, 195; support of colonization of Englishmen in India, 158
Mill, John Stuart: 2, 6, 11, 16, 24, 30–54 *passim*, 65, 92–6, 155, 161, 178, 193–217 *passim*, 219, 220, 221, 223, 224, 225, 228, 229, 230, 231, 232, 234, 251, 255, 257, 259, 260, 264, 268, 269, 271; appraisal of *A Plea for the Constitution*, 193–4; compares Bentham and Austin, 24; constitutional checks and colonial misrule, views of, 155–6; French Revolution of 1848 and JA, 206; impact of JA's residence in Germany, 33–4; interpretation of JA's jurisprudence, 2, 92, 95; James Mill and JA, 94; Malthus's principle of population, 161; philosophic radicals, 16; pledges to constituents, 200; paucity of statesmen in House of Commons, 214
Milton, John, 84
Mineka, Francis, 269
Mitrovich, George, 247, 249, 269
Montesquieu, Baron, 109
moral obligation, Austin's conception of vagueness of, 86
moral sense, JA's criticisms of, 66–7, 86
Morison, W.L., 5, 91, 92–8, 100, 109, 120, 223, 224, 225, 232, 238, 240, 242, 264, 269: *John Austin*, 5, 223, 224, 225, 232
Morrell, W.P., 269
Morris, Herbert, 223, 264
Moultrie, John, 11, 269
Mullett, Charles F., 246

Napier, Macvey, 209, 228, 248, 269
National Library of Wales, 271
natural law or rights: 32, 82; JA's criticisms of, 24, 66, 84–5, 87, 205, 206
neologisms, JA's disapproval of, 74
Nesbitt, George L., 226, 269
New York Court of Appeals, 125–6
New York Times Co. v. *Sullivan* (1964), 255, 271
Niebuhr, Barthold Georg, 31
Nino, C., 264
Normanby, Marquis of (Constantine Henry Phipps), 251, 256

Oliphant, Herman, 115, 138–9, 245, 264
Outline of a Course of Lectures on General Jurisprudence or the Philosophy of Positive Law, An (JA), 40, 56

Paley, William, 63–4, 65, 67, 193, 194, 195, 258
Parekh, Bhikhu, 269
Parliament, British: 22–3, 30, 42, 52, 81, 99, 147, 154, 155, 170, 173, 193, 197–200, 211, 214; JA's opposition to reform of, 196–7, 204, 206, 210–17, 218; omnipotence of, 52–3, 105; petitions to, from Malta, 147, 154; sovereign in Great Britain, 89
Paton, George W., 240, 269
Patterson, Edwin W., 225, 269
Patterson, Sir John, 14
Petersen, William, 252, 269
Phillimore, Joseph, 38
philosophic radicals, 16–17, 161, 195, 206, 218
philosophy of law, JA's, 1–5, 44–5, 61, 62–3, 71–6, 187, 219
Plea for the Constitution, A (JA), 6, 7, 55, 193–4, 197, 219, 221, 223, 225, 228, 232, 257, 258, 259, 260, 265
Plumb, J.H., 10, 224, 269
Pohlman, H.L., 223
political economy, 48, 53, 93, 201, 203; Chair in, University of Valetta, 165; JA's attitude toward, 47–8, 94–5, 165–6, 202
political thought, evolution of JA's, 34, 55–6, 189–90
Pollock, Sir Frederick, 18, 226, 264, 269
positive law or laws, 5, 36–7, 76, 78, 79, 80, 81, 97, 107, 108, 110, 131, 146; and codification, 130; impact of utility upon, 78, 79; JA's conception of, 40–1, 72; and judicial legislation, 110–12; and positive morality, 85–6, 87; and

sovereignty, 88, 89; *and see* law
positive morality, 83, 85–6, 87, 89
Posner, Richard, 269
Pound, Roscoe, 123, 133, 142, 244, 245, 246, 264, 269
poverty, 48, 164–5, 171
power, delegation of and local control, 52, 111
practice of law, JA's, 27–8
precedents, 128, 133, 140
Price, Charles A., 166, 252, 253, 269
primogeniture and entails, 6, 7, 18–22, 175–6, 219
progress, 23, 77, 150; and aristocracy, 209; and democracy, 200–1; extension of the suffrage as obstacle to, 201; and freedom of contract, 200; free press, indispensable for, 171; JA's attitude toward, 200
Province of Jurisprudence Determined, The (JA), 3, 13, 27, 37, 40, 56, 57, 60, 71, 77, 90, 162, 170, 184, 221, 222, 223, 224, 227, 229, 230, 231, 233, 234, 235, 237, 238, 239, 240, 241, 242, 243, 244, 245, 252, 254, 255, 256, 259, 260, 261, 264, 265; interpretations of, 60–2, 71–2; purpose and nature of, 40–1; reviews of, 41–2, 264–5
public law, JA's conception of, 81
public opinion, 145, 165, 181–3, 187–8
Puckler-Muskau, Hermann, 55, 232, 269

Radin, Max, 244, 264
Radzinowicz, Leon, 230, 269
ratio decidendi, JA's conception of, 114–15, 118, 127–8, 142
Rawls, John, 142, 246, 269
Raz, Joseph, 222, 243, 264, 267, 269
Read, Donald, 231, 269
Rees, John, 268
Reform Act of 1832, 197, 207, 211; of 1867, 210; of 1884, 210
'Report from the Council, Annual General Meeting of Proprietors', 229, 261
'Report from the Select Committee of the House of Lords appointed to consider the Law of Defamation and Libel', 255–6, 257, 271
'Report from the Select Committee on Legal Education', 33, 38, 43, 44, 229, 230, 271
Representation of the People Act of 1918, 211
resistance, JA's utilitarian approach to, 83–4, 86–7, 259–60
Revolution: American, 77; JA's attitude toward, 87, 207, 208
Ricardo, David, 20, 24
Riggs v. *Palmer*, 125–6, 243, 271
Roach, John, 48, 225, 231, 269
Robinson, Frederick John, Earl of Ripon, 159–60
Roebuck, J.A., 34
Roman Catholic Church, 164, 167, 179, 190, 191
Roman law, 142; JA's attitude toward, 32–3, 96, 98
Romilly, Sir John, 27, 34
Rosenberg, J. Mitchell, 242, 269
Rosenblum, Nancy L., 269
Ross, Janet, 11, 27, 30, 222, 224, 225, 227, 228, 229, 230, 231, 232, 235, 240, 253, 269
Royal Commission to Malta: 7, 46, 246, 247; appointment of, 248; types of reforms of, 145; contributions of, 192, 219; Council of Government, reforms for, 150–6, 249–51; difficulty of assignment of, 150; discussion of in House of Lords, 159–62; education, reforms for, 161–8; employment of natives, support for, 156–61; faith in progress of, 150, 171; importance of, 144–5; purpose and authority of, 147–8; *and see* 144–92
Ruben, Eira, 91, 98–100, 223, 224, 238, 239, 257, 265
Russell, Lord John, 150, 154, 155, 249, 250, 251
Ryan, Alan, 218, 251, 265

St Hilaire, M. Barthélemy, 45
Salmond, John, 269
Savigny, Friedrich Karl von, 32
Schlegel, Wilhelm von, 31
Schneewind, Jerome B., 234, 261, 269
Schuyler, Robert L., 270
Schwarz, Andreas, 31–2, 229, 265
Second Statement by the Council of the University of London, 235, 270
security, as end of political government and law, 103, 133
Seddall, Henry, 164, 247, 252, 253, 270
Select Committee on Legal Education (1846), 33, 38–9, 43–4
Senior, Nassau W., 36, 228, 230, 253, 271
sentiment of constitutionality, 204, 215
separation of law and morals, 24, 44, 61, 76, 80–7, 108
Shannon, H.A., 226, 227, 265
Shuman, Samuel I, 222, 270
Sidgwick, Henry, 270
Siebert, Frederick, 270
Simon, Brian, 252, 279
Simon, W.M., 270
slavery, 50, 82
Smart, J.J.C., 270
Smith, Adam, 24, 47, 201
Smith, F.B., 259, 265
Smith, Harrison, 247, 270
Smith, Sydney, 27
Smith, Vernon, 250
Socialism: and French Revolution of 1848, 208; influence of in Eng-

land, 208–9, 212; JA's conception and criticisms of, 201–2
Sovereign, sovereignty: and American revolution, 78; in Great Britain, locus of, 89, 92, 106, 117; implications of for censorship on Malta, 169–70; JA's conception of, 24, 41, 51–3, 61, 72, 73, 88–100, 102–8; and judicial legislation, 110–12, 140; and middle class, 98–100; tension with JA's limited role for state, 52; unlimited power of, 89–90, 96–7, 111
Stanlis, Peter J., 270
Stare decisis, 138–9
Stark, Werner, 270
Starkie, Thomas, 38
Statement by the Council of the University of London explanatory of the Nature and Objects of the Institution, 228, 270
Statute of Frauds, 120
Steintrager, James, 25, 227, 270
Stephen, Sir James, 248, 249
Stephen, Sir James Fitzjames, 4, 30, 174, 194, 228, 254, 255, 257, 265, 270
Stephen, Leslie, 29, 30, 92, 211, 216, 222, 228, 234, 252, 265, 270
Stoddart, Sir John, 189, 270
Stokes, Eric, 247, 251, 252, 270
Stone, Julius, 91–2, 94, 98, 100, 223, 238, 270
suffrage: evaluation of JA's critique of, 210–17; development of after 1959, 210–11; JA's opposition to extension of, 7, 196, 199, 201, 203, 204; Reform Act of 1832, impact upon, 197; *and see* 193–217
Summers, Robert S., 222, 265, 270
Supreme Court, USA, 177
Swiss Civil Code, 136
Sykes, Godfrey, 14

Taylor, Sarah – see Austin, Sarah
Thomas, William, 16, 225, 258, 270
Thompson, F.M.L., 226, 270
Tooke, William, 29
Treaty of Paris (1815), 146
Tucker, Robert C., 270
Tur, Richard, 222, 265
Turgot, 47
Twining, William, 242, 245, 270

Ulpian, 85
Uniform Commercial Code, 136
United Steeel Workers of America v. *Weber*, 271
University of London, 28, 75, 271; JA's appointment to and experience at, 29–31, 34–40
University of Valetta, 165
usery, JA's attitude toward, 24
utilitarianism: act, 67–8; and the Commissioners' reforms for Malta, 145, 155, 184–5; contribution to, by JA, 6, 219; ethical authority, basis of, 69; key to JA's thought, 6, 218; JA's commitment to, 6, 20, 24, 25, 108, 194, 218; relationship to JA's jurisprudence, 60–2, 73, 76, 77–8, 87, 100–8; rule, JA's support of, 66–8, 122–3, 134; varieties of, 63; *and see* utilitarians, utility
utilitarians: Bentham, JA, and J.S. Mill, comparison of, 220; colonial policies of, 7, 145, 155–6; economic and political views of, tension between, 203–4; liberty, conceptions of, 178; Malthusian views of, 161; parliamentary reform, opinions of, 215–7; political differences between, 168, 178, 194, 206, 218; political libels, attitude toward, 168; revolution, response to, 218; *and see* utilitarianism, utility
utility: basis of JA's opposition to reform of Parliament, 194, 196, 204–5, 216; basis of laymens' knowledge of law, 77; different interpretations of, 178, 218; and ends of government, 70–1; general, 71–2; guidance provided by, 83–4, 86–7, 195; index to law of God, 86–7; JA's justification of principle of, 79–80; legislation, impact on, 78–9; obedience and resistance to law, standard of, 77, 78, 83–4, 103–4; public, JA's use of as standard, 194, 196, 216–7; and sovereignty, 103–4; true theory of, 67; *and see* utilitarianism, utilitarians

Victorian critics of democracy, 6, 194, 200
Vigilante Committees, 205
Villiers, C.P., 34

war, 50
Wasserstrom, Richard, 123, 223, 270
Waterfield, Gordon, 25, 53, 224, 225, 227, 228, 231, 232, 270
Wellington, Duke of, 191–2
Weston, Corinne C., 270
White, Alan R., 223
Wickwar, William, 188, 256, 270
Wight, Martin, 247, 270
Williams, Bernard, 270
Williston, Samuel, 245
Winch, Donald, 223, 247, 251, 270
Winter, James, 257, 270

Yale University library, 271
Young, G.M., 15, 271